AF478677

# FOUNDATIONS OF
# GENETIC ALGORITHMS•3

# FOUNDATIONS OF
# GENETIC ALGORITHMS • 3

**EDITED BY**

## L. DARRELL WHITLEY
### AND
## MICHAEL D. VOSE

MORGAN KAUFMANN PUBLISHERS, INC.
SAN FRANCISCO, CALIFORNIA

**Executive Editor**   Bruce M. Spatz
**Production Manager**   Yonie Overton
**Production Editor**   Cheri Palmer
**Assistant Editor**   Douglas Sery
**Production Artist/Cover Design**   S.M. Sheldrake
**Printer**   Edwards Brothers, Inc.

## Morgan Kaufmann Publishers, Inc.

**Editorial and Sales Office**

340 Pine Street, Sixth Floor
San Francisco, CA 94104-3205
USA

Telephone   415 / 392-2665
Facsimile   415 / 982-2665
Internet   mkp@mkp.com



Library of Congress Catalogue-in-Publication is available for this book.
ISSN 1081-6593
ISBN 1-55860-356-5

# FOGA–94

## THE PROGRAM COMMITTEE

Michael Vose, *University of Tennessee*

Lashon Booker, *MITRE Corporation*

Melanie Mitchell, *Santa Fe Institute*

Robert E. Smith, *University of Alabama*

J. David Schaffer, *Philips Laboratories*

Gilbert Syswerda, *Optimax*

Worthy Martin, *University of Virginia*

Alden Wright, *University of Montana*

Larry Eshelman, *Philips Laboratories*

David Goldberg, *University of Illinois*

Darrell Whitley, *Colorado State University*

Kenneth A. De Jong, *George Mason University*

John Grefenstette, *Naval Research Laboratory*

Stephen F. Smith, *Carnegie Mellon University*

Gregory J.E. Rawlins, *Indiana University*

William Spears, *Naval Research Laboratory*

Nicholas Radcliffe, *University of Edinburgh*

Stephanie Forrest, *University of New Mexico*

Richard Belew, *University of California, San Diego*

# Contents

# Introduction

The third workshop on Foundations of Genetic Algorithms (FOGA) was held July 31 through August 2, 1994, in Estes Park, Colorado. These workshops have been held biennially, starting in 1990 (Rawlins 1991; Whitley 1993). FOGA alternates with the International Conference on Genetic Algorithms (ICGA) which is held in odd years. Both events are sponsored and organized under the auspices of the International Society for Genetic Algorithms.

Prior to the FOGA proceedings, theoretical work on genetic algorithms was found either in the ICGA proceedings or was scattered and difficult to locate. Now, both FOGA and the journal *Evolutionary Computation* provide forums specifically targeting theoretical publications on genetic algorithms. Special mention should also be made of the Parallel Problem Solving from Nature Conference (PPSN), which is the European sister conference to ICGA held in even years. Interesting theoretical work on genetic and other evolutionary algorithms, such as Evolution Strategies, has appeared in PPSN. In addition, the last two years have witnessed the appearance of several new conferences and special journal issues dedicated to evolutionary algorithms. A tutorial level introduction to genetic algorithm and basic models of genetic algorithms is provided by Whitley (1994).

Other publications have carried recent theoretical papers related to genetic algorithms. Some of this work, by authors not represented in the current FOGA volume, is mentioned here. In ICGA 93, a paper by Srinivas and Patnaik (1993) extends models appearing in FOGA · 2 to look at binomially distributed populations. Also in ICGA 93, Joe Suzuki (1993) used Markov chain analysis to explore the effects of elitism (where the individual with highest fitness is preserved in the next generation). Qi and Palmieri had papers appearing in ICGA (1993) and a special issue of the *IEEE Transactions on Neural Networks* (1994) using infinite population models of genetic algorithms to study selection and mutation as well as the diversification role of crossover. Also appearing in this *Tranactions* is work by Günter Rudolph (1994) on the convergence behavior of canonical genetic algorithms.

Several trends are evident in recent theoretical work. First, most researchers continue to work with minor variations on Holland's (1975) canonical genetic algorithm; this is because this model continues to be the easiest to characterize from an analytical view point. Second, Markov models have become more common as tools for providing supporting mathematical foundations for genetic algorithm theory. These are the early stages in the integration of genetic algorithm theory into mainstream mathematics. Some of the precursors to this trend include Bridges and Goldberg's 1987 analysis of selection and crossover for simple genetic algorithms, Vose's 1990 paper and the more accessible 1991 Vose and Liepins paper, T. Davis' Ph.D. dissertation from 1991, and the paper by Whitley et al. (1992).

One thing that has become a source of confusion is that non-Markov models of genetic algorithms are generally seen as infinite population models. These models use a vector $p^t$ to represent the expected proportion of each string in the genetic algorithm's population at generation $t$; component $p_i^t$ is the expected proportion of string $i$. As population size increases, the correspondence improves between the expected population predicted and the actual population observed in a finite population genetic algorithm.

Infinite population models are sometimes criticized as unrealistic, since all practical genetic algorithms use small populations with sizes that are far from infinite. However, there are other ways to interpret the vector $p$ which relate more directly to events in finite population genetic algorithms.

For example, assume parents are chosen (via some form of selection) and mixed (via some form of recombination and mutation) to ultimately yield one string as part of producing the next generation. It is natural to ask: Given a finite population with proportional representation $p^t$, what is the probability that the string $i$ is generated by the selection and mixing process? The same vector $p^{t+1}$ which is produced by the infinite population model also yields the probability $p_i^{t+1}$ that string $i$ is the result of selection and mixing. This is one sense in which infinite population models describe the probability distribution of events which are critical in finite population genetic algorithms.

Vose has proved that several alternate interpretations of what are generally seen as infinite population model are equally valid. In his book (in press), it is shown how some non-Markov models simultaneously answer the following basic questions:

1. What is the *exact sampling distribution* describing the formation of the next generation for a *finite* population genetic algorithm?

2. What is the *expected next generation*?

3. In the limit, as population size grows, what is the *transition function* which maps from one generation to the next?

Moreover, for each of these questions, the answer provided is exact, and holds for all generations and for all population sizes.

Besides these connections to finite population genetic algorithms, some non-Markov models occur as natural parts of the transition matrices which define Markov models. They are, in a literal sense, fundamental objects that make up much of the theoretical foundations of genetic algorithms.

Another issue that received a considerable amount of discussion at FOGA $\cdot$ 3 was the relationship between crossover as a local neighborhood operator and the landscape that is induced by crossover. Local search algorithms are based on the use of an operator that maps some current state (i.e., a current candidate solution) to a set of neighbors representing potential next states. For binary strings, a convenient set of neighbors is the set of $L$

strings reachable by changing any one of the $L$ bits that make up the string. A steepest ascent "bit climber," for example, checks each of the $L$ neighbors and moves the current state to the best neighbor. The process is then repeated until no improvements are found. Terry Jones (1995) has been exploring the neighborhoods that are induced by crossover. A current state in this case requires two strings instead of one. Potential offspring can be viewed as potential next states. The size of the neighborhood reachable under crossover is variable depending on what recombination operator is used and the composition of the two parents. If 1-point recombination of binary strings is used and the parents are complements, then there are $L - 1$ pairs of unique offspring pairs that are reachable. If the parents differ in $K$ bit positions (where $K > 0$) then 1-point recombination reaches $K - 1$ unique pairs of strings. Clearly not all points in the search space are reachable from all pairs of parents. But this point of view does raise some interesting questions. What is the relationship between more traditional local search methods, such as bit-climbers, and applying local search methods to the neighborhoods induced by crossover? Is there some relationship between the performance of a crossover-based neighborhood search algorithm and the performance of more traditional genetic algorithms?

As with FOGA $\cdot$ 2, the papers in these proceedings are longer than the typical conference paper. Papers were subjected to two rounds of reviewing; the first round selected which submissions would appear in the current volume, a second round of editing was done to improve the presentation and clarity of the proceedings. The one exception to this is the invited paper by DeJong, Spears and Gordon. One of the editors provided feedback on each paper; in addition, each paper was also read by one of the contributing authors.

Many people played a part in FOGA's success and deserve mention. The Computer Science Department at Colorado State University contributed materials and personnel to help make FOGA possible. In particular, Denise Hallman took care of local arrangements. She also did this job in 1992. In both cases, Denise helped to make everything run smoothly, made expenses match resources, and, as always, was pleasant to work with. We also thank the program committee and the authors for their hard work.

Darrell Whitley
Colorado State University, Fort Collins
whitley@cs.colostate.edu

Michael D. Vose
University of Tennessee, Knoxville
vose@cs.utk.edu

### References

Bridges, C. and Goldberg, D. (1987) An analysis of reproduction and crossover in a binary-coded genetic Algorithm. *Proc. 2nd International Conf. on Genetic Algorithms and Their Applications.* J. Grefenstette, ed. Lawrence Erlbaum.

Davis, T. (1991) Toward and Extrapolation of the Simulating Annealing Convergence Theory onto the Simple Genetic Algorithm. Doctoral Dissertation, University of Florida, Gainsville, FL.

Holland, J. (1975) Adaptation In Natural and Artificial Systems. University of Michigan Press.

Jones, T. (1995) Evolutionary Algorithms, Fitness Landscapes and Search. Doctoral Dissertation, University of New Mexico, Albuquerque, NM.

Qi, X. and Palmieri, F. (1993) The Diversification Role of Crossover in the Genetic Algorithms. *Proc. 5nd International Conf. on Genetic Algorithms.* S. Forrest, ed. Morgan Kaufmann.

Qi, X. and Palmieri, F. (1994) Theoretical Analysis of Evolutionary Algorithms with an Infinite Population Size in Continuous Space, Part I and Part II. *IEEE Transactions on Neural Networks.* 5(1):102-129.

Rawlins, G.J.E., ed. (1991) *Foundations of Genetic Algorithms.* Morgan Kaufmann.

Rudolph, G. (1994) Convergence Analysis of Canonical Genetic Algorithms. *IEEE Transactions on Neural Networks.* 5(1):96-101.

Srinivas, M. and Patnaik, L.M. (1993) Binomially Distributed Populations for Modeling GAs. *Proc. 5nd International Conf. on Genetic Algorithms.* S. Forrest, ed. Morgan Kaufmann.

Suzuki, J. (1993) A Markov Chain Analysis on A Genetic Algorithm. *Proc. 5nd International Conf. on Genetic Algorithms.* S. Forrest, ed. Morgan Kaufmann.

Vose, M.D. (in press) *The Simple Genetic Algorithm: Foundations and Theory.* MIT Press.

Vose, M.D. (1990) Formalizing Genetic Algorithms. *Proc. IEEE workshop on Genetic Algorithms, Neural Networks and Simulating Annealing applied to Signal and Image Processing.* Glasgow, U.K.

Vose, M. and Liepins, G., (1991) Punctuated Equilibria in Genetic Search. *Complex Systems* 5:31-44.

Whitley, D., (1994) A Genetic Algorithm Tutorial. *Statistics and Computing* 4:65-85.

Whitley, D., ed. (1993) *Foundations of Genetic Algorithms · 2.* Morgan Kaufmann.

Whitley, D., Das, R., and Crabb, C. (1992) Tracking Primary Hyperplane Competitors During Genetic Search. *Annals of Mathematics and Artificial Intelligence.* 6:367-388.

# PART 1

# SCHEMA BASED ANALYSES

# An Experimental Design Perspective on Genetic Algorithms

**Colin Reeves and Christine Wright**
Statistics and Operational Research Division
School of Mathematical and Information Sciences
Coventry University
UK
Email: CRReeves@cov.ac.uk

## Abstract

In this paper we examine the relationship between genetic algorithms (GAs) and traditional methods of *experimental design*. This was motivated by an investigation into the problem caused by epistasis in the implementation and application of GAs to optimization problems: one which has long been acknowledged to have an important influence on GA performance. Davidor [1, 2] has attempted an investigation of the important question of determining the degree of epistasis of a *given* problem. In this paper, we shall first summarise his methodology, and then provide a critique from the perspective of experimental design. We proceed to show how this viewpoint enables us to gain further insights into the determination of epistatic effects, and into the value of different forms of encoding a problem for a GA solution. We also demonstrate the equivalence of this approach to the *Walsh transform* analysis popularized by Goldberg [3, 4], and its extension to the idea of *partition coefficients* [5]. We then show how the experimental design perspective helps to throw further light on the nature of deception.

## 1   INTRODUCTION

The term *epistasis* is used in the field of genetic algorithms to denote the effect on chromosome fitness of a combination of alleles which is not merely a linear function of the effects of the individual alleles. It can be thought of as expressing a degree of non-linearity in the fitness function, and roughly speaking, the more epistatic the problem is, the harder it may be for a GA to find its optimum.

Table 1: Goldberg's 3-bit deceptive function

| String | Fitness |
|--------|---------|
| 0 0 0 | 7 |
| 0 0 1 | 5 |
| 0 1 0 | 5 |
| 0 1 1 | 0 |
| 1 0 0 | 3 |
| 1 0 1 | 0 |
| 1 1 0 | 0 |
| 1 1 1 | 8 |

Several authors [3, 4, 6, 8] have explored the problem of epistasis in terms of the properties of a particular class of epistatic problems, those known as *deceptive* problems—the most famous example of which is probably Goldberg's 3-bit function, which has the form shown in Table 1 (definitions of this function in the literature may differ in unimportant details).

The study of such functions has been fruitful, but in terms of solving a given practical problem *ab initio*, it may not provide too much help. What might be more important would be the ability to estimate the degree of epistasis in a given problem before deciding on the most suitable strategy for solving it. At one end of the spectrum, a problem with very little epistasis should perhaps not be solved by a GA at all; for such problems one should be able to find a suitable linear or quasi-linear numerical method with which a GA could not compete. At the other end, a highly epistatic problem is unlikely to be solvable by any systematic method, including a GA. Problems with intermediate epistasis would be worth attempting with a GA, although even here it would also be useful if one could identify particular varieties of epistasis. If one could detect problems of a deceptive nature, for instance, one might suggest using an approach such as the 'messy GA' of [9, 10].

There is another aspect to this too: it is well-known (see e.g. [7, 11]) that the *coding* used for a GA may be of critical importance in how easy it is to solve. In fact (as we shall also demonstrate later) a particular choice of coding may render a simple linear function epistatic. Conversely, by choosing a different coding, it may be possible to reduce the degree of epistasis in a problem. It would clearly be valuable to be able to compare the epistasis existing in different codings of the same problem.

In recent papers, Davidor [1, 2] has reported an initial attempt at estimating the degree of epistasis in some simple problems. His results are to some degree perplexing, and it is difficult to draw firm conclusions from them. In this paper, we hope to show that his methodology can be put on a firmer footing by drawing on existing work in the field of *experimental design* (ED), which can be used to give insights into epistatic effects, and into the value of different codings. Later we shall also show how this approach relates to the Walsh transform methodology and the analysis of deception.

We begin by summarising Davidor's approach to the analysis of epistasis.

## 2   DAVIDOR'S EPISTASIS METHODOLOGY

Davidor deals with populations of binary strings $\{S\}$ of length $l$, for which he defines several quantities, as summarised below:

The basic idea of his analysis is that for a given population $Pop$ of size $N$, the average fitness value can be determined as

$$\bar{V} = \sum_{S \in Pop} v(S)/N$$

where $v(S)$ is the fitness of string $S$. Subtracting this value from the fitness of a given string $S$ produces the excess string fitness value

$$E(S) = v(S) - \bar{V}.$$

We may count the number of occurrences of allele $a$ for each gene $i$, denoted by $N_i(a)$, and compute the average allele value

$$A_i(a) = \sum v(S)/N_i(a),$$

where the sum is over the strings whose $i^{th}$ gene takes the value $a$. The excess allele value measures the effect of having allele $a$ at gene $i$, and is given by

$$E_i(a) = A_i(a) - \bar{V}.$$

The genic value of string $S$ is the value obtained by summing the excess allele values at each gene, and adding $\bar{V}$ to the result:

$$A(S) = \bar{V} + \sum_{i=1}^{l} E_i(a).$$

(Davidor actually gives the sum in the above formula the name 'excess genic value', i.e.

$$E(A) = \sum_{i=1}^{l} E_i(a),$$

although this quantity is not necessary in the ED context; we include the definition here for completeness.) Finally, the epistasis value is the difference between the actual value of string $S$ and the genic value predicted by the above analysis:

$$\epsilon(S) = v(S) - A(S).$$

Thus far, what Davidor has done appears reasonably straightforward. He then defines further 'variance' measures, which he proposes to use as a way of quantifying the epistasis of a given problem. Several examples are given using some 3-bit problems, which demonstrate that using all 8 possible strings, his epistasis variance measure behaves in the expected fashion: it is zero for a linear problem, and increases in line with (qualitatively) more epistatic problems. However, when only a subset of the 8 possible strings is used, the epistasis measure gives rather problematic results, as evidenced by variances which are very hard to interpret.

In a real problem, of course, a sample of the $2^l$ possible strings is all we have, and an epistasis measure needs to be capable of operating in such circumstances. Below we re-formulate Davidor's analysis from an ED perspective, which we hope will shed rather more light on this problem.

## 3  AN EXPERIMENTAL DESIGN APPROACH

Davidor's analysis is complicated by the GA convention of describing a subset of strings as a *population*, when from a traditional statistical perspective it is actually a *sample*. Davidor uses the terms *Grand Population* and *sample population* to try to avoid this confusion. We propose instead to use the term *Universe* for the set of all possible $2^l$ strings, so that we can use the term population in the sense with which the GA community is familiar.

It is clear that Davidor is implicitly assuming an underlying linear model (defined on the bits) for the fitness of each string. This leads to a further problem in his analysis, linked to the above confusion between population and sample, in that he fails to distinguish between the *parameters* of this underlying model, and the *estimates* of those parameters which are possible for a given population. We can begin to explain this more clearly by first making the model explicit.

We can express the full epistatic model as

$$
\begin{aligned}
v(S) \;=\; & \text{constant} + \sum_{i=1}^{l} (\text{effect of allele at gene } i) \\
& + \sum_{i=1}^{l-1} \sum_{j=i+1}^{l} (\text{interaction between alleles at gene } i \text{ and gene } j) \\
& + \ldots \\
& + (\text{interaction between alleles at gene 1, gene 2, } \ldots, \text{ gene } l) \\
& + \text{random error}
\end{aligned}
$$

In conventional experimental design, the above model would actually be written in parametric form. For example, the model for a string of 3 binary bits could be written as follows:

$$
v_{pqrs} = \mu + \alpha_p + \beta_q + (\alpha\beta)_{pq} + \gamma_r + (\alpha\gamma)_{pr} + (\beta\gamma)_{qr} + (\alpha\beta\gamma)_{pqr} + \varepsilon_{pqrs} \tag{1}
$$

where $v_{pqrs}$ is the fitness of the string $(p, q, r)$, and the subscript $s$ denotes the replication number (i.e. the $s^{th}$ occurrence of the string). If there is no intrinsic noise, we can of course drop the subscript $s$. The parameters on the right-hand side are as follows:

| | |
|---|---|
| $\mu$ | average fitness |
| $\alpha_p$ | effect of allele $p$ at gene 1 |
| $\beta_q$ | effect of allele $q$ at gene 2 |
| $(\alpha\beta)_{pq}$ | joint effect of allele $p$ at gene 1 and allele $q$ at gene 2 |
| $\gamma_r$ | effect of allele $r$ at gene 3 |
| $(\alpha\gamma)_{pr}$ | joint effect of allele $p$ at gene 1 and allele $r$ at gene 3 |
| $(\beta\gamma)_{qr}$ | joint effect of allele $q$ at gene 2 and allele $r$ at gene 3 |
| $(\alpha\beta\gamma)_{pqr}$ | joint effect of allele $p$ at gene 1, allele $q$ at gene 2 and allele $r$ at gene 3 |
| $\varepsilon_{pqrs}$ | random error for replication $s$ of string $(p, q, r)$ |

Davidor assumes zero random error, which is reasonable in many, although not all, applications of GAs. We thus intend to ignore the possibility of random error here, although we hope to consider such problems at a later date.

We emphasize again that we must distingush two different situations, even when we assume zero random error. In the first case we know the fitness of every string in the Universe. In practice this is unrealistic—in reality we only know the fitness of every string in a subset of the Universe (i.e. our 'population', to use the conventional GA terminology, is merely a sample). Of course, in the first case, there is in one sense no problem: the optimal combination is obvious, and all the measures proposed by Davidor are constants. In the second case (which is the real situation) the various epistasis measures are only *estimates* of parameters, whose expectations and variances are important characteristics. Nevertheless, for purposes of exposition, we need to focus initially on the first case, and we shall postpone examination of the real situation to another paper.

## 3.1   An example

Suppose we have a 3-bit string, and the fitness of every string in the Universe is known. There are of course $2^3 = 8$ strings , and therefore 8 fitness values, but the experimental design model above has 27 parameters. It is thus essential to impose some side conditions if these parameters are to be estimated; the usual ones are the obvious constraints that at every order of interaction, the parameters sum to zero for each subscript. This results in an additional 19 independent relationships such as

$$\sum_p \alpha_p = 0$$

$$\sum_p (\alpha\beta)_{pq} = 0 \quad \text{for } q = 0, 1$$

$$\sum_p (\alpha\beta\gamma)_{pqr} = 0 \quad \text{for } q, r = 0, 1$$

and thus allows the 'solution' of the above model, in the sense that all the parameter values can be determined if we have observed every one of the 8 possible strings—the first case above. For example, we find that

$$\mu = v_{***}$$
$$\mu + \alpha_p = v_{p**} \quad \text{for } p = 0, 1$$
$$\mu + \beta_q = v_{*q*} \quad \text{for } q = 0, 1$$
$$\mu + \gamma_r = v_{**r} \quad \text{for } r = 0, 1$$

where the notation $v_{p**}$, for instance, means averaging over subscripts $q$ and $r$. The effects can be seen to be exactly equivalent to Davidor's 'excess allele values' as defined above. For instance, his $A_1(p) = v_{p**}$, so that $E_1(p) = \alpha_p$. Similarly, his 'excess genic values' $E(A)$ are found by summing $\alpha_p$, $\beta_q$ and $\gamma_r$ for each possible combination of $p, q, r$. Finally, his 'string genic value' is clearly

$$\mu + \alpha_p + \beta_q + \gamma_r.$$

The difference between the actual value and the genic value, $\epsilon(S)$, is therefore simply the sum of all the interaction terms. If there is no epistasis, then by definition the combinations of alleles $p, q, r$ will have no effect on chromosome fitness other than this simple linear sum, so that epistasis can be interpreted as the combined effect of the interaction terms.

## 3.2   Analysis of Variance

The normal procedure in experimental design is to perform an 'Analysis of Variance' (Anova), whereby the variability of the fitness values (measured by sums of squared deviations from mean fitness, and denoted by SS) is partitioned into orthogonal components from identifiable sources. In the table below, we give a conventional Anova table for our 3-bit example, with Davidor's notation alongside:

Table 2: Analysis of Variance Table

| Source of variation | Degrees of freedom | Sum of squares (SS) | Davidor's notation |
|---|---|---|---|
| Between alleles of gene 1 | 1 | $\sum_{pqr}(v_{p**} - v_{***})^2$ | $\sum[E_1(a)]^2$ |
| Between alleles of gene 2 | 1 | $\sum_{pqr}(v_{*q*} - v_{***})^2$ | $\sum[E_2(a)]^2$ |
| Between alleles of gene 3 | 1 | $\sum_{pqr}(v_{**r} - v_{***})^2$ | $\sum[E_3(a)]^2$ |
| Total main effects (i.e.'genic' effect) | 3 | sum of above | sum of above |
| Interactions (i.e.epistatic effect) | 4 | $\sum_{pqr}(v_{pqr} - v_{p**} - v_{*q*} - v_{**r} + 2v_{***})^2$ | $\sum[\epsilon(S)]^2$ |
| Total | 7 | $\sum(v_{pqr} - v_{***})^2$ | $\sum[E(S)]^2$ |

The *degrees of freedom* are the number of independent elements in the associated SS; for example, in the Total SS term, only 7 of the $(v_{pqr} - v_{***})$ terms are independent, since they must satisfy the relationship $\sum_{pqr}(v_{pqr} - v_{***}) = 0$.

It is well-known (and easy to prove) that

$$\text{Total SS} = \text{Main effects SS} + \text{Interactions SS}$$

and since Davidor has simply divided these values by a constant to obtain his 'variances', it is hardly surprising that he finds that

$$\text{Total 'variance'} = \text{Genic 'variance'} + \text{Epistasis 'variance'}.$$

(We note here that when we come to investigate the real situation, we shall see that this result *appears* no longer to be true using Davidor's definitions; the reason for this will be discussed in the second paper.)

Any standard statistical computing package will produce these Anova tables; below we give some examples obtained using MINITAB on Davidor's functions $f_1, f_2, f_3$ and $f_4$. These functions represent respectively a linear function, a delta function, a mixture of $f_1$ and $f_2$, and finally the deceptive function of Table 1.

We see from these results that in a qualitative sense (for these functions at least), the amount of epistasis can be inferred from the relative magnitudes of the SS terms, i.e. the SS values as a fraction of the total SS. In case $f_1$, the Anova table shows no epistasis at all, as would be expected, while $f_3$ appears to be much less epistatic than $f_2$. The case of $f_4$ (the deceptive function) is interesting: the *relative* magnitude of interactions SS is much greater than in the case of $f_2$ (the delta function)—that is, it is worse to have *misleading* information than to have no information at all. (We note here that Davidor [1] interprets the cases of $f_2$ and $f_4$ differently—arguing from the actual *numerical values* of his 'epistasis

Table 3: Anova results for Davidor's functions

|  | $f_1$ | | $f_2$ | | $f_3$ | | $f_4$ | |
| Source | df | SS | df | SS | df | SS | df | SS |
| --- | --- | --- | --- | --- | --- | --- | --- | --- |
| Main effects | 3 | 42.00 | 3 | 294.00 | 3 | 133.00 | 3 | 5.50 |
| 2-way interactions | 3 | 0.00 | 3 | 294.00 | 3 | 73.50 | 3 | 44.00 |
| 3-way interactions | 1 | 0.00 | 1 | 98.00 | 1 | 24.50 | 1 | 24.50 |
| Total | 7 | 42.00 | 7 | 686.00 | 7 | 231.00 | 7 | 74.00 |

variances' that the deceptive function is *less* epistatic than $f_2$. However, this would imply that epistasis is dependent on the measurement scale of the function, whereas it is clear that this should not influence the performance of a GA. We believe therefore that looking at the relative magnitudes in the Anova table is more informative. Whether we can then go on to infer that this indicator of epistasis necessarily means that the problem is hard for a GA to solve is of course a separate, although very important, issue—one to which we hope to return in a future paper.)

## 4    THE INFLUENCE OF CODING

Experimental design also helps to throw some light on the often-noticed influence of the adopted coding on the ease or difficulty of solving a given problem using GAs. We now consider 2 cases that have attracted attention in the GA literature: the influence of Gray coding, and the effect of using a binary rather than a $q$-ary alphabet ($q > 2$).

### 4.1    Gray coding

Another of Davidor's functions is a Gray-coded version of his function $f_1$. The case for Gray coding has been put persuasively by Caruana and Schaffer [16], but Davidor's example in [2] shows that it may not necessarily be helpful.

Consider the two representations of a 3-bit problem as tabulated below:

Table 4: Binary and Gray code versions of a 3-bit problem

| Binary representation | Fitness value | Gray representation |
| --- | --- | --- |
| 0 0 0 | $v_1$ | 0 0 0 |
| 0 0 1 | $v_2$ | 0 0 1 |
| 0 1 0 | $v_3$ | 0 1 1 |
| 0 1 1 | $v_4$ | 0 1 0 |
| 1 0 0 | $v_5$ | 1 1 0 |
| 1 0 1 | $v_6$ | 1 1 1 |
| 1 1 0 | $v_7$ | 1 0 1 |
| 1 1 1 | $v_8$ | 1 0 0 |

A useful experimental design concept here is that of a *contrast*, usually denoted by upper case Roman letters. For example, the contrast

$$A = \alpha_1 - \alpha_0$$

(where $\alpha_p$ is as previously defined), expresses the average fitness value when allele 1 is instantiated at gene 1, compared to the instantiation of allele 0. In terms of the vector of fitness values $\mathbf{v}$ in binary representation from the table above,

$$A = \frac{1}{4}(-1,-1,-1,-1,1,1,1,1)\mathbf{v}$$

$$B = \frac{1}{4}(-1,-1,1,1,-1,-1,1,1)\mathbf{v}$$

$$C = \frac{1}{4}(-1,1,-1,1,-1,1,-1,1)\mathbf{v}.$$

Similarly, we can define contrasts relating to the interaction effects, so that

$$AB = \frac{1}{4}(1,1,-1,-1,-1,-1,1,1)\mathbf{v}$$

expresses the average fitness value for cases where the instantiated alleles at genes 1 and 2 are the same, compared to those where they are different. The other contrasts are as follows:

$$AC = \frac{1}{4}(1,-1,1,-1,-1,1,-1,1)\mathbf{v}$$

$$BC = \frac{1}{4}(1,-1,-1,1,1,-1,-1,1)\mathbf{v}$$

$$ABC = \frac{1}{4}(-1,1,1,-1,1,-1,-1,1)\mathbf{v}.$$

The contrast $ABC$ can be regarded as the difference between $AB$ with allele 1 instantiated at gene 3 and $AB$ with allele 0 at gene 3. (Alternatively $ABC$ could be interpreted in terms of $AC$ or $BC$.) These 7 contrasts are each associated with 1 degree of freedom, and correspond to the information presented in Table 2; they are orthogonal, and can thus be determined simultaneously from the observed fitness values. In the case of Davidor's $f_1$, for example, they are $A = 4, B = 2, C = 1$ and all others 0.

Now consider the Gray-coded version of the same situation, where we denote the contrasts by the letters X,Y,Z. While it is clear that

$$X \equiv A,$$

the other contrasts are all different: for example,

$$Y = \frac{1}{4}(-1,-1,1,1,1,1,-1,-1)\mathbf{v},$$

so that

$$Y \equiv -AB.$$

Similar results can be found for the other contrasts, which can be summarised as follows:

$$A \equiv X, B \equiv -XY, C \equiv XYZ, AB \equiv -Y, AC \equiv YZ, BC \equiv -Z, ABC \equiv -XZ.$$

Thus, analysing Davidor's linear function $f_1$ using the above Gray code representation would result in non-zero contrasts for the interactions $XY$ and $XYZ$, and a conclusion from the Anova table that the function was epistatic. Of course, it would not be difficult to define a function for which a Gray code had the opposite effect—the 3-bit function displayed in Table 5 below is epistatic, but it is not difficult to show that using the Gray code of Table 4 would make the problem linear.

Table 5: Another 3-bit problem

| String (binary code) | Fitness |
|:---:|:---:|
| 0 0 0 | 8 |
| 0 0 1 | 5 |
| 0 1 0 | 1 |
| 0 1 1 | 4 |
| 1 0 0 | 5 |
| 1 0 1 | 2 |
| 1 1 0 | 6 |
| 1 1 1 | 9 |

We also note here a connection with the work of Liepins and Vose [6], who show that there is always a transformation of the coding of a 'fully deceptive' problem which transforms it into a 'fully easy' one (for a definition of these terms see [6]). In this sense, a Gray code transformation of a binary code is simply a special case of their more general result. In terms of experimental design, what they are saying is that there is always a way of converting interactions into main effects by a suitable transformation. The problem in practice, of course, is to know what that transformation is!

## 4.2   Binary versus $q$-ary coding

The issue of whether binary coding is to be preferred to using a larger $q$-ary alphabet ($q > 2$) has been widely debated, and it would be fair to say that it has not been resolved. Holland [14], and following him Goldberg [15], stressed the advantage of a binary alphabet, in that it allows the sampling of the maximum number of schemata per individual in the population. More recently, Antonisse has put forward a counter-argument in [17] by re-defining the concept of a schema, while Radcliffe's work [11] makes a very similar point. On the other hand, Reeves [18] has recently argued that there are certain theoretical advantages in using binary-coding in cases where GAs need to be limited to a small number of function evaluations. An ED approach throws a further interesting sidelight on the question.

Suppose we have a problem with 2 genes J and K, each of which has 4 alleles denoted by $\{0,1,2,3\}$. Then, defining the fitness vector as

$$\mathbf{v} = (v_{00}, v_{10}, \ldots, v_{33})^T,$$

we can determine 3 orthogonal contrasts for each gene

$$J_1 = (-1, -1, 1, 1, -1, -1, 1, 1, -1, -1, 1, 1, -1, -1, 1, 1)\mathbf{v},$$

$$J_2 = (1, -1, -1, 1, 1, -1, -1, 1, 1, -1, -1, 1, 1, -1, -1, 1)\mathbf{v},$$

$$J_3 = (-1, 1, -1, 1, -1, 1, -1, 1, -1, 1, -1, 1, -1, 1, -1, 1)\mathbf{v},$$

and

$$K_1 = (-1, -1, -1, -1, -1, -1, -1, -1, 1, 1, 1, 1, 1, 1, 1, 1)\mathbf{v},$$

$$K_2 = (1, 1, 1, 1, -1, -1, -1, -1, -1, -1, -1, -1, 1, 1, 1, 1)\mathbf{v}.$$

$$K_3 = (-1, -1, -1, -1, 1, 1, 1, 1, -1, -1, -1, -1, 1, 1, 1, 1)\mathbf{v},$$

The interpretation of these contrasts is a little more complicated than in the binary case, but it can easily be seen that $J_1$, for example, expresses the contrast between having alleles at 'high' levels at gene 1 rather then at 'low' levels. We could thus interpret $J_1$ (and, naturally, $K_1$) as indicating a 'linear' component, while the pattern of positive and negative signs for $J_2, K_2$ and $J_3, K_3$ suggest 'quadratic' and 'cubic' components respectively.

Suppose for a particular $\mathbf{v}$ the main effects give the only non-zero contrasts using this coding. For example, suppose the fitness is defined as

$$v_{jk} = 1 + 2j + k \qquad \text{for } j, k \in \{0, 1, 2, 3\}.$$

Consider what happens if the 4-ary code $\{jk\}$ is replaced by its binary equivalent $\{pqrs\} = (0000, 0100, 1000, \ldots, 1111)$. There will now be 4 genes P,Q,R,S leading to the following contrasts

$$P = (-1, -1, 1, 1, -1, -1, 1, 1, -1, -1, 1, 1, -1, -1, 1, 1)\mathbf{v},$$
$$Q = (-1, 1, -1, 1, -1, 1, -1, 1, -1, 1, -1, 1, -1, 1, -1, 1)\mathbf{v},$$
$$R = (-1, -1, -1, -1, -1, -1, -1, -1, 1, 1, 1, 1, 1, 1, 1, 1)\mathbf{v},$$
$$S = (-1, -1, -1, -1, 1, 1, 1, 1, -1, -1, -1, -1, 1, 1, 1, 1)\mathbf{v}.$$

These are seen to be identical to $J_1, J_3, K_1, K_3$ respectively, but what has happened to $J_2$ and $K_2$? It is in fact easily checked that the information contained in $J_2$ and $K_2$ will now be found in the contrasts PQ and RS, so that an Anova table based on a binary coding of such a function would again lead to the conclusion that the problem is epistatic.

In contrast to the binary versus Gray question, it would seem more doubtful that adoption of a binary coding could make an epistatic $q$-ary problem less so. Thus, to the extent that it is harder for a GA to solve an epistatic problem than a simple linear one (and we note that in the latter case we would not actually need to use a GA at all), we might argue that binary coding of the function is likely to increase epistasis, so that any supposed advantage from binary coding could be negated.

## 5    WALSH TRANSFORMS AND DECEPTION

Thus far we have seen that Davidor's linear decomposition of a bit-encoded function leads to a set of coefficients which are equivalent to the standard linear model of experimental design. Another linear decomposition which is often used in the analysis of GAs is the *Walsh transform*.

Bethke [19] introduced the idea of using Walsh transforms to analyse the process of a GA in the case of binary-coded strings. The ideas used were given greater impetus and wider currency in papers by Goldberg [3, 4]. More recently, Mason [5] has defined the concept of a *partition coefficient* as a generalization of the Walsh coefficients for non-binary strings. He proceeds to derive some theoretical results from this definition, which makes it clear that these coefficients are just the 'effects' as defined in the ED context, and his theoretical results are simply a derivation of the side constraints as outlined above. It further follows from this that the Walsh transform decomposition is also equivalent to that of experimental design. However, it is instructive to examine the relationship between Walsh transform analysis and experimental design rather more closely. We shall focus particularly on Goldberg's famous 3-bit deceptive problem, as in Table 1.

In Walsh transform analysis, the bits are usually numbered from right to left, so *in this section only* we shall adopt the same convention. The Walsh monomials are defined on the string positions $\{y_i\}$ coded for convenience as $+1$ or $-1$ rather than the usual 0 or 1:

$$\psi_j(y) = \Pi_{i=1}^{l}(y_i)^{j_i}$$

where $j_i$ is the $i^{th}$ bit (counting from the right) in the binary representation of the number $j$. The Walsh function representation of the fitness $v$ is

$$v(y) = \sum_{j=0}^{2^l-1} w_j \psi_j(y)$$

where $y$ encodes the bit positions as above. There are clearly the same number of independent coefficients in the ED decomposition as there are Walsh coefficients, so it is natural to ask how they are related.

The relationship is clearly illustrated in a 3-bit example. The Walsh coefficients can be found from the fitness averages for different schemata:

$$
\begin{aligned}
v_{***} &= w_0 \\
v_{**0} &= w_0 + w_1 \\
v_{**1} &= w_0 - w_1 \quad \text{etc}
\end{aligned}
$$

whereas from the experimental design viewpoint, we have

$$
\begin{aligned}
v_{***} &= \mu \\
v_{**0} &= \mu + \alpha_0 \\
v_{**1} &= \mu + \alpha_1 \quad \text{etc.}
\end{aligned}
$$

If we write out the full set of equations, we find that

$$
\begin{aligned}
\mu &= w_0 \\
\alpha_i &= (-1)^i w_1 \\
\beta_j &= (-1)^j w_2 \\
(\alpha\beta)_{ij} &= (-1)^{i+j} w_3 \\
\gamma_k &= (-1)^k w_4 \\
(\alpha\gamma)_{ik} &= (-1)^{i+k} w_5 \\
(\beta\gamma)_{jk} &= (-1)^{j+k} w_6 \\
(\alpha\beta\gamma)_{ijk} &= (-1)^{i+j+k} w_7
\end{aligned}
$$

The 'mapping' from the Walsh coefficient numbers to the appropriate 'effect' is given by writing the effects in what is known in experimental design as *standard order*: in this case $\{\mu, \alpha, \beta, \alpha\beta, \gamma, \alpha\gamma, \beta\gamma, \alpha\beta\gamma\}$. The general pattern is fairly obvious—on adding another factor the next set of effects is obtained by 'combining' the new factor with the effects already listed, in the same order. Thus in the case of a 4-bit problem, for example, the next 8 effects in standard order will be

$$\{\delta, \alpha\delta, \beta\delta, \alpha\beta\delta, \gamma\delta, \alpha\gamma\delta, \beta\gamma\delta, \alpha\beta\gamma\delta\}.$$

It is also fairly obvious that this order is a consequence of the definition of the Walsh monomials.

Thus in general, to convert from the Walsh representation to the ED coefficients, we first identify the appropriate coefficient as above, and its associated indices, and then multiply by $(-1)^{\sum \text{indices}}$.

### 5.1  Implications for deception

In his first paper [3], Goldberg uses Walsh coefficients to design the fully deceptive 3-bit function of Table 1. The requirement for this function is that while 111 is the optimal point, any schema containing 1s should be less fit than the corresponding schema which contains 0s: for example, $v_{**1} < v_{**0}$. We now consider this function from the ED viewpoint.

For example, the inequality $v_{**1} < v_{**0}$ can be decomposed as follows (remembering that the numbering is from right to left, so that the specified gene here corresponds to $\alpha$). $v_{**1} < v_{**0}$ implies that

$$v_{001} + v_{011} + v_{101} + v_{111} < v_{000} + v_{010} + v_{100} + v_{110}.$$

On substituting the ED model given in Equation 1, the left-hand-side of this inequality is

$$4\mu + 4\alpha_1 + 2[\beta_0 + \beta_1 + \gamma_0 + \gamma_1] + 2[(\alpha\beta)_{10} + (\alpha\beta)_{11}] + 2[(\alpha\gamma)_{10} + (\alpha\gamma)_{11}] +$$
$$(\beta\gamma)_{00} + (\beta\gamma)_{01} + (\beta\gamma)_{10} + (\beta\gamma)_{11} + (\alpha\beta\gamma)_{100} + (\alpha\beta\gamma)_{110} + (\alpha\beta\gamma)_{101} + (\alpha\beta\gamma)_{111}$$

while the right-hand-side is

$$4\mu + 4\alpha_0 + 2(\beta_0 + \beta_1 + \gamma_0 + \gamma_1) + 2[(\alpha\beta)_{00} + (\alpha\beta)_{01}] + 2[(\alpha\gamma)_{00} + (\alpha\gamma)_{01}] +$$
$$(\beta\gamma)_{00} + (\beta\gamma)_{01} + (\beta\gamma)_{10} + (\beta\gamma)_{11} + (\alpha\beta\gamma)_{000} + (\alpha\beta\gamma)_{010} + (\alpha\beta\gamma)_{001} + (\alpha\beta\gamma)_{011}.$$

Many of these terms cancel, while because of the side constraints terms such as $(\alpha\beta)_{10} + (\alpha\beta)_{11}$ vanish, and we are simply left with

$$\alpha_1 < \alpha_0.$$

The other order-1 schemata inequalities similarly reduce to

$$\beta_1 < \beta_0, \gamma_1 < \gamma_0$$

which, again because of the side constraints, simply mean that the effects with the '1' subscripts are the negative ones. Thus we could write

$$\alpha_1 = -a, \alpha_0 = a, \qquad \text{etc}$$

where it is to be understood that $a > 0$. It can also be shown that the order-2 inequalities lead to relationships of the form

$$
\begin{aligned}
\alpha_1 + (\alpha\beta)_{10} &< \alpha_0 + (\alpha\beta)_{00} \\
\beta_1 + (\alpha\beta)_{01} &< \beta_0 + (\alpha\beta)_{00} \\
\alpha_1 + \beta_1 + (\alpha\beta)_{11} &< \alpha_0 + \beta_0 + (\alpha\beta)_{00}
\end{aligned}
$$

The first two constraints reduce to

$$
\begin{aligned}
a + (ab) &> 0 \\
b + (ab) &> 0 \qquad \text{etc}
\end{aligned}
$$

where, because of the side constraints,

$$
\begin{aligned}
(\alpha\beta)_{00} &= (\alpha\beta)_{11} = (ab) \\
(\alpha\beta)_{01} &= (\alpha\beta)_{10} = -(ab), \qquad \text{etc.}
\end{aligned}
$$

The third constraint is redundant, as the interaction terms cancel.

Finally, we have the fact that $v_{111}$ is the optimum, leading to 7 inequalities generated by $v_{111} > v_{011}$ etc. After some algebra, these reduce to the following:

$$
\begin{aligned}
(ab) + (ac) &> b + c \\
(ab) + (ac) &> a + (abc) \\
(ab) + (bc) &> a + c \\
(ab) + (bc) &> b + (abc) \\
(ac) + (bc) &> a + b \\
(ac) + (bc) &> c + (abc) \\
(abc) &< -(a + b + c)
\end{aligned}
$$

The last inequality puts an upper bound on the third-order interaction, $(abc)$, and also forces it to be negative. The other conditions occur in pairs, each of them having the following interpretations:

- for each factor, the sum of the interactions with the other two factors must exceed the sum of the other two main effects;

- for each factor, the sum of the interactions with the other two factors and the third-order interaction must exceed that main effect (where we have used the fact that $(abc)$ is negative).

There are two comments here: firstly it is interesting that deception corresponds to 'large' interaction terms. There is a possible link here with the results of Liepins and Vose [6] who, although using yet another decomposition, found similar conditions for distinguishing between levels of epistasis. (It is obviously possible, although perhaps less interesting, to relate their polynomial decomposition to experimental design. The conditions on the coefficients in their decomposition do not have as 'nice' an interpretation as the above.)

The second comment relates to the relative transparency of this way of expressing the deception conditions. We would argue that they are rather more meaningful than when they are expressed by the rather anonymous Walsh coefficients. In fact, this analysis revealed an error in the specification given in Goldberg [3]—probably due to a typographical mistake which would be much harder to overlook using the ED formulation[1]. Remarkably, on comparing the ED decomposition to the Liepins and Vose representation, it was clear that there was also an error in one of the definitions in [6]!

## 6    CROSSOVER NON-LINEARITY RATIOS

Earlier, we referred to Mason's extension [5] of the Walsh transform decomposition to what he calls partition coefficients in the general (non-binary) case. These he denotes by symbols such as $\epsilon(i * *)$, which in ED terms represents the effect of allele $i$ at gene 1. That is, his $\epsilon(i * *)$ is just the term we have called $\alpha_i$.

In a more recent paper [21], Mason has taken this concept a stage further in an attempt to analyse the effect of traditional crossover and how this operator interacts with a given function. This is an important question, as it marks a step beyond the essentially static

---

[1]Goldberg [20] has confirmed that two inequalities which *should* read $w_3 + w_5 > w_1 + w_7$ and $w_3 + w_6 > w_2 + w_7$ have had their right-hand sides transposed in [3].

analysis of epistasis to a consideration of dynamic aspects. In Mason's terminology, if two strings $ab$ and $pq$ are crossed to produce $aq$ and $pb$, where $a, b, p, q$ may all represent *substrings* of several bits, we can form a *crossover non-linearity ratio*

$$\psi = \frac{|\epsilon(ab)|}{sign[\epsilon(a*)\epsilon(*b)][|\epsilon(a*)| + |\epsilon(*b)|]},$$

where the $\epsilon(a*)$ are now 'pseudo partition coefficients'. The purpose of this is to attempt to identify cases where crossover is likely to fail to combine building blocks usefully.

Unfortunately, he makes the assumptions that $\epsilon(a*) = -\epsilon(p*)$, $\epsilon(*b) = -\epsilon(*q)$ etc. These relations are perfectly valid in the case where $a, b, p, q$ represent single bits, but it does not follow when they represent several bits. We can see this quite easily from the ED viewpoint, if we take the simplest non-trivial case of 3-bit binary strings, where $a, p$ represent the first 2 bits, and $b, q$ the last one.

Using the ED decomposition of Equation 1, we can identify Mason's pseudo partition coefficients as follows (in an obvious notation):

$$
\begin{aligned}
\epsilon(a*) &= \alpha_{i_a} + \beta_{j_a} + (\alpha\beta)_{i_a j_a} \\
\epsilon(*b) &= \gamma_{k_b} \\
\epsilon(ab) &= (\alpha\gamma)_{i_a k_b} + (\beta\gamma)_{j_a k_b} + (\alpha\beta\gamma)_{i_a j_a k_b}
\end{aligned}
$$

Assuming that $a, p$ are not identical, it is clear we have two cases to consider. If *both* $i_a \neq i_p$ and $j_a \neq j_p$ then

$$\epsilon(a*) + \epsilon(p*) = 2(\alpha\beta)_{i_a j_a} \neq 0$$

because of the side constraints. Similarly, if just one of $i_a = i_p$ or $j_a = j_p$ is true, then we have

$$\epsilon(a*) + \epsilon(p*) = 2\alpha_{i_a} \neq 0 \quad \text{or} \quad \epsilon(a*) + \epsilon(p*) = 2\beta_{j_a} \neq 0$$

so that in neither case does the single-bit result follow through. There must consequently be some doubt as to the usefulness of $\psi$: a value of near zero is interpreted in [21] as indicating low epistasis and thus a situation where traditional one-point crossover is likely to be effective. However, it is clear from the above decomposition of his $\epsilon(ab)$ that a zero value of the $\psi$ ratio could result from an appropriate combination of interaction terms of different orders.

## 7    CONCLUSIONS

We have shown that there are considerable and interesting links between genetic algorithms and traditional experimental design methods, and that ED can help to illuminate the still inadequately understood nature of epistasis in GAs. These links have been adumbrated and explored in the context of three applications in the GA literature: Davidor's 'epistasis variance'; the Walsh transform analysis of Goldberg; and Mason's attempt to extend the latter to investigate the interaction between the characteristics of a function and the crossover operator. In each case, the ED perspective is helpful; it provides another way of formulating and understanding what the existing methodology is doing—a way which we would argue is more transparent and intuitive.

However, this approach has in common with existing methodology that it begs a very large question: in practice we have no knowledge of the Universe. This means that measures of epistasis, for instance, which assume such knowledge may give unpredictable and even contradictory results when we base them on sample information. In fact, experimental design has a long history of dealing with this problem, and in a further paper, currently in preparation, we hope to show how light can be thrown on this crucial question by drawing on the 50 years of experience which statisticians have accumulated in using experimental design. As already mentioned, it is also as yet far from certain whether the epistasis measures that have been developed actually do indicate cases which are in practice hard or easy for a GA (or indeed any other heuristic), but we hope that the ED approach will also enable this question to be more carefully addressed.

In summary, we believe that the experimental design perspective on GAs has much to commend it. At the very least it gives GA researchers another tool for approaching the analysis of GA performance. The history of the past decade has been of exciting and novel developments of genetic algorithms which have somewhat outstripped the development of tools for thinking theoretically about what GAs are doing. We hope that in a small way this paper will give the GA community something else to help in this endeavour.

# References


[1] Y.Davidor (1990) Epistasis variance: suitability of a representation to genetic algorithms. *Complex Systems*, **4**, 369-383.

[2] Y.Davidor (1991) Epistasis variance: a viewpoint on GA-hardness. *In* G.J.E.Rawlins (Ed.) (1991) *Foundations of Genetic Algorithms*, Morgan Kaufmann, San Mateo, CA.

[3] D.E.Goldberg (1989) Genetic algorithms and Walsh functions: part I, a gentle introduction. *Complex Systems*, **3**, 129-152.

[4] D.E.Goldberg (1989) Genetic algorithms and Walsh functions: part II, deception and its analysis. *Complex Systems*, **3**, 153-171.

[5] A.J.Mason (1991) Partition coefficients, static deception and deceptive problems for non-binary alphabets. *In* [23], 210-214.

[6] G.E.Liepins and M.D.Vose (1990) Representational issues in genetic optimization. *J.Exper. and Theor. Artificial Intelligence*, **2**, 101-115.

[7] M.D.Vose and G.E.Liepins (1991) Schema disruption. *In* [23], 237-242.

[8] D.Whitley(1992) Deception, dominance and implicit parallelism in genetic search. *Annals of Maths. and AI*, **5**, 49-78.

[9] D.E.Goldberg, B.Korb and K.Deb (1989) Messy genetic algorithms: motivation, analysis and first results. *Complex Systems*, **3**, 493-530.

[10] D.E.Goldberg, K.Deb and B.Korb (1990) Messy genetic algorithms revisited: studies in mixed size and scale. *Complex Systems*, **4**, 415-444.

[11] N.J.Radcliffe (1992) Non-linear genetic representations. *In* R.Männer and B.Manderick (Eds.) (1992) *Parallel problem-Solving from Nature 2.* Elsevier Science Publishers, Amsterdam.

[12] O.Kempthorne (1952) *The Design and Analysis of Experiments.* Wiley, New York.

[13] D.C.Montgomery (1991) *Design and Analysis of Experiments.* Wiley, New York.

[14] J.H.Holland (1975) *Adaptation in Natural and Artificial Systems.* University of Michigan Press, Ann Arbor.

[15] D.E.Goldberg (1989) *Genetic Algorithms in Search, Optimization, and Machine Learning.* Addison-Wesley, Reading, Mass.

[16] R.A.Caruana and J.D.Schaffer (1988) Representation and hidden bias: Gray vs. binary coding for genetic algorithms. In *Proc. 5th International Conference on Machine Learning.* Morgan Kaufmann, Los Altos, CA.

[17] J.Antonisse (1989) A new interpretation of schema notation that overturns the binary encoding constraint. *In* [22], 86-91.

[18] C.R.Reeves (1993) Using genetic algorithms with small populations. *In* [24], 92-99.

[19] A.D.Bethke (1981) *Genetic Algorithms as Function Optimizers.* Doctoral dissertation, University of Michigan.

[20] D.E.Goldberg (1993) Personal communication.

[21] A.J.Mason (1993) *Crossover Non-linearity Ratios and the Genetic Algorithm: Escaping the Blinkers of Schema Processing and Intrinsic Parallelism.* Report No. 535b, School of Engineering, University of Auckland, NZ.

[22] J.D.Schaffer (Ed.) (1989) *Proceedings of $3^{rd}$ International Conference on Genetic Algorithms.* Morgan Kaufmann, Los Altos, CA.

[23] R.K.Belew and L.B.Booker (Eds.) (1991) *Proceedings of $4^{th}$ International Conference on Genetic Algorithms.* Morgan Kaufmann, San Mateo, CA.

[24] S.Forrest (Ed.) (1993) *Proceedings of $5^{th}$ International Conference on Genetic Algorithms,* Morgan Kaufmann, San Mateo, CA.

# The Schema Theorem and Price's Theorem

**Lee Altenberg**
Institute of Statistics and Decision Sciences
Duke University, Durham, NC, USA 27708-0251
Internet: `altenber@acpub.duke.edu`

## Abstract

Holland's Schema Theorem is widely taken to be the foundation for explanations
of the power of genetic algorithms (GAs). Yet some dissent has been expressed as
to its implications. Here, dissenting arguments are reviewed and elaborated upon,
explaining why the Schema Theorem has no implications for how well a GA is
performing. Interpretations of the Schema Theorem have implicitly assumed that
a correlation exists between parent and offspring fitnesses, and this assumption
is made explicit in results based on Price's Covariance and Selection Theorem.
Schemata do not play a part in the performance theorems derived for representations and operators in general. However, schemata re-emerge when recombination
operators are used. Using Geiringer's recombination distribution representation
of recombination operators, a "missing" schema theorem is derived which makes
explicit the intuition for when a GA should perform well. Finally, the method
of "adaptive landscape" analysis is examined and counterexamples offered to the
commonly used correlation statistic. Instead, an alternative statistic — the transmission function in the fitness domain — is proposed as the optimal statistic for
estimating GA performance from limited samples.

## 1 INTRODUCTION

Although it is generally stated that the Schema Theorem (Holland, 1975) explains the power
of genetic algorithms (GAs), dissent to this view has been expressed a number of times
(Grefenstette and Baker 1989, Mühlenbein 1991, Radcliffe 1992). Mühlenbein points out
that "the Schema Theorem is almost a tautology, only describing proportional selection,"
and that "the question of why the genetic algorithm builds better and better substrings by
crossing-over is ignored." Radcliffe points out that

1. The Schema Theorem holds even with random representations, which cannot be expected to perform better than random search, whereas it has been used to claim that GAs perform better than random search;

2. The Schema Theorem holds even when the schemata defined by a representation may not capture the properties that determine fitness; and

3. The Schema Theorem extends to arbitrary subsets of the search space regardless of the kind of genetic operators, not merely the subsets defined by Holland schemata (Grefenstette 1989, Radcliffe 1991, Vose 1991).

The Schema Theorem, in short, does not address the search component of genetic algorithms on which performance depends, and cannot distinguish genetic algorithms that are performing well from those that are not. How, then, has the Schema Theorem been interpreted as providing a foundation for understanding GA performance?

What the Schema Theorem says is that schemata with above-average fitness (especially short, low order schemata), increase their frequency in the population each generation at an exponential rate when rare. The mistake is to conclude that this growth of schemata has any implications for the quality of the search carried out by the GA. The Schema Theorem's implication, as many have put it, is that the genetic algorithm is focusing its search on promising regions of the search space, and thus increasing the likelihood that new samples of the search space will have higher fitness. But the phrase "promising regions of the search space" is a construct through which hidden assumptions are introduced which are not implied by the Schema Theorem. What is a "region", and what makes it "promising"?

The regions are schemata, and "promising regions" are schemata with above-average fitness. Offspring produced by recombination will tend to be drawn from the same "regions" as their parents, depending on the disruption rate from recombination. The common interpretation of the Schema Theorem implicitly assumes that any member of an above-average schema is likely to produce offspring of above-average fitness, i.e. that there is a correlation between membership in an above-average schema and production of fitter offspring. But the existence of such correlations is logically independent of the validity of the Schema Theorem.

For example, consider a population with a needle-in-a-haystack fitness function, where exactly one genotype (the "needle") has a high fitness, and all the other genotypes in the search space (the "hay") have the same low fitness. Consider a population in which the "needle" has already been found. The needle will tend to increase in frequency by selection, while recombination will most likely generate more "hay". The Schema Theorem will still be seen to operate, in that short schemata with above-average fitness (those schemata containing the needle) will increase in frequency, even though the fitness of new instances of the schemata (more hay) will not be any more likely to have the high fitness of the needle.

It is the quality of the search that must be used to characterize the performance of a genetic algorithm. One basis for evaluation is to compare the ability of a GA to generate new, highly fit individuals with the rate at which they are generated by random search. A direct approach to measuring GA performance is to analyze the change in the fitness distribution as the population evolves. For a GA to perform better than random search, the upper tail of the fitness distribution has to grow in time to be larger than the tail produced by random search. Some initial efforts at characterizing the growth of the upper tail of the fitness distribution were provided in Altenberg (1994), where a notion of "evolvability" — the ability to produce individuals fitter than any existing — was introduced as a measure of GA performance. A basic result is that for a GA to perform better than random search, there has to be a correlation between the fitness of parents and the upper tail of the fitness distribution of their offspring. This was obtained by using Price's Covariance and Selection Theorem (Price 1970, 1972) with a particular measurement function that extracts the fitness distribution from the population.

In this paper, I first review the application of Price's Theorem to GA performance analysis. Then I show how Price's Theorem can be used to obtain the Schema Theorem by employing a measurement function that extracts the frequency of a schema from the population. The difference between the theorem that measures GA performance, and the Schema Theorem, which does not, is shown to be simply a choice of measurement functions.

In the process of deriving results that relate the parent-offspring correlations to the performance of the GA under a generalized transmission function, schemata disappear as pertinent entities. Therefore, "schema processing" is not a requirement for performance in evolutionary algorithms in general. However, under recombination operators, schemata reappear in the formula for the change in the fitness distribution. This "missing" schema theorem shows explicitly that there must be correlations between schema fitnesses and offspring fitness distributions for good GA performance. It gives a quantitative expression to the Building Blocks Hypothesis (Goldberg 1989) and suggests ways to modify recombination operators to improve genetic algorithm performance.

## 2    GENETIC ALGORITHM ANALYSIS USING PRICE'S THEOREM

The strategy I take here (see Altenberg (1994) for details) is to start with a general formulation of the "canonical" genetic algorithm dynamics, for arbitrary representations, operators, and fitness functions. *Measurement functions* are then introduced to extract macroscopic features of the population. The evolution of these features can be shown, using Price's Covariance and Selection Theorem, to depend on the covariance between the measurement function and fitness. The choice of one measurement function gives us the Schema Theorem, while the choice of another measurement function gives us the evolution of the fitness distribution in the population, which I refer to as the *Local Performance Theorem*. Thus, the inability of the Schema Theorem to distinguish GA performance can be seen simply as the consequence of the measurement function that was chosen.

### 2.1    A GENERAL MODEL OF THE CANONICAL GENETIC ALGORITHM

A "canonical" model of genetic algorithms has been generally used since its formulation by Holland (1975), which incorporates assumptions common to many evolutionary models in population genetics: discrete, non-overlapping generations, frequency-independent selection, and infinite population size. The algorithm iterates three steps: selection, random mating, and production of offspring to constitute the population in the next generation.

**Definition: Canonical Genetic Algorithm**
*The dynamical system representing the "canonical" genetic algorithm is:*

$$p(x)' = \sum_{y,z \in \mathcal{S}} T(x \leftarrow y, z) \frac{w(y)w(z)}{\overline{w}^2} p(y)p(z), \tag{1}$$

*where*

*$p(x)$ is the frequency of chromosome $x$ in the population, and $p(x)'$ is the frequency in the next generation;*

*$\mathcal{S}$ is the search space of $n$ chromosomal types;*

*$T(x \leftarrow y, z)$, the transmission function, is the probability that offspring genotype $x$ is produced by parental genotypes $y$ and $z$ as a result of the action of genetic operators on the representation, with $T(x \leftarrow y, z) = T(x \leftarrow z, y)$, and $\sum_x T(x \leftarrow y, z) = 1$ for all $y, z \in \mathcal{S}$;*

*$w(x)$ is the fitness of chromosome $x$; and*

*$\overline{w} = \sum_x w(x)p(x)$ is the mean fitness of the population;*

This general form of the transmission-selection recursion was used by Slatkin (1970), and has been used subsequently for a variety of quantitative genetic and complex transmission systems (Cavalli-Sforza and Feldman 1976, Karlin 1979, Altenberg and Feldman 1987), and has been derived independently in genetic algorithm analysis (Vose 1990, Vose and Liepins 1991).

No assumptions are made about the structure of the chromosomes — e.g. the number of loci, the number of alleles at each locus, or even the linearity of the chromosome. The specific structure of the transmission function $T(x \leftarrow y, z)$ will carry the information about the chromosomal structure and genetic operators that is relevant to the dynamics of the GA.

As a cross-reference, the "mixing matrix" defined by Vose (1990) is the $n$ by $n$ matrix

$$\left\| T(0 \leftarrow y_i, z_j) \right\|_{i,j=1}^{n},$$

where $0$ is the chromosome with all 0 alleles in the case of binary chromosomes, and chromosomes $y$ and $z$ are indexed from 1 to $n$. This is sufficient to characterize the transmission function in the case where mutation and recombination are symmetric with respect to either allele at each locus, by using $n$ permutations of the arguments.

### 2.1.1  A Note on Fitness

The term "fitness" has undergone a semantic shift in its migration from population biology to evolutionary computation. In population biology, fitness generally refers to the actual rate that an individual type ends up being sampled in contributing to the next generation. So the fitness coefficient $w(x)$ lumps together all the disparate influences from different traits, intraspecific competition, and environmental interaction that produce it. In the evolutionary computation literature, fitness has come to be used synonymously with one or more objective functions (e.g. Koza (1992)). Under this usage is there is no longer a word that refers specifically to the reproductive contribution of a genotype. Here I will keep the distinction between objective function and fitness, and use "fitness" in its sense in population biology.

The term "fitness proportionate selection" refers to fitnesses that are independent of chromosome frequencies. Many selection schemes, such as tournament and rank-based selection, truncation selection, fitness sharing, and other population-based rescaling, are examples of *frequency-dependent* selection (Altenberg (1991) contains further references). In frequency-dependent selection, the fitness $w(x)$ is a function not only of $x$ but of the composition of the population as well. All the theorems and corollaries in this paper apply to frequency-dependent selection. This is because they are all local, i.e. they apply to changes over a single generation based on the current composition of the population, so that any frequency-dependence in the fitness function $w(x)$ does not enter into the result.

The results on GA performance in this paper are defined directly in terms of the fitness distribution of the population. However, fitness functions are often defined in terms of an underlying objective function for the elements in the search space. This is the case with tournament selection, in which an individual's fitness equals the rank of their objective function in the population ($w = 1/N$ for the worst and $w = 1$ for the best individual in a population of size $N$). In these cases, GA performance ultimately is concerned with the distributions of objective function values in the population. The map from objective function to fitness would add an additional layer to the analysis of GA performance, and is not investigated here. However, numerous empirical studies have been undertaken to ascertain the effects of different selection schemes, with GA performance defined on underlying objective functions. So in the future such an analysis would be worthwhile.

### 2.1.2    Toward a Macroscopic Analysis

In the evolution of a population, individual chromosomes come and go, and their frequencies follow complex trajectories. These microscopic details are not the usual subject of interest when considering the performance of the GA (the one exception being the frequency of the fittest member of the search space). Rather, it is macroscopic properties, such as the population's mean fitness or fitness distribution, whose evolutionary trajectory is of interest. This is similar to the case of statistical mechanics, where one is interested not in the trajectories of individual molecules, but in the distribution of energies in the material.

It would be very useful if the evolutionary dynamics of the population could be defined solely at the macroscopic level — i.e. if the macroscopic description were *dynamically sufficient*. In GAs this will generally not be the case. However, let us consider one special condition when it is possible to describe the evolution of the fitness distribution solely in terms of the fitness distribution: when the fitness function $w(x)$ is invertible, i.e. no two genotypes have the same fitness. Then (1) can be transformed into a recursion in fitness domain:

$$f(w)' = \int_0^\infty T(w \leftarrow u, v)\frac{uv}{\overline{w}^2} f(u)\, f(v)\, du\, dv, \tag{2}$$

where $f(w)$ is the probability density of fitness $w$ in the population (integration may be over discrete measure), and $T(w \leftarrow u, v) = T(x \leftarrow y, z)$ when $w = w(x)$, $u = w(y)$, and $v = w(z)$.

For the purposes of statistical estimation of the performance of a GA, which will be an imprecise task to begin with, it may be sufficient to proceed as though the GA dynamics

Table 1: Measurement functions, $F(x)$ (some taking arguments), and the population properties measured by their mean in the population, $\overline{F}$.

| Population Property Measured by $\overline{F}$: | Measurement Function: |
|---|---|
| (1) Fitness distribution upper tail: | $F(x, w) = \begin{cases} 1 & w(x) > w \\ 0 & w(x) \le w \end{cases}$ |
| (2) Frequency of schema $\mathcal{H}$: | $F(x, \mathcal{H}) = \begin{cases} 1 & x \in \mathcal{H} \\ 0 & x \notin \mathcal{H} \end{cases}$ |
| (3) Mean fitness: | $F(x) = w(x)$ |
| (4) Fitness distribution's $n$-th non-central moment: | $F(x) = w(x)^n$ |
| (5) Mean phenotype (vector valued): | $F(x) \in \mathbb{R}^n$ |
| (6) Mean objective function: | $F(x) \in \mathbb{R}$ |

could be represented as in (2). That will be the strategy I suggest for statistically predicting the performance of a GA based on a limited sample from a GA run: an empirically derived estimate of $T(w \leftarrow u, v)$ may be used in (2) to approximate the dynamics of (1), in order to make predictions about GA performance. This is taken up in Section 4 on "adaptive landscape" analysis.

## 2.2   MEASUREMENT FUNCTIONS

A means of extracting macroscopic dynamics of a population from its microscopic dynamics (1) is the use of the appropriate *measurement functions*.

The fitness $w(x)$ is an example of a measurement function. Measurement functions need not be restricted to fitnesses, nor even scalar values. In general, let the measurement function $F(x)$ represent some property of genotype $x$, with $F : S \mapsto V$, where $V$ is a vector space over the real numbers (e.g. $\mathbb{R}^k$ or $[0, 1]^k$ for some positive integer $k$). The change in the population average of a measurement function is a measure of how the population is evolving:

$$\overline{F} = \sum_x F(x)\, p(x), \quad \overline{F}' = \sum_x F(x)\, p(x)' \tag{3}$$

A measurement function can be defined to indicate when a genotype instantiates a particular schema $\mathcal{H}$, by adding $\mathcal{H}$ as a parameter: $F(x, \mathcal{H}) = 1$ if $x \in \mathcal{H}$ and 0 otherwise. In general we can let $F : S \times \mathcal{P} \mapsto V$ be a parameterized family of measurement functions, for some parameter space $\mathcal{P}$.

Examples of different measurement functions and the population properties measured by $\overline{F}$ are shown in Table 1. Measurement functions (1) and (2) are the focus her: (1) extracts the fitness distribution of the population, and (2) extracts the frequency of a schema in the population.

## 2.3   PRICE'S THEOREM

Price (1970) introduced a theorem that partitions the effect of selection on a population in terms of covariances between fitness and the property of interest (allele frequencies were the property considered by Price) and effects due to transmission. Price's theorem has been applied in a number of different contexts in evolutionary genetics, including kin selection (Grafen 1985, Taylor 1988), group selection (Wade 1985), the evolution of mating systems (Uyenoyama 1988), and quantitative genetics (Frank and Slatkin 1990). Price's theorem gives the one-generation change in the population mean value of $F$:

**Theorem 1 (Covariance and Selection, Price, 1970)**
*For any parental pair $\{y, z\}$, let $\phi(y, z)$ represent the expected value of $F$ among their offspring. Thus:*

$$\phi(y, z) = \sum_x F(x)\, T(x \leftarrow y, z). \tag{4}$$

*Then the population average of the measurement function in the next generation is*

$$\overline{F}' = \overline{\phi} + \mathrm{Cov}[\phi(y, z),\, w(y)w(z)/\overline{w}^2] \tag{5}$$

*where*

$$\overline{\phi} = \sum_{y,z} \phi(y, z)\, p(y)p(z)$$

*is the average offspring value in a population reproducing without selection, and*

$$\mathrm{Cov}[\phi(y, z),\, w(y)w(z)/\overline{w}^2] = \sum_{y,z} \phi(y, z)\, \frac{w(y)w(z)}{\overline{w}^2}\, p(y)p(z) - \overline{\phi} \tag{6}$$

*is the population covariance (i.e. the covariance over the distribution of genotypes in the population) between the parental fitness values and the measured values of their offspring.*

*Proof.*   One must assume that for each $y$ and $z$, the expectation $\phi(y, z)$ exists (for measurement functions (1) and (2), the expectation always exists). Substitution of (1), (4), and (6) into (3) directly produces (5). ∎

Price's theorem shows that the covariance between parental fitness and offspring traits is the means by which selection directs the evolution of the population. Several corollaries follow:

**Corollary 1** *Let $C(y, z) = \phi(y, z) - [F(y) + F(z)]/2$ represent the difference between the mean of $F$ among parents $y$ and $z$, and the mean of $F$ in their offspring. Then*

$$\overline{F}' - \overline{F} = \mathrm{Cov}[F(x), w(x)/\overline{w}] + \overline{C} + \mathrm{Cov}[C(x, y), w(x)\, w(y)/\overline{w}^2],$$

*where $\overline{C} = \sum_{y,z} C(y, z)\, p(y)\, p(z)$.*

*Proof.*   The term $\mathrm{Cov}[F(x), w(x)/\overline{w}]$ uses the evaluation:

$$\sum_{y,z} \frac{1}{2}[F(y) + F(z)]\, \frac{w(y)w(z)}{\overline{w}^2}\, p(y)p(z) = \sum_y F(y)\, \frac{w(y)}{\overline{w}}\, p(y),$$

while the other terms follow from straightforward algebra. ∎

**Corollary 2 (Fisher's Fundamental Theorem, 1930)**
*Consider a population evolving in the absence of a genetic operator, so*

$$T(x \leftarrow y, z) = [\delta(x, y) + \delta(x, z)]/2,$$

*where*

$$\delta(x, y) = \begin{cases} 1 & \text{if } x = y \\ 0 & \text{if } x \neq y. \end{cases}$$

*Then $C(y, z) = 0$. For $F(x) = w(x)$, Corollary 1 gives:*

$$\overline{w}' - \overline{w} = \overline{w}\, \mathrm{Var}[w(x)/\overline{w}].$$

## 2.4   A LOCAL PERFORMANCE MEASURE FOR GENETIC ALGORITHMS

Price's theorem can be used to extract the change in the *distribution* of fitness values in the population by using the measurement function (1) from Table 1. Then

$$\overline{F}(w) = \sum_{x} F(x, w)\, p(x) = \sum_{x:\, w(x) > w} p(x)$$

is the proportion of the population that has fitness greater than $w$. Price's Theorem gives:

**Corollary 3 (Evolution of the fitness distribution)**
*The fitness distribution in the next generation is:*

$$\overline{F}(w)' = \overline{\phi}(w) + \mathrm{Cov}[\phi(y, z, w),\ w(y)w(z)/\overline{w}^2], \tag{7}$$

*where $\phi(y, z, w)$ is the proportion of offspring from parents $y$ and $z$ that with fitness greater than $w$.*

Note that $\phi(y, z, w)$ always exists, even when the distribution of fitnesses among the offspring of $y$ and $z$ has no expectation, i.e. when $\sum_{x} w(x)\, T(x \leftarrow y, z)$ is infinite.

The expression (7) can be made more informative by rewriting $\phi(y, z, w)$ as the sum of a random search term plus a *search bias* term that gives how parents $y$ and $z$ compare with random search in their offspring fitnesses. Let $\mathcal{R}(w)$ be the probability that random search produces an individual fitter than than $w$, and let the *search bias*, $\beta(y, z, w)$, be:

$$\beta(y, z, w) = \phi(y, z, w) - \mathcal{R}(w) = \sum_{x} F(x, w)\, T(x \leftarrow y, z) - \mathcal{R}(w).$$

The average search bias for a population before selection is $\overline{\beta}(w) = \sum_{y,z} \beta(y, z, w)\, p(y)\, p(z)$. The coefficient of regression of $\beta(y, z, w)$ on $w(y)\, w(z)/\overline{w}^2$ is

$$\mathrm{Reg}[\beta(y, z, w) \rightarrow w(y)\, w(z)/\overline{w}^2] = \mathrm{Cov}[\beta(y, z, w),\ w(y)\, w(z)/\overline{w}^2]\ /\ \mathrm{Var}[w(y)\, w(z)/\overline{w}^2].$$

It measures the magnitude of how $\beta(y, z, w)$ varies with $w(y)w(z)/\overline{w}^2$ in the population.

**Theorem 2 (Local Performance Measure)**
*The probability distribution of fitnesses in the next generation is*

$$\overline{F}(w)' = \mathcal{R}(w) + \overline{\beta}(w) + \mathrm{Reg}[\beta(y, z, w) \rightarrow w(y)\, w(z)/\overline{w}^2]\, \mathrm{Var}[w(y)\, w(z)/\overline{w}^2]. \tag{8}$$

Theorem 2 shows that in order for the GA to perform better than random search in producing individuals fitter than than $w$, the average search bias, plus the parent-offspring regression scaled by the fitness variance,

$$\overline{\beta}(w) + \mathrm{Reg}[\beta(y, z, w) \rightarrow w(y)\, w(z)/\overline{w}^2]\, \mathrm{Var}[w(y)\, w(z)/\overline{w}^2], \tag{9}$$

must be positive. As in the Schema Theorem, this is a local result because the terms in (8) other than $\mathcal{R}(w)$ depend on the composition of the population and thus change as it evolves.

Both the regression and the search bias terms require the transmission function to have "knowledge" about the fitness function. Under random search, the expected value of both these terms would be zero. Some knowledge of the fitness function must be incorporated in the transmission function for the expected value of these terms to be positive. It is this knowledge — whether incorporated explicitly or implicitly — that is the source of power in genetic algorithms.

## 2.5   THE SCHEMA THEOREM

Holland's Schema Theorem (Holland 1975) is classically given as follows. Let

$\mathcal{H}$ represent a particular schema as defined by Holland (1975),

$L$ be the length of the chromosome, and $L(\mathcal{H}) \leq L-1$ be the defining length of the schema;

$p(\mathcal{H}) = \sum_{x \in \mathcal{H}} p(x)$ be the frequency of schema $\mathcal{H}$ in the population, and

$\overline{w}(\mathcal{H}) = \sum_{x \in \mathcal{H}} w(x)p(x)/p(\mathcal{H})$ be the marginal fitness of schema $\mathcal{H}$.

**Theorem 3 (The Schema Theorem, Holland 1975)**
*In a genetic algorithm using a proportional selection algorithm and single point crossover occurring with probability $r$, the following holds for each schema $\mathcal{H}$:*

$$p(\mathcal{H})' \geq p(\mathcal{H})\frac{\overline{w}(\mathcal{H})}{\overline{w}} \left(1 - r\frac{L(\mathcal{H})}{L-1}\right) \tag{10}$$

Now, Price's Theorem can be used to obtain the Schema Theorem by using:

$$F(x, \mathcal{H}) = \begin{cases} 1 & \text{if } x \in \mathcal{H} \\ 0 & \text{if } i \notin \mathcal{H} \end{cases}$$

and $\phi(y, z, \mathcal{H}) = \sum_x F(x, \mathcal{H})T(x \leftarrow y, z)$, which represents the fraction of offspring of parents $y$ and $z$ that are in schema $\mathcal{H}$. Then $p(\mathcal{H}) = \overline{F}(\mathcal{H})$, and

**Corollary 4 (Schema Frequency Change)**

$$p(\mathcal{H})' = \overline{\phi}(\mathcal{H}) + \text{Cov}[\phi(y, z, \mathcal{H}), \ w(y)w(z)/\overline{w}^2], \tag{11}$$

Two sources can be seen to contribute to a change in schema frequency:

1. linkage disequilibrium, i.e. the schema frequency minus the product of the frequencies of the alleles comprising the schema. Negative linkage disequilibrium would produce $\overline{\phi}(\mathcal{H}) > p(\mathcal{H})$; and

2. covariance between parental fitnesses and the proportion of their offspring in the schema.

Equation (11) can be made more informative by rewriting $\phi(y, z, \mathcal{H})$ in terms of a "disruption" coefficient. A value $\alpha_{\mathcal{H}} \in [0, 1]$ can be defined that places a lower bound on the faithfulness of transmission of any schema $\mathcal{H}$:

$$\phi(y, z, \mathcal{H}) \geq \frac{1}{2}(1 - \alpha_{\mathcal{H}})[F(y, \mathcal{H}) + F(z, \mathcal{H})] \tag{12}$$

and

$$\alpha_{\mathcal{H}} = 1 - \min_{y \in \mathcal{H} \text{ or } z \in \mathcal{H}} \left[ \phi(y, z, \mathcal{H}) \frac{2}{F(y, \mathcal{H}) + F(z, \mathcal{H})} \right].$$

Actually, $\alpha_{\mathcal{H}}$ can be defined for any subset of the search space ("predicate" in Vose (1991) or "forma" in Radcliffe (1991)). For Holland schemata under single-point crossover, $\alpha_{\mathcal{H}} = r\,L(\mathcal{H})/(L-1)$ (the rate that crossover disrupts schema $\mathcal{H}$). Using (12) we obtain:

**Theorem 4 (Schema, Covariance Form)**
*The change in the frequency of any subset $\mathcal{H}$ of the search space (i.e. a schema) over one generation is bounded below by:*

$$p(\mathcal{H})' \geq \{p(\mathcal{H}) + \mathrm{Cov}[F(y, \mathcal{H}), w(x)/\overline{w}]\}\,(1 - \alpha_{\mathcal{H}}). \tag{13}$$

*Therefore, if*

$$\mathrm{Cov}\left[F(y, \mathcal{H}), \frac{w(x)}{\overline{w}}\right] > \frac{\alpha_{\mathcal{H}}}{1 - \alpha_{\mathcal{H}}}$$

*then schema $\mathcal{H}$ will increase in frequency.*

*Proof.*

$$
\begin{aligned}
\overline{F}(\mathcal{H})' &= \sum_{x,y,z} F(x, \mathcal{H}) T(x \leftarrow y, z) \frac{w(y)w(z)}{\overline{w}^2} p(y)p(z) \\
&= \sum_{y,z} \phi(y, z, \mathcal{H}) \frac{w(y)w(z)}{\overline{w}^2} p(y)p(z) \\
&\geq \frac{1}{2}(1 - \alpha_{\mathcal{H}}) \sum_{y,z} [F(y, \mathcal{H}) + F(z, \mathcal{H})] \frac{w(y)w(z)}{\overline{w}^2} p(y)p(z) \\
&= (1 - \alpha_{\mathcal{H}}) \sum_{y} F(y, \mathcal{H}) w(y) p(y)/\overline{w} = (1 - \alpha_{\mathcal{H}}) \left[\overline{F}(\mathcal{H}) + \mathrm{Cov}[F(y, \mathcal{H}), w(x)/\overline{w}]\right].
\end{aligned}
$$

∎

Thus, if there is a great enough covariance between fitness and being a member of a schema, the schema will increase in frequency.

Although both applications of Price's Theorem — to schema frequency change and change in the fitness distribution — involve covariances with parental fitness values, the crucial point is that the covariance term (from (13)), $\mathrm{Cov}[F(y, \mathcal{H}), w(x)/\overline{w}]$, and the covariance term (from (7)), $\mathrm{Cov}[\phi(y, z, w),\ w(y)w(z)/\overline{w}^2]$, are independently defined. So conditions that produce growth in the frequencies of different schemata are independent of conditions that produce growth in the upper tails of the fitness distribution.

For example, consider a fitness function with a random distribution being the one-sided stable distribution of index 1/2 (Feller, 1971): $R(w) = 2\mathcal{N}(a/\sqrt{w}) - 1$, where $\mathcal{N}(y)$ is the Normal distribution and $a$ is a scale parameter. This distribution is a way of generating "needles in the haystack" on all length scales. A GA with this fitness function will generically have schemata that obey (10), even though it is still random search.

# 3   RECOMBINATION AND THE RE-EMERGENCE OF SCHEMATA

In the local performance measure for the genetic algorithm, schemata disappear as relevant entities. No summations over hyperplanes or other subsets of the search space appear in Theorem 2. Schemata are therefore not informative structures for operators and representations in general. However, it is the recombination operator for which schemata have been hypothesized to play a special role. What I show in this section is that when one examines (7) using recombination operators specifically, schemata re-emerge in the local performance theorem, and they appear in a way that offers possible new insight into how schemata enter into GA performance. This "missing" schema theorem makes explicit the intuition, missing from the Schema Theorem, about what makes a good building block.

Recombination operators in a multiple-locus genetic algorithm can be generally characterized using the recombination distribution analysis introduced by Geiringer (1944), and developed independently by Syswerda (1989) (see also Karlin and Liberman 1978, Booker 1993, and Vose and Wright 1994). Consider a system of $L$ loci. Any particular recombination event can be described by indicating which parent the allele for each locus came from. This can be done with a mask, a vector $r \in \{0,1\}^L$, of binary variables $r_i \in \{0,1\}$, which indicate the loci that are transmitted together from either parent. So all loci with $r_i = 0$ are transmitted from one parent, while the remainder of the loci, with $r_i = 1$, are transmitted from the other parent. The vectors $r = 0 = (0\ldots0)$ and $r = 1 = (1\ldots1)$ correspond to an absence of recombination in transmission. With $r$ representing the recombination event that occurred in transmission, the offspring $x$ of parental chromosomes $y$ and $z$ can be expressed as:

$$x = r \circ y + (1-r) \circ z,$$

where $\circ$ is the Schur product: $u \circ v = (u_1 v_1 \ldots u_L v_L)$ (allele multiplication and addition is just for the convenience of notation; it is defined only with 0 as the other operand).

The action of any particular recombination operator can be represented as a probability distribution, $R(r)$, over the set $r \in \{0,1\}^L$. Thus $\sum_{r \in \{0,1\}^L} R(r) = 1$. Using $R(r)$ the transmission probabilities can be written:

$$T(x \leftarrow y, z) = \sum_{r \in \{0,1\}^L} R(r)\, \delta(x, r \circ y + (1-r) \circ z).$$

Because the order of the parents is taken to be irrelevant, $r$ and $1-r$ represent the same recombination event, hence $R(r) = R(1-r)$, which gives $T(x \leftarrow y, z) = T(x \leftarrow z, y)$.

Often with genetic algorithms, the genetic operator is applied to only a proportion, $\alpha$, of the population. In this case one would have:

$$T(x \leftarrow y, z) = (1-\alpha)[\delta(x, y) + \delta(x, z)]/2 + \alpha \sum_{r \in \{0,1\}^L} R(r)\, \delta(x, r \circ y + (1-r) \circ z).$$

**Examples.**   Uniform crossover (Ackley 1987, Syswerda 1989), i.e. free recombination (Charlesworth *et al.* 1992, Goodnight 1988), is described by $R(r) = 2^{-L}$. Single-point crossover is described (Karlin and Liberman 1978) by:

$$R(r) = \begin{cases} 1/(L-1) & \text{if } \sum_{i=1}^{L-1} |r_{i+1} - r_i| = 1, \\ 0 & \text{otherwise.} \end{cases}$$

Single-point shuffle crossover (Eshelman *et al.* 1989) is described by:

$$R(r) = \begin{cases} 1/(L-1)\binom{L}{n(r)} & \text{if } n(r) = 1, \ldots, L-1, \\ \\ 0 & \text{if } n(r) = 0 \text{ or } L, \end{cases}$$

where $n(r) = \sum_{i=1}^{L} r_i$ is the number of 1s in $r$.

Note that each $r$ partitions the loci into two sets. Let us collect from $x$ the loci with $r_i = 0$ to make a vector $x_0(r)$, and similarly collect the loci with $r_i = 1$ to make a vector $x_1(r)$. Let $\mathcal{H}(r)$ denote the set of schemata with defining positions $\{i : r_i = 1\}$. Thus the vectors $x_0(r) \in \mathcal{H}(1-r)$ and $x_1(r) \in \mathcal{H}(r)$ represent Holland schemata. For notational brevity I henceforth write simply $x_0$ and $x_1$, with the dependence on $r$ being understood.

The marginal fitnesses of the schemata are:

$$\overline{w}_0(x_0) = \sum_{x_1 \in \mathcal{H}(r)} w(x_0, x_1)\, p(x_0, x_1)/p_0(x_0),$$

and

$$\overline{w}_1(x_1) = \sum_{x_0 \in \mathcal{H}(1-r)} w(x_0, x_1)\, p(x_0, x_1)/p_1(x_1),$$

where

$$p_0(x_0) = \sum_{x_1 \in \mathcal{H}(r)} p(x_0, x_1) \quad \text{and} \quad p_1(x_1) = \sum_{x_0 \in \mathcal{H}(1-r)} p(x_0, x_1).$$

At this point we can express (7) in Corollary 3 using the marginal fitnesses of schemata defined by each $r$.

**Theorem 5 (Evolution of the fitness distribution under recombination)**
*The change in the fitness distribution over one generation under the action of selection and recombination is:*

$$\overline{F}(w)' - \overline{F}(w) = \sum_{r \in \{0,1\}^L} R(r)\, \mathrm{Cov}[F(x,w), \frac{\overline{w}_0(x_0)\,\overline{w}_1(x_1)}{\overline{w}^2}] \tag{14}$$

$$- \sum_{r \in \{0,1\}^L} R(r) \sum_{\substack{x_0 \in \mathcal{H}(1-r) \\ x_1 \in \mathcal{H}(r)}} [p(x) - p_0(x_0)\,p_1(x_1)]\, [F(x,w) - \overline{F}(w)]\, \frac{\overline{w}_0(x_0)\,\overline{w}_1(x_1)}{\overline{w}^2},$$

*where the partition of $x$ into vectors $x_0$ and $x_1$ is understood to be determined by each transmission vector $r$ in the sum.*

The proof is given in the Appendix.

Theorem 5 is what I have referred to as the "missing" schema theorem. Equation (14) shows a number of features:

**The covariance term.** The change in the fitness distribution $\overline{F}(w)$ depends on the covariance between the schema fitnesses $\overline{w}_0(x_0)\,\overline{w}_1(x_1)$ and $F(x,w)$. Thus a positive covariance between the fittest schemata and the fittest offspring will contribute toward an increase in the upper tail of the fitness distribution.

**Not all schemata are "processed".** Not all possible Holland schemata appear in (5), but only the ones for which the recombination event $r$ occurs with some probability (i.e. $R(r) > 0$). In the case of classical single-point crossover, only $L - 1$ recombination events may occur out of the $2^{L-1} - 1$ possible recombination events (subtracting transmission of intact chromosomes and symmetry in the parents). Thus, the schemata from only $L - 1$ different configurations of defining positions contribute to (14). So, with two alleles at each locus, only $2(2^1 + 2^2 + \ldots + 2^{L-1}) = 2^{L+1} - 4$ schemata are involved in (14) under single-point crossover. This is compared to a possible $3^L - 2^L$ schemata (subtracting the highest order schemata, i.e. chromosomes) that could result from a recombination event in the case of uniform crossover.

**Schemata enter as complementary pairs.** Schema fitnesses always occur in complementary pairs whose defining positions encompass all the loci.

**Disruption is quantified by the linkage disequilibrium.** The *linkage disequilibrium* between schemata $x_0$ and $x_1$ is the term $p(x) - p_0(x_0)p_1(x_1)$. It is a measure of the co-occurrence of schemata $x_0$ and $x_1$ in the population. If $p(x) > p_0(x_0)p_1(x_1)$, then recombination event $r$ disrupts more instances of genotype $x$ than it creates. If in addition, $F(x, w) > \overline{F}(w)$, then this term contributes negatively toward the change in $\overline{F}(w)$. Conversely, if a combination of schemata has a deficit in the population (i.e. $p(x) < p_0(x_0)p_1(x_1)$), and the measurement function for this combination is greater than the population average (i.e. $F(x, w) - \overline{F}(w)$), then the recombination event $r$ will contribute toward in increase in $\overline{F}(w)$.

If all loci were in linkage equilibrium, exhibiting *Robbins proportions* $p(x) = \prod_{i=1\ldots L} p_i(x_i)$ (Robbins 1918, Christiansen 1987, Booker 1993), then (14) reduces to:

$$\overline{F}(w)' - \overline{F}(w) = \sum_{r \in \{0,1\}^L} R(r) \operatorname{Cov}[F(x, w), \frac{\overline{w}_0(x_0)\,\overline{w}_1(x_1)}{\overline{w}^2}]. \tag{15}$$

Robbins proportions are assumed in much of quantitative genetic analysis, both classically (Cockerham 1954), and more recently (Bürger 1993), because linkage disequilibrium presents analytical difficulties. Asoh and Muhlenbein (1994) and Mühlenbein and Schlierkamp-Vosen (1993) assume Robbins proportions in their quantitative-genetic approach to GA analysis. Using $F(x) = w(x)$ as the measurement function, they show that under free recombination, a term similar to (15) evaluates to a sum of variances of epistatic fitness components derived from a linear regression.

Except under special assumptions, however, selection will generate linkage disequilibrium that produces departures from the results that assume Robbins proportions (Turelli and Barton 1990). The only recombination operator that will enforce Robbins proportions in the face of selection is Syswerda's "simulated crossover" (Syswerda 1993). Simulated crossover produces offspring by independently drawing the allele for each locus from the entire population after selection. One may even speculate that the performance advantage seen in simulated crossover in some way relates to it producing a population that exhibits "balanced design" from the point of view of analysis of variance, allowing estimation of the epistasis components (Reeves and Wright, this volume).

The epistasis variance components from Asoh and Muhlenbein (1994) figure into the parent-offspring covariance in fitness. In their covariance sum, higher order schemata appear with exponentially decreasing weights. Thus, the lowest order components are most important in determining the parent-offspring correlation. These epistasis variance components, it should be noted, appear implicitly in the paper by Radcliffe and Surry (this volume). They constitute the increments between successive forma variances shown in their Figure 2. Radcliffe and Surry find that the rate of decline in the forma variances as forma order increases is a good predictor of the GA performance of different representations. This is equivalent to there being large epistasis components for low order schemata, which produces the highest parent-offspring correlation in fitness in the result of Asoh and Muhlenbein (1994).

**Guidance for improving the genetic operator.** The terms

$$\mathrm{Cov}[F(x, w), \frac{\overline{w}_0(x_0)\,\overline{w}_1(x_1)}{\overline{w}^2}] \tag{16}$$

$$- \sum_x [p(x) - p_0(x_0)p_1(x_1)]\,[F(x, w) - \overline{F}(w)]\,\frac{\overline{w}_0(x_0)\,\overline{w}_1(x_1)}{\overline{w}^2},$$

for each recombination event, $r$, provide a rationale for modifying the recombination distribution to increase the performance of the GA. Probabilities $R(r)$ for which terms (16) are negative should be set to zero, and the distribution $R(r)$ allocated among the most positive terms (16). The best strategy of modifying $R(r)$ presents an interesting problem: I propose that a good strategy would be to start with uniform recombination and progressively concentrate it on the highest terms in (16).

## 4    ADAPTIVE LANDSCAPE ANALYSIS

The "adaptive landscape" concept was introduced by Wright (1932) to help describe evolution when the actions of selection, recombination, mutation, and drift produce are multiple attractors in the space of genotypes or genotype frequencies. Under the rubric of "landscape" analysis, a number of studies have employed covariance statistics as predictors of the performance of evolutionary algorithms (Weinberger 1990, Manderick *et al.* 1991, Weinberger 1991a,b, Mathias and Whitley 1992, Stadler and Schnabl 1992, Stadler and Happel 1992, Stadler 1992, Menczer and Parisi 1992, Fontana *et al.* 1993, Weinberger and Stadler 1993, Kinnear 1994, Stadler 1994, Grefenstette, this volume). I consider first some general aspects of the landscape concept, and then examine the use of covariance statistics to predict the performance of the GA.

### 4.1    THE LANDSCAPE CONCEPT

The "adaptive landscape" is a visually intuitive way of describing how evolution moves through the search space. A search space is made into a landscape by defining closeness relations between its points, so that for each point in the search space, neighborhoods of "nearby" points are defined. The purpose of doing this is to represent the attractors of the evolutionary process as "fitness peaks", with the premise that selection concentrates a population within a domain of attraction around the fittest genotype in the domain. The concepts of local search, multimodal fitness functions, and hill climbing are all landscape concepts.

Definitions of closeness relations are often derived from metrics that are seemingly natural for the search space, for example, Hamming distances for binary chromosomes, and Euclidean distance in the case of search spaces in $\mathbb{R}^n$. However, in order for closeness relations to be relevant to the evolutionary dynamics, they must be based on the transmission function, since it is the transmission function that connects one point in the search space to another by defining the transition probabilities between parents and offspring. In the adaptive landscape literature, this distinction between extrinsically defined landscapes and landscapes defined by the transmission function is frequently omitted.

Application of the landscape metaphor is difficult, if not infeasible, for sexual transmission functions. For this reason, some authors have implicitly used mutation to define their adaptive landscape even when recombination is the genetic operator acting. The definition of closeness becomes problematic because the distribution of offspring of a given parent depends on the frequency of other parents in the population. For example, consider a mating between two complementary binary chromosomes when uniform recombination is used. The neighborhood of the chromosomes will be the entire search space, because recombinant offspring include every possible chromosome. Since the neighborhood of a chromosome depends on chromosomes that it is mated with, the adaptive landscape depends on the composition of the population, and could thus be described as frequency-dependent. The sexual adaptive landscape will change as the population evolves on it.

The concept of multimodality illustrates the problem of using metrics extrinsic to the transmission function to define the adaptive landscape. Consider a search space in $\mathbb{R}^n$ with a multimodal fitness function. The function is multimodal in terms of the Euclidean metric on $\mathbb{R}^n$. But the Euclidean neighborhoods may be obliterated when the real-valued phenotype is encoded into a binary chromosome and neighborhoods are defined by the action of mutation or recombination. For example, let $a, b \in \mathbb{R}^n$ be encoded into binary chromosomes $x, y \in \{0,1\}^L$. The Hamming neighborhoods $H(x, y) \leq k$ may have no correspondence to Euclidean neighborhoods $|a - b| \leq c$. Thus multimodality under the Euclidean metric is irrelevant to the GA unless the transmission function preserves the Euclidean metric. Multimodality should not be considered a property of the fitness function alone, but only of the relationship between the fitness function and the transmission function.

### 4.1.1    An Illustration of Multimodality's Relation to Transmission

Consider the fitness function from p. 34 in Michalewicz (1994):

$$w(x_1, x_2) = 21.5 + x_1 \sin(4\pi x_1) + x_2 \sin(20\pi x_2),$$

defined on the variables $x_1, x_2$. In terms of the normal Euclidean neighborhoods about $(x_1, x_2)$, $w(x_1, x_2)$ is highly multimodal, as can be seen in Figure 1. There are over 500 modes on the area defined by the constraints

$$-3 \leq x_1 \leq 12.1 \text{ and } 4.1 \leq x_2 \leq 5.8.$$

A transmission function that could be said to produce the Euclidean neighborhoods is a Gaussian mutation operator that perturbs $(x_1, x_2)$ to $(x_1 + \epsilon_1, \ x_2 + \epsilon_2)$ with probability density

$$C \exp[-(\epsilon_1^2 + \epsilon_2^2)/2\sigma^2], \tag{17}$$

with $\sigma$ small and C the normalizing constant. The adaptive landscape could be said to be multimodal with respect to this genetic operator.

Suppose we change the representation into four new variables, integers $n_1, n_2$ and fractions $\phi_1, \phi_2 \in [0, 1)$:

$$n_1 = \text{Int}(2x_1), \text{ and } \phi_1 = 2x_1 - n_1,$$

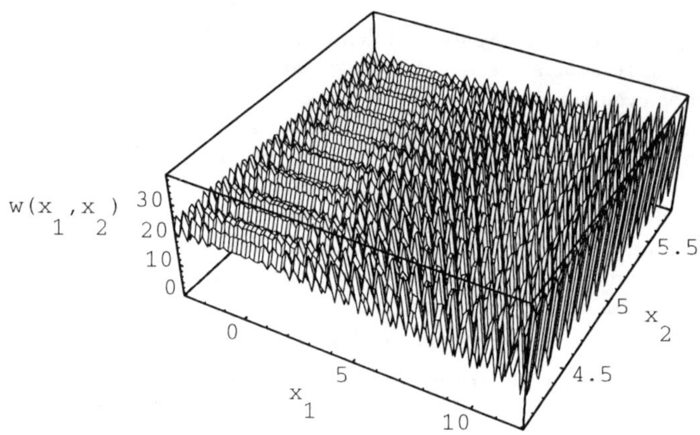

**Figure 1**: The fitness function $w(x_1, x_2) = 21.5 + x_1 \sin(4\pi x_1) + x_2 \sin(20\pi x_2)$ is highly multimodal in terms of the Euclidean neighborhoods on $(x_1, x_2)$.

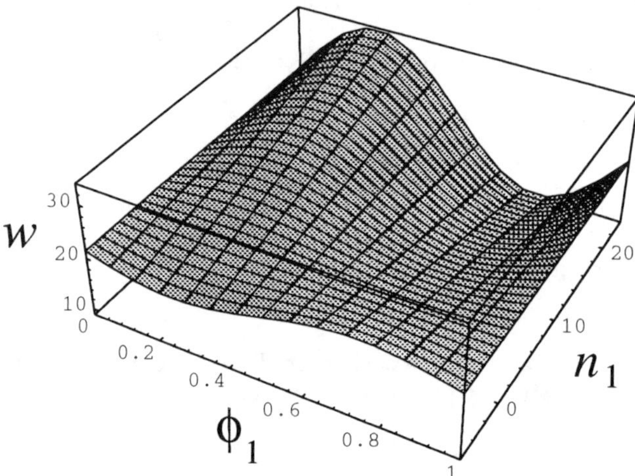

**Figure 2**: The "adaptive landscape" produced from mutation operators acting on the transformed representation $(n_1, \phi_1, n_2, \phi_2)$, where $x_1 = (n_1 + \phi_1)/2$, and $x_2 = (n_2 + \phi_2)/10$. Over the same region as in Figure 1, $w$ has few modes, as seen in this slice through the 4 dimensional space, setting $n_2 = 50$, $\phi_2 = 0$.

$$n_2 = \text{Int}(10x_2), \text{ and } \phi_2 = 10x_2 - n_2,$$

where $\text{Int}(v)$ is the largest integer not greater than $v$. Thus $x_1 = (n_1 + \phi_1)/2$, and $x_2 = (n_2 + \phi_2)/10$.

This transformation of variables uses our *a priori* knowledge about the fitness function to produce a smoother adaptive landscape. Neighborhoods for the new representation are produced by using a mutation operator that increases or decreases $n_1$ or $n_2$ by 1, or perturbs $\phi_1$ or $\phi_2$ in a Gaussian manner. In this new topography, the fitness function has very few modes, as shown in Figure 2.

Instead of changing the representation to produce a smooth landscape, one can keep the native variables $x_1$ and $x_2$, but change the mutation operator. The new mutation operator perturbs $(x_1, x_2)$ to $(x_1 + \epsilon_1 + \nu_1, \ x_2 + \epsilon_2 + \nu_2)$ with probability densities $f(\nu_1) = 1/2$ for $\nu_1 = 1/2$ or $-1/2$, and $f(\nu_2) = 1/2$ for $\nu_2 = 1/10$ or $-1/10$, and

$$f(\epsilon_1, \epsilon_2) = C \exp[-(\epsilon_1^2 + \epsilon_2^2)/2\sigma^2],$$

with $\sigma$ small and C the normalizing constant. This change in the genetic operator produces evolutionary dynamics identical to that produced by the change in the representation. This exemplifies the duality between representations and operators (Altenberg 1994).

Rather than trying to push the landscape metaphor further, it may be more fruitful to return to the roots of the concept, which is the existence of multiple attractors in evolutionary dynamics (or metastable states, in the case of stochastic evolutionary systems). The task of producing a smooth adaptive landscape is, in effect, to design operators and representations that yield a single domain of attraction, where all populations converge to the fittest member of the search space. In order to evaluate an adaptive landscape that contains multiple attractors, one needs a way of characterizing the attractors. This is the goal of adaptive landscapes statistics that have been developed.

## 4.2  LANDSCAPE STATISTICS

It would be useful to be able to predict the performance of a GA, or of particular representations or operators used by a GA, based on a limited number of sample points. I will review previous work toward this goal, pose some counterexamples to the statistics that have been developed, and offer a new statistic that solves some of the difficulties.

A number of studies have employed the statistical technique introduced by Weinberger (1990) toward predicting the performance of a GA. They rely on the autocorrelation statistic:

$$\rho_{op}(\tau) = \frac{\text{Cov}[w(\boldsymbol{x}_\tau), w(\boldsymbol{x}_0)]}{(\text{Var}[w(\boldsymbol{x}_\tau)] \ \text{Var}[w(\boldsymbol{x}_0)])^{1/2}}, \tag{18}$$

where $\boldsymbol{x}_\tau$ is derived from $x_0$ by $\tau$ iterations of the genetic operator, Cov and Var are taken over some measure, $m(\boldsymbol{x}_\tau, \boldsymbol{x}_0)$, on the search space $\mathcal{S}$:

$$\text{Cov}[w(\boldsymbol{x}_\tau), w(\boldsymbol{x}_0)] = \int_{\mathcal{S}} w(\boldsymbol{x}_\tau) \, w(\boldsymbol{x}_0) \, dm(\boldsymbol{x}_\tau, \boldsymbol{x}_0) - \int_{\mathcal{S}} w(\boldsymbol{x}_\tau) \, dm(\boldsymbol{x}_\tau, \boldsymbol{x}_0) \int_{\mathcal{S}} w(\boldsymbol{x}_0) \, dm(\boldsymbol{x}_\tau, \boldsymbol{x}_0).$$

The measure $m(\boldsymbol{x}_\tau, \boldsymbol{x}_0)$ derives from the way samples of the search space are taken. Weinberger uses random walks over the search space generated by iteration of asexual genetic operators. Manderick *et al.* (1991) point out that only asexual genetic operators allow one to generate the random walks that produce the sequence $\boldsymbol{x}_\tau$, precluding this technique from sexual genetic operators.

In order to use $\rho_{op}(\tau)$ as a predictor of evolution on the landscape, Weinberger notes that one must assume that the landscape is statistically isotropic, and that the fitness distribution of the sequence of points in the search space is stationary. He points out, however, that stationarity is violated in the presence of selection, and that landscapes will depart to varying degrees from isotropy.

Others have avoided this problem by using a single-generation correlation statistic, where $\tau = 1$. One can then incorporate sexual genetic operators by defining a function $g(u, v)$ that combines the fitnesses $(u, v)$ of the two parents. Typically, $g(u, v) = (u + v)/2$, giving:

$$\rho_{op} = \frac{\mathrm{Cov}[w, (u + v)/2]}{(\mathrm{Var}[w]\ \mathrm{Var}[u]/2)^{1/2}},$$

where $w$ is the fitness of offspring from parents with fitness $u$ and $v$, and Cov and Var are with respect to some measure over the search space.

No one has claimed that the autocorrelation statistic would be an exact estimator of the performance of complex GAs, which is why empirical studies of its applicability have been undertaken. However, as shown in Theorem 2, the properly defined covariance statistics are exact estimators of evolutionary change in the population. The autocorrelation function uses the fitness, $w(\boldsymbol{x})$, as a measurement function. When $w(\boldsymbol{x})$ is used as the measurement function in Price's Theorem, one obtains the change in the population mean fitness (see Table 1). However, what is more important to the performance of the GA is the change in the upper tail of the fitness distribution, which is obtained by using $F(\boldsymbol{x}, w)$ as in Theorem 2. This suggests circumstances in which $\rho_{op}$ may be fooled.

### 4.2.1   Counterexamples for $\rho_{op}$

I give two constructed examples of landscapes in which $\rho_{op}$ fails to predict GA performance. In them I will define the transmission functions $T(w \leftarrow u, v)$ directly in the fitness domain, as in (2). Thus $T(w \leftarrow u, v)$ contains all the information about the fitness landscape.

It should be noted that the value of $\rho_{op}$ is derived not from the total transmission function $T(w \leftarrow u, v)$, but from just the portion of $T(w \leftarrow u, v)$ that results from application of the genetic operator. In typical GAs, the genetic operator acts with probability $\alpha < 1$. The canonical recursion in the fitness domain (2) is then written:

$$p(w)' = (1 - \alpha)\, p(w)\, w/\overline{w} + \alpha \int_0^\infty P(w \leftarrow u, v)\, \frac{uv}{\overline{w}^2}\, p(u)\, p(v)\, du\, dv, \qquad (19)$$

where the transmission function $P(w \leftarrow u, v)$ represents the action of the genetic operator and is referred to as the *search kernel* (Altenberg 1994). Therefore, the values of $\alpha$ and $P(w \leftarrow u, v)$ contain all the information about the landscape that affects performance. The statistic $\rho_{op}$ is always taken with respect to the search kernel $P(w \leftarrow u, v)$.

The following are two cases in which $\rho_{op}$ errs in describing the evolutionary performance of the GA:

1. One case with a maximal parent-offspring correlation, but which gives poor GA performance, because parents never produce offspring fitter than what already exists, and

2. A second case with no correlation between the fitnesses of parents and their offspring, but which nevertheless gives excellent GA performance, because the proportion of offspring that are fitter than their parents is a constant, even as the parental fitnesses increase.

**High parent-offspring correlation but no evolvability.** Suppose the fitness of an offspring produced by the genetic operator is always the average of the parental fitnesses. If one uses $q(u, v) = (u + v)/2$, so that $\rho_{op}$ is the correlation between mean parental fitness and offspring fitness, then $\rho_{op} = 1$.

However, this is classical blending inheritance, in which the fitness variance of the population rapidly decays. Furthermore, the fittest member of the population will never be greater than the fittest in the first generation. Thus, although the mean fitness of the population will increase initially, it has no evolvability.

**Zero parent-offspring correlation but high evolvability.** In this example there is no correlation between parent and offspring fitness, yet there is high evolvability because each pair of parents has the same chance of producing still fitter offspring, no matter how fit the parents are within a certain limit. This is achieved with a lognormal distribution:

$$P(w \leftarrow u, v) = \frac{1}{w\, \sigma(u, v)\sqrt{2\pi}} \exp\left\{ -\frac{[\ln[w] - \mu(u, v)]^2}{2\sigma(u, v)^2} \right\},$$

where $\mu(u, v)$ and $\sigma(u, v)$ are scalar functions of $u$ and $v$, derived as follows.

To obtain the desired value $\rho_{op} = 0$, the mean offspring fitness $\phi(u, v)$ is set to a constant for all parents:

$$\phi(u, v) = \int_0^\infty w\, P(w \leftarrow u, v)\, dw = \exp\left[\mu(u, v) + \sigma(u, v)^2\right] = \hat{w} \quad \text{for all } u, v. \quad (20)$$

This requires:

$$\mu(u, v) = \ln[\hat{w}] - \sigma(u, v)^2/2. \quad (21)$$

The desired high evolvability is obtained by ensuring that a constant proportion of offspring are fitter than some function $g(u, v)$ of the parents' fitnesses. This requires:

$$\mathcal{N}\left[\frac{\ln[g(u, v)] - \mu(u, v)}{\sigma(u, v)}\right] = C, \quad (22)$$

where $\mathcal{N}[\,]$ is the normal distribution. The choice of $g(u, v)$ is arbitrary, but reasonable examples for defining evolvability would include $g(u, v) = (u + v)/2$, or $g(u, v) = \sqrt{uv}$, or $g(u, v) = \max[u, v]$. Equation (22) gives the condition:

$$\mu(u, v) = \ln[g(u, v)] - s\, \sigma(u, v) \quad (23)$$

where $s$ is the value giving $\mathcal{N}[s] = C$. Together conditions (21) and (23) are solved by:

$$\sigma(u, v) = s - \sqrt{s^2 - 2\ln[g(u, v)/\hat{w}]}. \quad (24)$$

This requires $g(u, v)$ be constrained to $g(u, v) \leq \hat{w}\, e^{s^2/2}$.

Let $\rho_{op}$ be computed as $\mathrm{Cov}[w, q(u, v)]/(\mathrm{Var}[w]\, \mathrm{Var}[q(u, v)])^{1/2}$ for some arbitrary function $q(u, v)$ of the parents' fitnesses $u, v$, where $w$ is the offspring fitness. Condition (20) gives

$\rho_{op} = 0$, since

$$
\begin{aligned}
\mathrm{Cov}[w, q(u,v)] \;=\;& \int_0^\infty w\, q(u,v)\, P(w \leftarrow u, v)\, p(u)\, p(v)\, du\, dv\, dw \\[2mm]
& - \int_0^\infty w\, P(w \leftarrow u, v)\, p(u)\, p(v)\, du\, dv\, dw \int_0^\infty q(u,v)\, p(u)\, p(v)\, du\, dv \\[2mm]
\;=\;& \int_0^\infty q(u,v)\, p(u)\, p(v) \left[ \int_0^\infty w\, P(w \leftarrow u, v)\, dw \right] du\, dv \\[2mm]
& - \int_0^\infty p(u)\, p(v) \left[ \int_0^\infty w\, P(w \leftarrow u, v)\, dw \right] du\, dv \int_0^\infty q(u,v)\, p(u)\, p(v)\, du\, dv \\[2mm]
\;=\;& \hat{w} \int_0^\infty q(u,v)\, p(u)\, p(v)\, du\, dv - 1 * \hat{w} * \int_0^\infty q(u,v)\, p(u)\, p(v)\, du\, dv \\[2mm]
\;=\;& 0.
\end{aligned}
$$

Yet with a reasonably small value of $\alpha$ in (19), the fitness distribution will keep increasing in the upper tail, up to fitnesses of at least $\hat{w}\, e^{d^2/2}$, because of the constant rate of producing offspring fitter than $g(u,v)$ even as $u, v$ grow. Even though $\rho_{op} = 0$, this landscape could be described as very smooth, because below the limit $g(u,v) \leq \hat{w}\, e^{s^2/2}$, the neighborhood of any genotype (i.e. its offspring) includes a portion that are fitter than it. Therefore, none of the lower fitnesses can be "local" optima, and the population evolves toward the global limit. So $\rho_{op}$ in this example is not providing an estimate of landscape smoothness either.

### 4.2.2   A New Statistic

In order to predict the performance of a GA based solely on sampled fitness values, one must assume that the fitnesses are dynamically sufficient, as described in Section 2.1.2. However, in general this assumption will be rendered only an approximation by the occurrence of noninvertibility in the fitness function. In many actual cases, though, it may be a good enough approximation to yield good predictions.

The most complete description of the transmission function in the fitness domain — one which loses no information (assuming the invertibility of $w(\boldsymbol{x})$) — is simply $T(w \leftarrow u, v)$. Other statistics such as $\rho_{op}$ involve averages that already lose information. Therefore I propose the following:

**Conjecture:**   *When attempting to predict the performance of a genetic algorithm using the fitnesses of a limited sample of points, the best statistic to use should be an estimate of the search kernel*

$$
\hat{P}(w \leftarrow u, v) \approx P(w \leftarrow u, v),
$$

*produced using the values of $w(\boldsymbol{y})$, $w(\boldsymbol{z})$ of parents and $w(\boldsymbol{x})$ of offspring sampled during the GA.*

A simple way to proceed in predicting the future course of a GA is to take the estimate of the search kernel $\hat{P}(w \leftarrow u, v)$ and insert it in recursion (19) to simulate the progress of the GA, and predict the evolution of the fitness distribution (an approach also taken by Grefenstette, this volume). It may be possible to analyze the search kernel more directly to predict the performance of the GA. I would propose in addition:

**Conjecture:**    *The critical determinant of GA performance is how rapidly the evolvability — i.e., the likelihood of parents being able to produce offspring fitter than themselves — decays with increasing parental fitness.*

One could classify different representations and operators by the decay rates of the search kernels they produce (e.g. exponential, hyperbolic, etc.). Search kernels with the least decay ought to exhibit the best GA performance.

If there are multiple domains of attraction in the dynamics of the GA, different initial populations may yield divergent estimates of $P(w \leftarrow u, v)$, even when $P(w \leftarrow u, v)$ is dynamically sufficient. A general caveat, therefore, is that the feasibility of predicting the performance of the GA depends on some level of regularity in the adaptive landscape.

The estimation of $P(w \leftarrow u, v)$ based on the fitnesses of a limited sample of points in a run of a genetic algorithm is a problem of generalization. Inference must be made on the sample search kernel. A Bayesian approach toward producing the search kernel estimator would be to begin with a prior distribution over a family of functions $\hat{P}(w \leftarrow u, v)$, and use the sampled data to form a posterior distribution. The function with the maximum posterior likelihood could be taken as the best estimator of $P(w \leftarrow u, v)$. The ability to generalize from the sampled data depends on ones prior distribution (Solla 1990). Generalization requires some knowledge that allows one to narrow the prior distribution to a smaller universe of distribution functions $\hat{P}(w \leftarrow u, v)$, within which one believes the actual function $P(w \leftarrow u, w)$ is likely to be found.

## 5    CONCLUSIONS

This paper begins with a critique of the Schema Theorem describing why it does not come to bear on the performance of genetic algorithms. The Schema Theorem does not capture the intuitive idea about what makes a GA work — that offspring with above-average fitness can be produced by recombining schemata with above-average fitness. There is a "missing" theorem needed to capture this intuition, and this is Price's Covariance and Selection Theorem. Price's theorem is used to show how changes in different macroscopic properties of populations in a genetic algorithm can be derived by using the microscopic dynamics of the GA combined with the appropriate measurement function. When the measurement function is a fitness indicator function, one obtains the evolution of the fitness distribution over one generation. When the measurement function is a schema indicator function, one obtains the evolution of the schema frequency. Thus, the Schema Theorem can be expressed using Price's theorem. However, the fact that schemata with above-average fitness increase in frequency says nothing about the performance of the GA. The ability for a GA to increase the upper tail of the fitness distribution is necessary for good performance.

This is expressed in a local performance theorem for genetic algorithms. Schemata do not appear in this performance theorem for general representations and operators. When one examines recombination operators specifically, however, schemata reappear in the performance theorem in a way that shows some qualitatively novel aspects of schema processing.

This "missing" schema theorem is obtained by using the recombination distribution representation of transmission introduced by Geiringer (1944). It makes explicit the intuition about how schema processing can provide a GA with good performance, namely: (1) that the recombination operator determines which schemata are being recombined; and (2) that there needs to be a correlation between complementary schemata of high fitness and the fitness distributions of their recombinant offspring in order for the GA to increase the chance of sampling fitter individuals. It also shows the influence of linkage disequilibrium on the performance of the GA.

Finally, the "adaptive landscape" approach to understanding GA performance is discussed. I examine some of the problems that ensue when one defines the landscape using metrics extrinsic to the transmission function. While the properly defined covariance statistics give quantitative estimates for the change in the fitness distribution, as shown in the local performance theorem, the autocorrelation statistics commonly used in landscape analysis do not, and this is illustrated with two examples of landscapes that give GA performance exactly contrary to that predicted by these statistics. I propose that the best estimator for predicting the behavior of a GA is simply the approximation of the transmission function in the fitness domain, and that it is the rate of decay of evolvability as parents increase in fitness that is the critical feature of the transmission function for GA performance. With these statistics calculated for the transmission functions produced by different operators and representations, one may be able to better design genetic algorithms.

## APPENDIX

### PROOF OF THEOREM 5

The general recursion (1) with the recombination operator becomes:

$$p(x)' = \sum_{r \in \{0,1\}^L} R(r)\, q(x|r), \tag{25}$$

where

$$q(x|r) = \sum_{y,z} \delta(x,\, r \circ y + (1-r) \circ z)\frac{w(y)\,w(z)}{\overline{w}^2}\, p(y)\, p(z). \tag{26}$$

The representation of the recursion for the general multi-locus, selection-recombination system was first obtained by Karlin and Liberman (1979) in a form similar to (25). Vose (1990) and Vose and Liepins (1991) independently developed a different representation for (25) assuming two alleles at each locus, which has been called the "exact schema theorem" (Juliany and Vose 1994).

The term $q(x|r)$ evaluates to:

$$
\begin{aligned}
q(x|r) \;&=\; \sum_{y,z} \delta(x,\, r \circ y + (1-r) \circ z)\frac{w(y)\,w(z)}{\overline{w}^2}\, p(y)\, p(z)\\[2ex]
&=\; \sum_{\substack{y_0 \in \mathcal{H}(1-r)\\ y_1 \in \mathcal{H}(r)}} \frac{w(x_0, y_1)\, w(y_0, x_1)}{\overline{w}^2}\, p(x_0, y_1)\, p(y_0, x_1)\\[2ex]
&=\; \sum_{y_1 \in \mathcal{H}(r)} \frac{w(x_0, y_1)}{\overline{w}} p(x_0, y_1) \sum_{y_0 \in \mathcal{H}(1-r)} \frac{w(y_0, x_1)}{\overline{w}} p(y_0, x_1)\\[2ex]
&=\; \overline{w}_0(x_0)\, p_0(x_0)\, \overline{w}_1(x_1)\, p_1(x_1)/\overline{w}^2.
\end{aligned}
$$

Equation (26) gives:

$$\overline{F}(w)' = \sum_{x} F(x, w)\, p(x)' = \sum_{r \in \{0,1\}^L} R(r) \sum_{x} F(x, w)\, q(x|r). \qquad (27)$$

The sum on the right evaluates to:

$$
\begin{aligned}
\sum_{x} F(x, w)\, q(x|r) &= \sum_{\substack{x_0 \in \mathcal{H}(1-r) \\ x_1 \in \mathcal{H}(r)}} F(x, w) \frac{\overline{w}_0(x_0)\,\overline{w}_1(x_1)}{\overline{w}^2} p_0(x_0)\, p_1(x_1) \\[2mm]
&= \overline{F}(w) + \mathrm{Cov}[F(x, w),\, \frac{\overline{w}_0(x_0)\,\overline{w}_1(x_1)}{\overline{w}^2}] \\[2mm]
&\quad - \sum_{\substack{x_0 \in \mathcal{H}(1-r) \\ x_1 \in \mathcal{H}(r)}} [F(x, w) - \overline{F}(w)][p(x) - p_0(x_0) p_1(x_1)] \frac{\overline{w}_0(x_0)\,\overline{w}_1(x_1)}{\overline{w}^2}.
\end{aligned}
$$

Substitution into (27) gives the result.

## Acknowledgements

I thank Roger Altenberg, Wayne Altenberg, and Darrell Whitley for their consideration during the completion of this paper. Thanks to Heinz Mühlenbein and Michael Vose for incisive comments, Marcy Uyenoyama, Eric Jakobsson, the Hawaii Institute of Geophysics, and the Maui High Performance Computing Center for infrastructural support, and the American Dance Festival for inspiration.

## References


Ackley, D. H. 1987. *A Connectionist Machine for Genetic Hillclimbing*. Kluwer Academic Publishers, Boston, MA.

Altenberg, L. 1991. Chaos from linear frequency-dependent selection. *American Naturalist* 138: 51–68.

Altenberg, L. 1994. The evolution of evolvability in genetic programming. In K. E. Kinnear, editor, *Advances in Genetic Programming*, pages 47–74. MIT Press, Cambridge, MA.

Altenberg, L. and M. W. Feldman. 1987. Selection, generalized transmission, and the evolution of modifier genes. I. The reduction principle. *Genetics* 117: 559–572.

Asoh, H. and H. Mühlenbein. 1994. Estimating the heritability by decomposing the genetic variance. Technical Report 94-02-12, GMD, Sakt Augustin, Available by ftp from anonymous@omega.gmd.de under /gmd/as/ga/paper.

Booker, L. B. 1993. Recombination distributions for genetic algorithms. In L. D. Whitley, editor, *Foundations of Genetic Algorithms 2*, pages 29–44. Morgan Kaufmann, San Mateo, CA.

Bürger, R. 1993. Predictions of the dynamics of a polygenic character under directional selection. *Journal of Theoretical Biology* 162: 487–513.

Cavalli-Sforza, L. L. and M. W. Feldman. 1976. Evolution of continuous variation: direct approach through joint distribution of genotypes and phenotypes. *Proceedings of the National Academy of Science U.S.A.* 73: 1689–1692.

Charlesworth, D., M. T. Morgan, and B. Charlesworth. 1992. The effect of linkage and population size on inbreeding depression due to mutational load. *Genetical Research* 59(1): 49–61.

Christiansen, F. B. 1987. The deviation from linkage equilibrium with multiple loci varying in a stepping-stone cline. *Journal of Genetics* 66: 45–67.

Cockerham, C. C. 1954. An extension of the concept of partitioning hereditary variance for analysis ofcovariances among relatives when epistasis is present. *Genetics* 39: 859–882.

Eshelman, L. J., R. A. Caruana, and J. D. Schaffer. 1989. Biases in crossover landscape. In J. D. Schaffer, editor, *Proceedings of the Third International Conference on Genetic Algorithms*, pages 10–19, San Mateo, CA. Morgan Kaufmann.

Feller, W. 1971. *An Introduction to Probability Theory and Its Applications.* John Wiley and Sons, New York, page 27.

Fisher, R. A. 1930. *The Genetical Theory of Natural Selection.* Clarendon Press, Oxford, pages 30–37.

Fontana, W., P. F. Stadler, E. G. Bornberg-Bauer, T. Griesmacher, I. L. Hofacker, M. Tacker, P. Tarazona, E. D. Weinberger, and P. Schuster. 1993. RNA folding and combinatory landscapes. *Physical Review E* 47(3): 2083–2099.

Frank, S. A. and M. Slatkin. 1990. The distribution of allelic effects under mutation and selection. *Genetical Research, Cambridge* 55: 111–117.

Geiringer, H. 1944. On the probability theory of linkage in mendelian heredity. *Annals of Mathematical Statistics* 15: 25–57.

Goldberg, D. 1989. *Genetic Algorithms in Search, Optimization and Machine Learning.* Addison Wesley.

Goodnight, C. J. 1988. Epistasis and the effect of founder events on the additive genetic variance. *Evolution* 42(3): 441–454.

Grafen, A. 1985. A geometric view of relatedness. *Oxford Surveys in Evolutionary Biology* 2: 28–89.

Grefenstette, J. 1989. Conditions for implicit parallelism. In G. Rawlins, editor, *Foundations of Genetic Algorithms*, pages 252–261. Morgan Kaufmann, San Mateo, CA.

Grefenstette, J. J. 1995. Using fitness distributions of genetic operators to predict performance. In D. Whitley and M. D. Vose, editors, *Foundations of Genetic Algorithms 3.* Morgan Kaufmann, San Mateo, CA.

Grefenstette, J. J. and J. E. Baker. 1989. How genetic algorithms work: a critical look at implicit parallelism. In J. D. Schaffer, editor, *Proceedings of the Third International Conference on Genetic Algorithms*, pages 20–27, San Mateo, CA. Morgan Kaufmann.

Holland, J. H. 1975. *Adaptation in Natural and Artificial Systems*. University of Michigan Press, Ann Arbor.

Juliany, J. and M. D. Vose. 1994. The genetic algorithm fractal. *Evolutionary Computation* 2(2): 165–180.

Karlin, S. 1979. Models of multifactorial inheritance: I, Multivariate formulations and basic convergence results. *Theoretical Population Biology* 15: 308–355.

Karlin, S. and U. Liberman. 1978. Classifications and comparisons of multilocus recombination distributions. *Proceedings of the National Academy of Sciences of the U.S.A.* 75(12): 6332–6336.

Karlin, S. and U. Liberman. 1979. Central equilibria in multilocus systems. I. Generalized nonepistatic selection regimes. *Genetics* 91: 777–798.

Kinnear, K. E. 1994. Fitness landscapes and difficulty in genetic programming. In J. D. Schaffer, H. P. Schwefel, and H. Kitano, editors, *Proceedings of the IEEE World Congress on Computational Intelligence*, pages 142–147, Piscataway N.J.

Koza, J. R. 1992. *Genetic Programming: On the Programming of Computers by Means of Natural Selection*. MIT Press, Cambridge, MA.

Manderick, B., M. de Weger, and P. Spiessens. 1991. The genetic algorithm and the structure of the fitness landscape. In R. K. Belew and L. B. Booker, editors, *Proceedings of the Fourth International Conference on Genetic Algorithms*, pages 143–150, San Mateo, CA. Morgan Kaufmann Publishers.

Mathias, K. and D. Whitley. 1992. Genetic operators, the fitness landscape and the traveling salesman problem. In R. Männer and B. Manderick, editors, *Parallel Problem Solving from Nature, 2*, pages 219–228, Amsterdam. North-Holland.

Menczer, F. and D. Parisi. 1992. Evidence of hyperplanes in the genetic learning of neural networks. *Biological Cybernetics* 66(3): 283–289.

Michalewicz, Z. 1994. *Genetic Algorithms + Data Structures = Evolution Programs*. Springer-Verlag, Berlin.

Mühlenbein, H. 1991. Evolution in time and space — the parallel genetic algorithm. In G. Rawlins, editor, *Foundations of Genetic Algorithms*, pages 316–338. Morgan Kaufmann, San Mateo, CA.

Mühlenbein, H. and D. Schlierkamp-Vosen. 1993. The science of breeding and its application to the breeder genetic algorithm (BGA). *Evolutionary Computation* 1(4): 335–360.

Price, G. R. 1970. Selection and covariance. *Nature* 227: 520–521.

Price, G. R. 1972. Extension of covariance selection mathematics. *Annals of Human Genetics* 35: 485–489.

Radcliffe, N. 1991. Equivalence class analysis of genetic algorithms. *Complex Systems* 5(2): 183–205.

Radcliffe, N. J. 1992. Non-linear genetic representations. In R. Männer and B. Manderick, editors, *Parallel Problem Solving from Nature, 2*, pages 259–268, Amsterdam. North-Holland.

Radcliffe, N. J. and P. D. Surry. 1995. Fitness variance of formae and performance prediction. In D. Whitley and M. D. Vose, editors, *Foundations of Genetic Algorithms 3*. Morgan Kaufmann, San Mateo, CA.

Reeves, C. and C. Wright. 1995. An experimental design perspective on genetic algorithms. In D. Whitley and M. D. Vose, editors, *Foundations of Genetic Algorithms 3*. Morgan Kaufmann, San Mateo, CA.

Robbins, R. B. 1918. Some applications of mathematics to breeding problems III. *Genetics* 3: 375–389.

Slatkin, M. 1970. Selection and polygenic characters. *Proceedings of the National Academy of Sciences U.S.A.* 66: 87–93.

Solla, S. A. 1990. Supervised learning and generalization. In *Neural Networks: Biological Computers or Electronic Brains*, pages 21–28. Springer-Verlag, Paris, France.

Stadler, P. F. 1992. Correlation in landscapes of combinatorial optimization problems. *Europhysics Letters* 20(6): 479–482.

Stadler, P. F. 1994. Linear operators on correlated landscapes. *Journal de Physique I* 4(5): 681–696.

Stadler, P. F. and R. Happel. 1992. Correlation structure of the landscape of the graph-bipartitioning problem. *Journal of Physics A: Math. Gen.* 25: 3103–3110.

Stadler, P. F. and W. Schnabl. 1992. The landscape of the traveling salesman problem. *Physics Letters A* 161: 337–344.

Syswerda, G. 1989. Uniform crossover in genetic algorithms. In J. D. Schaffer, editor, *Proceedings of the Third International Conference on Genetic Algorithms*, pages 2–9, San Mateo, CA. Morgan Kaufmann.

Syswerda, G. 1993. Simulated crossover in genetic algorithms. In L. D. Whitley, editor, *Foundations of Genetic Algorithms 2*, pages 239–255. Morgan Kaufmann, San Mateo, CA.

Taylor, P. D. 1988. Inclusive fitness models with two sexes. *Theoretical Population Biology* 34: 145–168.

Turelli, M. and N. H. Barton. 1990. Dynamics of polygenic characters under selection. *Theoretical Population Biology* 38: 1–57.

Uyenoyama, M. K. 1988. On the evolution of genetic incompatibility systems: incompatibility as a mechanism for the regulation of outcrossing distance. In R. E. Michod and B. R. Levin, editors, *The Evolution of Sex*, pages 212–232. Sinauer Associates, Sunderland, MA.

Vose, M. D. 1990. Formalizing genetic algorithms. In *Proceedings of the IEEE workshop on Genetic Algorithms, Neural Networks, and Simulated Annealing Applied to Problems in Signal and Image Processing*, Glasgow, UK.

Vose, M. D. 1991. Generalizing the notion of schema in genetic algorithms. *Artificial Intelligence* 50(3): 385–396.

Vose, M. D. and G. E. Liepins. 1991. Punctuated equilibria in genetic search. *Complex Systems* 5(1): 31–44.

Vose, M. D. and A. Wright. 1994. The walsh transform and the theory of the simple genetic algorithm. *Pattern Recognition* In press.

Wade, M. J. 1985. Soft selection, hard selection, kin selection, and group selection. *American Naturalist* 125: 61–73.

Weinberger, E. D. 1990. Correlated and uncorrelated fitness landscapes and how to tell the difference. *Biological Cybernetics* 63: 325–336.

Weinberger, E. D. 1991a. Local properties of Kauffman's N-k model, a tuneably rugged energy landscape. *Physical Review A* 44(10): 6399–6413.

Weinberger, E. D. 1991b. Fourier and Taylor series on fitness landscapes. *Biological Cybernetics* 65: 321–330.

Weinberger, E. D. and P. F. Stadler. 1993. Why *some* fitness landscapes are fractal. *Journal of Theoretical Biology* 163: 255–275.

Wright, S. 1932. The roles of mutation, inbreeding, crossbreeding, and selection in evolution. *Proceedings of the Sixth International Congress on Genetics* 1: 356–366.

# Fitness Variance of Formae and Performance Prediction


**Nicholas J. Radcliffe**
njr@epcc.ed.ac.uk
Edinburgh Parallel Computing Centre
University of Edinburgh
King's Buildings
EH9 3JZ
Scotland

**Patrick D. Surry**
pds@epcc.ed.ac.uk
Edinburgh Parallel Computing Centre
University of Edinburgh
King's Buildings
EH9 3JZ
Scotland


## Abstract


Representation is widely recognised as a key determinant of performance in evolutionary computation. The development of families of representation-independent operators allows the formulation of formal representation-independent evolutionary algorithms. These formal algorithms can be instantiated for particular search problems by selecting a suitable representation. The performance of different representations, in the context of any given formal representation-independent algorithm, can then be measured. Simple analyses suggest that fitness variance of formae (generalised schemata) for the chosen representation might act as a performance predictor for evolutionary algorithms. This hypothesis is tested and supported through studies of four different representations for the travelling sales-rep problem (TSP) in the context of both formal representation-independent genetic algorithms and corresponding memetic algorithms.


## 1  Motivation

The subject of this paper is representation in the context of evolutionary search. In particular, it explores questions such as what it might mean to talk about the quality of a representation, what the interaction between operators and representations might be, how one set of operators might be said to be better in some problem domain than some other set of (possibly "standard") operators, and—most importantly—what are the characteristics of representations that make evolutionary search easier or harder. The particular problem domain on which the paper will focus will be the travelling sales-rep problem (TSP), and results will be presented for preliminary empirical studies of this problem. This should not, however, distract from the primary goal, which will be to understand more about the nature of representations in evolutionary search.

This work grows out of previous work on *forma analysis* (Radcliffe, 1992, 1994), which is a generalisation of schema analysis (Holland, 1975). Forma analysis as developed thus far allows the generation of a (formal) "genetic" representation through the characterisation of a problem class. Significant effort has been devoted to understanding the kinds of representations that can result from arbitrary characterisation of general problem classes (though the discussions have tended to be couched in terms of "search spaces" rather than "problem classes") and a family of generic recombination operators has been developed. Each of the recombination operators in this family can be applied to any search problem given only a (sufficiently rich) characterisation of the problem class. This paper, together with Radcliffe & Surry (1994), extends this family of recombination operators and augments it with representation-independent forms of mutation and hill-climbing algorithms.

The result of having created representation-independent forms for all the classes of operators in common use in evolutionary computing is that formal, representation-independent algorithms can be defined. This permits variation of representation as an independent variable in the context of a fixed formal algorithm, allowing the influence of representation to be isolated and measured. This is achieved by comparing the performance of algorithms that are identical in all respects other than the representation chosen—ones that execute the same reproductive plan, with the same set of operators and the same parameters. This paper addresses the exploitation of evolutionary algorithms for search and optimisation, and is thus, in the terminology favoured by DeJong (1992), concerned with GAFO's (Genetic Algorithms for Function Optimisation) or perhaps ECFO's (Evolutionary Computing For Optimisation). In particular, it is formal genetic and memetic algorithms that will be considered, memetic algorithms being genetic algorithms that include local optimisers as operators (Moscato & Norman, 1992; Radcliffe & Surry, 1994).

There is considerable freedom in choosing exactly how to measure the performance of evolutionary algorithms. For example, it would be possible to choose to consider rate of convergence, time to solution, or robustness of results, off-line or "best seen" performance, number of evaluations or wall-clock time in almost any combination. Moreover, robustness is an issue not only with respect to differently seeded stochastic runs, but also as a function of different problem instances, perhaps of quite different complexities, and it may be that different relative performances will be achieved by different representations as the parameters of the algorithm, the operators used and the particular problem instance are varied. Despite this panoply of choices, it seems reasonable to expect that for at least some classes of problem there will be a broad congruence of results over these different measures. For other problem classes it might be possible to rank the performance of different representations with respect to a particular performance measure and some chosen set of parameters and operators.

The principal aim of this paper is to find and measure properties of representations that are well-correlated with their performance in evolutionary search. If this could be achieved it would both allow some level of performance prediction and increase understanding of the search techniques themselves. A key motivation for the development of forma analysis was a set of observations about the schema theorem (Holland, 1975) in its generalised form (Radcliffe, 1991; Vose & Liepins, 1991). These suggest that representations based on formae (generalised schemata) with lower fitness variance would be expected—other things being equal—to allow more effective search than those based on formae with higher fitness variance. Fitness variance of formae thus forms a natural candidate for a measure to act as a predictor of representation performance. This paper goes on to explore whether or not this proposition is supported through studies of the TSP.

Hofmann (1993) began to test fitness variance of formae as a performance predictor by studying the travelling sales-rep Problem (TSP). He compared instantiations of random assorting recombination (RAR; Radcliffe, 1994) using various representations, and the *strategic edge crossover,* SEX, developed by Moscato & Norman (1992) as an extension of edge recombination (Whitley *et al.,* 1989). The present work develops these tests significantly further by considering fully representation-independent genetic and memetic algorithms with a range of representations.

## 2    A Review of Forma Analysis

Forma analysis provides methods for constructing representations of problems and for defining operators with respect to those representations. Radcliffe (1994) provides a detailed and precise formulation of forma analysis, while Radcliffe (1992) gives a more descriptive overview. The present section summarises only those parts necessary for the immediate goals of formulating and analysing representation-independent evolutionary algorithms.

### 2.1    Problem Class and Search Space

Let $T$ be a class of search problems. In the present paper $T$ will be the set of all travelling sales-rep problems. More specifically, let $T$ be the set of all problem instances in the class, where a problem instance takes the form of the search space, $S$, to which it gives rise. Given a particular collection of cities, the search space $S$ is the set of all possible paths that visit every city exactly once—the set of all possible tours—and the aim is to find the shortest with respect to some metric. More precisely still, since there is no interest in the $2n$ equivalent paths through $n$ cities that arise from the freedom to choose the starting city and the direction of travel, $S$ is the set of all *non-equivalent* tours. For example, given a set of four particular cities labelled 1 to 4, chosen for illustration to sit at the corners of a square,

$$S = \left\{ \begin{matrix} {}^4 \quad {}^3 \\ \square \\ {}_1 \quad {}_2 \end{matrix}, \begin{matrix} {}^4 \quad {}^3 \\ \times \\ {}_1 \quad {}_2 \end{matrix}, \begin{matrix} {}^4 \quad {}^3 \\ \bowtie \\ {}_1 \quad {}_2 \end{matrix} \right\} . \tag{1}$$

A convenient way to represent a tour is by listing the sequence of city labels in the order in which they are visited, so that the first tour shown in the set might be represented by 1234. This is called the *permutation representation,* denoted $p$.

It is important to be able to distinguish between the representative of a solution under some representation (the formal chromosome, or genotype) and the solution itself (the phenotype). For a particular representation $\rho$, the set of all chromosomes in this representation will be denoted $\mathcal{C}^\rho$. Given a chromosome $X \in \mathcal{C}^\rho$, and the solution $x \in S$ to which it corresponds, the notation $X^\rho$ will be used to mean "the solution represented by $X$ in representation $\rho$". Thus $X^\rho$ is a member of $S$, and in the current example $X^\rho = x$. It is thus accurate to write

$$S = \{1234^p, 1243^p, 1324^p\} . \tag{2}$$

In general, a TSP over $n$ cities has an associated search space of size $n!/2n = (n-1)!/2$, arising from the $n!$ different permutations of the city labels and the $2n$ equivalent forms for any tour. In this paper, tours shown in the permutation representation will be shown starting with city 1, followed by the lower-numbered of city 1's two neighbours.

### 2.2    Representation

It is necessary to be rather precise about representations in this study. For present purposes, a distinction will be made between *genetic* representations and *allelic* representations. A genetic representation includes a collection of *genes*, each of which has a well-defined value for every chromosome in $C^p$. As usual, the values that genes take will be termed *alleles*, and will formally be labelled with the gene to which they correspond. It is a requirement of a (formal) genetic representation that given all the gene values it be possible to identify the unique solution to which they collectively correspond (if they do correspond to some solution). If all combinations of alleles correspond to solutions in $S$ the genes (and the representation) are said to be *orthogonal*. It is *not* a requirement that representations be orthogonal, and indeed all of the representations that will be used in this paper are non-orthogonal. The permutation representation of the TSP used in equation 2 qualifies as a formal genetic representation under this definition. For an $n$-city TSP, is has $n$ genes, $(g_1, g_2 \ldots, g_n)$, the $i$th of which describes the city that is visited $i$th in the tour. Notice that not all combinations of alleles correspond to solutions—for example, 1223 does not—so the representation is non-orthogonal.

In an *allelic* representation, genes are *not* required. Instead, a set of properties is defined, each of which a solution may or may not have, and a solution is represented by the set of properties it has. For example, in the *undirected edge representation* of the TSP, denoted $u$, a solution is represented by the set of the edges that it contains. Thus, the tour $1234^p$ contains the (undirected) edges 12, 23, 34 and 14, so

$$1234^p = \{12, 23, 34, 14\}^u. \tag{3}$$

Each of the chosen properties will be referred to as an *allele* and it is a requirement of an allelic representation that every collection of alleles corresponds to a unique solution (if it does correspond to some solution). This use of the term allele is non-standard, and arguably an abuse, but is natural and convenient for the purposes of this paper.

Having introduced both (formal) genetic representations and (formal) allelic representations the notion of a *chromosome* (or genotype, or genome) can be made precise. In the case of genetic representations this is more-or-less the familiar object, though formally will consist simply of the set of alleles characterising a solution, usually together with an ordering of the genes. Thus, using a tuple $(a, b)$ to specify that the $a$th city visited is the city with label $b$, the formal chromosome corresponding to $1243^p$ is $\{(1, 1), (2, 2), (3, 4), (4, 3)\}$. In the case of an allelic representation, again the chromosome corresponding to a solution is simply the set of alleles that the solution contains.

It should be mentioned briefly that when (formal) genetic and allelic representations are discussed in this paper there is no intended implication that the actual coding used to store individuals in a computer need take the form described. The formal representation or representations that an evolutionary computation uses are defined by the actions of operators on individuals rather than any details of implementation.

### 2.3    Formae

A *forma* is a generalisation of the familiar concept of a *schema*. A forma can be viewed for present purposes as any collection of solutions in which the corresponding chromosomes share particular alleles. Formae are typically given names such as $\xi$, and specified through a *description set* denoted $\langle \xi \rangle$. The description set is simply the set of alleles that a chromosome must have in order for the solution it represents to be a member of the forma in question, and is thus closely related to the set of defining positions (and defining values) familiar from schema analysis. Since the formal chromosome used here is precisely the set of alleles, it is clear that

$$\xi = \{X^p \in S \mid X \supset \langle \xi \rangle\}. \tag{4}$$

For example, working in the permutation representation for a 4-city TSP, the forma containing all tours that have city 2 in their second position would be given by

$$\xi = \{1234^p, 1243^p\} \tag{5}$$

and described by

$$\langle \xi \rangle = \{(2,2)\}, \tag{6}$$

This is probably more familiar to most readers as the $o$-schema $\square 2\square\square$ (Goldberg & Lingle, 1985). Similarly, in the undirected edge representation the forma $\xi'$ consisting of those tours that contain the 12 edge is

$$\xi' = \{1234^p, 1243^p\} = \{\{12, 23, 34, 14\}^u, \{12, 24, 34, 13\}^u\}, \tag{7}$$

which is conveniently described by

$$\langle \xi' \rangle = \{12\}. \tag{8}$$

### 2.4   Recombination, Respect, Transmission and Assortment

Evolutionary computing has given rise to a large and growing collection of recombination operators. When the representations used are orthogonal, certain properties tend to be common to almost all such operators, and seem barely worthy of comment. When non-orthogonal representations are used, however, these properties are much less universal and become more salient. The three properties of respect, transmission and assortment are of particular relevance and are defined below. These are normally discussed with respect to formae, but are here discussed with reference instead to a representation.

A recombination operator is said to *respect* a representation if and only if every child it produces contains all the alleles common to its two parents.

A recombination operator is said to *transmit genes* with respect to a given (formal) *genetic* representation if and only if each allele in every child it produces is present in at least one of that child's parents. It is easy to see that a recombination operator that transmits *genes* is respectful.

A recombination operator is said to *transmit alleles* with respect to a given (formal) *allelic* representation if and only if each allele in every child it produces is present in at least one of its parents. It is *not* necessarily the case that an operator that transmits *alleles* for an allelic representation is respectful.

The distinction between gene transmission and allele transmission is important. For example, the Edge Recombination Operator in its original form (Whitley *et al.*, 1989) sought to transmit as many undirected edges from the two parents as possible, and was thus striving to achieve allele transmission, which it did typically with over 99% success. The operator was then modified to achieve strict respect by placing all edges common to the parents in the child at the start (Whitley *et al.*, 1991), resulting in a quite different (and apparently more successful) operator.

A recombination operator is said to be *assorting* (with respect to a given representation) if and only if it is possible for it to produce any solution that contains only alleles present in the two parents. It is not necessary for it to be possible to achieve this in a single recombination: repeated incestuous recombination may be required. In the latter case, the operator is said to be *weakly,* rather than *properly,* assorting.

The most familiar crossover operators from genetic algorithms (such as $N$-point crossover, reduced-surrogate crossover (Booker, 1987), parameterised uniform crossover (Spears & DeJong, 1991), shuffle crossover (Schaffer *et al.*, 1989) etc. are respectful, transmitting and assorting with respect to familiar string representations, which are typically orthogonal. However, for non-orthogonal representations assortment is often incompatible with respect and gene transmission. Many operators for non-orthogonal representations fail to have some or any of these properties.

## 3   Representation-independent Recombination

Three representation-independent recombination operators have previously been introduced, under the names of *random respectful recombination* ($R^3$), *random transmitting recombination* (RTR) and *random assorting recombination* (RAR). As the names suggest, $R^3$ is always respectful, RTR is always transmitting and RAR is always assorting, in each case with respect to the representation for which they are instantiated. For orthogonal representations, RAR and RTR are equivalent and thus assort, transmit and respect, and are in fact equivalent to uniform crossover. In the special case of binary representations, RTR reduces to $R^3$.

For all the representations of the TSP considered here, RAR is the most relevant operator of the family. It is described in detail in Radcliffe (1994), and may be thought of as a generalisation of uniform crossover. A newer representation-independent form of recombination is *Generalised N-point Crossover* (GNX), which is now described.

### 3.1   Generalised N-point Crossover

In constructing a generalised form of $N$-point crossover, it is convenient to consider only genetic representations. The difficulty in applying conventional crossover operators is that not all combinations of gene values are legal. Let $\mathcal{L} = \{\ell_1, \ell_2, \ldots, \ell_N\}$ be a set of cross points, with $0 < \ell_1 < \ell_2 < \cdots < \ell_N < n$. This breaks a parent (genetic) chromosome $X$ into the $N + 1$ segments

$$(X_1, X_2, \ldots, X_{\ell_1-1}), \ (X_{\ell_1}, X_{\ell_1+1}, \ldots, X_{\ell_2-1}), \ \ldots, \ (X_{\ell_N}, X_{\ell_N+1}, \ldots, X_n), \qquad (9)$$

and breaks the second parent chromosome, $Y$, into corresponding segments.

The first phase of GNX's operation uses the same genetic material as ordinary $N$-point crossover, i.e., alternate segments from the two parents. It proceeds by picking a random order to visit the $N + 1$ segments (irrespective of the parents to which these segments are assigned). Within each segment, the alleles are "tested" in a random order. An allele is "tested" by seeing whether it can be placed in the child—i.e. whether it is compatible with those alleles that have already been accepted. If compatible, the new allele is inserted, otherwise it is discarded. Because in general after this process has terminated the child will still be incomplete, a second phase then commences in which the genetic material discarded by ordinary $N$-point crossover (the 'complementary' alternating sections) is used to try to fill in any gaps. The segments are again visited in a random order and the alleles within them are tested in random sequence. If the child is still not fully specified after this, it is completed at random from amongst the legal combinations of alleles, or by some other patching method. In this study, patching is always random. The general pattern of progress of GNX is shown in figure 1.

An example using the TSP may help to clarify this. Consider the permutation representation for the TSP and G2X with cross points 3 and 6 with parents given by

$$\begin{aligned} X &= (1, 2, 3 \mid \underline{4}, \underline{5}, \underline{6} \mid 7, 8), \\ Y &= (\underline{1}, \underline{5}, \underline{4} \mid 3, 8, 7 \mid \underline{2}, \underline{6}), \end{aligned} \qquad (10)$$

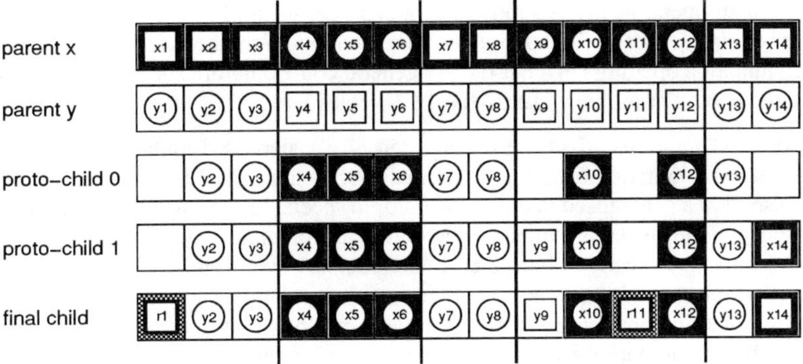


Figure 1: GNX first copies gene values from alternating segments (circled) of the parent chromosomes, visiting the segments and testing the genes within these segments in a random order. Gene values are copied to the child only if they are compatible with those already present. In this example, genes 2–8, 10, 12 and 13 are assigned in this way, resulting in proto-child 0. For genes not set by this process, alleles from the unused segments (boxed) of the parents are then tested for inclusion, again in random sequence. In the example, genes 9 and 14 are assigned thus, to give proto-child 1. Genes still not fixed after this process are assigned either at random from the set of legal combinations, or by some heuristic or other patching procedure. In this example, genes 1 and 11 fall into this category.

where the underlined alleles are the ones that would normally be chosen by $N$-point crossover. Suppose the order in which the segments are tested is $(2, 3, 1)$. Then the second segment of $X$ will be inserted whole, giving the proto-child $(\Box, \Box, \Box, 4, 5, 6, \Box, \Box)$. Alleles in the third segment from $Y$ will then be tested in a random order. Whichever order is chosen in this case, the 2 will be accepted and the 6 rejected, giving the proto-child $(\Box, \Box, \Box, 4, 5, 6, 2, \Box)$. The first segment of $Y$ is then tested, and only the 1 will be accepted, giving the final proto-child, $Z_0$, at the end of the first phase as

$$Z_0 = (1, \Box, \Box, 4, 5, 6, 2, \Box). \tag{11}$$

The untested segments are then visited in random order, Only the first and third segments from $X$ are relevant here, and whatever the order of testing, the 3 and the 8 will be accepted, and the 2 and the 7 will be rejected, giving the proto-child at the end of the second phase

$$Z_1 = (1, \Box, 3, 4, 5, 6, 2, 8). \tag{12}$$

Since this child is still incomplete, it must be patched. In this case however, only one legal chromosome has the required allele pattern, so the final child is given by

$$Z = (1, 7, 3, 4, 5, 6, 2, 8). \tag{13}$$

## 4    Representation-independent Mutation and Hill-climbing

No effort has previously been devoted—to the best of the authors' knowledge—to defining representation-independent mutation and hill-climbing operators. Since mutation is widely recognised as playing a vital rôle in evolutionary search it is clearly essential to the aim of this paper to include such an operator; given a move operator in the form of mutation, the construction of a hill-climber is a simple matter. The present section attempts to set the discussion of representation-independent mutation operators in a reasonably general context before specialising to construct one pertinent to the particular problem class—the TSP—considered.

A number of considerations affect the formulation of a generalised mutation operator, including the characteristics of mutation operators in normal use, the perceived function of mutation and the behaviour desired of a generalised mutation operator in special limits (such as the case of orthogonal representations). The different strands of evolutionary computing use rather different sorts of mutation operators. One nearly universal characteristic, however, is that they ensure ergodicity, i.e. that the entire search space remains accessible from any population, and indeed from any individual. In most cases mutation operators can actually move from any point in the search space to any other point directly, but the probability of making "large" moves is very much smaller than that of making "small" moves (at least with small mutation rates). For example, in evolution strategies mutation is typically Gaussian on a parameter-by-parameter basis, while in genetic algorithms with orthogonal representations a probability of (uniformly) choosing a new value for each gene is most commonly used, giving rise to a binomial distribution for the number of mutations made. It is a characteristic of most mutation schemes that relatively unlikely "large" moves can be effected by a series of smaller moves, thus making large, potentially fruitful moves possible with reasonable probability through iteration provided that the intermediate points (solutions) are themselves viable in the context of the reproductive plan used.

In order to clarify notions of "large" and "small" mutations, a metric (distance measure) will be introduced over the representation space $C^\rho$. In the case of genetic representations, this is straightforward. A distinction is first made between *cardinal* and *ordinal* genes. The alleles for ordinal genes are naturally ordered, as, for example, when the gene represents a continuous or contiguous variable, and in this case it makes sense to define a variable distance between alleles (normally the Euclidean distance). With cardinal genes, such as those found in all the genetic representations of the TSP considered, there is no particular relationship between the various alleles for a given gene, so the discrete metric is used, making the distance between any pair of distinct alleles one. The distance between solutions is then computed simply by summing the distances between the gene values at each locus. For cardinal genes, this measure reduces to the familiar Hamming distance.

Allelic representations are a little more complex to handle. It is implicit in the definition of genes that every chromosome has the same number of alleles, because every gene has precisely one well-defined value for each solution (and there is no other source of alleles). In the case of allelic representations this need not be the case. For example, if the search space consists of sets of variable size, it would sometimes seem appropriate to take the (variable number of) elements of the set as alleles. A satisfactory approach for allelic representations is to define an overlap or similarity measure in the first instance by counting the number of alleles that are common to the two solutions in question. A distance is then formed by subtraction, possibly after normalisation, from a suitable number, being careful to ensure that a solution's distance from itself is zero. In the particular case of the TSP, the only allelic representation used in this paper (the undirected edge representation) has the property that every solution has the same number of alleles, so this complication may be ignored.

### 4.1  Binomial Minimal Mutation

The specific form of mutation required for present purposes is a generalisation of the standard gene-wise mutation operator from genetic algorithms since the TSP representations considered are all essentially cardinal. The *binomial minimal mutation* operator (BMM) can be defined for any representation—genetic or allelic—provided that the following conditions are met.

1. Every solution has the same number, $n$, of alleles. The distance between two chromosomes $X$ and $Y$ will be taken to be $n$ minus the number of alleles that they share and will be written $D(X, Y)$.

2. It is computationally feasible to identify *minimal mutations*. Considering a pair of chromosomes $X$ and $Y$, $Y$ will be said to be a minimal mutation of $X$ provided that there is no solution $Z$ $(\neq X)$ for which $D(X, Z) < D(X, Y)$. Although not absolutely required, BMM is formulated primarily for the case in which the distance between a chromosome and each of its minimal mutations is the same for all chromosomes, and every chromosome has the same number of minimal mutations.

3. A sequence of minimal mutations from any point in the representation space $\mathcal{C}^\rho$ can generate any point in $\mathcal{C}^\rho$, and thus any point in $\mathcal{S}$.

*Binomial minimal mutation* takes a single parameter $p_m \in [0, 1]$, which is a probability. If the conditions listed above are met, BMM proceeds by first choosing a number of minimal mutations to make by sampling the binomial distribution $B(n, p_m)$, where, as before, $n$ is the number of alleles in each chromosome. It then generates the mutated child by repeatedly choosing a randomly (uniformly) selected minimal mutation until the requisite number have been performed.

There are a few points worth noting about this operator. First, in the limit of orthogonal genes, standard mutation is recovered provided that no mutation in the sequence is accepted if it generates a chromosome already visited in the sequence of minimal mutations. While this check is technically desirable, it is relatively troublesome to implement in general. For small values of $p_m$ and for representations in which the number of minimal mutations for each chromosome is large, the check makes little practical difference, merely distorting the binomial distribution slightly, so in the experiments for this paper, checks for previously visited mutations have not been performed.

Secondly, notice that there is no suggestion that the minimal mutations should have distance 1 from the solution to be mutated; indeed, while this will clearly be the case for orthogonal genetic representations, it is the case for none of the four representations considered in this paper.

Finally, given chromosomes $X$, $Y$ and $Z$, it is not necessarily the case that $D(X, Y) < D(X, Z)$ implies that $Y$ can be generated from $X$ in fewer minimal mutations than can $Z$.

### 4.2  Representation-independent Hill-climbing and Memetic Algorithms

Given a move operator, which in the present case will be taken to be the minimal mutation operator, it is a simple matter to define a family of hill-climbing operators. A hill-climber can be obtained by repeatedly trying moves generated by the move operator, in some sequence, and accepting all those that improve upon the current solution. This process continues until none of the moves that the operator can generate improves the solution. Numerous strategies are possible for generating the moves, but in the authors' experience the more random the order, the better will be the expected performance. The method used here generates moves in a pre-determined order for any particular hill-climbing, but this order changes each time the hill-climber is invoked. Davis (1991) has argued that it is usually desirable to accept neutral moves (ones that have no effect on fitness), but this is not central to the current discussion, and since neutral moves are unlikely in general TSP instances, this has not been allowed.

The application of a local optimiser such as the hill-climber described always succeeds in generating a local optimum (with respect to minimal mutations). Following Radcliffe & Surry (1994), which also contains further details of the hill-climbing techniques used, a *memetic algorithm* is defined to be a genetic algorithm in which local optimisation is applied to all solutions before evaluation. This can be thought of as a genetic algorithm applied in the subspace of local optima, with local optimisation acting as a repair mechanism for children lying outside this subspace (i.e. not being locally optimal). Because the evaluation function for the TSP is decomposable—the length of a child tour similar to its parent can be computed more easily given the length of the parent tour—hill-climbing is relatively cheap, so memetic algorithms might be expected to perform relatively better than genetic algorithms for this problem.

## 5    Formae and Performance Prediction

The primary aim in this work is to find measurable properties of representations that are correlated with the performance of an evolutionary algorithm. The candidate indicator studied will be fitness variance of the formae associated with the chosen representation. One motivation for this choice derives from the Schema Theorem (Holland, 1975), which has been shown both by Vose (1991) and Radcliffe (1991) to apply to general subsets of the representation space provided that disruption coefficients are computed appropriately. This motivation has previously been described in detail, so here the focus is instead on the interactions between formae, genetic operators and population update mechanisms.

Consider first those formae whose members in the current population are fitter than average. Along with the chromosomes that instantiate them, these formae are selected for reproduction more often, or selected for deletion less often, than formae with lower observed performance. Consider now the effects of applying genetic operators. If the recombination operator used respects the representation, this will ensure that whenever two parents are recombined their child will instantiate all formae of which they share membership. If the recombination operator is not very disruptive, even when only a single parent is a member of such formae the probability of generating new instances of them is relatively high. If the recombination operator is non-respectful, the extent to which these arguments apply depends on the degree to which respect is violated. Similarly, for (typical) low mutation rates, a child produced by mutation will share membership of most formae of low to medium order with its parent. Finally, although hill-climbing from a random starting point will usually produce a chromosome very different from its parent, when the parent is in the vicinity of a local optimum (with respect to that hill-climbing operator) as will tend to be the case after recombination in an effective memetic algorithm, it is likely that hill-climbing will not change a very large number of alleles, so forma membership is still to some extent preserved.

Turning now to forma construction—i.e., the sampling of chromosomes in formae of which the parents are not instances—observe that such newly sampled formae are likely to overlap in their allele composition with formae currently seen to be performing well, particularly to the extent that the recombination operator used is respectful. This is important because the way in which evolutionary (and particularly genetic) search is thought to proceed is by sampling smaller (higher order) formae that are intersections (compositions) of larger (lower order) formae of high relative fitness. Thus recombination is thought of as gradually building up complex solutions by combining "fit" components. While challenging search problems will exhibit some possibly large degree of non-linearity, so that combining components that are observed to be (relatively) fit will not always result in ever-fitter individuals, this approach retains some validity.

If the recombination operator used is transmitting, it can further be observed that alleles common to chromosomes and formae exhibiting above average performance at the current time step are also preferentially selected, both individually and collectively. The essence of the notion of assortment is that assorting recombination operators are capable of bringing together any compatible (non-competing) formae from the parents in a child. This seems to be essential given the model of genetic (and more widely evolutionary) search considered, the wide-spread use of non-assorting recombination operators for non-orthogonal representations notwithstanding. Needless to say, in the presence of selective pressure towards better solutions and formae, the new formae of which instances are created tend to be intersections of fitter, larger (lower order) formae.

Though somewhat imprecise, these arguments suggest that there are important senses in which evolutionary algorithms are directed by observed forma fitnesses, especially when recombination plays a major rôle, and when the recombination operators are (more strongly) respectful, transmitting and assorting. The schema theorem also points to the important rôle observed forma fitnesses play in guiding the search. Given this, the distribution of fitnesses within formae would seem to be central to how search proceeds. It is therefore worth considering the distributions that might be expected or desired.

First, it seems clear that for any challenging search problem large formae will have wide distributions of fitnesses, while if the search is to be guided by forma fitnesses it would be helpful if smaller formae had narrower distributions. Indeed, if formae were simply random collections of solutions from the search space it would be impossible to collect any useful directional information from collecting fitness samples from formae. Ultimately, of course, the interest is really in the fitness of the fittest member of each sampled forma, but unfortunately that is unavailable without exhaustively searching each forma. It is therefore probably necessary to restrict consideration to statistical measures available from sampling formae. Of these, the variance is the most familiar measure of spread, and it is this that will be considered.

These considerations suggest that the variance and other moments of formae from any representation in which the genes carry useful fitness information would be a maximum for large formae and fall towards zero for very small formae. More importantly, however, it might be further expected that representations for which fitness variance tends to fall more quickly as a function of increasing forma order would give evolutionary search algorithms stronger and more exploitable information than those with broader fitness distributions. For this reason the experiments in this paper will measure fitness variance and various other fitness moments for formae in four different representations for the TSP in the hope that these moments will tend to be inversely correlated with the performance of the algorithm. Related experiments have been conducted previously by Hofmann (1993), though he did not use a fully representation-independent algorithm and was more concerned with the comparison between RAR and a domain-specific operator, the Strategic Edge Crossover operator (SEX; Moscato & Norman, 1992), which is a variant of the Edge Recombination operator (Whitley *et al.*, 1989).

## 6    Representations for the TSP

In the empirical tests that follow, four representations of the TSP will be used. Two have already been introduced—the permutation representation $p$ (section 6.1), which gives rise to traditional $o$-schemata and is a (formal) genetic representation, and the undirected edge representation $u$ (section 6.2), which is allelic. Additionally, a directed edge (genetic) representation $d$ will be used (section 6.3) as well as a genetic variation $c$ of the undirected edge representation (section 6.4), that uses compound genes and is equivalent to the corner representation suggested by Hofmann (1993). These four representations are then characterised in sections 6.5–6.7.

## 6.1   The Permutation Representation

The permutation representation is a formal genetic representation, and has already been introduced in section 2.2. Here the $i$th gene identifies the $i$th city in the tour. Thus

$$1324^P = \phantom{} \tag{14}$$

The first gene is fixed to have allele 1 and is thus formally redundant but this will not prove problematical. A complication does arise, however, from the freedom to choose the direction in which a tour is traversed. While this degeneracy can be formally removed with the convention introduced previously (always choosing the second city to have a lower numbered label than the $n$th), this is not wholly satisfactory. This problem is discussed in section 6.6.

The $\mathrm{RAR}^P$ and $\mathrm{GNX}^P$ operators are easy to implement for this representation, while the definition of $\mathrm{BMM}^P$ depends on the observation that the minimal mutation of a permutation is generated by exchanging the positions of two cities. An example of such an exchange would be

$$143526^P \overset{\mathrm{BMM}^P}{\longmapsto} 153426^P, \tag{15}$$

by exchange of genes 2 and 4. Minimal mutations are at distance 2 from their parents in this representation. (In terms of the number of edges broken, this corresponds to a four-change.) It is easy to see that all permutations can be generated by a sequence of such city exchanges, so the conditions for BMM are satisfied.

Gene transmission is incompatible with assortment in this representation, as the reader will be able to verify by trying to construct a member of the forma described by $\{(3,3),(5,2)\}$ from parents $123456^P$ and $134526^P$ without violating transmission.

## 6.2   The Undirected Edge Representation

The undirected edge representation has also been introduced previously and is allelic. In this representation a tour is represented by the set of undirected edges it contains. As an example of the representation,

$$1324^P = \{13, 23, 24, 14\}^u. \tag{16}$$

$\mathrm{RAR}^u$, while somewhat harder to construct than for the permutation representation, is straightforward, and the factor of 2 that is problematical for the permutation representation does not arise since the representation makes no reference to the direction in which a tour is traversed.

It is easy to see that the minimal mutation for this representation is the reversal of a sub-tour, which is a 2-change in terms of the number of edges broken. For example,

$$\{14, 34, 35, 25, 26, 16\}^u = 143526^P \overset{\mathrm{BMM}^u}{\longmapsto} 125346^P = \{12, 34, 35, 25, 46, 16\}^u, \tag{17}$$

reversing the section from positions 2 to 5 inclusive. (In general, solutions are written in the permutation representation in this paper, even when they are being manipulated with respect to other representations.) Minimal mutations are at distance 2 from their parents in this representation. Although this operator is often referred to as *inversion,* this term will be avoided here because of possible confusion with the general re-linking operator (Holland, 1975).

To see that transmission is incompatible with assortment in this representation, observe that generating an instance of the forma described by $\{24, 23\}$ from parents $123456^p$ and $124356^p$ is impossible without violating transmission.

It is possible to apply $\mathrm{GNX}^u$ to the undirected edge representation by constructing an associated *pseudo-genetic representation.* This is achieved by arranging the edges in the order and sense in which they are encountered following the tour they describe in an arbitrarily chosen direction. The resulting list of edges will have every city exactly once as the "first" end of an edge, and can thus be used for alignment, allowing application of $\mathrm{GNX}^u$. While the chromosome resulting from this process is the same as that used in the directed edge representation, the edge is still considered to be undirected, so that when determining whether an edge can be added to a proto-child, its sense may be reversed if necessary. Thus, $\mathrm{GNX}^u$ based on undirected edges is different from the the same operator for directed edges.

### 6.3 The Directed Edge Representation

The directed edge representation is a (formal) genetic representation and represents a tour by the set of directed edges it contains. It is genetic because genes are well defined, the $i$th corresponding to the city visited after city $i$. Thus, identifying this representation by the superscript $d$,

$$1423^p = \{\overrightarrow{14}, \overrightarrow{23}, \overrightarrow{31}, \overrightarrow{42}\}^d. \tag{18}$$

As with the permutation representation, the degeneracy arising from the freedom to choose the direction in which to traverse the tour may be formally removed by convention, but again this is not wholly satisfactory. This is discussed in section 6.6.

The construction of $\mathrm{RAR}^d$ and $\mathrm{GNX}^d$ for this representation is again straightforward. The minimal mutations for the directed edge representation are 3-changes, for example,

$$143526^p \stackrel{\mathrm{BMM}^d}{\longmapsto} 142356^p, \tag{19}$$

which corresponds to cycling the edges $\{\overrightarrow{43}, \overrightarrow{52}, \overrightarrow{26}\}$ to become $\{\overrightarrow{42}, \overrightarrow{56}, \overrightarrow{23}\}$. Minimal mutations are at distance 3 in this representation. The reader will quickly become convinced that such 3-changes suffice to generate all tours, and that 1-changes and 2-changes are not possible in this representation.

Attempting to construct an instance of the forma described by $\{\overrightarrow{23}, \overrightarrow{31}\}$ from parents $123456^p$ and $126543^p$ should convince the reader that transmission is incompatible with assortment here also.

### 6.4 The Corner Representation

The final representation is in some ways the most complex, and is again based on undirected edges, but forms a (formal) genetic representation, denoted $c$. In this case, there is a gene corresponding to each city, each of which takes compound alleles consisting of the unordered pair of edges centred on that city. For example,

$$1423^p = \left\{(1, \{3, 4\}), (2, \{3, 4\}), (3, \{1, 2\}), (4, \{1, 2\})\right\}^c \tag{20}$$

where a tuple $(a, \{b, c\})$ indicates that city $a$ has neighbours $b$ and $c$. Defining $\text{RAR}^c$ and $\text{GNX}^c$ is straightforward.

The minimal mutation is sub-tour reversal (a 2-change), so the same example as for undirected edges may be used, specifically

$$143526^p \overset{\text{BMM}^c}{\longmapsto} 125346^p \tag{21}$$

Notice, however, that in this case the new solution is at distance 4 from its parent in this representation.

The incompatibility of transmission and assortment may be verified for this representation by attempting to generate an instance of the forma described by $\{(4, \{3, 5\}), (6, \{3, 7\})\}$ from parents $12345678^p$ and $12367458^p$.

### 6.5  Linkage Considerations

The positioning of genes on a chromosome defines its *linkage*. With crossover operators based on transferring contiguous portions of the genome from parents to children, such as $N$-point crossover, linkage can significantly affect algorithmic performance. In the case of the permutation representation, where the $i$th gene specifies the $i$th city visited, the static linkage achieved by placing the $i$th gene at the $i$th locus seems natural. With the other genetic representations—directed edges and corners—and the pseudo-genetic representation based on undirected edges, it is less clear that placing the $i$th gene at the $i$th locus is sensible. This is because in each of these cases, the $i$th gene is associated with the $i$th-*labelled* city, rather than the $i$th city in the tour, and the city labels are (usually) arbitrary. A simple way to determine the linkage adaptively is to re-link the genome in one of the two possible orders achieved by following the tour in a consistent direction. It seems at least possible that GNX using this linkage will perform better than using the essentially random linkage achieved by determining locus from city number. Both forms of linkage will therefore be tried with GNX.

### 6.6  Redundancy and Degeneracy

In order to classify representations further, it is useful to introduce the distinct notions of redundancy and degeneracy. These notions are often confused, a failing of which the authors, amongst others, have previously been guilty.

A representation is said to exhibit *redundancy* if a solution can be uniquely determined from a subset of its genes (or in the case of allelic representations, its alleles). All four representations considered contain some redundancy, because the last allele value can always be determined from the others (owing to the cyclic nature of the tour). The corner representation, however, contains vastly more than the other representations, actually specifying each edge twice. Thus fully half of the genetic material in the corner representation is formally redundant—specifying every other corner in the tour would suffice. Notice, however, that no *fixed* set of corners (those centred on a particular half of the cities) would be adequate, which is why the representation used specifies the corner for each city. High redundancy necessarily gives rise to a high degree of non-orthogonality, but it is not clear to what extent—if any—this inhibits the search.

In contrast, a representation is said to exhibit *degeneracy* if more than one chromosome is used to represent the same solution, (i.e. if the genotype-phenotype mapping is non-injective). Both the permutation representation and the directed edge representation exhibit degeneracy, while the undirected edge representation and the corner representation do not. While folding out the factor of

$n$ arising from the need to fix a starting city is easily handled, the degeneracy associated with the direction of travel is more problematical.

There are a number of possible responses to degeneracy:

1. *Gauge Fixing.* As has been stated earlier, the problem can be removed formally by a convention such as that used in this paper—always choosing the direction so that the second city has a lower numeric label than the $n$th. The problem with this is that some very similar solutions have almost maximally different representations. For example, $162453^P$ is a minimal mutation of $126453^P$, but in standard form is represented as $135426^P$. This is a practical problem for recombination, which will fail to recognise that the two solutions have anything in common except the redundant first gene and equidistant fourth gene, and leads to a certain "brittleness".

2. *Ignore the problem.* It is possible simply to leave the evolutionary search to use two different representatives for each solution. This avoids the brittleness of the "gauge fixing" approach, but at the cost of searching a larger space with two optima, and (more importantly) failing to allow recombination to recognise even when it is manipulating identical parent solutions. While there is some evidence that evolutionary search is still reasonably effective in these circumstances, it is hard to avoid the suspicion that its efficiency is reduced.

3. *Align before Recombination.* The practical difficulties of degeneracy manifest themselves during recombination. An alternative approach involves computing the distance between the first parent the second traversed in one sense, and then computing the distance with the second parent reversed. Recombination is performed with second parent in the sense that minimises the distance. This is similar in spirit to an approach used by Montana & Davis (1989) for removing the well-known hidden node degeneracy in feed-forward neural networks before recombination. This avoids the problem of brittleness and recombination's consequent inability to recognise certain very similar solutions, but is arguably somewhat arbitrary.

All of these options have drawbacks. For this study, the second option has been chosen as the simplest.

## 6.7   Characteristics of TSP Representations

Before proceeding to the experimental results, it will prove useful to summarise the key characteristics of the four representations considered. These are presented in table 1.

# 7   Experiments and Results

Figure 2 shows the standard deviation of fitness within formae as a function of order for the four different representations. Each point is based on 100 samples from each of 100 formae of the given order, for the 100-city Krolak 'C' problem from TSPLIB (Reinelt, 1990). Graphs of higher fitness moments are qualitatively rather similar, and are not shown.

TSP optimisation experiments were then conducted using both genetic and memetic algorithms, using $RAR_2$ and G2X for recombination, as well as edge recombination for a domain-specific comparison. For all representations except permutations, G2X was applied with both fixed linkage and the "tour-following" scheme described in section 6.5. The order of application of operators was recombination (with probability 1.0) of two parents chosen by probabilistic binary tournament selection, followed by BMM (defined with respect to the chosen representation) with a rate chosen so

| representation | rep. type | cardinality | degeneracy redundancy | | mutation-order (edges) | (genes) | linkage | variance |
|---|---|---|---|---|---|---|---|---|
| permutation | genetic | $O(n)$ | low | $\times 2$ | 4 | 2 | good | high |
| directed edge | genetic | $O(n)$ | low | $\times 2$ | 3 | 3 | random | medium |
| undirected edge | allelic | — | low | none | 2 | 2 | none | medium |
| undirected edge | pseudo | $O(n)$ | low | $\times 2$ | 2 | 2 | random | medium |
| corner | genetic | $O(n^2)$ | high | none | 2 | 4 | random | low |

Table 1: This table shows the main characteristics of the representations studied for the TSP. Cardinality indicates the number of allele values per gene (where applicable). Degeneracy and redundancy are discussed in section 6.6. Mutation order lists first the number of edges and second the number of gene values changed by a minimal mutation. The linkage column describes the appropriateness of the "natural" linkage for the representation, and variance gives the relative fitness variance of formae, as shown in figure 2. Note that the undirected edge representation is shown twice, once in its allelic form and once as the pseudo-genetic representation discussed in section 6.2.

that the mean number of mutations per chromosome was one. In the case of the memetic algorithms, minimal-mutation-based hill-climbing was then performed to find a local optimum. A panmictic population of size of 100 was used with a steady state update scheme. All performance results are averages over 20 runs, and show the length of the best tour in the population relative to the optimum. Each representation started from the same set of 20 randomly-generated populations. Error bars are omitted since they are in all cases smaller than the tick sizes.

Both the 100-city Krolak 'C' and the 442-hole PCB drilling problem from TSPLIB were studied. The genetic algorithm for the smaller problem used probabilistic binary tournaments with $p = 0.7$ for selection and replacement, with elitism, and allowed duplicates. Results for these runs are shown in figures 3, 4 and 5. A memetic algorithm (not shown) solves this problem to optimality extremely quickly.

The larger problem used a more aggressive GENITOR-style plan adapted from Whitley *et al.* (1989), using tournament selection with probability 1.0, and replacement of the worst individual. Duplicate solutions were forbidden. For edge recombination only, a zero mutation rate was used in line with its creators' recommendation (to achieve maximal edge transmission). Both genetic and memetic algorithms were used for this problem, with genetic results shown in figures 6 and 7 and memetic results in figure 8.

In general, the results show fitness variance of formae to be a powerful indicator of algorithmic performance. The results expected on this basis would be that for any fixed algorithm, corners should perform best, permutations worst, and the edge representations somewhere in between. The only discrepancies that need to be explained are now addressed in turn.

First, in four of the five direct comparisons, undirected edges out-perform directed edges despite similar forma variance. Factors explaining this might include the difference in mutation operators (two-changes for undirected edges versus three-changes for directed edges) and the greater disruptiveness of recombination for directed edges. The one case in which directed edges do better is a very aggressive plan with RAR. Here, it is possible that mutation is performing a more important search rôle, and greater recombinative disruption effectively increases the mutation rate advantageously.

Secondly, while permutations generally perform poorly, as forma variance would suggest, in one case (GNX on the 100 city problem) they perform rather better than might be expected. This is probably in part because GNX takes long contiguous chunks from parents, thus effectively transmitting many edges even for permutations. As noted in figure 2, if the formae considered are restricted to be those with contiguous defining positions, forma variance falls almost exactly to that for the edge-based representations, largely explaining this anomaly.

The final discrepancy concerns the performance of the corner representation relative to that of undirected edges. Here, the general pattern is that when good linkage is used and maintained, performance is very similar, but when poorer linkage is used, or is severely disrupted (as with RAR), corners significantly outperform edges. This is wholly understandable since corners intrinsically carry much more linkage information, in the sense that every corner specifies an adjacency of two edges. The only case in which this pattern breaks down is for the smaller problem where corners and undirected edges perform similarly with RAR.

Other points evident from the results are that GNX consistently out-performs RAR, linkage effects are (perhaps unsurprisingly) rather strong and the memetic algorithms produce dramatically better results in absolute terms than do genetic algorithms on the problems considered. More surprisingly, GNX with both the corner and undirected edge representations, even with non-optimised parameters, appears at least competitive with, and arguably superior to, edge recombination.

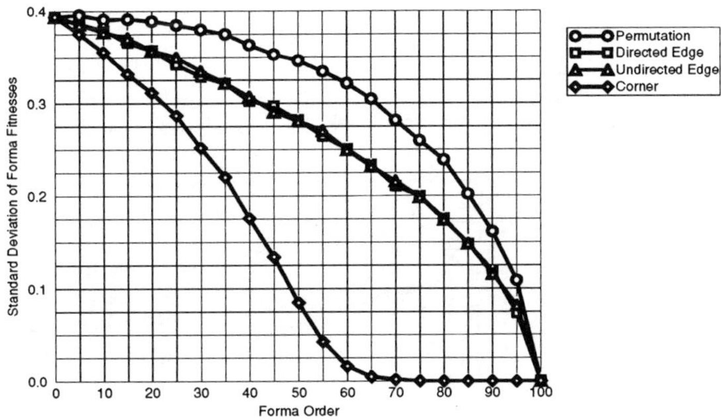


Figure 2: The graph shows the mean standard deviation of fitness for 100 samples drawn from 100 randomly generated formae at each order shown for the four representations considered. They are based on the 100 city Krolak 'C' problem. Note that if the graphs were shown as functions of forma size, rather than forma order, the corner line would be coincident with those for the edge representations. Further, if the formae are restricted to have adjacent defining positions, the permutation line becomes almost coincident with the edge lines. Confidence intervals (standard errors) are omitted as they are smaller than the tick marks shown.

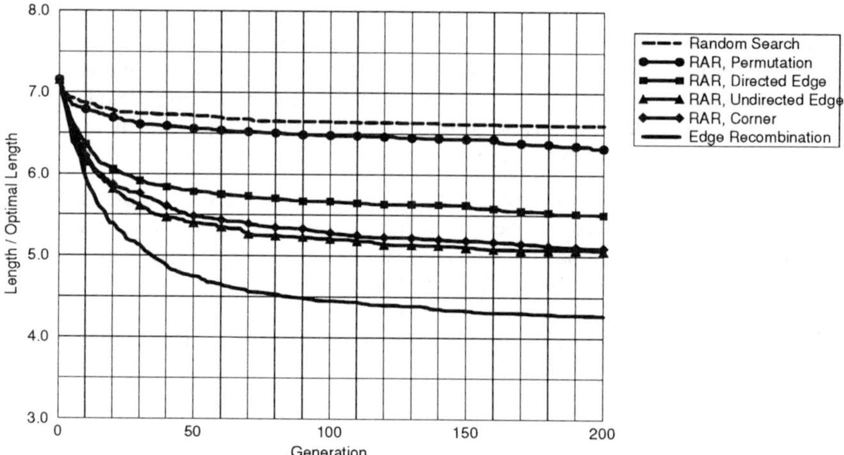

Figure 3: The graph shows the results produced by representation-independent genetic algorithms on the 100-city Krolak 'C' problem, instantiated with four representations using the RAR recombination operator. For comparison, a curve for random search is shown, as is Whitley *et al.*'s edge recombination operator, modified by deferring patching of tour fragments until all parent edges are exhausted.

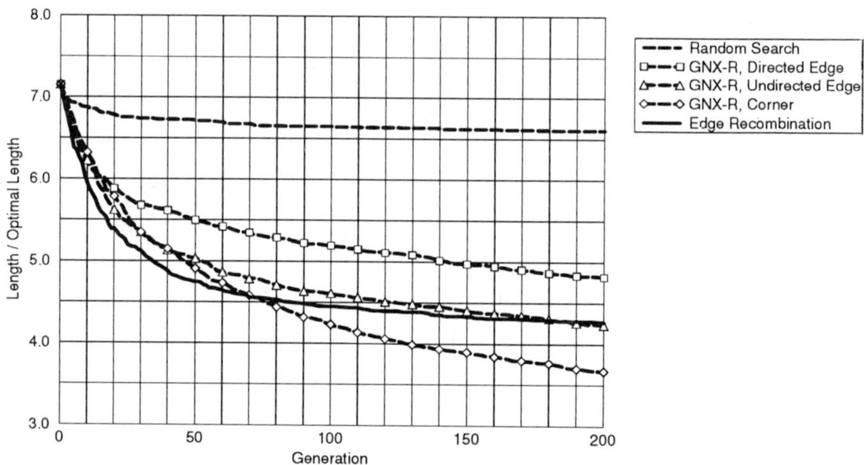

Figure 4: The graph shows the results produced by representation-independent genetic algorithms on the 100-city Krolak 'C' problem, using the GNX-R recombination operator (c.f. figure 3). These runs use the "natural" linkage associated with the representation. For the edge-based and corner representations, this linkage is essentially random (the gene's locus being determined by its city label).

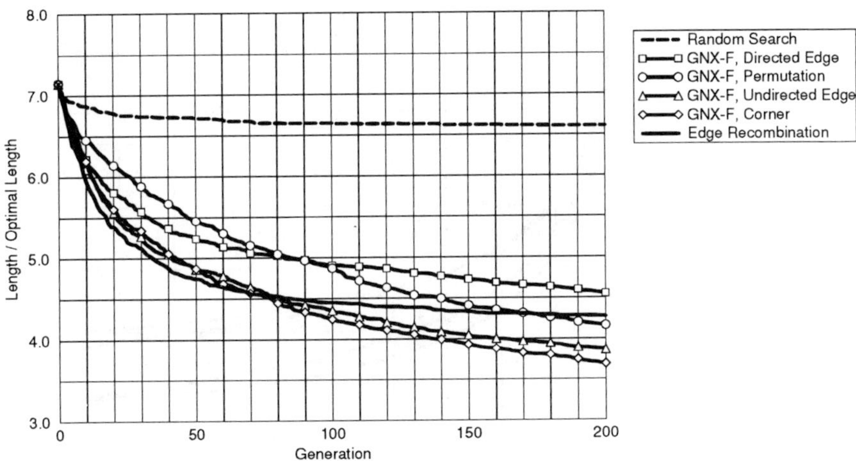


Figure 5: The graph shows the results produced by representation-independent genetic algorithms on the 100-city Krolak 'C' problem, using the GNX-F recombination operator (c.f. figures 3, 4). These runs use a dynamic "tour-following" linkage.

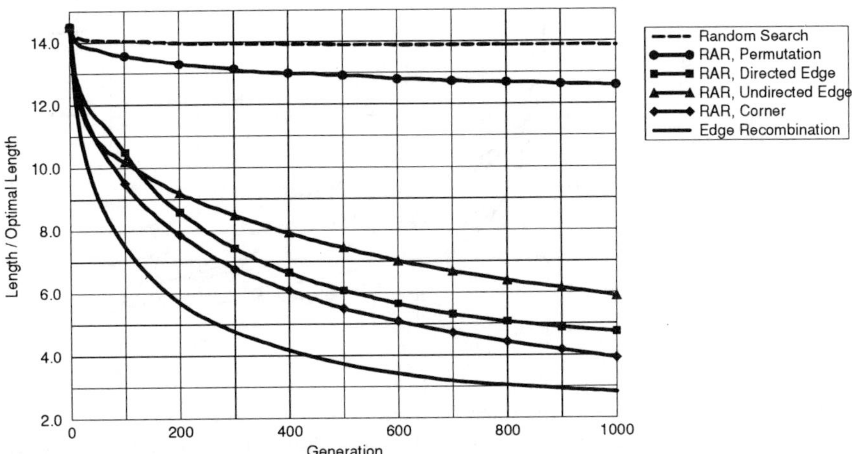


Figure 6: The graph shows results for a GENITOR-style genetic algorithm with RAR on the 442-hole PCB drilling problem corresponding to those in figure 3.

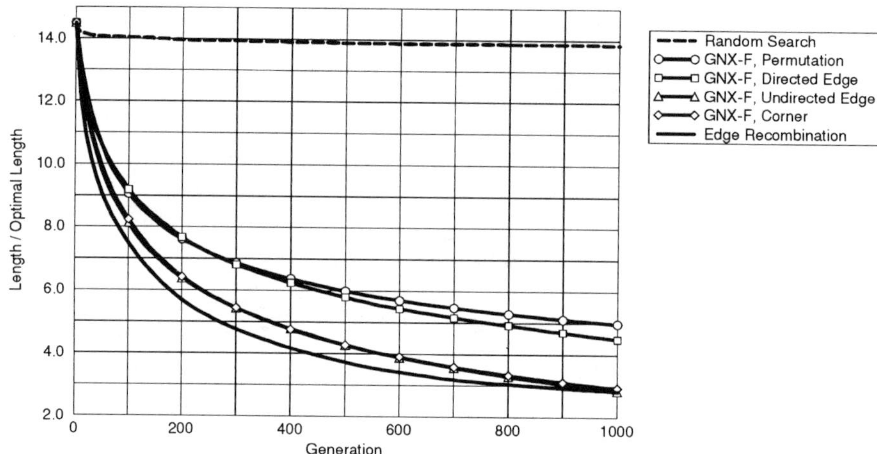

Figure 7: The graph shows results for a GENITOR-style genetic algorithm with GNX on the 442-hole PCB drilling problem corresponding to those in figure 5. Results for the inferior random linkage corresponding to figure 4 are omitted.

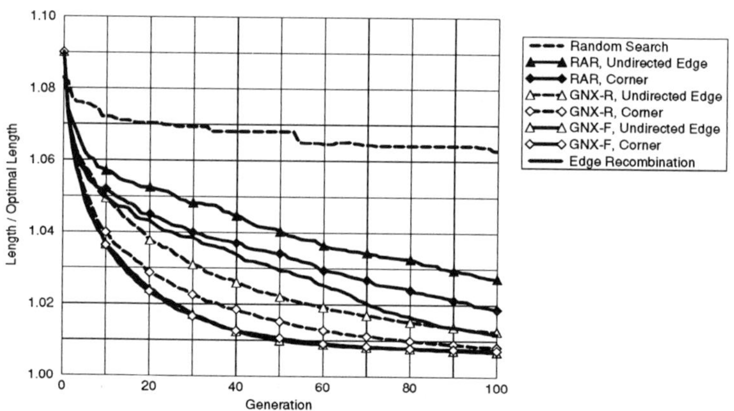

Figure 8: The graph shows the same problem as is presented in figures 6 and 7, but now using a memetic algorithm that applies full minimal-mutation-based optimisation before each evaluation. Note the different scales used on the axes. Results for the permutation representation are omitted owing to the extremely long generation times required. Furthermore, even on a per-generation comparison, results are not competitive with those shown. Results are also omitted for directed edges, again because of excessive compute times required. These arise because the minimal mutation for this representation is a 3-change, which requires at least $O(n)$ more computation than the 2-changes needed for undirected edges and corners.

## 8   Discussion and Conclusions

The general pattern of results supports the hypothesis that the fitness variance of forma exhibited by a representation acts as a good predictor of its performance in formal genetic and memetic algorithms. Indeed, given the large number of potentially relevant differences between the four representations considered, the predictive power of forma variance is rather impressive. While results have only been gathered for one problem class (the travelling sales-rep problem) and a limited range of representation-independent algorithms, they provide a powerful case for corresponding studies in other problem domains.

The best results overall were produced with the corner representation, which has a number of unusual features. Principal among these is its extremely high cardinality and compound allele structure. The results therefore provide further evidence that the traditional advocacy of low cardinality representations as universally appropriate is misguided.

The results obtained with GNX are at least competitive with, and arguably superior to, those obtained with edge recombination. Since this is widely regarded as the best form of recombination for the TSP when a genetic algorithm without local search is used, this is a significant finding. Moreover, since GNX is applicable to *any* (formal) genetic representation (including non-orthogonal representations) it may well prove effective in other problem domains. These studies have demonstrated that the construction of formal representation-independent operators and algorithms is not merely of theoretical import, but can provide competitive practical search tools.

Linkage has long been recognised as an important theoretical characteristic of chromosomes in the context of recombination, but has rarely been shown to have a major effect on performance in practice. These experiments have clearly demonstrated linkage effects, and shown that adaptive linkage strategies—albeit not the traditional inversion-based approach—can yield superior performance. The best results achieved were with corners, which contain intrinsic linkage information, and undirected edges when linked by tour following.

Finally, these results strongly confirm the dramatically superior performance that can be achieved by incorporating local search in genetic algorithms for TSP to yield memetic algorithms. The TSP is a natural candidate for memetic search because the fitness function is decomposable, allowing very cheap testing of minimal mutations, but it should be noted that even if full evaluation is performed at each memetic step the overall performance of the memetic algorithms discussed is still superior.

## References


Lashon Booker, 1987. Improving search in genetic algorithms. In Lawrence Davis, editor, *Genetic Algorithms and Simulated Annealing*. Pitman (London).

Lawrence Davis, 1991. Bit-climbing, representational bias, and test suite design. In *Proceedings of the Fourth International Conference on Genetic Algorithms*. Morgan Kaufmann (San Mateo).

Kenneth A. De Jong, 1992. Genetic algorithms are NOT function optimizers. In Darrell Whitley, editor, *Foundations of Genetic Algorithms 2*. Morgan Kaufmann (San Mateo, CA).

David E. Goldberg and Robert Lingle Jr, 1985. Alleles, loci and the traveling salesman problem. In *Proceedings of an International Conference on Genetic Algorithms*. Lawrence Erlbaum Associates (Hillsdale).

Reimar Hofmann, 1993. Examinations on the algebra of genetic algorithms. Diploma Thesis, Technical University of Munich, Department of Computer Science.

John H. Holland, 1975. *Adaptation in Natural and Artificial Systems.* University of Michigan Press (Ann Arbor).

David J. Montana and Lawrence Davis, 1989. Training feedforward neural networks using genetic algorithms. In *Proceedings of the Eleventh International Joint Conference on Artificial Intelligence*, pages 762–767.

Pablo Moscato and Michael G. Norman, 1992. A "memetic" approach for the travelling salesman problem — implementation of a computational ecology for combinatorial optimisation on message-passing systems. In *Proceedings of the International Conference on Parallel Computing and Transputer Applications.* IOS Press (Amsterdam).

Nicholas J. Radcliffe and Patrick D. Surry, 1994. Formal memetic algorithms. In Terence C. Fogarty, editor, *Evolutionary Computing: AISB Workshop*, pages 1–16. Springer-Verlag, Lecture Notes in Computer Science 865.

Nicholas J. Radcliffe, 1991. Equivalence class analysis of genetic algorithms. *Complex Systems*, 5(2):183–205.

Nicholas J. Radcliffe, 1992. Non-linear genetic representations. In R. Männer and B. Manderick, editors, *Parallel Problem Solving from Nature 2*, pages 259–268. Elsevier Science Publishers/North Holland (Amsterdam).

Nicholas J. Radcliffe, 1994. The algebra of genetic algorithms. *Annals of Maths and Artificial Intelligence*, 10:339–384.

Gerhard Reinelt, 1990. TSPLIB. Available by anonymous FTP from softlib.rice.edu.

J. David Schaffer, Richard A. Caruana, Larry J. Eshelman, and Rajarshi Das, 1989. A study of the control parameters affecting online performance of genetic algorithms for function optimisation. In *Proceedings of the Third International Conference on Genetic Algorithms.* Morgan Kaufmann (San Mateo).

William M. Spears and Kenneth A. De Jong, 1991. On the virtues of parameterised uniform crossover. In *Proceedings of the Fourth International Conference on Genetic Algorithms*, pages 230–236. Morgan Kaufmann (San Mateo).

Michael D. Vose and Gunar E. Liepins, 1991. Schema disruption. In *Proceedings of the Fourth International Conference on Genetic Algorithms*, pages 237–243. Morgan Kaufmann (San Mateo).

Michael D. Vose, 1991. Generalizing the notion of schema in genetic algorithms. *Artificial Intelligence.*

Darrell Whitley, Timothy Starkweather, and D'Ann Fuquay, 1989. Scheduling problems and traveling salesmen: The genetic edge recombination operator. In *Proceedings of the Third International Conference on Genetic Algorithms.* Morgan Kaufmann (San Mateo).

Darrell Whitley, Timothy Starkweather, and Danial Shaner, 1991. The traveling salesmen and sequence sheduling: Quality solutions using genetic edge recombination. In Lawrence Davis, editor, *Handbook of Genetic Algorithms.* Van Nostrand Reinhold (New York).

# The Troubling Aspects of a Building Block Hypothesis for Genetic Programming


**Una-May O'Reilly**
Santa Fe Institute
Santa Fe, NM, 87501

**Franz Oppacher**
School of Computer Science
Carleton University, Ottawa, CANADA


## Abstract


In this paper we carefully formulate a Schema Theorem for Genetic Programming (GP) using a schema definition that accounts for the variable length and the non-homologous nature of GP's representation. In a manner similar to early GA research, we use interpretations of our GP Schema Theorem to obtain a GP Building Block definition and to state a "classical" Building Block Hypothesis (BBH): that GP searches by hierarchically combining building blocks. We report that this approach is not convincing for several reasons: it is difficult to find support for the promotion and combination of building blocks solely by rigourous interpretation of a GP Schema Theorem; even if there were such support for a BBH, it is empirically questionable whether building blocks always exist because partial solutions of consistently above average fitness and resilience to disruption are not assured; also, a BBH constitutes a narrow and imprecise account of GP search behavior.


## 1 INTRODUCTION

In this paper we precisely define a schema in GP and derive a lower bound on the growth of the expected number of instances of a GP-schema from one generation to the next. Following GA precedent, we refer to this as the GP Schema Theorem (GPST). We also wish to show that, although a notion of building blocks arises from an interpretation of the GPST, it is questionable whether such building blocks reliably exist throughout the course of a GP run. Finally, we emphasize that, as with GAs, hypothesizing building block combination requires greater liberty with the interpretation of the Schema Theorem than is justifiable.

Our investigation is motivated by the historical precedent of the Schema Theorem and BBH as an explanation of the search power of GAs [Holland 1975/1992, Goldberg 1989]. Holland's analyses have been the foundation for more precise explanations (some diverging from a schema-based approach) of GA search behavior. GA theory promises to be a useful source of analogy for GP because both models use the same central algorithm loop which applies the basic evolution-based genetic operators and both act as a "shell" which accepts fitness function and problem encoding as parameters. Both GA and GP use genetic exchange within the population (crossover) and fitness-based selection (and both have been widely employed with fitness proportional selection). The similarity of operators and central algorithm make it worthwhile to formulate a GP theory along the lines of GA theory.

Some recent experimental [Mitchell,Forrest,Holland 1991, Forrest,Mitchell 1992] and theoretical [Goldberg 1989, Radcliffe 1991, Grefenstette,1992, Vose 1993, Altenberg 1994a, Altenberg 1994b] research has questioned the value of the Schema Theorem and BBH as a description of how the GA searches or as the source of the GA's power. In this paper we confirm that the GPST and a GP BBH similarly fail to provide an adequate account of GP's search behavior and that various plausible interpretations of the GPST fail to support a GP BBH. Some reasons for the inadequacy of the interpretations are the same as for GAs, others pertain more directly to GP, and are due to its representation and crossover operator. We hope, however, that is investigation of how interpretations of the GPST fall short of supporting a GP BBH will provide insights for subsequent improved accounts of GP's search behavior.

The paper is organized as follows:

Section 2 discusses various options for a schema definition, and a more general definition than the one given in [Koza 1992] is chosen. We also give formal definitions of GP-schemas and of schema order and defining length.

Section 3 presents the GPST as a recurrence relation that expresses the lower bound on expected instances of GP-schemas from one generation to the next.

In Section 4 we discuss the approximations and questionable assumptions involved in interpreting the GPST to hypothesize that a building block process characterizes GP search.

Section 5 concludes the paper.

## 2    SCHEMA DEFINITION AND RELATED CONCEPTS

The first question to be considered is: what schema definition in GP is useful in formulating a description of GP search? Schemas, or similarity templates, are simply one way of defining subsets of the search space. There are obviously many ways in which the GP search space could be partitioned (e.g. according to function, fitness, number of nodes in tree, height of tree) but it is logical to stay close to the spirit of the GA schema definition because it permits a description of the crossover operator's behavior to be incorporated into the recurrence relation that counts the schema instances each generation. For example, if we were to instead choose to define subsets of the space according to fitness, we would not be able to explicitly formulate how many instances within a partition of a given fitness would propagate to the next generation since it is not known how crossover affects the samples of this partition.

The first schema definition we will consider is from [Koza 1992, p. 117–118]. According to Koza, a *schema* in GP is the set of all individual trees from the population that contain, as subtrees, one or more specified trees. A schema is a set of LISP S-expressions (i.e., a set of rooted, point-labeled trees with ordered branches) sharing common features.

The distinctive aspect of Koza's schema definition is that a schema is a number of S-Expressions each of which is isomorphic to a tree. See Tree A of Figure 1. It can be parsed inorder to form the S- Expression (IF (< 3 4) (+ 1 2) (dec x)) where IF, <, +, and dec are names of S-Expressions with 3, 2, 2 and 1 argument, respectively.

Koza's definition implies that no schema is defined by an incompletely specified S-Expression such as (+ # 2) where "#" is a wildcard denoting the substitution of any S-Expression. There are wildcards implicit in the Koza definition but they are restricted to S-Expressions which enclose the schema rather than lie within it. Thus, the schema can also be written correctly as (# (IF (< 3 4) (+ 1 2) (dec x))), with the interpretation that the wildcard can be matched by any S-Expression which has at least one argument matching the schema. In other words, the schema can be embedded as a sub-tree anywhere in a larger tree. In consideration of the variable length representation in GP a wildcard can also be null (i.e. represent nothing and the parentheses which match it are eliminated). In this case the schema defines a partition of one instance.

There are less restrictive schema definitions which are worthy of consideration. First, while this schema definition seems intuitive because subtrees or syntactically complete S-Expressions are swapped by GP crossover, it ignores the possibility of an incompletely specified S-Expression such as (+ # b) or (+ (# 3 4) b). This sort of S-Expression has a specific name (or root in the corresponding tree, + in this example) but some parts within it are not specified because of the presence of internal wildcards. One obvious example of such an incompletely specified S-Expression is the part of the parent tree "left behind" to be joined with a subtree taken from the other parent. We call the hierarchical structure (which is not strictly a tree) corresponding to what is left intact by repeated crossovers a **tree fragment** or simply a **fragment**. An example is Fragment B of Figure 1 which corresponds to a schema (# (IF (< # #) (+ 1 #) (dec #))).

A fragment is essentially a tree that has at least one leaf that is a wildcard. It corresponds to an incomplete S-Expression with wildcards inside it. There is always a wildcard at the root of a fragment to denote that it can be fully embedded in a tree.

It should be noted that the root wildcard (implicit in Koza's schema definition) can be matched more freely than a fragment's leaf wildcard. Although both kinds of wildcard eventually match with a primitive, a primitive can match a leaf wildcard only if it is in a specified position of an argument list. A primitive can match the root wildcard each time one of its arguments matches the specified part of the schema. This is because the schema definition does not state what position the specified part has in the root primitive's argument list. For example, both (− (+ 3 4) 5) and (− 5 (+ 3 4)) are instances of the schema (# (+ 3 4)) because the definition does not state which argument (+ 3 4) must match. The schema definition is not restricted so as to require a specific argument position, such as the first, or the n-th, to match because, in order to designate the match, wildcards of different arity would have to be introduced. This, in turn, would defeat the generality a wildcard is supposed to provide. Instead this ambiguity is accepted as a natural consequence of a representation which does not use fixed positioning.

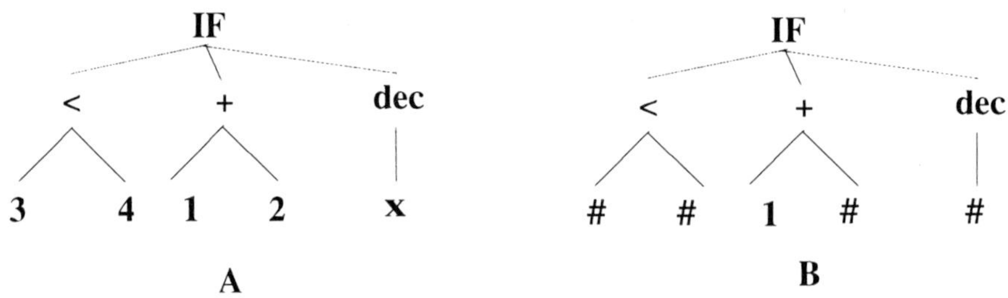

Figure 1: Tree *(A)* versus Fragment *(B)*

A is a tree because it can be parsed inorder to form a syntactic ally complete S-Expression. All of A's leaves are variables, constants or primitives that do not require arguments. B is a fragment, not a tree, because it has wildcards as leaves.

Considering fragments, an even more general schema definition is possible. A schema may be defined as an unordered collection of both completely defined S-Expressions (as in Koza's definition) and incompletely defined S-Expressions (i.e., fragments). The schema definition does not specify exactly how the fragments or S-Expressions are linked within an instance but it requires that they must all be matched.

For example, consider the unordered 3 element collection of $(+\ 3\ 4)$, $(+\ 3\ 4)$ and $(-\ \#\ \#)$ and three individuals:

1. $(\text{IF}\ (+\ 3\ 4)\ (+\ 3\ 4)\ (-\ \text{x}\ 2))$,

2. $(\text{IF}\ (-\ \text{x}\ 2)\ (+\ 3\ 4)\ (+\ 3\ 4))$ and

3. $(\text{AND}\ (+\ 3\ 4)\ (+\ 3\ 4)\ (+\ 3\ 4)\ (-\ \text{x}\ \text{y}))$

Individuals 1 and 2 instantiate the schema once and individual 3 actually instantiates it three times because there are three combinations of two $(+\ 3\ 4)$ subtrees and one $(-\ \#\ \#)$ fragment. Figure 2 shows a different example in terms of trees.

This general schema can be written more simply as a set (i.e. an unordered collection without duplicates) of pairs by pairing each fragment or completely defined S-Expression with the number of its occurrences that must be matched by an instance, and the root wildcard is implicitly assumed. In the above example, the schema would be represented as $\{((+\ 3\ 4),2),\ (-\ \#\ \#),1)\}$.

The more general schema definition is relevant because it allows the description of partial solutions in GP, i.e., of combinations that persist for more than one generation as crossover dissects and substitutes the parts of a tree corresponding to wildcards. Another reason is this: Consider that GP estimates the fitness of a schema by sampling the fitness of its instantiations (i.e. by sampling the fitness of a program each time the schema is found in it). The accuracy of the estimate depends on how many different samples GP processes. Other considerations being equal, the accuracy of the estimate is not related to whether the schema is a complete S-Expression tree or multiple fragments and trees.

We therefore choose to define GP-schemas as follows:

> A **GP-schema** $H$ is a set of pairs. Each pair is a unique S-Expression tree or fragment (i.e., incomplete S-Expression tree with some leaves as wildcards) and a corresponding integer that specifies how many instances of the S-Expression tree or fragment comprise H.

An individual program in the population **instantiates** a GP-schema once **for each way** it matches the number of occurrences of trees and fragments in the GP-schema. For example, in Program ii of Figure 2 schema $H =\{((+\ 3\ 4),\ 2)\}$ is matched by six different combinations of two subtrees and, thus, Program ii instantiates $H$ six times. While argument position is not considered when placing a fragment into the parse tree, the order of the arguments found inside a fragment must match the order of the arguments in the target subtree. Thus the program $(+\ 4\ 3)$ does not match with the schema $\{((+\ 3\ 4),\ 1)\}$.

We stress that a program instantiates a GP-schema once **for each way** it matches the GP-schema because we are ultimately interested in counting the expected occurences of a program pattern. Our GP-Schema definition captures the notion of a program pattern and, due to GP's representation, a program pattern (i.e., GP-schema) can occur more than once in a program. Consider a program $h$. An **instantiation** of a schema H by a program h, $inst(h, H)$, is an element of $Inst(h, H)$, which, in turn, is a function that produces a set of all matches of H by the target program h, based on the matching procedure described above. Figure 2 shows 6 instantiations of $H =\{((+\ 3\ 4),\ 2)\}$ by Program ii. Though an instantiation designates one specific match of the GP- schema, the notation $inst(h, H)$ does not specify the designation. The designation is, however, important and should be implicitly noted because it is later required in counting the edges connecting the GP-schema instantiation to determine its *defining length*.

Once a GP-schema definition has been adopted, the next task - in analogy to GA theory - is to define measures of GP-schema specificity or order and of GP-schema defining length. These two concepts are used together - again in analogy to GA theory - to determine the likelihood that a GP-schema will be disrupted by crossover. The notion of order makes it possible to compare the relative sample sizes of schemas, and can be transferred directly from GA theory. The notion of defining length, however, can not be directly lifted from the GA domain because of the variable structure of trees and fragments.

The **order** of a GP-schema is the number of nodes in the graphs corresponding to its S-expressions and fragments. For example, in Figure 2 the schema $H =\{((+\ 3\ 4),\ 2)\}$ has order 6, the schema $\{((IF\ \#\ \#\ \#),\ 1)\}$ has order 1, and the schema $\{((IF\ a\ \#\ \#),\ 1)\}$ has order 2.

Order is a straight-forward concept for GP-schemas. Schemas of higher order or greater specificity, other considerations being equal, will have fewer instances in a population than those of lower order or lesser specificity.

The **defining length D** of a GP-schema instantiation is the sum of its variable and fixed defining lengths:

$$D(inst(h, H), H) = D_{fixed}(H) + D_{var}(inst(h, H), H)$$

Below, we let $D(h, H)$ be short for $D(inst(h, H), H)$, and $D_{var}(h, H)$ be short for $D_{var}(inst(h, H), H)$.

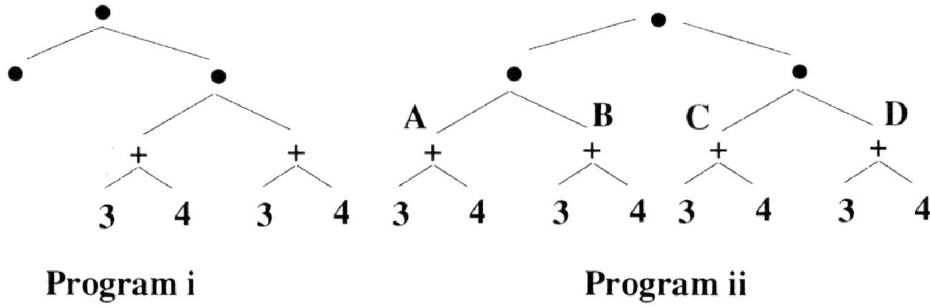



Figure 2: GP-schemas

The GP-schema $H = \{((+34), 2)\}$ has one instance in Program i and six instances in Program ii (AB, AC, AD, BC, BD, CD). The order of $H$ is 6 and $D_{fixed}(H) = 4$. In Program i $D_{var}(h) = 2$. The instances in Program ii (see previous list) have $D_{var}(h) = 2, 4, 4, 4, 4, 2$ respectively.

The **fixed defining length** of a GP-schema H, $D_{fixed}(H)$, is the number of edges within each S-expression or fragment of H, not including edges connected to a wildcard. It is derivable from the GP-schema alone, independently of any program. For example, in schema $H = \{((+ 3\ 4), 2)\}$ of Figure 2, $D_{fixed}(H)$ equals 4.

The **variable defining length** of a GP-schema instantiation, $D_{var}(h, H)$, is the number of edges which connect together the S-expressions or fragments in H, i.e., the sum of the lengths of the shortest paths between a schema fragment and the deepest common ancestor of all the schema fragments in the instantiation. $D_{var}(h, H)$ must be calculated for each instantiation and depends upon how the schema instance is embedded in the program. For example, in Program ii in Figure 2, instantiations AB and CD have a variable defining length of 2 and the others have a variable defining length of 4.

**Disruption** of a GP-schema instantiation $inst(h, H)$ occurs when a node in $h$ is selected as a crossover point and the swapping of the subtree rooted at the crossover point with a subtree from another program changes $h$ sufficiently so that it no longer instantiates $H$.

Let the sample space of disruption of a GP-schema instantiation be the number of nodes in program $h$, $Size(h)$, and let $P_d(h, H)$ be short for $P_d(inst(h, H), H)$. The upper bound on the probability of disruption under crossover of a GP-schema instantiation is its defining length divided by the number of nodes in $h$:

$$P_d(h, H) = \frac{D_{fixed}(H) + D_{var}(h, H)}{Size(h)}$$

Proof: The defining length of a GP-schema instantiation equals the number of crossover events that can destroy it. $Size(h)$ is the number of available crossover locations. In the worst case, no subtree swapped in will re-create the instantiation. $\square$

For example, when $h$ = Program i in Figure 2 and $H = \{((+ 3\ 4), 2)\}$, $P_d(h, H) = \frac{2}{3}$ since

$D(h, H) = 6$ ($D_{var}(h, H) = 2$, $D_{fixed}(H) = 4$) and the total program consists of 9 nodes.

Most reported experiments of GP are run with a probabilistic bias in the crossover point selection. Leaf crossover points are probabilistically selected with a leaf bias $L_b = 0.1$ and interior points are probabilistically selected with bias $1 - L_b = 0.9$. Let the number of leaf nodes in a schema $H$ be $V(H)$. Since the changing of a leaf node by crossover is accounted for by $D_{fixed}(H)$ and not $D_{var}(h, H)$, the probability of disruption can now be biased accordingly to yield the more precise formulation of $P_d(h, H)$:

$$P_d(h, H) = \frac{L_b V(H) + (1 - L_b)(D(h, H) - V(H))}{Size(h)}$$

Proof: The probability that a leaf in schema $H$ will be chosen as a crossover point is $L_b V(H)$. The probability that an interior point in schema $H$ will be chosen is $(1 - L_b)(D(h, H) - V(H))$. The space of all crossover events is $Size(h)$. $\square$

For example, using again Program i in Figure 2 as $h$, $P_d(h, H) = 0.24$ since $L_b V(H) = 0.4$ ($L_b = 0.1$ and $V(H) = 4$) and the program consists of 9 nodes.

We define the **compactness** of a GP-schema instantiation as the converse of its probability of disruption: $c(h)$ equals $1 - P_d(h, H)$. Thus, when the probability of schema disruption of an instantiation is high, its compactness is low, and, when the probability of disruption of an instantiation is low, its compactness is high. Since $P_d(h, H)$ is a upper bound on the probability of disruption, $c(h, H)$ is the lower bound on the compactness.

In summary, in this section we have motivated and introduced a general GP-schema definition and defined concepts of specificity, disruption and compactness relating to this definition.

## 3    A GP SCHEMA THEOREM

This section formulates a GP Schema Theorem (GPST) that expresses the lower bound of the growth of the expected number of instances of a GP-Schema.

Recall that the GA Schema Theorem expresses the lower bound on growth in expected membership of a schema in the population from time $t$ to $t + 1$. It has three factors:

1. the expected membership of the schema at time $t$ in a population of $n$ strings,

2. the reproductive factor of the expected membership of a schema contributed by fitness proportional selection, and

3. the lower bound estimate of whether a schema member will survive crossover and mutation.

To formulate a similar lower bound for GP the following adjustments are required.

1. The GA Schema Theorem refers to expected **members** of a schema. Membership is appropriate in GAs because a string instantiates a given schema at most once. The GPST needs to count the expected **instances** of a GP-schema because a program may instantiate a given schema more than once (see Section 2). Let $i(H, t)$ be the number of instances (by virtue of instantiation) of schema $H$ at time $t$ in the population of programs. $E[i(H, t)]$ denotes the expected number of instances of schema $H$.

2. The expected number of instances of a schema $H$ that are reproduced via fitness proportional selection of programs must be calculated. Let $\hat{f}(H,t)$ denote the estimated average fitness of schema H at time t.

**Lemma 1**  $E[i(H, t+1)] = i(H, t)\frac{\hat{f}(H,t)}{\bar{f}(t)}$ .

Proof: Let $n$ denote the population size and $\bar{f}(t)$ the average fitness of all programs in the population. Let $f(j)$ denote the fitness of program j. Since the number of times a program $h$ instantiates schema $H$ can be calculated as $|Inst(h, H)|$, the number of instantiations of $H$ in the population at generation t, $i(H,t)$, is given by $i(H,t) = \sum_k |Inst(k, H)|$. Fitness proportional selection reproduces a program k with probability:

$$\frac{f(k)}{\sum_{j=1}^{n} f(j)}$$

The expected number of times that program k will be copied into the next generation is:

$$n\frac{f(k)}{\sum_{j=1}^{n} f(j)}$$

and the number of instantiations of H that will be in the next generation because of program k is:

$$n\frac{f(k)}{\sum_{j=1}^{n} f(j)}|Inst(k, H)|$$

Thus, the expected total number, $E[i(H, t+1)]$, of instantiations of H in the next generation, is:

$$E[i(H, t+1)] = \sum_{k=1}^{n} n\frac{f(k)}{\sum_{j=1}^{n} f(j)}|Inst(k, H)|$$

Since $\bar{f}(t) = \frac{\sum_{j=1}^{n} f(j)}{n}$,

$$E[i(H, t+1)] = \frac{1}{\bar{f}(t)}\sum_{k=1}^{n} f(k)|Inst(k, H)|$$

$$E[i(H, t+1)] = \frac{i(H,t)}{\bar{f}(t)}\sum_{k=1}^{n} \frac{f(k)|Inst(k, H)|}{I(H,t)}$$

Since the estimated average fitness is:

$$\hat{f}(H,t) = \sum_{k=1}^{n} \frac{f(k)|Inst(k, H)|}{I(H,t)}$$

Therefore, $E[i(H, t+1)] = i(H, t)\frac{\hat{f}(H,t)}{\bar{f}(t)}$ $\square$

To see how a schema that appears several times in a program can be expected to reproduce in proportion to its fitness via fitness proportional selection on programs, it is important to realize that the average fitness of a schema $H$ is the sum of the partial contributions of the fitnesses of programs that instantiate $H$. The fitness contribution of a program is proportional to the number of instantiations the program adds to the total instantiations of $H$ in the population. If the above divisor were the number of programs that are members of the schema, rather than $i(H,t)$, fitness proportional selection would not guarantee expected reproduction relative to estimated average fitness.

3. Because the standard GP [Koza 1992] does not use mutation, we do not account for it. We define an estimate of the probability of disruption of any instantiation of $H$ because $P_d(h, H)$ is not the same for every GP-instantiation involving $H$. The upper bound probability of disruption of any instantiation of $H$ is defined as follows:

$$P_d(H, t) = \sup P_d(h, H) \text{ at time t.}$$

$P_d(H, t)$ is a very conservative upper bound. The GPST would be more precisely bounded if the probability of disruption of schema instances were more accurately represented.

The modifications result in the following GP Schema Theorem, where $E[i(H, t)]$ denotes the expected number of instances, not members, of $H$ at $t$, $\hat{f}(H, t)$ is the observed average fitness of the instances of the GP-schema $H$, $\bar{f}(t)$ is the average fitness of the population, $P_d(H, t)$ is the upper bound on the probability of schema disruption, and $P_{xo}$ is the probability of using crossover:

**GP SCHEMA THEOREM:**    $E[i(H, t+1)] \geq i(H, t)\frac{\hat{f}(H)}{\bar{f}(t)}(1 - P_{xo}P_d(H, t))$

Proof: By Lemma 1, without crossover, the expected reproduction of schema $H$ is $i(H, t)\frac{\hat{f}(H,t)}{\bar{f}(t)}$. With crossover, the lower bound probability that schema $H$ survives intact is $(1 - P_{xo}P_d(H, t))$ because $P_d(H, t)$ is an upper bound on the probability that a schema $H$ will be disrupted. $\square$

On first glance, the above recurrence is the same as the GA Schema Theorem but an interesting difference is due to the "**crossover survival term**" $(1 - P_{xo}P_d(H, t))$. This is an **estimate** of the minimal number of schema instances that survive crossover. As in GAs, the **actual** minimum likelihood of survival may be greater than the estimate and may change each generation. Whether this is indeed the case depends upon the composition of the population from which mates are drawn. Given an appropriate subtree from its mate, a schema disrupted by removing a subtree at the crossover point can be "repaired" and reinstantiated. The estimate of crossover survival in both GAs and GP is inaccurate because it does not account for such an event.

However, in GP, the inaccuracy of the crossover survival term is further exacerbated by the fact that both the size and shape of a program containing a schema instance can change in a generation even when the schema instance is not disrupted. As a consequence of the variable length representation and the behaviour of the crossover operator, the defining length of a schema and the size of the program in which it is embedded both can change. These changes will also impact the observed probability of disruption.

Not only is crossover probabilistic, but fitness proportional selection is not explicitly correlated to program size and height[1]. These facts, together with the facts stated in the previous paragraph, imply that the probability of disruption of a schema - while an upper bound can be formulated - changes so drastically from generation to generation, and in such an unpredictable fashion, that it can best be represented as a random variable. Since the term $P_d(H, t)$ in the GPST can be considered a random variable, we refer to it as $\tilde{D}_t$.

---

[1] Fitness proportional selection is probably implicitly correlated to program size and height but the relationship is not known and it may differ for each GP problem.

$\tilde{D}_t$ represents the observed probability of disruption of schema $H$ in the population at time $t$. We use $\tilde{D}_t$ to formulate definitions of disruption and compactness. This allows us to interpret the GPST with respect to the allocation of trials among schemas.

**Schema Disruption**: Let $R$ be the event that, at time t, $\tilde{D}_t$ is less than $\beta$, a constant. The disruption likelihood of a schema $H$ is defined as the probability of event $R$, $P_R$. For $P_R < \alpha$, a constant, a schema is disruption prone.

**Schema Compactness**: Compactness is defined as $1 - P_R$. If, at time t, $P_R > \alpha$, a constant, a schema is compact. Intuitively a schema is compact if its maximum probability of disruption is low regardless of the size and structure of the programs which contain it.

## 4    BUILDING BLOCK DEFINITION and BUILDING BLOCK HYPOTHESIS

In this section we propose and critically examine a definition of GP building blocks and a GP Building Block Hypothesis (BBH). Both the definition and the hypothesis result from an interpretation of the GPST and are intended to be fully analogous to the definition of GA building blocks and to the GA BBH. However, as will be pointed out below, our seemingly straightforward interpretation of the GPST rests on several questionable assumptions. Without these assumptions, no GP BBH can be formulated in analogy with the GA BBH.

**GP building blocks:** GP building blocks are low order, consistently compact GP schemas with consistently above average observed performance that are expected to be sampled at increasing or exponential rates in future generations.

**GP Building Block Hypothesis (BBH):** The GP BBH states that GP combines building blocks, the low order, compact highly fit partial solutions of past samplings, to compose individuals which, over generations, improve in fitness.

Thus, the source of GP's power, (i.e., when it works), lies in the fact that selection and crossover guide GP towards the evolution of improved solutions by discovering, promoting and combining building blocks.

Let us now review the assumptions presupposed by the GP BBH.

1. The GP BBH refers to the combining of schemas yet the GPST, by referring to the expected instances of only one schema, fails to describe the interactions of schemas. In this respect, the GP BBH is not supported by any interpretation of the GPST.

   Previous GA work [Grefenstette,Baker 1989, Liepins and Vose 1991, Whitley 1991] has made this point in much more detail. Many complicated interactions between competing schemas and hyperplanes take place in the course of a GA run. None of this activity can be described by a Schema Theorem because the latter simply considers one schema in isolation. Since the GPST does not differ from the GA Schema Theorem in this respect, the above argument applies with equal strength to GP.

   Vose has pointed out that, without knowing the composition of the population in a GA, it is impossible to precisely state how schemas combine and how many schemas can be expected [Vose 1993]. Again, this point applies equally to GP.

2. The GPST also fails to lend support to the GP BBH because hyperplane competition in GP is not well defined. In GAs, trial allocation competition takes place among

hyperplanes which have common features but where each "competitor" differs in the expression of that feature. The lack of a feature-expression orientation in the GP representation (i.e., GPUs non-homologous nature) results in an unclear notion of which hyperplanes compete for trial allocation. This inherent lack of clarity concerning hyperplane competition seems to indicate that schema processing may not be the best abstraction with which to analyze GP behavior.

3. Grefenstette [Grefenstette,1992] has called the classic GA BBH a "Static Building Block Hypothesis". This he states as

> Given any short, low order hyperplane partition, a GA is expected to converge to the hyperplane with the best static fitness (the "expected winner").
> [Grefenstette,1992, p. 78 ]

Static fitness is defined as the average of every schema instance in the entire search space to distinguish it from the observed fitnesses the GA uses as an estimate of static schema fitness. He argues that "the dynamic behavior of a GA cannot in general be predicted on the basis of static analysis of hyperplanes"[Grefenstette,1992, p. 76 ]. Two of the reasons that the true dynamics of a GA is not estimated by the static fitness of schemas are "collateral convergence" and high fitness variance within schemas. The first reason is that, once the population begins to converge even a little, it becomes impossible to estimate static fitness using the information present in the current population. The second reason is that, in populations of realistic size, high fitness variance within schemas, even in the initial generation, can cause the estimate and static fitness to become uncorrelated.

This argument applies to GP. Furthermore, the issue of high fitness variance within a schema may be especially important in GP. As far as we know, the amount of fitness variance for GP schemas has not been empirically sampled. To discuss the issue, one must consider that schemas in GP are "pieces of program". A schema instance acquires the fitness of the program which embeds it. If the primitives are functionally relatively insensitive to context, there may be schemas in the search space that are also relatively insensitive to program embedding and thus have low fitness variance among their instances. GP is also known to evolve large programs full of functionally inert material. This material may act to shield partial solutions from interference with each other and prevent their fitness from changing when surrounding code is sampled [2]. In contrast, it intuitively seems that rearranging code or simply inserting a new statement into a program can lead to drastic changes in its fitness. This argues that the fitness variance of a schema's instances may be high.

4. The assumption of expected increasing or exponential trials for building blocks requires certain behavior to be constant over more than one time step. The GPST does not describe behaviour for more than one time step and it is not the case that the required behaviour is constant.

The inaccuracy in the assumption arises from estimating the long term behavior of the reproduction and crossover survival terms in the GPST. In fact, the GPST describes behaviour for only one step and this hides important dependencies in the iteration [3]. The GPST states that **in the next generation** schema $H$ grows or decays depending

---

[2] Admittedly this is simplistic; in programs it is difficult to ever clearly state that pieces of code do not interact.

[3] See [Altenberg 1994b] for a different and crucial Schema Theorem dependency

upon a multiplication factor that is the product of two terms: the probability of the schema being reproduced (i.e. the schema's fitness relative to the population average) and the probability that the schema is not disrupted.

$$\textbf{MultiplicationFactor}: \frac{\hat{f}(H,t)}{\bar{f}(t)}(1 - P_{xo}P_d(H,t)) \tag{1}$$

Clearly if the Multiplication Factor (1) is greater or equal to 1, the expected trials of a schema will increase **in the next generation**.

Interpreting the GPST to describe the expected allocation of trials to a schema **asymptotically** or **over more than one generation** relies on interpreting the Multiplication Factor in the GPST for more than one time step. If the time dependence of the terms were ignored by assuming that the margin by which a schema's estimated average fitness is better than the population average is constant and that $P_d(H,t)$ never changes, the claim of expected **exponentially** increasing trial allocation would be justified.

If we resist ignoring the time dependence of the two terms (because they are a reality!) to avoid misleading over-simplification, the assumption that the expected number of trials will grow exponentially is weakened by the qualification that the Multiplication Factor must be stationary:

$$\frac{\hat{f}(H,t)}{\bar{f}(t)}(1 - P_{xo}P_d(H,t)) = \frac{\hat{f}(H,t+1)}{\bar{f}(t+1)}(1 - P_{xo}P_d(H,t+1))$$

and the crucial time dependent relationship is the logarithmic growth of the reproductive term relative to the negative logarithmic growth of the crossover survival term:

$$\Delta \log \frac{\hat{f}(H,t)}{\bar{f}(t)} = -\Delta \log (1 - P_{xo}P_d(H,t))$$

5. As a schema starts dominating, the margin by which it is fitter than the average fitness of the population decreases. The only thing that enables it to continue growing is a decrease in its probability of disruption. The problem is that there is no guarantee that $\tilde{D}_t$ decreases at a rate ensuring positive growth of expected allocation of trials over the same interval.

   We can only consider the plausibility of this decrease in the upper bound on disruption likelihood in this situation. An exact answer is not possible[4]. Consider the growth of programs in GP runs: In GP the maximum height or size of a program is set to a lower value for the initial population than the value crossover is constrained to use in creating trees in subsequent generations. This allows programs to grow larger each generation (up to the maximum). We cannot make precise statements about the size and height distribution of a schema's instances but if one assumes they are uniformly distributed within the population, program growth in each generation may indeed cause the upper bound on the probability of disruption to decrease. Whatever the circumstances of program growth, in GP any decrease in the likelihood of disruption is fortuitous or roundabout rather than explicit in the algorithm. That is, the crossover operator and selection process do not explicitly control the size and shape of programs in a correlation with fit schemas. It should be noted that the decrease in probability of disruption caused by program growth also works in favor of unfit program fragments.

---

[4] Because it requires an account of population composition that is lacking in the GPST.

Because of the variable length representation of GP, the 'cushioning' of unfit programs due to program growth is more of a problem than it would be in GAs.

6. Building blocks may only exist for a time interval of the GP run because the estimated fitness relative to the population fitness and upper bound probability of disruption of a schema vary with time.

   Consider an interpretation of the GPST that is intended to explain why a particular GP run did not find an optimal solution. An explanatory hypothesis might be that consistently highly fit partial solutions are not consistently compact. Or, that consistently compact partial solutions are not highly fit. These hypotheses reveal a caveat of the BBH : a partial solution is a building block only if its sample is consistently **both** above the population average in fitness and compact (i.e., consistently has a low maximum probability of disruption). When the Multiplication Factor is not greater than one, **despite fit partial solutions or compact partial solutions**, building blocks **do not exist**.

   To elaborate further, consider an interval when a schema's margin of fitness above the population stays constant. This could happen when the observed average fitness of the schema increases (due to updated sampling) at the same rate as the population fitness. In this interval, the upper bound probability of the schema's disruption becomes the crucial factor in determining whether it will be a building block. Relative to its fitness, the schema could be allocated fewer trials for one interval than a comparable schema because the tree sizes and shapes of its instances have changed. This implies that, in some sense, **partial solutions can be inert as building blocks at some generations and active at others**. It is not a conceded fact that a building block persists in the subsequent course of the run. Indeed, in the described circumstance highly fit partial solutions may never be building blocks because, despite reproduction, they could be too prone to disruption.

7. The BBH assumes that solutions can be arrived at through linear combination of highly fit partial solutions. This is a statement about the problem of program induction rather than GP. There is no basis for assuming that a solution's sub-components are independent. The BBH is a statement about how GP works only if there is linearity in the solution.

The basic lesson is that the GPST (and any similar schema theorem) omits important dependencies from the recurrence and is, thus, bound to oversimplify GP dynamics. In particular, the dynamics of crossover and selection that are of interest last longer than one time step. The BBH also assumes the existence of the same building blocks throughout a run and is not specific about the dynamics of building block discovery, promotion and combination in the course of a run.

In summary of Section 4, we presented a definition of GP building blocks and a GP Building Block Hypothesis. We then discussed crucial issues in their usefulness and credibility. The most serious issue concerns the time dependent behavior of schema disruption and observed average fitness relative to the population fitness. We also have cautioned that there are times when the BBH will not hold because the BBH presupposes the existence of building blocks despite the fact that compactness and consistent fitness are not guaranteed.

## 5   CONCLUSION AND FUTURE WORK

We conclude that the GP BBH is not forthcoming without untenable assumptions. Our critical discussion has led us to identify what we take to be perhaps the major problem of GP: it exerts no control over program size but program size directly affects disruption probability. Furthermore, how the probability of disruption of a schema changes over time, even from one generation to the next, is unpredictable. This time dependent behavior is almost certainly a stochastic process (i.e., it may have underlying structure but is primarily driven by randomness): while selection and crossover determine the structure of individuals for the next generation, they control program size - which affects disruption probability - in only a roundabout way. A more useful and precise GP building block definition should state something about the time dependent behavior of the probability of disruption but this is not quantifiable without some empirical data or simulation.

The doubts raised in this paper about the GP BBH and the appropriateness of schema processing as a perspective for comparing GP as a search technique to other program discovery methods are confirmed by our empirical results. Rather than assuming that GP is better than other techniques on the general grounds that it accumulates good partial solutions in parallel and hierarchically combines them, we have empirically tested GP against single point mutation based search such as Stochastic Iterated Hill Climbing and Simulated Annealing. The results from all of these program discovery methods are comparable [O'Reilly,Oppacher 1994b, O'Reilly,Oppacher 1994c].

Our ongoing research focuses on the comparison of program discovery methods and on schema-based experimentation [O'Reilly,Oppacher 1994a]. We continue to search for better explanations as to when and why GP is indeed a superior program search technique.

### Acknowledgments

U.M.O'R. wishes to thank S. Forrest, R. Hightower, T. Jones, B. Macready, M. Mitchell, R. Palmer, P. Stadler, and the members of the UNM study group for their insightful contributions. She greatly appreciates the stimulating environment provided by the Santa Fe Institute. Both authors thank M. Wineberg and the referees.

## References

[Altenberg 1994a] Altenberg, L. (1994). The evolution of evolvability in genetic programming. In K.A. Kinnear Jr. (ed), *Advances in Genetic Programming*, Ch. 3. Cambridge, MA: MIT Press.

[Altenberg 1994b] Altenberg, L. (1994). The Schema Theorem and Price's Theorem. In these proceedings.

[Forrest,Mitchell 1992] Forrest, S. and M. Mitchell (1992). Relative building-block fitness and the building block hypothesis. In D. Whitley (ed), *Foundations of Genetic Algorithms 2*, 109-126. San Mateo, CA: Morgan Kaufmann.

[Grefenstette,Baker 1989] Grefenstette, J. J. and J. E. Baker (1989). How genetic algorithms work: a critical look at implicit parallelism. In J.D. Schaffer (ed), *Proceedings of the Third International Conference on Genetic Algorithms*, San Mateo, CA: Morgan Kaufmann.

[Grefenstette,1992] Grefenstette, J. J. (1992). Deception Considered Harmful, In D. Whitley (ed), *Foundations of Genetic Algorithms 2*, 109-126. San Mateo, CA: Morgan Kaufmann.

[Goldberg 1989] Goldberg, D. E. (1989). *Genetic Algorithms in Search, Optimization, and Machine Learning*. Reading, MA: Addison-Wesley.

[Holland 1975/1992] Holland, J. H. (1975/1992). *Adaptation in Natural and Artificial Systems*. Cambridge, MA: MIT Press, (1st Edition 1975, Ann Arbor, U. of Michigan Press).

[Koza 1992] Koza, J. R. (1992). *Genetic Programming; On the Programming of Computers by Means of Natural Selection*. Cambridge, MA: Bradford Books.

[Liepins and Vose 1991] Liepins, G. and Vose, M. (1990) Representation Issues in Genetic Optimization. J. Experimental and Theoretical A.I. 2(1990) 101-115.

[Mitchell,Forrest,Holland 1991] Mitchell, M., S. Forrest, J. Holland. (1991). The royal road for genetic algorithms: fitness landscapes and genetic algorithm performance. In F. Varela and P. Bourgine (eds), *Proceedings of the First European Conference on Artificial Life*, 245-254. Cambridge, MA: Bradford Books.

[O'Reilly,Oppacher 1994a] O'Reilly, U. M. and F. Oppacher (1994). *Building block functions to confirm a building block hypothesis for Genetic Programming*, Santa Fe Institute Working Report 94-04-020, Santa Fe Inst itute, NM.

[O'Reilly,Oppacher 1994b] O'Reilly, U. M. and F. Oppacher (1994). Program search with a hierarchical variable length representation: genetic programming, simulated annealing and hill climbing, In *Parallel Problem Solving from Nature -PPSN III*, 397-406. New York: Springer.

[O'Reilly,Oppacher 1994c] O'Reilly, U. M. and F. Oppacher (1994). *Program search with a hierarchical variable length representation: genetic programming, simulated annealing and hill climbing*, Santa Fe Institute Working Report 94-04-021 (unabridged version of [O'Reilly,Oppacher 1994b]), Santa Fe Institute, NM.

[Radcliffe 1991] Radcliffe, N. J. (1991). Formal Analysis and Random Respectful Recombination. In R.K. Belew and L.B. Booker (eds), *Proceedings of the Fourth International Conference on Genetic Algorithms*. San Mateo, CA: Morgan Kaufman.

[Vose 1993] Vose, M. (1993). "A Critical Examination Of The Schema Theorem", University of Tennesse Technical Report CS-93-212.

[Whitley 1991] Whitley, L. D. (1991). "Fundamental Principles in Deception of Genetic Search", In G. Rawlins (ed), *Foundations of Genetic Algorithms*. San Mateo, CA: Morgan Kaufmann.

# PART 2

# CONVERGENCE AND PREDICTIVE MODELS

# Order Statistics for Convergence Velocity Analysis of Simplified Evolutionary Algorithms

**Thomas Bäck**
Informatik Centrum Dortmund
Joseph von Fraunhofer Straße 20
D–44227 Dortmund, Germany
`baeck@ls11.informatik.uni-dortmund.de`

## Abstract

The theory of *order statistics* is utilized in this paper to analyze the convergence velocity $\varphi$ of simplified evolutionary algorithms based on mutation and $(\mu \overset{+}{,} \lambda)$-selection. A general, representation-independent way of theoretical analysis is outlined and put in concrete terms for two specific objective functions: The binary counting ones objective function and the continuous sphere model. This way, the same method of theoretical analysis describes the behavior of a search strategy similar to a genetic algorithm as well as a search strategy similar to an evolution strategy. The resulting convergence velocity graphics exhibit a striking similarity, such that the underlying principles of evolutionary search seem to be valid independently of the particular search space. The expectations $\mathbf{E}(Z_{\nu:\lambda})$ of the $\nu$-th order statistics turn out to be of paramount importance for determining the convergence velocity $\varphi$. The expectation $\mathbf{E}(Z_{\lambda:\lambda})$ for the continuous normal case is identical to Rechenberg's *progress coefficient* $c_{1,\lambda}$, and the averages of the $\mu$ upper order statistics are known as the *selection differential* in the literature. For the case of an underlying normal distribution (as in evolution strategies) many of the results from order statistics can be utilized e.g. to determine the asymptotic behavior of an $(1,\lambda)$-strategy, while in the discrete case no such result is available. The order statistics approach turns out to be a very useful theoretical framework for the derivation of quite general results (including upper bounds) on the convergence velocity of evolutionary algorithms.

## 1   SIMPLIFIED EVOLUTIONARY ALGORITHMS

Throughout this paper, a simplified concept of an evolutionary algorithm is assumed. The algorithm, which is denoted a $(\mu \overset{+}{,} \lambda)$-EA in the following, is solely based on the operators mutation and selection. More specifically, we consider the deterministic, extinctive $(\mu+\lambda)$-selection and $(\mu,\lambda)$-selection operators introduced by Schwefel for evolution strategies (see [18], pp. 118–120). In case of $(\mu+\lambda)$-selection, $\mu$ parents create $\lambda$ offspring (in the standard evolutionary algorithms, this works by means of recombination and mutation) and the $\mu$ best out of offspring and parents are chosen to become parents of the next generation. For a $(\mu,\lambda)$-selection ($\lambda \geq \mu$) the $\mu$ best offspring individuals are selected to survive. The offspring population is generated in our simplified algorithm by repeating a uniform, random choice of a parent individual for $\lambda$ samples and applying mutation to each of these parents. The following pseudocode formulation of the algorithm denotes individuals $\vec{a}_i^t \in I$, where $t$ is the generation counter and $I$ a space of individuals. Populations $P^t \in I^\mu$ (or $P^t \in I^\lambda$) are collections $\{\vec{a}_1^t, \ldots, \vec{a}_\mu^t\}$ of individuals, and mutation and selection are represented by operators $m : I \to I$ (mutation) and $s_{(\mu,\lambda)} : I^\lambda \to I^\mu$ ($s_{(\mu+\lambda)} : I^{\lambda+\mu} \to I^\mu$, selection) (see also [5] for pseudocode descriptions of complete standard EAs).

ALGORITHM 1   $((\mu \overset{+}{,} \lambda)$-EA$)$

$$
\begin{aligned}
&t := 0; \\
&initialize\ P^0 := \{\vec{a}_1^0, \ldots, \vec{a}_\mu^0\} \in I^\mu; \\
&evaluate\ P^0 \colon \{f(\vec{a}_1^0), \ldots, f(\vec{a}_\mu^0)\}; \\
&\textbf{while not } terminate \textbf{ do} \\
&\qquad mutate\colon \forall i = 1, \ldots, \lambda : \vec{a}_i'^t = m(\vec{a}_u^t); \\
&\qquad\qquad u \sim U(1, \ldots, \mu); \\
&\qquad P'^t := \{\vec{a}_1'^t, \ldots, \vec{a}_\lambda'^t\}; \\
&\qquad evaluate\colon \{f(\vec{a}_1'^t), \ldots, f(\vec{a}_\lambda'^t)\}; \\
&\qquad select\colon P^{t+1} := \quad s_{(\mu,\lambda)}(P'^t)\ or \\
&\qquad\qquad\qquad\qquad\quad s_{(\mu+\lambda)}(P'^t \cup P^t); \\
&\qquad t := t + 1; \\
&\textbf{od}
\end{aligned}
$$

$f : I \to \mathbb{R}$ denotes the objective function, and $u$ is a uniform random variable over $\{1, \ldots, \mu\}$.

In order to analyze the convergence velocity of such an algorithm, we use the approach to concentrate on the average objective function value $\bar{f}_\mu$ of the $\mu$ best individuals. Of course, $\bar{f}_\mu$ represents a hypothetical individual $\bar{a}$. Furthermore, to obtain a common probability density function for all mutations, the offspring individuals $\vec{a}_i'^{t+1}$ are interpreted as results of mutating $\bar{a}$ rather than different individuals. This situation is graphically shown in figure 1 for a (3,6)-strategy.

The simplification yields a conservative appproximation, i.e. a lower bound of the convergence velocity, because the (on average) $\lambda/\mu$ individuals which are created from a parent with a better $f$ than $\bar{f}_\mu^t$ are neglected. However, currently no better method is known for analyzing the convergence velocity $\varphi$ of population-based algorithms. $\varphi$ can be defined either as the expectation of the change of the distance towards the optimum (as done by Rechenberg for the (1+1)-ES [15] and by Schwefel for the $(1 \overset{+}{,} \lambda)$-ES [18]; see also [6]) or as the expectation of the change of the objective function value (as performed by Beyer

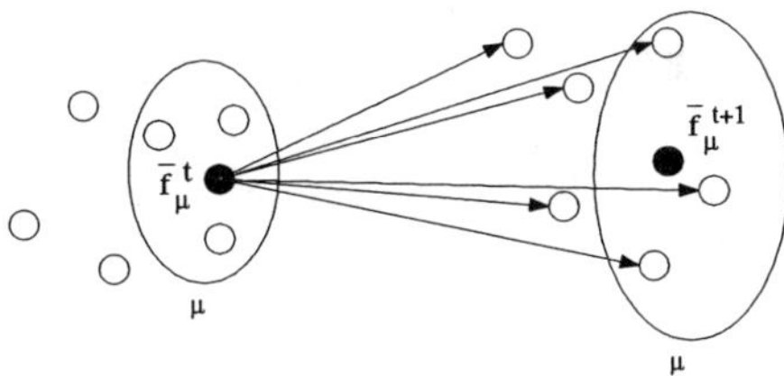

Figure 1: Schematic Diagram of the Simplified Interpretation of a $(\mu \overset{+}{,} \lambda)$-Strategy.

for the $(1 \overset{+}{,} \lambda)$-ES with noisy function evaluations and by Bäck, Rudolph and Schwefel for the $(1 \overset{+}{,} \lambda)$-ES [4]). In the following, we use the second method, starting from $f := \bar{f}_\mu^t$ at generation $t$, and define

$$\varphi(\mu, \lambda, f, p(z)) := \mathbf{E}(\bar{f}_\mu^{t+1} - f) \quad . \tag{1}$$

Notice that, besides its obvious dependency on $\mu$ and $\lambda$, $\varphi$ is a local measure that depends on the actual objective function value $f$ and the probability density function $p(z)$ of the change of $f$ by applying mutation. In the next section, we derive an explicit expression for $\varphi$.

## 2   CONVERGENCE VELOCITY

Starting from the definition of $\varphi$ as presented in equation (1), we use the theory of *order statistics* to proceed further. According to the assumptions introduced in section 1, the population $P^{t+1}$ consists of the fitness values $f_1 = f + Z_1, f_2 = f + Z_2, \ldots, f_\lambda = f + Z_\lambda$, where $Z_1, Z_2, \ldots, Z_\lambda$ are random variables with a common probability density function $p(z)$ (which characterizes the mutation operator). In the following, we concentrate on the changes $Z_\nu$ rather than the absolute values $f_\nu$. Arranging the $Z_\nu$ in nondecreasing order, the reordering $Z_{1:\lambda} \leq Z_{2:\lambda} \leq \ldots \leq Z_{\lambda:\lambda}$ is called the order statistics of $Z_1, \ldots, Z_\lambda$. The theory of order statistics is helpful to find an expression for $p_{\nu:\lambda}(z)$, the probability density function of $Z_{\nu:\lambda}$. In order to determine $\varphi$, the probability density functions of those individuals which achieve a maximum improvement are of interest, i.e., $\nu \in \{\lambda - \mu + 1, \ldots, \lambda\}$. According to this argumentation, we obtain

$$\varphi \;=\; \mathbf{E}(\bar{f}_\mu^{t+1}) - f = \mathbf{E}\left(\frac{1}{\mu} \sum_{\nu=\lambda-\mu+1}^{\lambda} f_{\nu:\lambda}^{t+1}\right) - f = \frac{1}{\mu} \sum_{\nu=\lambda-\mu+1}^{\lambda} \mathbf{E}(Z_{\nu:\lambda}) \quad . \tag{2}$$

The expression $D(\mu, \lambda) := \sum_{\nu=\lambda-\mu+1}^{\lambda} f_{\nu:\lambda}/\mu$ is known as the *selection differential* (see [14]), and its distribution function does not have a closed analytical form. While the selection differential is based on the top $\mu$ function values, the term *truncation selection* refers to a method where all $f$-values exceeding a specified value are selected [14] (in contrast to this, Mühlenbein et al. use the term truncation selection to denote a method where the $T\%$ best individuals are selected as parents — which is identical to a $(\mu, \lambda)$-selection with $\mu = T\lambda/100$ [13]).

To proceed further, the expectations $\mathbf{E}(Z_{\nu:\lambda})$ are needed, where of course

$$\mathbf{E}(Z_{\nu:\lambda}) = \int_{z_{\min}}^{z_{\max}} z \cdot p_{\nu:\lambda}(z)dz \tag{3}$$

for a continuous probability density function $p(z)$ (with support $[z_{\min}, z_{\max}]$) and

$$\mathbf{E}(Z_{\nu:\lambda}) = \sum_{z=z_{\min}}^{z_{\max}} z \cdot p_{\nu:\lambda}(z) \tag{4}$$

for a discrete probability density function $p(z)$.

In case of a discrete probability density function $p(z)$ for mutations — as occurring for genetic algorithms — the expression for $p_{\nu:\lambda}(z)$ becomes quite complex due to the possibility of ties: More than just one offspring individual may represent a change of $f$ by the same value, i.e., may occupy the same position in the order statistics. Using $P(z) = \mathcal{P}(Z \le z)$ to denote the cumulative density function and $P(z-) = \mathcal{P}(Z < z)$ (a distinction which is only needed for the discrete case), one obtains (see also [1], p. 42):

$$p_{\nu:\lambda}(z) = \sum_{i=0}^{\nu-1} \binom{\lambda}{\nu-1-i} \sum_{j=0}^{\lambda-\nu} \binom{\lambda-(\nu-1-i)}{\lambda-\nu-j} [p(z)]^{i+j+1} [P(z-)]^{\nu-1-i} [1 - P(z)]^{\lambda-\nu-j} .$$

$$\tag{5}$$

**Proof:** An improvement by $z$ may occur for the $(\lambda-\nu+1)$-th best individual in $\nu \cdot (\lambda-\nu+1)$ different ways: $\nu - i - 1$ outcomes are less than $z$ with probability $P(z-)$ per outcome $(i = 0, 1, \ldots, \nu - 1)$, $\lambda - \nu - j$ outcomes are larger than $z$ with probability $1 - P(z)$ per outcome $(j = 0, 1, \ldots, \lambda - \nu)$, and the remaining $\lambda - (\nu - i - 1) - (\lambda - \nu - j) = i + j + 1$ outcomes equal $z$. There are $\binom{\lambda}{\nu-1-i}$ possibilities for the $\nu - i - 1$ outcomes less than $z$ and $\binom{\lambda-(\nu-1-i)}{\lambda-\nu-j}$ possibilities for the better ones. $\qquad\square$

From equation (5), the expression for a continuous probability density function $p(z)$ — as occurring for evolution strategies — is obtained as a special case by excluding the possibility of ties. In other words, exactly one single $(\lambda - \nu + 1)$-th best outcome exists, such that $i = j = 0$ in equation (5), and the equation reduces to

$$p_{\nu:\lambda}(z) = \lambda \binom{\lambda - 1}{\nu - 1} p(z) [P(z)]^{\nu-1} [1 - P(z)]^{\lambda-\nu} . \tag{6}$$

With the exception of an index transformation ($\nu \mapsto \lambda-\nu+1$), this equation (6) was already derived by Schwefel to describe the change of the distance towards the optimum for a $(\mu \overset{+}{,} \lambda)$-ES (see [18], pp. 121–124). He interpreted the indices $1, \ldots, \mu$ rather than $\lambda - \mu + 1, \ldots, \lambda$ to denote the best individuals, and his (only approximate) result was obtained without the order statistics approach as used here.

Notice that for $\mu = 1$ the convergence velocity approximation introduced in equations (1) and (2) becomes exact, resulting in the equation $\varphi = \mathbf{E}(Z_{\lambda:\lambda})$. For a continuous probability density function $p(z)$, we obtain

$$\varphi_{(1\overset{+}{,}\lambda)} = \lambda \int_{z_{\min}}^{z_{\max}} z \cdot p(z) \cdot [P(z)]^{\lambda-1} dz = \int_{z_{\min}}^{z_{\max}} z \cdot \frac{d}{dz} [P(z)]^{\lambda} dz , \tag{7}$$

an equation which was used by several authors with slightly different interpretations of the random variable $Z$ to derive the convergence velocity of a $(1\overset{+}{,}\lambda)$-ES on the sphere model (see [4, 6, 18]). In section 4, we will demonstrate how to derive the corresponding result for the sphere model by using the method presented here, which is much simpler than the methods used by the authors mentioned above.

In case of a discrete $p(z)$ and $\mu = 1$, equation (5) simplifies according to

$$
\begin{aligned}
p_{\lambda:\lambda}(z) &= \sum_{i=0}^{\lambda} \binom{\lambda}{\lambda - i - 1} [p(z)]^{i+1} [P(z-)]^{\lambda - i - 1} \\
&= [P(z)]^{\lambda} - [P(z-)]^{\lambda} ,
\end{aligned}
\tag{8}
$$

such that

$$
\varphi_{(1\overset{+}{,}\lambda)} = \sum_{z=z_{\min}}^{z_{\max}} z \cdot \left( [P(z)]^{\lambda} - [P(z-)]^{\lambda} \right) .
\tag{9}
$$

This expression was presented (in a different, but equivalent form) in [2] for the concept of a $(1\overset{+}{,}\lambda)$-GA and used by Yanagiya to analyze the convergence velocity (and optimal mutation rates) for some pseudoboolean functions [19].

So far, the structure of the fitness function was not taken into account. The concrete fitness function is hidden in the probability density function $p(z)$. Clearly, especially the topological difficulties of the objective function are hidden in $p(z)$, and explicit analytical expressions for $p(z)$ can be derived only for very simple examples. Nevertheless, such investigations yield insight into the behavior of evolutionary algorithms and the impact of parameter settings on the efficiency of the search.

In the next sections, we present convergence velocity derivations based on the knowledge of $p(z)$ both for the case of a discrete objective function (i.e., the application domain of genetic algorithms; section 3) and for the case of a continuous objective function (i.e., the application domain of evolution strategies; section 4).

## 3    A DISCRETE OBJECTIVE FUNCTION

The counting ones problem $f : \{0,1\}^n \rightarrow \{0,1,\ldots,n\}$, $f(a_1 a_2 \ldots a_n) = \sum_{i=1}^{n} a_i$, is an example of a discrete fitness function for which the probability density function for the mutation operator in genetic algorithms is explicitly known. We assume mutation to invert a bit with probability $p$ and define $q = 1 - p$ and $f := f(\bar{a})$ where $\bar{a}$ is the hypothetical average individual introduced in section 1. Then, as shown in [2], the probability density function $p(z)$, $-f \leq z \leq n - f$, is given by

$$
p(z) = \begin{cases}
\displaystyle\sum_{i=0}^{f} \binom{f}{i} \binom{n-f}{i+z} p^{2i+z} q^{n-2i-z} & , \quad z \geq 0 \\[2ex]
\displaystyle\sum_{i=0}^{n-f} \binom{n-f}{i} \binom{f}{i-z} p^{2i-z} q^{n-2i+z} & , \quad z < 0 .
\end{cases}
\tag{10}
$$

Consequently, $P(z) = \sum_{k=-f}^{z} p(k)$ and $P(z-) = P(z) - p(z)$. In contrast to the continuous example (presented in section 4) where assumptions about the objective function will be used in early stages of the derivation of $\varphi$ (equations (11) and (12)), the counting ones objective function is completely hidden in $p(z)$. From equations (2), (4), (5), and (10), the convergence velocity $\varphi_{(\mu \overset{+}{,} \lambda)}$ can be calculated numerically if the mutation rate $p$, problem dimension $n$, and fitness value $f$ of the ancestor individual $\bar{a}$ are specified.

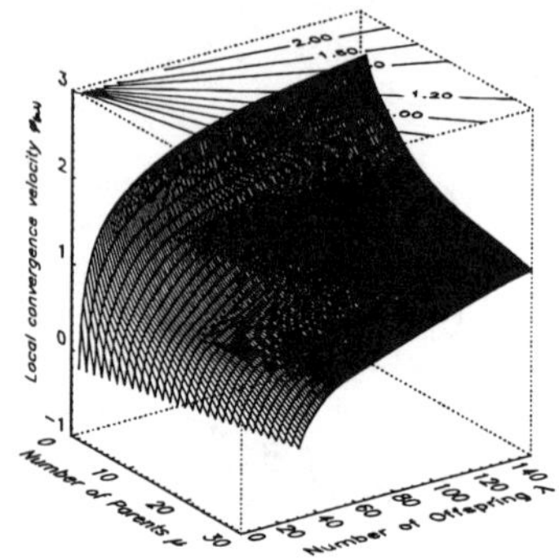
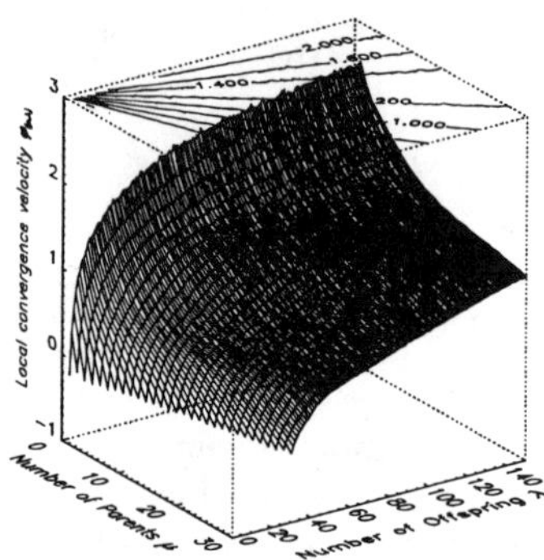

Figure 2: Theoretical (Left) and Experimental (Right) Values of the Local Convergence Velocity $\varphi_{(\mu,\lambda)}$ for $p = 0.01$, $n = 100$, $f = 60$, $\mu \in \{1, \ldots, 30\}$, and $\lambda \in \{\mu, \ldots, 150\}$.

The distinction between $(\mu+\lambda)$-selection and $(\mu,\lambda)$-selection is introduced to the mathematical formulation by specifying the lower summation index in equation (4). For $(\mu+\lambda)$-selection a worsening of fitness is not accepted, i.e., $z_{\min} = 0$. In contrast to this, $z_{\min} = -f$ for $(\mu,\lambda)$-selection, where in principle all $f$ correct bits may get lost due to mutation. The upper index is given by $z_{\max} = n - f$ in the counting ones example, since this is the number of still incorrect bits in $\bar{a}$.

A numerical evaluation of $\varphi_{(\mu,\lambda)}$ was performed for $n = 100$ and an objective function value $f = 60$ of the hypothetical parent individual $\bar{a}$ with $\mu \in \{1, \ldots, 30\}$ and $\lambda \in \{\mu, \ldots, 150\}$. $\varphi_{(\mu,\lambda)}$ was also evaluated for other values of $f$, and the results clarify that theory and practice match well for arbitrary values of $f$. Furthermore, the shape of the $\varphi_{(\mu,\lambda)}$-landscape is qualitatively independent of the actual value of $f$.

Following the results presented by Mühlenbein, a mutation rate $p = 1/n = 0.01$ [12] is utilized for the results summarized in figure 2. In contrast to this, the results presented in figure 3 are based on a mutation rate $p = 1/(2(f + 1) - n) = 0.045$, which is a better approximation of the optimal mutation rate [3].

Both figures 2 and 3 show a graphic of the local convergence velocity $\varphi_{(\mu,\lambda)}$ over $\mu$ and $\lambda$ for constant values of $p$, $n$, and $f$. The left graphics are obtained by numerical evaluation of equation (2) (using equations (4), (5), and (10)), while the graphics in the right part represent the results of a computer experiment. According to figure 1, this experiment works by generating $\lambda$ offspring individuals from a parent individual with fitness value $f$ and determining the average fitness value of the $\mu$ best out of the offspring. For each combination of $\mu$ and $\lambda$, the experimental value reflects the average of $N = 1000$ such experiments (offspring generation and evaluation of $\bar{f}_{\mu}^{t+1}$).

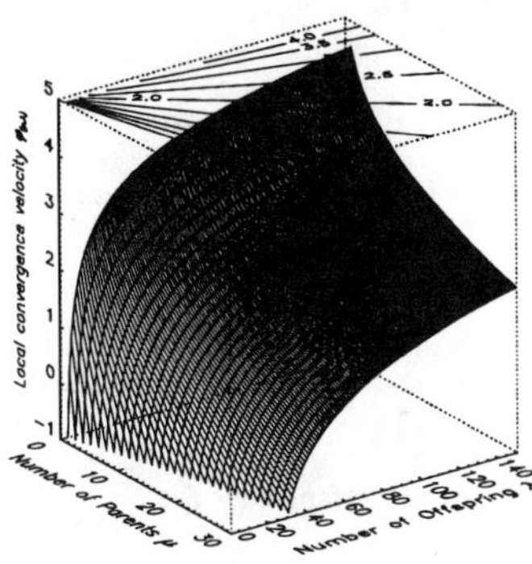
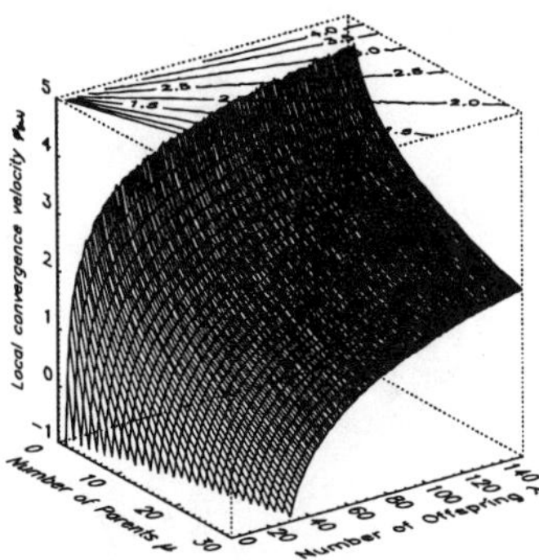

Figure 3: Theoretical (Left) and Experimental (Right) Values of the Local Convergence Velocity $\varphi_{(\mu,\lambda)}$ for a Near Optimal Mutation Rate $p = 0.045$, $n = 100$, $f = 60$, $\mu \in \{1, \ldots, 30\}$, and $\lambda \in \{\mu, \ldots, 150\}$.

The agreement between theory and experiment is striking and confirms the usefulness of the order statistics method for analyzing convergence velocities. The smooth topology of the convergence velocity landscape meets our expectation insofar as a decrease of $\varphi$ as $\mu$ increases and an increase of $\varphi$ as $\lambda$ increases are obvious for a unimodal topology of the fitness function. More interesting, the lines of constant convergence velocity shown at the top of all graphics demonstrate that $\varphi_{(\mu,\lambda)}$ is constant if and only if the ratio $\lambda/\mu$ — the selective pressure — is held constant.

## 4    A CONTINUOUS OBJECTIVE FUNCTION

In the following, we demonstrate the generality of the order statistics method by a further application to the $(\mu \overset{+}{,} \lambda)$-ES in the continuous sphere model case $f : \mathbb{R}^n \to \mathbb{R}$, $f(\vec{x}) = \sum_{i=1}^{n}(x_i - x_i^*)^2 = r^2$ where $r$ denotes the distance between $\vec{x}$ and the optimum point $\vec{x}^*$ (here, we assume $\vec{x}^* = \vec{0}$). By using the order statistics approach, the existing convergence velocity analysis can be simplified considerably.

Notice that the definition of $f$ implies a minimization task, such that we start with equation (2) in the form $\varphi = \mathbf{E}(f - \bar{f}_\mu^{t+1})$ in order to associate positive values of $\varphi$ with a rapprochement of the optimum point. To be consistent with the notation used by Beyer [6], we define $f := f(\bar{a}) := R^2$ and obtain:

$$\varphi_{(\mu \overset{+}{,} \lambda)} = \mathbf{E}\left(R^2 - \frac{1}{\mu}\sum_{\nu=\lambda-\mu+1}^{\lambda} r_{\nu:\lambda}^2\right) = \frac{1}{\mu}\sum_{\nu=\lambda-\mu+1}^{\lambda} \mathbf{E}\left(R^2 - r_{\nu:\lambda}^2\right) . \tag{11}$$

The principal topological situation is shown in figure 4, where only one offspring individual and the parent individual are indicated. $O$ denotes the origin of the coordinate system, i.e., the location of the optimum.

From geometrical considerations (using the two right-angled triangles shown in figure 4),

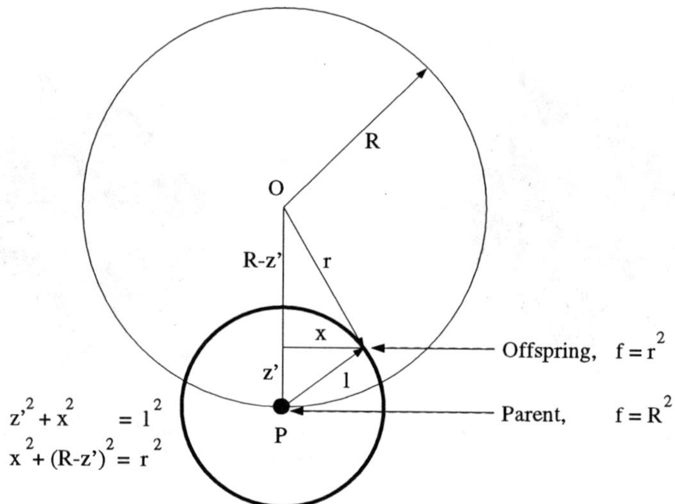



Figure 4: Topological Parent-Offspring Situation in Case of the Sphere Model.

it is known that the expectation $l$ of the length of an $n$-dimensional normally distributed mutation and the random variable $Z'$ (notice that $Z$, $Z'$ denote random variables, while lower case letters $z$ and $z'$ are used to denote their realizations) which denotes the progress towards the optimum achieved by the mutation are related by

$$r^2 \;=\; l^2 + R^2 - 2RZ' \tag{12}$$

(see [6], p. 169). Assuming a standard deviation $\sigma$ for mutations, it is known that $l = \sigma\sqrt{n}$ for large $n$ [6]. As a third prerequisite we use the fact that $Z'$, as a marginal distribution of the $n$-dimensional normal distribution, is again normally distributed (see e.g. [8], p. 84), i.e. $p(z') = \exp(-z'^2/(2\sigma^2))/(\sigma\sqrt{2\pi})$. Substituting equation (12) in (11), we obtain

$$
\begin{aligned}
\varphi_{(\mu\overset{+}{,}\lambda)} &= \frac{1}{\mu} \sum_{\nu=\lambda-\mu+1}^{\lambda} \mathbf{E}\left(2R \cdot Z'_{\nu:\lambda} - l^2\right) \\
&= \frac{1}{\mu} \sum_{\nu=\lambda-\mu+1}^{\lambda} \mathbf{E}\left(2R\sigma \cdot Z_{\nu:\lambda} - \sigma^2 n\right) ,
\end{aligned}
\tag{13}
$$

where $p(z) = \exp(-z^2/2)/\sqrt{2\pi} = \phi(z)$ is the probability density function of the standardized normal variable $Z$. From the definition of the expectation $\mathbf{E}(\cdot)$, we obtain:

$$
\varphi_{(\mu\overset{+}{,}\lambda)} = \frac{1}{\mu} \sum_{\nu=\lambda-\mu+1}^{\lambda} \left[ 2R\sigma \int_{z_{\min}}^{z_{\max}} z \cdot p_{\nu:\lambda}(z)\,dz - \sigma^2 n \int_{z_{\min}}^{z_{\max}} p_{\nu:\lambda}(z)\,dz \right] .
\tag{14}
$$

For the special case $\mu = 1$, which has gained most attention so far, equation (14) yields with

$p_{\lambda:\lambda}(z) = \frac{d}{dz}\left[\Phi(z)\right]^{\lambda}$ (from equation (6)):

$$\varphi_{(1\overset{+}{,}\lambda)} \;=\; 2R\sigma \int_{z_{\min}}^{z_{\max}} z \cdot \frac{d}{dz}\left[\Phi(z)\right]^{\lambda} dz - \sigma^2 n \int_{z_{\min}}^{z_{\max}} \frac{d}{dz}\left[\Phi(z)\right]^{\lambda} dz \;. \tag{15}$$

For the $(1,\lambda)$-ES, $z_{\min} = -\infty$ and $z_{\max} = \infty$ (in principle, the domain of possible mutations is unrestricted in case of a $(\mu,\lambda)$-selection mechanism because each mutation is accepted), and equation (15) yields

$$\varphi_{(1,\lambda)} \;=\; 2R\sigma \cdot \mathbf{E}(Z_{\lambda:\lambda}) - \sigma^2 n \;, \tag{16}$$

where

$$\mathbf{E}(Z_{\lambda:\lambda}) \;=\; \int_{-\infty}^{\infty} z \cdot \frac{d}{dz}\left[\Phi(z)\right]^{\lambda} dz \;. \tag{17}$$

The value $c_{1,\lambda} := \mathbf{E}(Z_{\lambda:\lambda})$ was called *progress coefficient* by Rechenberg [16]. In the theory of order statistics, the moments $c_{1,\lambda}$ for the case of a standardized normal distribution $\phi(z)$ are well investigated (see [7], pp. 30–32). Only for $\lambda \leq 5$, closed arithmetical expressions for $c_{1,\lambda}$ are known (see [1], pp. 88-90). Numerically evaluated values of $c_{1,\lambda}$ for $\lambda \leq 400$ can be found in [10].

For the sphere model the progress measure $\varphi$ in terms of the objective function value can easily be converted into a progress measure $\tilde{\varphi}$ in terms of the distance towards the optimum by using a linear approximation based on the local slope of the tangent, i.e., $\varphi = 2R\tilde{\varphi}$. Additionally, we introduce dimensionless, normalized variables $\tilde{\varphi}' = \tilde{\varphi}n/R$ and $\sigma' = \sigma n/R$ and obtain from equation (16):

$$\tilde{\varphi}'_{(1,\lambda)} \;=\; c_{1,\lambda} \cdot \sigma' - \sigma'^2/2 \;, \tag{18}$$

which is the convergence velocity expression for a $(1,\lambda)$-ES in the form as presented by Scheel [17] or Beyer [6]. Notice that, for a $(\mu,\lambda)$-ES, equation (14) yields the generalization

$$\tilde{\varphi}'_{(\mu,\lambda)} \;=\; \frac{\sigma'}{\mu} \sum_{\nu=\lambda-\mu+1}^{\lambda} \mathbf{E}\left(Z_{\nu:\lambda}\right) - \sigma'^2/2 \;=\; \sigma' \cdot \mathbf{E}(D(\mu,\lambda)) - \sigma'^2/2 \tag{19}$$

of equation (18), which clarifies the relation between convergence velocity and the expectation of the selection differential (2) for a standardized normal distribution. Notice that the optimal standard deviation $\sigma'^*$, which maximizes $\tilde{\varphi}'_{(\mu,\lambda)}$, is given by $\sigma'^* = \mathbf{E}(D(\mu,\lambda))$ with $\tilde{\varphi}'^*_{(\mu,\lambda)} = [\mathbf{E}(D(\mu,\lambda))]^2/2$.

According to equation (19), the expectations $\sigma'^*$ of the selection differential provide a universal characterization of the $(\mu,\lambda)$-strategy. In the left part of figure 5, numerically evaluated values of $\sigma'^*$ are graphically presented for $\mu \in \{1,\ldots,30\}$ and $\lambda \in \{\mu,\ldots,150\}$. Starting with $\mathbf{E}(D(\lambda,\lambda)) = 0$, all curves for a constant value of $\mu$ and varying $\lambda$ have identical shapes which scale down as $\mu$ increases. Notice that, in contrast to figure 2 and 3 where the chance of ties increases as $\mu$ is growing, the curves for large values of $\mu$ do not show the relatively long region of linear dependency of $\lambda$ as observed in figure 2 (but not in figure 3, where the mutation rate is optimal). As for the discrete case, the curves of constant values of

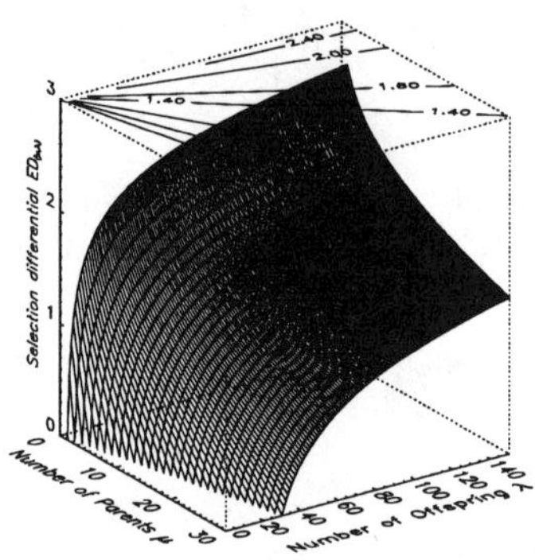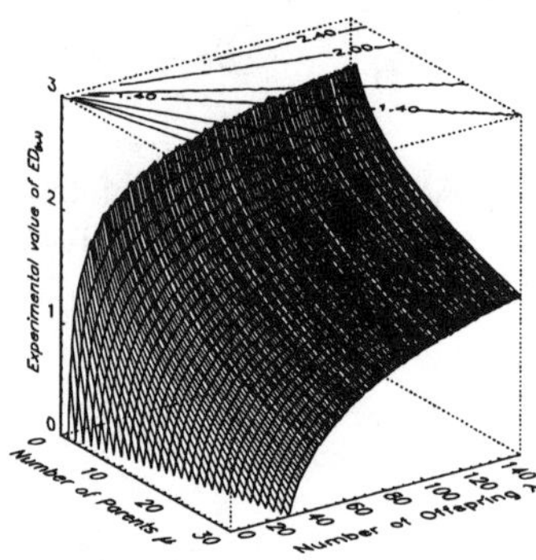

Figure 5: Theoretical (left) and Experimental (right) Expected Values of the Selection Differential $D(\mu, \lambda)$ for $\mu \in \{1, \ldots, 30\}$ and $\lambda \in \{\mu, \ldots, 150\}$.

$\mathbf{E}(D(\mu, \lambda))$ are lines, and the general similarity between figures 5 and figures 2 and 3 is striking.

Again, the theoretical results are confirmed by experimental data shown in the right part of figure 5. The hypothetical parent individual was initialized with $n = 100$, $x_i = 10$ $\forall i \in \{1, \ldots, 100\}$ (i.e., $f = 10,000$), and mutation was performed by utilizing the optimal standard deviation $\sigma^* = \mathbf{E}(D(\mu, \lambda))\sqrt{f}/n$ (i.e., $\sigma^* = \mathbf{E}(D(\mu, \lambda))$ for the values of $f$ and $n$ used here). For each combination of $\mu$ and $\lambda$, the experimental value for $\varphi_{(\mu,\lambda)}$ reflects the average of $N = 1000$ experiments. From the measured values of $\varphi_{(\mu,\lambda)}$, we calculated the measured values of $\mathbf{E}(D(\mu, \lambda)) = (\varphi_{(\mu,\lambda)} \cdot n/f)^{1/2}$, which are shown in the graphic. The measured data confirms the validity of the theoretical model well.

For a $(1+\lambda)$-strategy, we use equation (15) with a lower bound of integration $z_{\min} = \frac{\sigma n}{2R}$ (which results for $r = R$ from equation (12) by taking into account that for $r < R$ an offspring individual is accepted as improvement and that $z_{\min} = z'_{\min}/\sigma$ is a normalized lower bound). This way, we obtain the convergence velocity equation

$$\varphi_{(1+\lambda)} \;=\; 2R\sigma \int_{\frac{\sigma n}{2R}}^{\infty} z \frac{d}{dz} \left[\Phi(z)\right]^\lambda dz - \sigma^2 n \cdot \left(1 - \left[\Phi\left(\frac{\sigma n}{2R}\right)\right]^\lambda\right), \tag{20}$$

which can easily be normalized in the same way as performed to obtain equation (18). Notice that equation (20) neither has a closed form nor can results from order statistics be utilized to simplify it further.

## 5 ASYMPTOTICS AND SUCH

The theory of order statistics provides a tool to derive some very general results concerning the simplified instances of Evolutionary Algorithms discussed here. For instance, from extreme value theory one easily obtains the result $c_{1,\lambda} \to \sqrt{2\ln\lambda}$ as $\lambda \to \infty$ (see e.g. [1], p. 216) for the continuous normal case (equation (18)). As shown in [4], this estimate can still be improved. Unfortunately, in case of a discrete probability density function $p(z)$ no such asymptotic expression can be derived because the limit distribution is degenerate (see [1], pp. 216–217).

Furthermore, the case $\mu = \lambda$ can be analyzed by utilizing order statistics results. Following [1] (p. 110), the identity

$$\sum_{i=1}^{\lambda} \mathbf{E}(Z_{i:\lambda}) \;\; = \;\; \lambda \cdot \mathbf{E}(Z_{1:1}) \tag{21}$$

holds for the discrete as well as the continuous case. This result immediately yields $\varphi_{(\lambda,\lambda)} = \varphi_{(1,1)}$ and $\varphi_{(\lambda+\lambda)} = \varphi_{(1+1)}$ for the counting ones example (using equation (2)) and $\tilde{\varphi}'_{(\lambda,\lambda)} = -\sigma'/2$ for the sphere model (equation (19)). Notice that this result indicates that a $(\lambda,\lambda)$-strategy can yield a positive convergence velocity in the discrete case, which is impossible in the continuous case.

# 6  CONCLUSIONS

Deterministic, extinctive selection mechanisms — $(\mu \overset{+}{,} \lambda)$-selection — in evolutionary algorithms are theoretically formalizable in an elegant way by means of order statistics. Moreover, the theory can be applied independently of the underlying search space ($I\!\!R^n$ for evolution strategies respectively $\{0,1\}^n$ for genetic algorithms), if the probability density function $p(z)$ for mutation is known. The striking similarity of the general shape of the convergence velocity graphics (figures 2, 3, and 5) clarifies that some very general, representation-independent principles determine the behavior of evolutionary algorithms. The identification and analysis of these general principles are important tasks for further research and may help to formulate a general theory of direct random search algorithms based on the principles of mutation, selection, and recombination.

Such a theory will also help to discover the limits of evolutionary algorithms. For instance, it is known that $\mathbf{E}(Z_{\lambda:\lambda}) \le (\lambda - 1)/\sqrt{2\lambda - 1}$, *independently of the probability density function* $p(z)$ (e.g. [7], p. 47). This is a general upper bound which can not be exceeded by whatever mutation operator may be proposed. If a symmetrical $p(z)$ is assumed, the upper bound can be sharpened considerably (for a numerical comparison of the quality of both bounds, see [7], p. 50).

The most obvious next steps in order to develop the proposed theory consist in incorporating population diversity and recombination. These are two major hurdles where the order statistics approach may prove to be helpful too.

### Acknowledgements

This work was performed as a part of the project EVOALG. The author gratefully acknowledges support by the BMFT, grant 01IB403A. The author would like to thank Ulrich Hammel for valuable discussions related to this work.

### References

[1] B. C. Arnold, N. Balakrishnan, and H. N. Nagaraja. *A First Course in Order Statistics.* Wiley Series in Probability and Mathematical Statistics. Wiley, New York, 1992.

[2] Th. Bäck. The interaction of mutation rate, selection, and self-adaptation within a genetic algorithm. In Männer and Manderick [11], pages 85–94.

[3] Th. Bäck. Optimal mutation rates in genetic search. In Forrest [9], pages 2–9.

[4] Th. Bäck, G. Rudolph, and H.-P. Schwefel. Evolutionary programming and evolution strategies: Similarities and differences. In D. B. Fogel and W. Atmar, editors, *Proceedings of the 2nd Annual Conference on Evolutionary Programming*, pages 11–22. Evolutionary Programming Society, San Diego, CA, 1993.

[5] Th. Bäck and H.-P. Schwefel. An overview of evolutionary algorithms for parameter optimization. *Evolutionary Computation*, 1(1):1–23, 1993.

[6] H.-G. Beyer. Towards a theory of evolution strategies: Some asymptotical results from the $(1 \overset{+}{,} \lambda)$-theory. *Evolutionary Computation*, 1(2):165–188, 1993.

[7] H. A. David. *Order Statistics*. Wiley, New York, 2 edition, 1981.

[8] W. Feller. *An Introduction to Probability Theory and Its Applications*. Wiley Series in Probability and Mathematical Statistics. Wiley, New York, 2 edition, 1971.

[9] S. Forrest, editor. *Proceedings of the 5th International Conference on Genetic Algorithms*. Morgan Kaufmann Publishers, San Mateo, CA, 1993.

[10] H. L. Harter. Expected values of normal order statistics. *Biometrika*, 48(1,2):151–165, 1961.

[11] R. Männer and B. Manderick, editors. *Parallel Problem Solving from Nature 2*. Elsevier, Amsterdam, 1992.

[12] H. Mühlenbein. How genetic algorithms really work: I. mutation and hillclimbing. In Männer and Manderick [11], pages 15–25.

[13] H. Mühlenbein and D. Schlierkamp-Voosen. Predictive models for the breeder genetic algorithm. *Evolutionary Computation*, 1(1):25–49, 1993.

[14] H. N. Nagaraja. Selection differentials. In S. Kotz, N. L. Johnson, and C. B. Read, editors, *Encyclopedia of Statistical Sciences*, volume 8, pages 334–338. Wiley, New York, 1988.

[15] I. Rechenberg. *Evolutionsstrategie: Optimierung technischer Systeme nach Prinzipien der biologischen Evolution*. Frommann–Holzboog, Stuttgart, 1973.

[16] I. Rechenberg. The evolution strategy – a mathematical model of Darwinian evolution. In H. Frehland, editor, *Synergetics – From Microscopic to Macroscopic Order*, volume 22 of *Springer Series in Synergetics*, pages 122–132. Springer, Berlin, 1984.

[17] A. Scheel. *Beitrag zur Theorie der Evolutionsstrategie*. Dissertation, Technische Universität Berlin, 1985.

[18] H.-P. Schwefel. *Numerical Optimization of Computer Models*. Wiley, Chichester, 1981.

[19] M. Yanagiya. A simple mutation-dependent genetic algorithm. In Forrest [9], page 659.

# Stability of Vertex Fixed Points and Applications

**Michael D. Vose**
C. S. Dept., 107 Ayres Hall
The University of Tennessee
Knoxville, TN 37996-1301

**Alden H. Wright***
Computer Science Dept.
The University of Montana
Missoula, MT 59812-1008

## Abstract

In the Infinite Population Simple Genetic Algorithm, stability of fixed points is considered when mutation is zero. The analysis is based on the spectrum of the differential of the mapping which defines the transition from one generation to the next. Based on a simple formula for this spectrum, fully nondeceptive functions having exponentially many non-optimal fixed points are constructed.

## 1   INTRODUCTION

This paper is concerned with properties of a function $\mathcal{G}$ (defined in the next section) which can be regarded as answering the following fundamental questions for a simple genetic algorithm:

1. What is the *exact sampling distribution* describing the formation of the next generation?

2. What is the *expected next generation*?

3. In the limit, as population size grows, what is the *transition function* which maps from one generation to the next?

For each of these questions, the answer provided by $\mathcal{G}$ is exact. In a sense, $\mathcal{G}$ *is a GA*: anything that ever could be proved about the simple genetic algorithm (for arbitrary population sizes, finite or infinite) corresponds to some property of $\mathcal{G}$. It is not unnatural to refer to $\mathcal{G}$ as the "Infinite Population Simple Genetic Algorithm" since, by answering the third question above, it is the transition function in the infinite population case. In terms of a finite population GA, an alternate interpretation is that the sequence

$$x, \ \mathcal{G}(x), \ \mathcal{G}^2(x), \ \mathcal{G}^3(x), \ \ldots$$

---

*This work was done while the second author was visiting the Computer Science Department of the University of Tennessee is essentially the most probable transient behavior from initial population $x$ when the population size is large. An introduction to various interpretations of $\mathcal{G}$ can be found in [4].

The relationship between the finite and infinite population GA (i.e., the connection between the behavior of a finite population GA and what the corresponding relevant properties of $\mathcal{G}$ are) is an active area of research. The most complete results to date can be found in [9].

The iterative procedure $x$, $\mathcal{G}(x)$, ... is an example of a discrete dynamical system. A basic goal in the theory of dynamical systems is to understand the nature of the sequence of iterates. *Fixed points*, solutions to $\mathcal{G}(x) = x$, frequently indicate destinations towards which trajectories may converge. It is not known whether iterates of $\mathcal{G}$ typically converge for every initial population $x$ (i.e., for arbitrary fitness functions and typical GA parameters) but it is conjectured that this is the case, and empirical evidence supports this conjecture.

Assuming iterates of $\mathcal{G}$ converge, fixed points represent populations towards which an infinite population GA may evolve. Approximately the same may be said concerning a large finite population GA, except being constrained to occupy points in population space corresponding to its finite population size and being subject to stochastic effects (from selection, crossover, and mutation) would keep it from converging. Fixed points nevertheless locate regions within population space where a finite population GA spends much of its time. Details concerning this type of connection between finite population behavior and fixed points of $\mathcal{G}$ can be found in [7].

This paper is primarily concerned with the stability of fixed points. Roughly speaking, a stable fixed point attracts neighboring populations, while an unstable fixed point tends to repel them. A rough analogy for an unstable fixed point is a pencil balanced on its tip. When truly balanced, it may be stable in the sense of not moving, but the slightest random perturbation is expected to send it diverging towards quite a different state. A stable equilibrium is like a pendulum hanging downwards and at rest. No small perturbation will send it off on a divergent course. While it is possible for a dynamical system to follow a trajectory leading to an unstable fixed point, that is atypical behavior. The analysis in [9] indicates that with positive mutation, there is a strong sense in which unstable fixed points may be ignored.

Although mutation has a more profound influence on GA behavior than is generally recognized [10], it also complicates analysis. For this reason, the results we consider are for the zero mutation case. Because of continuous dependence on parameters, our results may still apply when the mutation rate is low. We also assume that strings have distinct fitness, though the differences may be arbitrarily small.

An application of our stability analysis is in the last section, where "fully nondeceptive" fitness functions are constructed for which $\mathcal{G}$ has exponentially many stable fixed points. The point is not the well known fact that functions may be difficult for a GA even when they are fully nondeceptive (see sections 5 through 7 of [6] for a discussion of various GA failure modes). The purpose is to illustrate our theoretical results with a concrete application. The particular example is important by establishing just how bad things can get; it is extremal in the sense of having the maximum possible number of stable suboptimal attractors.

## 2  BASICS

We consider a generalization of the infinite population GA model introduced in [8]. The domain $\Omega$ is the set of length $\ell$ binary strings. Let $n = 2^\ell$ and note that elements of $\Omega$ correspond to integers in the interval $[0, n)$. They are thereby thought of interchangeably as integers or as bit strings which are regarded as column vectors. Because of frequent use, it is convenient to let $\mathbf{1}$ denote the vector $n - 1$ (the vector of all ones).

Let $\oplus$ denote the bitwise exclusive-or operation, and let $\otimes$ denote the bitwise and operation on $\Omega$. For $x \in \Omega$, the ones-complement of $x$ is denoted by $\overline{x}$. Note that $\overline{x} = \mathbf{1} \oplus x$. If $expr$ is an experssion that is either true or false, then

$$[expr] = \begin{cases} 1 & \text{if } expr \text{ is true} \\ 0 & \text{otherwise} \end{cases}$$

Let $\delta_{ij} = [i = j]$. The $n \times n$ permutation matrix whose $i, j$ th entry is $\delta_{i \oplus k, j}$ is denoted by $\sigma_k$. Note that $(\sigma_k x)_i = x_{i \oplus k}$. The $j$ th column of the $n \times n$ identity matrix is the vector $e_j$. Indexing of vectors and matrices begins with 0.

A *population* is a real-valued vector $x$ indexed over $\Omega$, where $\sum x_i = 1$ and $x_i \geq 0$. The probability (or proportion) of string $i$ in population $x$ is $x_i$ (keep in mind that indexing begins with 0). The set of all populations is the unit simplex $\Lambda$ in $R^n$. For $\ell = 2$, $\Lambda$ is a solid tetrahedron. In general, $\Lambda$ is the smallest convex set containing the unit basis vectors. The vertices of $\Lambda$ correspond to populations consisting entirely of one string type.

The following diagram illustrates the string length 2 case. Here $n = 4$ and $\Omega = \{0, 1, 2, 3\}$, so the ambient space is four dimensional. Thus the projection of the coordinate axes – the rays tipped with arrows – are being viewed. The vertices of the solid tetrahedron are at the basis vectors and correspond (respectively, counterclockwise from top) to populations consisting entirely of: the element 0, the element 1, the element 2, and the element 3.

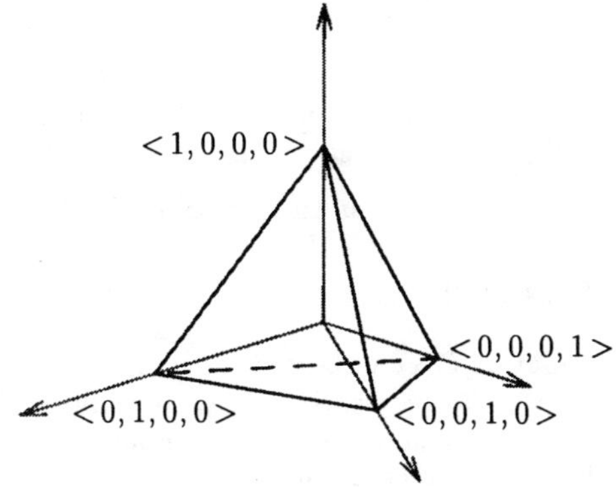


A $n \times n$ *mixing matrix* $M$ implements mutation and crossover. $M$ is defined so that $x^T M x$ is the probability that the result of doing crossover and mutation based on population $x$ is 0. Thus $M_{i,j}$ is the probability that 0 is the result produced by parents $i$ and $j$.

Since this paper only considers zero mutation, we define $M$ for that special case (the general formula can be found in [11]). Considering $k \in \Omega$ as a *crossover mask* used with parents $i, j \in \Omega$, the children are $(i \otimes k) \oplus (j \otimes \overline{k})$ and $(j \otimes k) \oplus (i \otimes \overline{k})$. We assume one child is kept (with equal probability). If $\chi_k$ denotes the probability that mask $k$ is used, then $M$ is given by

$$M_{i,j} = \sum_{k \in \Omega} \frac{\chi_k + \chi_{\overline{k}}}{2} [(i \otimes k) \oplus (j \otimes \overline{k}) = 0]$$

The *twist* of an $n \times n$ matrix $A$, denoted by $A_*$, has entries $(A_*)_{i,j} = A_{i \oplus j, i}$.

**Proposition 2.1**  *The matrix $M_*$ is upper triangular.*

**Proof:** If $i \otimes j \neq 0$, then either $i \otimes j \otimes k \neq 0$ which implies $i \otimes k \neq 0$, or $i \otimes j \otimes \overline{k} \neq 0$ which implies $j \otimes \overline{k} \neq 0$. In either case $(i \otimes k) \oplus (j \otimes \overline{k}) \neq 0$ and hence $M_{i,j} = 0$.

Thus, $(M_*)_{i,j} = M_{i \oplus j, i}$ can be nonzero only when $(i \oplus j) \otimes i = 0$, which is equivalent to $\overline{j} \otimes i = 0$, which implies $j \geq i$. ∎

The *recombination function* $\mathcal{M} : \Lambda \longrightarrow \Lambda$ is defined by the component equations

$$e_i^T \mathcal{M}(x) = (\sigma_i x)^T M \sigma_i x = \sum_{u,v} x_u x_v M_{u \oplus i, v \oplus i}$$

**Proposition 2.2**  *The differential of $\mathcal{M}$ at $x \in \Lambda$ is given by $d\mathcal{M}_x = 2 \sum_u \sigma_u M_* \sigma_u x_u$.*

**Proof:** First note that $(\sigma_u M_* \sigma_u)_{i,j} = M_{i \oplus j, u \oplus i}$. Next, the $i, j$ th entry of $d\mathcal{M}_x$ is

$$\frac{\partial}{\partial x_j} \sum_{u,v} x_u x_v M_{u \oplus i, v \oplus i} = \sum_{u,v} (\delta_{u,j} x_v + \delta_{v,j} x_u) M_{u \oplus i, v \oplus i} = 2 \sum_u x_u M_{i \oplus j, u \oplus i}$$

∎

Assuming a *fitness function* $f : \Omega \longrightarrow R^+$, proportional selection is the mapping from $\Lambda$ into $\Lambda$ defined by $x \mapsto Fx / 1^T Fx$, where $F$ is the $n \times n$ diagonal matrix $F_{i,j} = \delta_{i,j} f(i)$.

The *Infinite Population Simple Genetic Algorithm* is defined as the mapping $\mathcal{G} : \Lambda \longrightarrow \Lambda$ where

$$\mathcal{G}(x) = \mathcal{M}(Fx / 1^T Fx)$$

As indicated in the introduction, an infinite population GA can be defined in a very natural way via the limit of a finite population GA as population size increases. It follows that such a GA is deterministic (the stochastic variations average out as the population size grows) and the next generation is given by the expected next generation. This expected next generation, given current population $x$, is given by $\mathcal{G}(x)$ as defined above.

**Proposition 2.3**  *The differential of $\mathcal{G}$ at $x \in \Lambda$ is given by*

$$d\mathcal{G}_x = \frac{1}{1^T Fx} d\mathcal{M}_{\frac{Fx}{1^T Fx}} FP \qquad where \qquad P = I - x \frac{1^T F}{1^T Fx}$$

**Proof:** The differential of $h(x) = x/\mathbf{1}^T x$ is

$$dh_x = \frac{I}{\mathbf{1}^T x} - x\frac{\mathbf{1}^T}{(\mathbf{1}^T x)^2}$$

Applying the chain rule to $\mathcal{G} = \mathcal{M} \circ h \circ F$ yields

$$d\mathcal{G}_x = d\mathcal{M}_{h \circ Fx}\, dh_{Fx}\, F$$

Since $dh_{Fx} F = FP/\mathbf{1}^T Fx$, the formula for the differential follows. ∎

# 3  THE SPECTRUM OF $d\mathcal{G}$

A fixed point $x \in \Lambda$ of $\mathcal{G}$ is *stable* if for any neighborhood $U$ of $x$, there is a neighborhood $V$ of $x$ such that for each $q \in V$ the trajectory $q, \mathcal{G}(q), \mathcal{G}^2(q), \dots$ lies in $U$. The fixed point $x$ is *asymptotically stable* if it is stable and all trajectories beginning in some neighborhood of $x$ converge to $x$.

The *spectral radius* of a square matrix $A$, denoted by $\rho(A)$, is the largest modulus of the eigenvalues of $A$. A standard result of dynamical systems theory is that (for any differentiable map $\mathcal{G}$) if $x$ is a fixed point of $\mathcal{G}$ and $\rho(d\mathcal{G}_x) < 1$, then $x$ is asymptotically stable, where $\mathcal{G}$ considered as a map from $R^n$ into itself. Moreover, $x$ is unstable if the spectral radius is greater than 1 (see [2], for example). Therefore information about the *spectrum* of $d\mathcal{G}_x$ (its set of eigenvalues) is important to the stability of a fixed point $x$.

**Lemma 3.1** *The matrix $\sigma_k F \sigma_k - e_0 f^T \sigma_k$ is diagonal except for row 0.*

**Proof:** The matrix $\sigma_k F \sigma_k$ is diagonal, and $e_0 f^T \sigma_k$ is nonzero only in row 0. ∎

**Lemma 3.2** *The matrix $\sigma_k d\mathcal{G}_{e_k} \sigma_k$ is given by $\frac{2}{f_k} M_*(\sigma_k F \sigma_k - e_0 f^T \sigma_k)$.*

**Proof:** We will apply Proposition 2.3 at $x = e_k$. First note that $\mathbf{1}^T F = f^T$, $Fx = f_k e_k$, and $\mathbf{1}^T Fx = f_k$. Thus

$$\sigma_k FP\sigma_k = \sigma_k F\sigma_k - \sigma_k e_k f^T \sigma_k = \sigma_k F\sigma_k - e_0 f^T \sigma_k$$

By Proposition 2.2,

$$d\mathcal{M}_{e_k} = 2\sum (e_k)_i \sigma_i M_* \sigma_i = 2\sigma_k M_* \sigma_k$$

so that $\sigma_k d\mathcal{M}_{e_k} \sigma_k = 2M_*$. Appealing to proposition 2.3 gives

$$\sigma_k d\mathcal{G}_{e_k} \sigma_k = \frac{1}{f_k}(\sigma_k d\mathcal{M}_{e_k} \sigma_k)(\sigma_k FP\sigma_k) = \frac{2}{f_k} M_*(\sigma_k F\sigma_k - e_0 f^T \sigma_k)$$

∎

**Corollary 3.3** *If mutation is zero, the matrix $D = \sigma_k d\mathcal{G}_{e_k} \sigma_k$ has the following properties:*

1. *Column 0 of $D$ is zero.*

2. *$D$ is upper triangular, with diagonal $D_{i,i} = \frac{f_{k \oplus i}}{f_k} \sum_u (\chi_u + \chi_{\overline{u}})[u \otimes i = 0]$ for $i > 0$.*

3. *Row 0 of $D$ is nonpositive (i.e., $D_{0,j} \le 0$ for $1 \le j < n$).*

4. *The other rows of $D$ are nonnegative (i.e., $D_{i,j} \ge 0$ for $1 \le i < n$, $i \le j < n$).*

**Proof:** By Proposition 2.1, $M_*$ is upper triangular. By Lemma 3.1, so too is $\sigma_k F \sigma_k - e_0 f^T \sigma_k$. The product of upper triangular matrices is upper triangular. Hence, by lemma 3.2, $D$ is upper triangular.

The 0,0 th entry of both $\sigma_k F \sigma_k$ and $e_0 f^T \sigma_k$ is $f_k$, hence their difference is zero. Thus, column 0 of $\sigma_k F \sigma_k - e_0 f^T \sigma_k$ is zero which, by lemma 3.2, implies column 0 of $D$ is zero.

By lemma 3.2, $D_{0,j} = 2((M_*)_{0,j} - (M_*)_{0,0}) f_{j \oplus k} / f_k = 2(M_{j,0} - M_{0,0}) f_{j \oplus k} / f_k$ for $j > 0$. But $M_{0,0} = 1$ and $M_{j,0} \leq 1$, so this quantity is nonpositive.

By lemma 3.2, $D_{i,j} = 2(M_*)_{i,j} f_{k \oplus j} / f_k = 2 M_{i \oplus j,i} f_{k \oplus j} / f_k$ for $j \geq i > 0$, and this quantity is nonnegative. The diagonal entries are $2 M_{0,i} f_{k \oplus i} / f_k$ for $i > 0$. ∎

**Theorem 3.4** *If mutation is zero, then the spectrum of $d\mathcal{G}_{e_k}$ is given by:*

$$spec(d\mathcal{G}_{e_k}) = \left\{ \frac{f_{i \oplus k}}{f_k} \sum_u (\chi_u + \chi_{\overline{u}})[u \otimes i = 0] \; : \; i = 1, 2, \ldots, n - 1 \right\} \bigcup \{0\}$$

**Proof:** Since the spectrum is invariant under conjugation, the spectrum of $d\mathcal{G}_{e_k}$ is the same as that of $\sigma_k d\mathcal{G}_{e_k} \sigma_k$. The spectrum of a triangular matrix is the set of diagonal entries. These entries are given by Corollary 3.3. ∎

## 4 STABILITY IN THE SIMPLEX

Theorem 3.4 can be used to compute $\rho(d\mathcal{G}_{e_k})$ and thus characterize the stability at $e_k$ of $\mathcal{G}$ as a map from $R^n$ to $R^n$. One might wonder, however, if a fixed point of $\mathcal{G}$ could be unstable in this sense, but stable when the domain of $\mathcal{G}$ is restricted to $\Lambda$. Among other things, this section shows that cannot happen.

Before proceeding, we review some facts concerning the Jordan canonical form. A $m \times m$ *simple Jordan submatrix* is identical to a constant times the identity matrix, except that the subdiagonal consists of 1's. For example,

$$\begin{pmatrix} a & 0 & 0 \\ 1 & a & 0 \\ 0 & 1 & a \end{pmatrix}$$

is a $3 \times 3$ simple Jordan submatrix. Given any square matrix $A$, there exists a similarity transformation $P$ such that $J = P^{-1} A P$ is in *Jordan canonical form*: it is block diagonal with simple Jordan submatrices along the diagonal. The diagonal entries of a block are eigenvalues and the columns of $P$ corresponding to the columns occupied by a block (in $J$) form a basis for a space invariant under $A$.

We apply the Jordan canonical form to $d\mathcal{G}_{e_k}$, dividing the simple Jordan blocks into two categories: *stable* blocks corresponding to eigenvalues $\lambda$ with $|\lambda| \leq 1$, and *unstable* blocks corresponding to eigenvalues $\lambda$ with $|\lambda| > 1$. The columns of $P$ (the matrix of the similarity transformation) corresponding to stable blocks form a basis for the *stable space* $S$. The columns corresponding to unstable blocks form a basis for the *unstable space* $U$. Thus $R^n$ is decomposed into the direct sum of $S$ and $U$, and each is invariant under $d\mathcal{G}_{e_k}$. Let $\pi_S : R^n \longrightarrow S$ and $\pi_U : R^n \longrightarrow U$ be the projections into these subspaces.

Let $\|\cdot\|_S$ and $\|\cdot\|_U$ denote norms on $S$ and $U$ respectively. Given $\theta > 0$, we define the s-region $r(\theta) = \{x \in R^n : \|\pi_S(x)\|_S < \theta\|\pi_U(x)\|_U\}$. Note that $r(\theta)$ depends on the choice of norms on $U$ and $S$ as well as on the parameter $\theta$.

**Theorem 4.1** *Let $x$ be a fixed point of $f : R^n \longrightarrow R^n$ such that $\rho(df_x) > 1$. Let $U$ and $S$ be the unstable and stable spaces corresponding to the differential $df_x$. For all $\theta > 0$, there exist norms on $S$ and $U$ and a corresponding s-region $r(\theta)$ such that if $V$ is a sufficiently small neighborhood of $x$, then $y \in V \cap (x + r(\theta))$ implies that $f^i(y) \notin V$ for some $i$.*

**Proof:** We first choose appropriate norms. Let $D_S = df_x|S$ and let $D_U = df_x|U$. Then $\rho(D_S) \le 1$ and all eigenvalues of $D_U$ are greater than 1 (thus $D_U$ is invertible and $\rho(D_U^{-1}) < 1$). Choose norms $\|\cdot\|_S$ and $\|\cdot\|_U$ so that $\|D_U^{-1}\|_U = \beta^{-1} < 1$ and $\|D_S\|_S = \alpha < \beta$ (the norm can be chosen arbitrarily close to the spectral radius, see for example [2]). It follows that $\|df_x s\|_S = \|D_S s\| \le \alpha\|s\|_S$ and $\|df_x u\| = \|D_U u\|_U \ge \beta\|u\|_U$ for all $s \in S$, $u \in U$. Define the norm $\|\cdot\|$ on $R^n$ by $\|x\| = \|s + u\| = \|s\|_S + \|u\|_U$. These norms will be assumed throughout the rest of the proof, and their subscripts will be dropped to streamline notation.

The next step is to show that for any $\theta > 0$, there exists a neighborhood $V$ of $x$ such that if $y \in V \cap (x + r(\theta))$ then $f(y) \in x + r(\theta)$.

Suppose $y \in V \cap (x + r(\theta))$ and let $y - x = s + u$ where $s \in S$ and $u \in U$. By the definition of the differential, $f(y) - x = df_x(y - x) + o(y - x) = df_x s + df_x u + o(y - x)$. Choose $\eta > 0$ such that $\alpha\theta + (\theta + 1)\eta \le \theta(\beta - (\theta + 1)\eta)$. Now choose the neighborhood $V$ sufficiently small that $y \in V \implies \|o(y - x)\| < \|y - x\|\eta$. It follows that

$$
\begin{aligned}
\|\pi_S(f(y) - x)\| \;&\le\; \|df_x s\| + \|\pi_S(o(y - x))\| \\
&\le\; \alpha\|s\| + (\|s\| + \|u\|)\eta \\
&\le\; \alpha\theta\|u\| + (\theta\|u\| + \|u\|)\eta \\
&\le\; \|u\|(\alpha\theta + (\theta + 1)\eta) \\
&\le\; \theta\|u\|(\beta - (\theta + 1)\eta) \qquad \text{by the choice of } \eta \\
&\le\; \theta(\|u\|\beta - (\|s\| + \|u\|)\eta) \\
&\le\; \theta(\|df_x u\| - \|y - x\|\eta) \\
&\le\; \theta(\|df_x u\| - \|\pi_U(o(y - x))\|) \\
&\le\; \theta\|\pi_U(f(y) - x)\|
\end{aligned}
$$

Finally, we show that if $y \in V \cap (x + r(\theta))$ then $f^t(y) \notin V$ for some $t$. Otherwise, the trajectory $y, f(y), f^2(y), \ldots$ lies in $V \cap (x + r(\theta))$ by what has already been shown. Applying $\|\pi_U(f(y) - x)\| \ge \|u\|(\beta - (\theta + 1)\eta)$ (which follows from the inequalities above) we conclude that $\|\pi_U(f^k(y) - x)\| \ge \|u\|(\beta - (\theta + 1)\eta)^k$ for all $k$. Since $\eta$ may be chosen so that $\beta - (\theta + 1)\eta > 1$, this contradicts that $V$ is a bounded neighborhood. $\blacksquare$

**Lemma 4.2** *For $i \ne k$, if $f_i \sum_u (X_u + X_{\bar{u}})[u \otimes (i \oplus k) = 0] > f_k$ then the stable space of $d\mathcal{G}_{e_k}$ does not intersect $\{p \in \Lambda : p_i > 0\} - e_k$.*

**Proof:** Abbreviate $\sigma_k d\mathcal{G}_{e_k}\sigma_k$ by $D$ and let $p \in \Lambda$ be such that $p_i > 0$. We first show $e_i^T d\mathcal{G}_{e_k}(p-e_k) > e_i^T(p-e_k)$. By assumption, $D_{i\oplus k,i\oplus k} > 1$ (see corollary 3.3).

$$
\begin{aligned}
e_i^T d\mathcal{G}_{e_k}(p - e_k) &= e_i^T \sigma_k(\sigma_k d\mathcal{G}_{e_k}\sigma_k)\sigma_k(p - e_k) \\
&= (\sigma_k e_i)^T D(\sigma_k p - e_0) \\
&= e_{i\oplus k}^T D\sigma_k p - e_{i\oplus k}^T De_0
\end{aligned}
$$

By Corollary 3.3, column 0 of $D$ is zero. Hence $e_{i\oplus k}^T De_0 = 0$. The term corresponding to $u = i \oplus k$ in

$$
e_{i\oplus k}^T D\sigma_k p = \sum_u D_{i\oplus k,u}p_{u\oplus k}
$$

is $D_{i\oplus k,i\oplus k}\, p_i$, which is greater than $p_i$ (since $D_{i\oplus k,i\oplus k} > 1$). The remaining terms are nonnegative since row $k\oplus i$ of $D$ is. This establishes $e_i^T d\mathcal{G}_{e_k}(p-e_k) > e_i^T(p-e_k)$.

Applying this inequality recursively yields $e_i^T d\mathcal{G}_{e_k}^j(p - e_k) > e_i^T(p - e_k)$ for all $j$. Thus $p - e_k$ can not lie in the stable space of $d\mathcal{G}_{e_k}$. ∎

We say a fixed point $p$ of $\mathcal{G} : \Lambda \longrightarrow \Lambda$ is *unstable* if there exists a relative neighborhood[1] $V$ in $\Lambda$ of $p$ such that for any neighborhood $V'$ of $p$, there exists a $q \in V'$ and an integer $t$ such that $\mathcal{G}^t(q) \notin V$.

**Theorem 4.3** *If the spectral radius of $d\mathcal{G}_{e_k}$ is greater than 1, then $e_k$ is an unstable fixed point of $\mathcal{G}$, considered as a map from $\Lambda$ to $\Lambda$.*

**Proof:** We use the same notation and conventions as in the proof of Theorem 4.1. By Lemma 4.2, the translate by $e_k$ of the stable space of $d\mathcal{G}_{e_k}$ does not intersect the interior of $\Lambda$. Choose norms for $R^n$ as in the proof of Theorem 4.1 and let $p - e_k = s + u$ where $p$ is in the interior of $\Lambda$. Then $\|u\| > 0$ and $p \in e_k + r(\theta)$ for some $\theta$. Now for sufficiently small $\delta$ with $\delta(p - e_k) + e_k \in V$, there exists $t$ such that $\mathcal{G}^t(\delta p) \notin V$ (here $V$ is the neighborhood given by Theorem 4.1). ∎

The importance of theorem 4.3 is that if $\rho(d\mathcal{G}_{e_k}) > 1$, then populations arbitrarily close to $e_k$ are expected to follow an evolutionary trajectory moving away from $e_k$. In fact, the proof shows all nearby interior points of $\Lambda$ are expected to behave in this way.

It appears as though the stability analysis just presented covers only the fixed points of $\mathcal{G}$ found at vertices of $\Lambda$. However, when mutation is zero, we do not know of any examples where stable fixed points are not at vertices.

**Conjecture 4.4** *If mutation is zero, the only stable fixed points of $\mathcal{G}$ are at vertices of $\Lambda$.*

The *basin of attraction* of a fixed point $x$ is the set of points whose trajectories converge to $x$. A fixed point is *hyperbolic* if the differential has no eigenvalues of modulus 1. For hyperbolic fixed points, it is shown in [1] that the translate of the stable space of the differential is tangent to the basin of attraction of $x$. Recall that Lemma 4.2 shows the translate of the stable space of the differential does not intersect the interior of $\Lambda$. This motivates the following generalization.

**Conjecture 4.5** *If mutation is zero, the basin of attraction of an unstable vertex fixed point of $\mathcal{G}$ does not intersect the interior of the simplex.*

---

[1] A relative neighborhood of $p$ in $\Lambda$ is the intersection of a neighborhood of $p$ in $R^n$ with $\Lambda$.

# 5   APPLICATIONS

In this section we specialize the formula of Theorem 3.4 to one-point and uniform crossover. Then an example is given of a "fully nondeceptive" fitness function (defined below) that has exponentially many stable fixed points (exponential in the string length).

For one-point crossover, the crossover mask probabilities are

$$\chi_u = \begin{cases} 1 - \chi & \text{if } u = 0 \\ \chi/(\ell - 1) & \text{if } u = 2^k - 1 \text{ for some integer } k, 1 \le k < \ell \\ 0 & \text{otherwise} \end{cases}$$

where $\chi$ is the crossover rate. For uniform crossover, the crossover mask probabilities are given by $\chi_u = \delta_{u,0}(1-\chi)+\chi/n$. Here $\chi$ is used both as a vector, to specify the probability $\chi_i$ that crossover mask $i$ is used, and as a scalar, to specify the crossover rate. This overloading of $\chi$ does not take long to get used to because context makes its meaning clear.

For $i \neq 0$, let $\text{lo}(i)$ and $\text{hi}(i)$ be the smallest and largest $k$ such that $i \otimes 2^k \neq 0$. Note that $\text{lo}(i)$ and $\text{hi}(i)$ are the smallest and largest nonzero bit positions in $i$. Define $\delta(i) = \text{hi}(i) - \text{lo}(i) + 1$. The following lemma is a special case of a formula proved by Gary Koehler [5].

**Lemma 5.1** *For $i \neq 0$ and one-point crossover,*

$$\sum_u (\chi_u + \chi_{\overline{u}})[u \otimes i = 0] = 1 - \chi + \chi \frac{\ell - \delta(i)}{\ell - 1}$$

**Lemma 5.2** *For $i \neq 0$ and uniform crossover,*

$$\sum_u (\chi_u + \chi_{\overline{u}})[u \otimes i = 0] = 1 - \chi + \chi 2^{1-|i|}$$

*where $|i| = 1^T i$ is the number of nonzero bits in $i$.*

**Proof:** The cardinality of the set $\{u : u \otimes i = 0\}$ is $2^{\ell-|i|}$. If $i \neq 0$, then the sets $\{u : u \otimes i = 0\}$ and $\{\overline{u} : u \otimes i = 0\}$ are disjoint. Hence their union has cardinality $2^{\ell-|i|+1}$. Thus

$$\sum_u (\chi_u + \chi_{\overline{u}})[u \otimes i = 0] = 1 - \chi + 2^{\ell-|i|+1}\chi/n$$

∎

Two schema are said to be *competing* if they have the same fixed positions but different fixed bits. Let $S_1$ and $S_2$ be competing and suppose $S_1$ contains the maximum. A fitness function has been called *fully nondeceptive* if for every such pair, $S_1$ has the higher average fitness. We now give a family of fully nondeceptive fitness functions which have $2^{\ell-1}$ stable fixed points.

If $|k|$ is even (i.e., $k$ has even parity), let $f_k = a$, and if $|k|$ is odd, let $f_k = b$ where $a > b > 0$. Any schema with more than one element contains equal numbers of even and odd parity strings. Hence, all nontrivial schemata have equal average fitness. Now modify $f$ to $f_k = a + c(\ell - |k|)$ for even parity $k$. If $c > 0$ then 0 is the unique point of maximum fitness and $f$ is fully nondeceptive. Under appropriate choice of $a$, $b$, and $c$, this function will have the required properties.

For any crossover type, define

$$h = \max_{|i|>1} \sum (\chi_u + \chi_{\overline{u}})[u \otimes i = 0]$$

In the case of one-point crossover, $h = 1 - \chi/(\ell - 1)$. For uniform crossover, $h = 1 - \chi/2$.

**Proposition 5.3** *If $0 < c < \frac{a}{\ell}(\frac{1}{h} - 1)$, then $f$ as defined above is fully nondeceptive. If $|k|$ is even, then $e_k$ is a stable fixed point of $\mathcal{G}$ given any crossover for which $h < 1$.*

**Proof:** The function $f$ is fully nondeceptive by construction. If $|k|$ is even and $|i| > 1$, then

$$\frac{f_{i \oplus k}}{f_k} \sum_u (\chi_u + \chi_{\overline{u}})[u \otimes i = 0] \quad \leq \quad \frac{a + c\ell}{a} h < 1$$

If $|k|$ is even and $|i| = 1$, then $|k \oplus i|$ is odd, $f_{k \oplus i} = b < a = f_k$, and the summation above is 1. These considerations together with Theorem 3.4 show $\rho(d\mathcal{G}_{e_k}) < 1$. Hence $e_k$ is stable.

∎

The next proposition shows that if fitnesses are distinct then $2^{\ell-1}$ is the maximum possible number of stable fixed points.

**Proposition 5.4** *Suppose $|j \oplus k| = 1$ ($j$ and $k$ differ by exactly one bit). If $f_j \neq f_k$, then at most one of $e_j$ and $e_k$ is stable.*

**Proof:** Without loss of generality, assume $f_j > f_k$. Let $i = j \oplus k$ and consider the eigenvalue of $d\mathcal{G}_{e_k}$ given by $\frac{f_{i \oplus k}}{f_k} \sum_u (\chi_u + \chi_{\overline{u}})[u \otimes i = 0]$. Since the summation is 1, the eigenvalue is $f_j/f_k > 1$, and $e_k$ can not be stable. ∎

In particular, proposition 5.3 implies that the classical taxonomy of two bit problems [3] is incomplete. There are two bit problems for which:

- The schema containing the optimum wins every uniform schema competition.
- From some initial population containing every string type, a GA may converge to a suboptimal with probability which approaches 1 as the population size grows.

Although the analysis in this paper is limited to zero mutation, examples of this kind are not. The following function is an example for crossover rate 0.6 and mutation rate 0.00001

$$0 \mapsto 1.6, \quad 1 \mapsto 1.0, \quad 2 \mapsto 1.0, \quad 3 \mapsto 1.1$$

# 6 CONCLUSION

In the case of no mutation, we have defined $\mathcal{G}$, the infinite population Simple Genetic Algorithm. We have produced a formula for the spectrum of $d\mathcal{G}$ that allows the determination of the stability of fixed points at vertices of $\Lambda$. Fixed points are important because they represent populations towards which populations may evolve. When a fixed point $p$ is stable, one would expect a GA could become trapped there. If $p$ were unstable, it would be less likely that convergence to $p$ would take place (for large populations).

Even though our method applies only to vertex fixed points (populations consisting of a single string type), we believe that all stable fixed points are in fact vertices when mutation is zero and fitnesses are distinct. We have made related conjectures concerning these matters (see conjectures 3.4 and 3.5) which identify important open questions.

In the final section, our analysis is applied to construct functions which are – from a "static schema analysis perspective" – totally easy, yet have exponentially many suboptimum stable fixed points. We also show these functions to be extremal in the sense of having the maximum number of stable fixed points possible.

## Acknowledgements

This research was supported by the National Science Foundation IRI-9224917.

## References

[1] Ethan Akin (1993). *The General Topology of Dynamical Systems*. Americal Mathematical Society.

[2] G. R. Belitskii and Yu. I. Lyubich (1988). *Matrix Norms and their Applications*. Birkhäuser.

[3] Goldberg, D. E. (1987). "Simple Genetic Algorithms and the Minimal, Deceptive Problem". L. Davis (Ed.), *Genetic Algorithms and Simulated Annealing*. London: Pitman.

[4] J. Juliany & M. D. Vose (1994). "The Genetic Algorithm Fractal". Evolutionary Computation, v. 2, no. 2, 165-180.

[5] G. Koehler (1992). "A Proof of the Vose-Liepins Conjecture". *Annals of Mathematics and Artificial Intelligence 5*.

[6] G. E. Liepins & M. D. Vose (1990). "Representational Issues in Genetic Optimization". *Journal of Experimental and Theoretical Artificial Intelligence*, 2, 101-115

[7] A. Nix & M. D. Vose (1992). "Modeling Genetic Algorithms With Markov Chains". *Annals of Mathematics and Artificial Intelligence* 5, 79-88.

[8] M. D. Vose (1990). "Formalizing Genetic Algorithms". *Proc. IEEE wksp. on G.A.s, N.N.s, & S.A. applied to problems in Signal & Image Processing*, May 1990, Glasgow, U.K.

[9] M. D. Vose (1993). "Modeling Simple Genetic Algorithms". Submitted to *Evolutionary Computation*.

[10] M. D. Vose (1994). "A Closer Look At Mutation In Genetic Algorithms". *Annals of Mathematics and Artificial Intelligence* 10, 423-434

[11] M. D. Vose and A. H. Wright (1993). "Simple Genetic Algorithms with Linear Fitness". Submitted to *Evolutionary Computation*.

# Using Markov Chains to Analyze GAFOs


**Kenneth A. De Jong**
Computer Science Department
George Mason University
Fairfax, VA 22030
E-mail: kdejong@gmu.edu

**William M. Spears**
**Diana F. Gordon**
Navy Center for Applied Research in Artificial Intelligence
Code 5510
Naval Research Laboratory
Washington, D.C. 20375-5320
E-mail: spears,gordon@aic.nrl.navy.mil


## Abstract


Our theoretical understanding of the properties of genetic algorithms (GAs) being used for function optimization (GAFOs) is not as strong as we would like. Traditional schema analysis provides some first order insights, but doesn't capture the non-linear dynamics of the GA search process very well. Markov chain theory has been used primarily for steady state analysis of GAs. In this paper we explore the use of transient Markov chain analysis to model and understand the behavior of finite population GAFOs observed while in transition to steady states. This approach appears to provide new insights into the circumstances under which GAFOs will (will not) perform well. Some preliminary results are presented and an initial evaluation of the merits of this approach is provided.

## 1  INTRODUCTION

At the previous FOGA workshop the claim was made that our theoretical understanding of the properties of genetic algorithms (GAs) being used for function optimization (i.e., GAFOs) was quite weak (De Jong, 1992). Traditional schema analysis provides insight into the optimal allocation of trials when maximizing cumulative profits is the goal (Holland, 1975), but doesn't say much about global function optimization. Static analysis of functions regarding their "deceptiveness" provides some insights into what kinds of functions are difficult to optimize with a GA (Goldberg, 1987), but is a "first order" theory in the sense that it doesn't include the effects of the non-linear dynamics of the GA search process. Traditional Markov chain analysis provides insight into the long term, steady state behavior of large population GAs (Davis and Principe, 1991; Nix and Vose, 1992; Vose, 1992; Suzuki, 1993; Rudolph, 1994), but says little about the transient observable behavior of implementable GAFOs. Markov chains have also been used to model specific features of GAs, such as selection, genetic drift, niching, etc. (De Jong, 1975; Goldberg and Segrest, 1987; Mafoud, 1993; Horn, 1993).

We feel that recent theoretical developments along with advances in computational power have set the stage for a more complete analysis of GAFOs via Markov chains. In this paper we present our ideas as to how previous Markov chain analyses can be extended to provide a stronger GAFO theory capable of explaining and predicting the behavior of GAFOs on various classes of optimization problems. We feel that such a theory must simultaneously take into account the characteristics of the particular GAFO being used (generational, elitist, etc.), the internal search space representation (binary, gray code, etc.), the operators used (form and rate of crossover, etc.), the non-linear dynamics of the search process, and the characteristics of the function to be optimized.

As a consequence, we are uncomfortable with the notion of a "GA-hard problem" independent of these other details, unless we mean by such a phrase that *no* choice of GA properties, representations, and operators exist that make such a problem easy for a GAFO to solve. There are such problems, of course. Needle-in-a-haystack problems are the canonical example, but are equally difficult for any other optimization algorithm.

As soon as we leave this class of hard search problems, we find ourselves in situations in which the difficulty of finding the optimum is a function of both the particular GAFO being used as well as the optimization problem. Changes to either can increase or decrease the observed difficulty. Said another way, the difficulty of a particular GAFO situation is strongly correlated to how well matched the features of a particular GAFO are to the characteristics of a given problem. High degrees of consonance correspond to our informal notion of a GA-easy situation, and significant dissonance results in GA-hard situations. As GAFO engineers we can and do frequently increase the consonance of a particular situation by changing representations, operators, etc.

From this perspective a GAFO theory should provide ways of measuring degrees of hardness of a particular situation. It should provide insight into the effects that changes in representation, operators, etc. have on hardness, and for a given GAFO make predictions about the kinds of problems with which it will have difficulties. We present the initial steps toward such a theory in the remaining sections.

## 2  MEASURING GA PERFORMANCE AND HARDNESS

The standard measures of performance for optimization algorithms involve convergence properties (i.e., the ability to find an optimum) as well as convergence rates (how quickly they are found). Since GAFOs are parallel, population-based stochastic search procedures, there are a number of possible definitions of convergence. The simplest notion is that ultimately a GAFO population converges to a uniform population consisting of $n$ copies of a single individual which may or may not correspond to a global optimum.

Since most GAFOs are run with non-zero mutation rates, this simple form of convergence seldom occurs, unless one "anneals" the mutation rate over time. Without an annealing mechanism GAFOs settle into a dynamic equilibrium in which the exploratory pressures of mutation and crossover are balanced by the exploitative pressure of selection. Moreover, since mutation is active, every point in the space has some non-zero probability of being visited. Hence, it is trivial to show that a global optimum will be visited infinitely often when a GAFO is left to run in this state of dynamic equilibrium.

As a consequence, most GAFO practitioners measure performance in terms of the average (or best) points in the current population, or in terms of monotonically non-decreasing ''best so far'' curves which plot, as a function of the number of samples (or generations), the best point found so far in the search process regardless of whether or not that point is currently represented in the population.

Some natural questions related to such performance measures immediately arise. How likely is it that, if I look at the contents of the $k$th generation, it will contain a copy of the optimum? What is the expected waiting time until a global optimum is encountered for the first time? How long must we wait before a point is encountered that is within some error tolerance of the optimum? How much variance is there in such measures from run to run? How much are such measures affected by changes in population size, mutation rates, etc.?

As GA practitioners we constantly look for ways to improve the performance of our GAFOs with respect to these measures. Situations which exhibit shorter mean waiting times and smaller variances correspond to our notion of GA-easy situations, and situations with longer mean waiting times and higher variances are viewed as harder. Consequently, these statistics appear to be natural quantitative measures of the difficulty of a particular GAFO situation.

## 3  MARKOV MODELS OF SIMPLE GAs

If we are to use such statistics as the mean and variance of waiting times as measures of hardness, random process theory would seem to provide an appropriate set of tools for describing the behavior of stochastic GAFOs. Historically, it has been quite natural to model simple GAs as Markov processes in which the ''state'' of the GA is given by the contents of the current population (De Jong, 1975; Goldberg & Segrest, 1987). One can then imagine a state space of all possible populations and study the characteristics of the population trajectories (the Markov chains) a GA produces from randomly generated initial populations.

Most of the analytic results obtained from this approach are derived using infinite population models and involve characterizing steady state behavior (Davis and Principe, 1991; Vose, 1992; Suzuki, 1993; Rudolph, 1994). It is considerably more difficult to get analytic results concerning means and variances of waiting times for Markov models of finite population GAFOs. However, increases in computer technology now permit the visualization and computational exploration of such models as the first steps in developing such a theory. We explore such an approach in this paper.†

Among the many papers on Markov models of GAs, the Nix and Vose model (1992) is particularly well suited to serve as the basis for our GAFO theory. We begin with a brief summary of their model and notation.

### 3.1    Summary of the Nix and Vose Markov Model

The Nix and Vose Markov model is intended to represent a simple generational GA consisting of a finite population, a standard binary integer representation, standard mutation and crossover operators, and fitness-proportional selection. Fitness scaling, elitism, and other GAFO-oriented features are not modeled.

If $l$ is the length of the binary strings, then $r = 2^l$ is the total number of possible strings. If $n$ is the population size, then the number of possible populations, $N$, corresponding to the number of possible states is:

$$N = \begin{bmatrix} n + r - 1 \\ r - 1 \end{bmatrix} \tag{1}$$

The possible populations are described by the matrix $Z$, which is an $N$ x $r$ matrix.‡ The $i$th row $\phi_i = <z_{i,0}, \ldots, z_{i,r-1}>$ of $Z$ is the incidence vector for the $i$th population. In other words, $z_{i,y}$ is the number of occurrences of string $y$ in the $i$th population, where $y$ is the integer representation of the binary string. For example, suppose $l = 2$ and $n = 2$. Then $r = 4$, $N = 10$, and the $Z$ matrix would be:

|         | Binary | String |    |    |
|---------|--------|--------|----|----|
| State   | 00     | 01     | 10 | 11 |
| P1      | 0      | 0      | 0  | 2  |
| P2      | 0      | 0      | 1  | 1  |
| P3      | 0      | 0      | 2  | 0  |
| P4      | 0      | 1      | 0  | 1  |
| P5      | 0      | 1      | 1  | 0  |
| P6      | 0      | 2      | 0  | 0  |
| P7      | 1      | 0      | 0  | 1  |
| P8      | 1      | 0      | 1  | 0  |
| P9      | 1      | 1      | 0  | 0  |
| P10     | 2      | 0      | 0  | 0  |

Table 1: The $Z$ matrix when $n = 2$ and $l = 2$.

---

† This approach is similar in spirit to Whitley's executable GA models (Whitley, 1992).
‡ For programming convenience we transpose the $Z$ matrix of Nix and Vose (1992).

Nix and Vose then define two mathematical operators, $F$ and $M$, where $F$ is determined from the fitness function, and $M$ depends on the mutation rate $\mu$, crossover rate $\chi$, and form of crossover and mutation used.†

With $F$ and $M$ defined, they are now able to calculate exact state transition probabilities $Q_{i,j}$ via:

$$Q_{i,j} = n! \prod_{y=0}^{r-1} \frac{\left\{ M \left[ \frac{F \phi_i}{|F \phi_i|} \right]_y \right\}^{z_{j,y}}}{z_{j,y}!} \tag{2}$$

That is, given $F$ and $M$, $Q_{i,j}$ specifies how likely it is that a simple GA in state $i$ (the current population) will be in state $j$ in the next generation.

If the mutation rate is non-zero, all states have some non-zero probability of being reached. Hence all the entries of $Q$ are non-zero making the Markov chain ergodic. It is a theorem that any ergodic Markov chain has a limiting distribution called the "steady state distribution". This implies that, in the limit of many generations (time steps), the probability of being in any state does not depend on the starting state of the GA.


## 3.2  GAFO-related Extensions

While these results provide us with useful insights about long term steady state behavior, they don't directly answer the GAFO-related questions raised earlier, such as how likely is it that the optimum will be present in the $k$th generation, or long will it take on the average before a global optimum is encountered for the first time. To answer such questions we need to concentrate on the transient behavior of the Markov chain (i.e., the time *before* steady state behavior is reached).

To see how this can be done, let us review what the $Q$ matrix tells us. First, $Q_{i,j}$ is the probability that the GA will be in state $j$ at time $t + 1$, given that it is in state $i$ at time $t$. One consequence of this is that the powers of $Q$ yield the probabilistic behavior for larger jumps in time. Thus $Q_{i,j}^k$ is the probability that the GA will be in state $j$ at time $t + k$, given that it is in state $i$ at time $t$. The matrix $Q^k$ is often referred to as the $k$ step probability transition matrix. The fact that $Q$ is ergodic (as noted earlier) implies that $Q^k$ approaches the steady state distribution as $k$ increases.

However, as we will show, many interesting GAFO-related questions can be answered using $Q^k$ before it reaches steady state. Closed form characterizations of transient $Q^k$ are difficult in general. However, considerable insight into transient behavior can be obtained computationally by computing and analyzing $Q^k$ directly. Unfortunately, the size of the $Q$ matrix for typical GAFO applications is computationally unmanageable since the number of states $N$ grows rapidly with population size $n$ and string length $l$ (see equation 1 and table 2). However, we have obtained promising initial results from models involving small values of $n$ and $l$ which appear to hold as the models scale up to more realistic sizes.

---

† In their paper they assume a standard bit flipping mutation operator and a 1-point crossover which produces a single offspring, although $M$ can be generalized to other operators.

| Popsize n | String length $l$ | | | | |
|---|---|---|---|---|---|
| | 1 | 2 | 3 | 4 | 5 |
| 1 | 2 | 4 | 8 | 16 | 32 |
| 2 | 3 | 10 | 36 | 136 | 528 |
| 3 | 4 | 20 | 120 | 816 | 5,984 |
| 4 | 5 | 35 | 330 | 3,876 | 52,360 |
| 5 | 6 | 56 | 792 | 15,504 | 376,992 |
| 6 | 7 | 84 | 1,716 | 54,264 | 2,324,784 |
| 7 | 8 | 120 | 3,432 | 170,544 | 12,620,256 |
| 8 | 9 | 165 | 6,435 | 490,314 | 61,523,748 |
| 9 | 10 | 220 | 11,440 | 1,307,504 | 273,438,880 |
| 10 | 11 | 286 | 19,448 | 3,268,760 | 1,121,099,408 |

Table 2: The value of $N$ as a function of $l$ and $n$.

## 4  Visualizing Markov Models

Before we develop our GAFO theory in more detail, we take a slight diversion to indicate a side benefit to having $Q^k$ directly available, namely to allow for visualization of the changing probability distributions $Q^k$ represents. We have been pleasantly surprised at the insight even simple visualization techniques provide concerning the effects that various GA and fitness function features have on $Q^k$. † We illustrate this briefly with an example involving visualizing $Q^k$ as an image, where the gray level of coordinate $(i,j)$ reflects the probability that the GA will move from state $i$ to state $j$ in $k$ steps. White indicates high probability, while black indicates low probability.

Figures 1-4 illustrate this for various $Q^k$ in which $n = 3$ and $l = 3$. To highlight the effects of genetic operators, Figures 1 and 2 show $Q^k$ with a flat fitness function (i.e., no selection pressure). Figure 1 shows $Q^k$ when only mutation is active ($\mu = 0.01$ and $\chi = 0.0$). The left most image, representing $Q^1$, has two interesting features. A bright diagonal line is clearly visible, indicating that significant changes in the population in one generation are very unlikely. Also, notice the interesting fractal-like patterns exhibited. This appears to be an artifact of the particular lexicographic ordering of states (given by Nix and Vose, 1992). We are currently exploring other potentially more natural orderings.

As one scans the images from left to right, notice that the changes in the probability distribution are already evident in $Q^4$ and quite striking in $Q^{10}$. The emerging vertical lines represent the particular populations at which the steady state distribution will accumulate most of its probability mass, i.e., those populations most likely to be observed when the GA settles into its dynamic equilibrium.

Figure 2 shows the change in $Q^k$ when crossover is activated ($\mu = 0.01$ and $\chi = 1.0$). It is interesting to compare $Q^1$ in Figure 1 with $Q^1$ in figure 2. The visual effect of turning on crossover is to make $Q^1$ more diffuse, matching our intuition that crossover can make larger changes more easily.

---

† For additional evidence of the usefulness of visualizing $Q$, see Horn, Goldberg & Deb (1994).

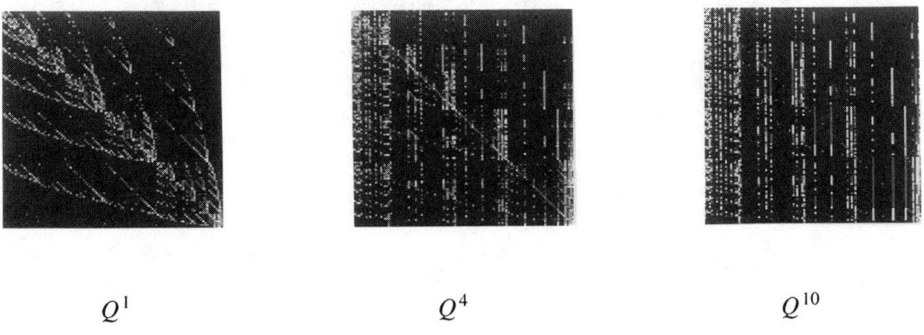

$Q^1$  $Q^4$  $Q^{10}$

Figure 1: $Q^k$ with no selection, $\mu = 0.01$ and $\chi = 0.0$.

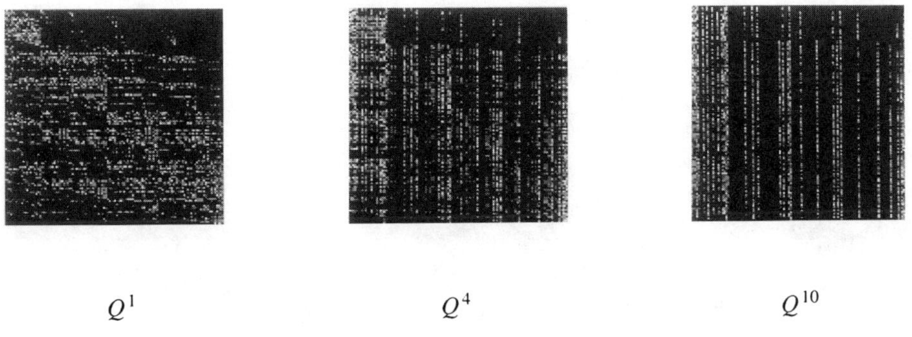

$Q^1$  $Q^4$  $Q^{10}$

Figure 2: $Q^k$ with no selection, $\mu = 0.01$ and $\chi = 1.0$.

Figure 3 illustrates the added effects of selection pressure on $Q^k$ by replacing the flat fitness function with $f(y) = integer(y) + 1$, where $integer(y)$ returns the integer equivalent of the bit string $y$. Notice the visual confirmation of our intuition that selection has an increasing effect on the probability distributions as the number of generations ($k$) increases.

Finally, figure 4 illustrates the effects of increasing the mutation rate from $\mu = 0.01$ to $\mu = 0.1$. Notice that the vertical lines in $Q^{10}$ form a different and much sharper pattern than they did in figure 3. This reflects the fact that increasing $\mu$ not only changes the steady state probability distribution, but also decreases the number of generations required to achieve a steady state distribution. Note that this does not imply that the

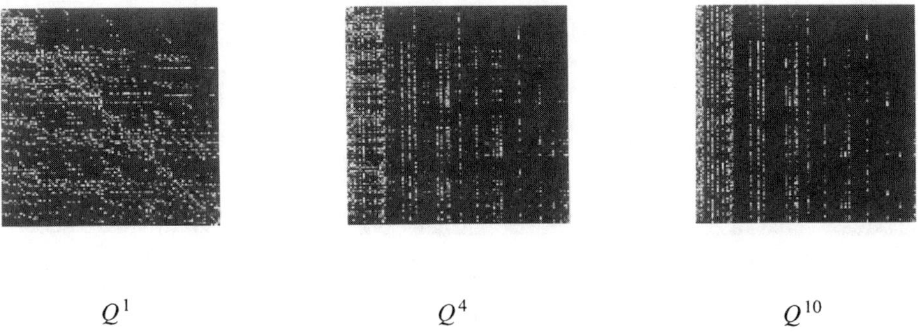

$Q^1$        $Q^4$        $Q^{10}$

Figure 3: $Q^k$ with selection, $\mu = 0.01$, and $\chi = 1.0$.

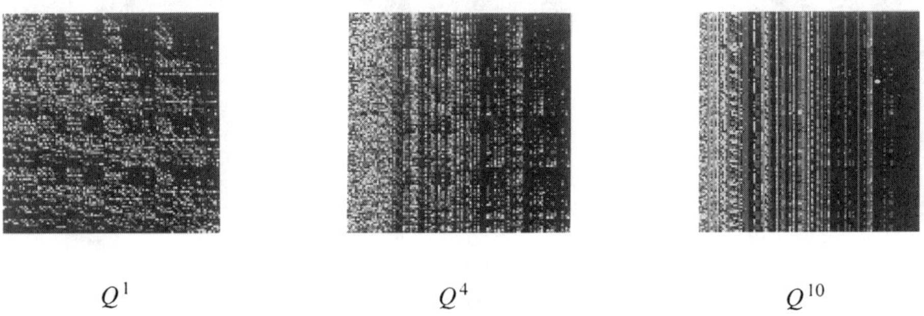

$Q^1$        $Q^4$        $Q^{10}$

Figure 4: $Q^k$ with selection, $\mu = 0.1$, and $\chi = 1.0$.

number of generations required to find the optimum has also decreased. This is easily seen by observing that in the limit of $\mu = 0.5$ the steady state distribution is reached immediately in generation 1 (i.e., $Q = Q^k$ for all $k$). In this extreme case the steady state probabilities are precisely the *a priori* probabilities given in equation 3 in the next section, since $\mu = 0.5$ is equivalent to randomly initializing a population.

## 5  GAFO THEORY

We now show how $Q^k$ can be used to characterize the transient behavior of GAs. This in turn allows us to answer many questions related to the observable behavior of finite population GAFOs. For the sake of clarity we will develop these results in two steps.

First, in this section, we will use $Q^k$ to give probabilistic answers to questions concerning the expected behavior of a GA at a particular point in time (i.e., during a particular generation), and illustrate how that can provide considerable insight into issues such as GA hardness.

Then, in section 6, we will extend these ideas to describe cumulative GA behavior extending over multiple generations, which provides *exact* answers to GAFO-related questions such as the expected waiting time until an optimum is first encountered.


### 5.1    Expected Behavior during the *k*th Generation

In this section we develop the theory which will allow us to answer questions such as:

1) What is the probability that the GA population will contain a copy of the optimum at generation $k$?

2) What is the probability that the GA population will have average fitness greater than some value at generation $k$?

3) What is the probability that the GA population will have diversity less than some value at generation $k$?

4) What is the expected best individual at generation $k$?

To answer such questions, we need only combine $Q^k$ with a set of initial conditions concerning a GA at generation 0. For this paper we make the reasonable assumption that GA populations are randomly initialized. Thus, the *a priori* probability of the GA being in state $i$ at time 0, denoted as $P(i \ @ \ 0)$, is:

$$P(i \ @ \ 0) = \frac{n\,!}{z_{i,0}! \cdots z_{i,r-1}!} \left[\frac{1}{r}\right]^n \tag{3}$$

Since there are $r = 2^l$ possible strings, each string has a probability of $r^{-1}$ of occurring, there are $n$ strings in the population, and the multinomial distribution takes into account the different ways the strings can be inserted into the population to create a unique state.

Given this, we can now compute the probability that the GA will be in a particular state $j$ at time $k$:

$$P(j \ @ \ k) = \sum_i P(i \ @ \ 0) \, Q^k_{i,j} \tag{4}$$

by simply considering the probability of each possible $k$ step transition, appropriately weighted by the *a priori* probabilities.

We can also compute probabilities over a set of states. Define a predicate $Pred_J$ and the set $J$ of states that make $Pred_J$ true. Then the probability that the GA will be in one of the states of $J$ at time $k$ is:

$$P(J \ @ \ k) = \sum_{j \in J} P(j \ @ \ k) \tag{5}$$

It is also straightforward to compute related conditional probabilities such as the probability that the GA is in one of the states of $J$ at time $t + k$, given that it is in state $i$ at time $t$:

$$P(J @ t + k \mid i @ t) = \sum_{j \in J} Q_{i,j}^k \tag{6}$$

This is easily generalized to give the probability that the GA will transition from one set of states to another. Let $Pred_I$ be another predicate over the states, and denote $I$ to be the set of states that make $Pred_I$ true. Then the probability that the GA will be in one of the states of $J$ at time $t + k$, given that it is in one of the states of $I$ at time $t$, is:

$$P(J @ t + k \mid I @ t) = \frac{\sum_{i \in I} \left[ P(i @ t)\, P(J @ t + k \mid i @ t) \right]}{P(I @ t)} \tag{7}$$

which involves a renormalization over the states indexed by $I$. Note that equation 7 simplifies to equation 6 when $I$ is composed of one state, and is similar to equation 4 when $I$ is composed of all the states.

The nice feature of this formalization is that *any* predicate over the states (populations) can be used. Thus, if we are interested in optimality, we can define the set of states that contain at least one copy of an optimum, and compute the probability that the GA will actually be in one of these states at generation $k$. We can also define predicates that select states based on average fitness, fitness variance, diversity, and so on.

In fact we can generalize further to arbitrary functions $f$ over the states and compute, for example, the expected value of that function, at time $k$:

$$E[f_k] = \sum_j P(j @ k)\, f(j) \tag{8}$$

This allows us to compute for the $k$th generation the expected best fitness value, the expected average fitness, expected diversity, or any other measure of interest that is defined over the states.

We conclude this section by illustrating how these results can be used to answer the four questions posed at the beginning of this section:

1) To compute the probability that a GA will have in the population at time $k$ at least one copy of the optimum, use equation 5 with $J$ as the set of all populations containing at least one copy of the optimum.

2) To compute the probability that a GA will have at time $k$ a population with an average fitness greater than $X$, use equation 5 with $J$ as the set of all populations having average fitness greater than $X$.

3) To compute the probability that a GA will have at time $k$ a population with diversity less than $X$, use equation 5 with $J$ as the set of all populations having diversity less than $X$.

4) To compute the expected best fitness value in the population at time $k$, use equation 8 with $f$ defined to return the maximum fitness in a given population.

## 5.2    Transient Behavior of GAs

These results can be used directly to provide insight into the effects that fitness functions, choice of operators, etc. have on the transient behavior of GAs. For example, to understand GAFO behavior better we might consider plotting the probability that a GA will have a copy of the optimum in its population at generation $k$ for $k = 1,...,K$ using equation 5 above.

Figure 5 illustrates this for the simple case of $l = 2$, $n = 5$ and the fitness function $f(y) = integer(y) + 1$. Using random search as a baseline, we show how the probability of having a copy of the optimum in the population at generation $k$ changes dynamically over time, and how these probability curves are affected by turning crossover off ($\chi = 0.0$) and on ($\chi = 1.0$) while holding the mutation rate fixed at $\mu = 0.1$.

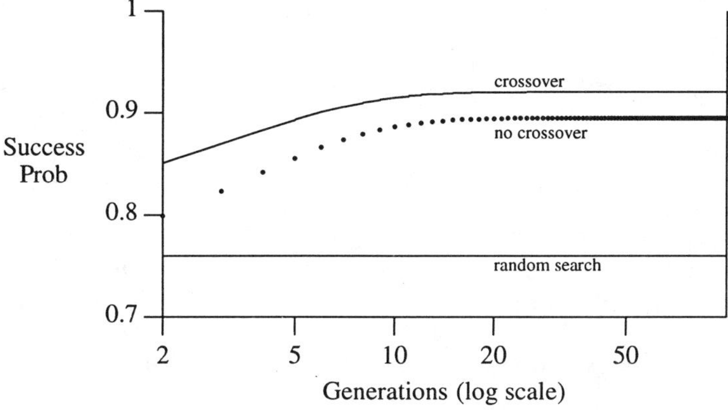


Figure 5: GA behavior on $f(y) = integer(y) + 1$

The probability curve for random search is included for comparative purposes. Since we are focusing on generation-oriented questions, we conceptualize random search as a GA which produces $n$ random strings each generation. If there is a unique optimum among the $r = 2^l$ strings, then the probability that this random process will contain at least one copy of the optimum string in generation $k$ is constant and given by:

$$1 - \left[ \frac{r-1}{r} \right]^n$$

There are several interesting observations one can draw from the probability curves in figure 5. First, note that these are not cumulative probabilities indicating whether or not the optimum has been encountered at least once by generation $k$. Rather, they predict the likelihood of generation $k$ containing a copy of the optimum regardless of whether or not the optimum appeared in an earlier generation. These curves confirm our intuition that GAs settle into a dynamic steady state in which there are no changes in the probability of producing an optimal string.

They also confirm our notion that there are situations in which crossover clearly improves the likelihood of generating optimal strings, and that even without crossover a

GA with moderate mutation rates is more likely to do so than random search.

These probability curves can also be used to study the effect that different classes of fitness functions have on the "hardness" of the situation. To illustrate this, we simply permute the fitness values assigned to the $r = 2^l$ strings by the original fitness function. In the previous example $f$ assigned the values $\{1,2,3,4\}$ to the strings $\{00,01,10,11\}$ respectively. Permuting the 4 fitness values produces $4! = 24$ distinct fitness functions.

Although not true in general, in this simple 2-bit case the 24 fitness functions fall into three equivalence classes, each containing eight functions producing identical probability curves.† Figures 6 and 7 show the corresponding curves for the two equivalence classes not containing the fitness function used in figure 5.

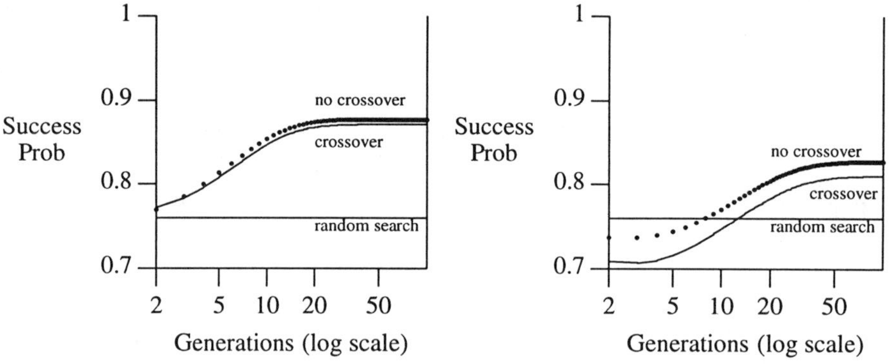


Figure 6: GA behavior on class 2.        Figure 7: GA behavior on class 3.

The first thing to note is that crossover only clearly helps on the first of the three equivalence classes. The reason for this is not clear until one considers both the effects of crossover and fitness on this equivalence class. It turns out that the strings that have 2nd and 3rd highest fitness can be combined via crossover to yield the optimum string. This is not true of the other two equivalence classes. This supports our intuitions that crossover will exploit useful building blocks when they are present, but can actually degrade performance when they are not present.

It is easy to show that none of these three equivalence classes obtained by permuting the values $\{1,2,3,4\}$ are "deceptive" in the sense of static schema analysis (Goldberg, 1987) as indicated in table 3.

However, note that while a GA is uniformly better than random search on the first two equivalence classes, its probability curves are actually worse than random search on class 3 in the early generations. This is an example of a situation where the fitness landscape is leading the GA away from the optimum initially, but the GA subsequently recovers. Clearly the dynamics of the situation are quite subtle and complex. If we observed a GA over the first 10 generations, we might conclude that we have a "GA-hard" situation, whereas running a GA longer might shift that perception.

---

† For the sake of brevity we omit an explanation of why this occurs, other than to note that it is caused by a relationship between fitness rankings of strings and the Hamming distance between them.

| Class | Fitness | Function | | | | Schema | Fitness | |
| --- | --- | --- | --- | --- | --- | --- | --- | --- |
| | f(00) | f(01) | f(10) | f(11) | f(0*) | f(1*) | f(*0) | f(*1) |
| 1 | 1 | 2 | 3 | 4 | 1.5 | 3.5 | 2.0 | 3.0 |
| 2 | 2 | 1 | 3 | 4 | 1.5 | 3.5 | 2.5 | 2.5 |
| 3 | 3 | 1 | 2 | 4 | 2.0 | 3.0 | 2.5 | 2.5 |

Table 3: Static schema analysis for the three equivalence classes.

## 5.3  Dynamic Properties of Deception

The fact that we were seeing interesting dynamic behavior on three classes of non-deceptive functions lead us naturally to apply these transient GA analysis tools to the Type I and Type II deceptive problems defined by Goldberg (1987). Figures 8 and 9 illustrate the performance of a GA with $n = 5$, $l = 2$, $\mu = 0.01$ and $\chi = 1.0$.

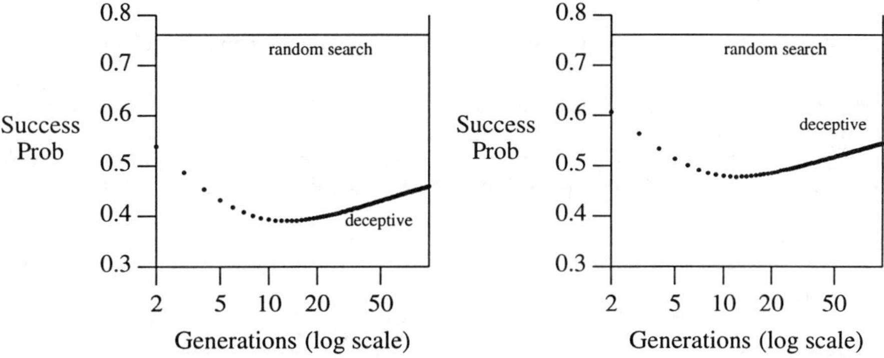


Figure 8: Type I deception.  Figure 9: Type II deception.

It is interesting to note that the deceptive functions yield a ''U''-shaped curve that is very similar to that shown by Goldberg, in which he considers the expected proportion of the optimum string in the population. The explanation for this is that the expected proportion of the optimum string at generation $k$ directly effects the probability that the GA population will contain at least one copy of that optimum at generation $k$. If the expected proportion is high (low), so is the associated probability that we are measuring.

Note that, unlike the results obtained in the previous section, the probability curves of the GA in this case are uniformly worse than random search. This certainly confirms our notion that these deceptive problems create hard situations for simple GAs.

This same analysis can be used to show that there are other classes of fitness functions which create similar difficulties for simple GAs, but which are not deceptive in the static sense. We illustrate this by modifying the fitness value of one string in both of the deceptive functions so that they are statically non-deceptive. However, care was taken to ensure that the ranking of strings by fitness was still the same. The intuition here was that such a minimal change was not likely to significantly change the dynamic behavior of a simple GA. Table 4 summarizes both the original deceptive functions as well as their modified non-deceptive counterparts.

| Class | f(00) | Fitness Function f(01) | f(10) | f(11) |
|---|---|---|---|---|
| TypeI | 1.0 | 1.05 | 0.1 | 1.1 |
| NotTypeI | 1.0 | 1.05 | 0.975 | 1.1 |
| TypeII | 1.0 | 0.9 | 0.5 | 1.1 |
| NotTypeII | 1.0 | 0.9 | 0.85 | 1.1 |

| Class | f(0*) | Schema Fitness f(1*) | f(*0) | f(*1) |
|---|---|---|---|---|
| TypeI | 1.025 | 0.6 | 0.55 | 1.075 |
| NotTypeI | 1.025 | 1.0375 | 0.9875 | 1.075 |
| TypeII | 0.95 | 0.8 | 0.75 | 1.0 |
| NotTypeII | 0.95 | 0.975 | 0.925 | 1.0 |

Table 4: Static schema analysis for deceptive and non-deceptive problems

Figures 10 and 11 illustrate the behavior of a simple GA on these two non-deceptive functions in comparison with the deceptive functions. If we consider situations in which GAs perform uniformly worse than random search as one possible definition of "GA hard", we see that statically deceptive functions are not the only sources of difficulty.

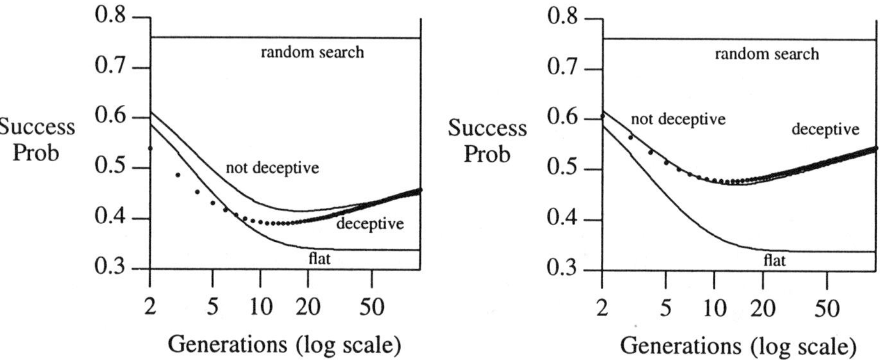


Figure 10: Type I deception      Figure 11: Type II deception

To further illustrate this point, we allowed a GA to attempt to find the hardest such function in the following sense. We fixed the optimum at string "11", with a fitness value of 1.0. We then allowed a GA to modify the fitness values of the other three strings in the range (0, 1) and rewarded values that generated low probability curves. The result was an "almost" flat fitness function (where all strings have fitness as close as possible to 1.0). The resulting probability curve for this function is also illustrated in figures 10 and 11. Note that the probability curve for this nearly flat fitness function is in fact lower than the probability curves for the other four problems in table 4, especially in later generations. The difficulty with it, of course, is that there is no differential feedback whatsoever. On the other hand, if one were measuring difficulty in terms of "best so far" curves, this would certainly look "easy" since near-optimal solutions are abundant already in the first generation.

Finally, we were curious to see how sensitive these results were to population size, since increasing population size is a standard way to overcome low-order deceptiveness. Figure 12 illustrates typical results obtained with increasing population sizes, confirming our expectations that the dynamic characteristics of deception remain, but that the difficulty of the situation (as measured by the probability curves) decreases.

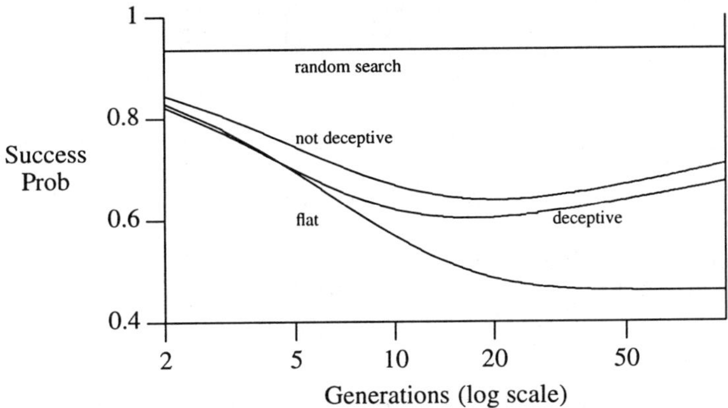


Figure 12: Type II deception with $n = 10$, $\mu = 0.01$, $\chi = 1.0$

## 6   WAITING TIME ANALYSIS

The probability curve analysis of the previous section provides some interesting and important insights into the non-linear interactions of the various components of a GAFO situation. However, as we have seen, it doesn't precisely capture "hardness" in a form that a GAFO practitioner would necessarily care about. Generally, such a person would be much more interested in ''best so far'' curves and in knowing how long the GA would have to run on average before first encountering the optimum. In this section we extend the theory developed in the previous sections to provide exact answers to such questions.

### 6.1   Expected Waiting Time Theory

The theory extension needed to obtain the expected waiting time until an event of interest is first observed is based on the observation that the $Q$ matrix can be used to compute ''mean first passage times'' for going from state $i$ to state $j$ (for a nice discussion of this, see Winston 1991). Questions involving waiting times to convergence using a 1-bit Markov model with mutation and selection were considered in the paper by

Goldberg and Segrest (1987). Our work extends these earlier formulations.

More precisely, we wish to compute the length of time that it takes (on the average) to reach state $j$ for the first time, given that the process is currently in state $i$. Answering such questions involves solving the set of simultaneous equations:

$$m_{i,j} = Q_{i,j} + \sum_{k \neq j} Q_{i,k} (1 + m_{k,j}) \tag{9}$$

where $m_{i,j}$ denotes the mean first passage time from state $i$ to state $j$. To understand the equation, consider transitioning from state $i$ to $j$ in one move. This occurs with probability $Q_{i,j}$ and requires only one step. However, suppose the GA transitions from state $i$ to state $k$, where $k$ is not equal to $j$. This occurs with probability $Q_{i,k}$ and requires one step. However, there now remain $m_{k,j}$ steps to state $j$.

As before, if we are interested in a set $J$ of states, we can compute the mean first passage time for the GA to first enter that set of states, given that it is currently outside that set:

$$m_{i,J} = \sum_{j \in J} Q_{i,j} + \sum_{k \notin J} Q_{i,k} (1 + m_{k,J}) \tag{10}$$

where $m_{i,J}$ denotes the mean first passage time from state $i$ to any of the states in set $J$, and $i$ is not in $J$. This is very similar to equation 9, with the exception that the probability of entering state $J$ in one step is simply the sum of the probabilities of entering each state within $J$.

Once this system of simultaneous equations is solved, we can calculate the "expected waiting time" to reach a state in $J$, given a random initial state, via:

$$EWT(J) = \sum_{i \in J} P(i \ @ \ 0) \, 0 + \sum_{i \notin J} P(i \ @ \ 0) \, m_{i,J} \tag{11}$$

There are two parts to Equation 11. The first part reflects the possibility that a random initial population is in state $J$, and hence has a zero waiting time. The second part reflects the mean passage time from initial populations not in $J$, to a state in $J$. Clearly this simplifies to:

$$EWT(J) = \sum_{i \notin J} P(i \ @ \ 0) \, m_{i,J} \tag{12}$$

As we noted in section 5, equation 12 hold for any set of states $J$, and thus can be used to provide expected waiting times for a variety of "interesting" events such as: the first time an optimum is encountered, the first time the average fitness of the population exceeds a given threshold, the first time the population diversity falls below a given threshold, etc.

### 6.2    Expected Waiting Times for GAFOs

Clearly, an interesting GAFO event involves the first time an optimal string is produced. Following the same approach as section 5, we define $J$ to be the set of states containing at least one copy of the optimum string. Then $EWT(J)$ is the expected number of generations until the optimum is first encountered. To us, this scalar quantity is a natural measure of the difficulty of a GAFO situation, with longer *EWTs* representing more difficult situations. We explore this view in more detail in this section.

As a starting point, table 5 provides the *EWTs* for the same three equivalence classes of fitness functions studied in section 5 and illustrated in figures 5-7. Recall that in these situations $l = 2$, $n = 5$ and $\mu = 0.1$.

| Class | No Crossover | Crossover | Random |
|-------|--------------|-----------|--------|
| 1 | 0.71 | 0.52 | 0.31 |
| 2 | 0.89 | 0.75 | 0.31 |
| 3 | 1.42 | 1.19 | 0.31 |

Table 5: $EWT(J)$ for $l = 2$ and $n = 5$.

There are several interesting observations about the $EWT$ results in table 5. First, note that the $EWT$ analysis agrees with the probability curve analysis (figures 5-7) with respect to ranking the "difficulty" of the equivalence classes. However, there are also some striking disagreements. Notice that, unlike the probability curve analysis, crossover improves the situation (decreases $EWT(J)$) on all three classes. It is also interesting to note that random search yields the best $EWT$ performance on all three of these classes of 2-bit functions.†

One would expect that the $EWT(J)$ results should be highly correlated with the corresponding probability curves. After all, if a GA always has a higher probability of seeing the optimum at every generation than random search on some particular problem (e.g., figure 5), then shouldn't we expect the GA to first see the optimum in less time? Similarly, if a GA with crossover yields lower probability curves (e.g., figures 6 and 7), shouldn't this be reflected in table 5?

To understand better this apparent contradiction consider two simple Markov processes, $R_{explore}$ and $R_{exploit}$ whose transition matrices are given by:

| | $Q_{R_{explore}}$ | | $Q_{R_{exploit}}$ | |
|---|------|------|------|------|
| | **I** | **J** | **I** | **J** |
| **I** | 0.50 | 0.50 | 0.75 | 0.25 |
| **J** | 0.50 | 0.50 | 0.25 | 0.75 |

Table 6: The transition matrices.

$R_{explore}$ is the more explorative of the two because its probability of going from one state to a different state is higher than $R_{exploit}$, which is more likely to remain in a given state. For simplicity of illustration, we assume each of the processes has just two states $I$ and $J$ in which state $J$ is analogous to being in the $J$ set of states containing the optimum, as discussed earlier. We also assume that each of the processes has identical *a priori* probabilities of being in one of the two states. Hence, any behavioral differences are due only to the different $Q$ matrices (transition probabilities).

---

† Again, random search is equivalent to running the GA with $\mu = 0.5$. In this case crossover and selection do not affect the results.

From equation 4 we have the probability of being in state $J$ at time $k$ given by:

$$P(J \text{ @ } k) = \sum_s P(s \text{ @ } 0)\, Q^k_{s,J}$$

If we assign equal *a priori* probabilities to both states, this simplifies to:

$$P(J \text{ @ } k) = 0.5 \sum_s Q^k_{s,J}$$

Since each of the $Q$ matrices are symmetric, so are their powers $Q^k$. Hence their columns (as well as their rows) sum to 1.0, leading to a further simplification:

$$P(J \text{ @ } k) = 0.5$$

Hence, in spite of their different transition probabilities, both processes have identical probability curves with respect to their likelihood of being in state $J$ at time $k$, namely, at any given time each process has a 50/50 chance of being in state $J$.

However, when we calculate expected waiting times until these processes *first* enter state $J$, we observe something quite different. Using equations 10, we compute the mean first passage time from state $I$ to state $J$ for process $R_{explore}$:

$$m_{I,J} = 0.5 + (0.5)(1.0 + m_{I,J})$$

the solution of which yields $m_{I,J} = 2.0$. The expected waiting time until state $J$ is first encountered is then easily calculated via equation 12 in which the mean first passage times are normalized by the 0.5 probability of being in state $I$ at time zero, yielding $EWT_{explore}(J) = 1.0$.

Similar calculations yield an $EWT(J)$ of 2.0 for $R_{exploit}$, producing the curious situation that, although each process has a 50/50 chance of being in state $J$ at any given instant in time, $EWT_{explore}(J) < EWT_{exploit}(J)$.

To see why that is the case, consider the sequence of states visited by one of these random processes over time:

$$s_1, s_2, s_3, ..., s_k, \cdots$$

Both processes have a 50/50 chance of starting out in state $J$. If that's the case, then we have identical $EWT(J)$s of zero. However, if both processes start out in state $I$, then $R_{explore}$ is much more likely to switch to state $J$, resulting in a shorter average waiting time until the *first J* occurs in the sequence.

Interestingly, this effect can be made even more dramatic by changing the *a priori* probabilities of being in states $I$ and $J$. For example, consider the effects of setting $P(I \text{ @ } 0) = 0.25$ and $P(J \text{ @ } 0) = 0.75$ while keeping the two $Q$ matrices the same as before. In this case $P_{explore}(J \text{ @ } k) < P_{exploit}(J \text{ @ } k)$ while their relative rankings with respect to $EWT(J)$ remains unchanged (we omit the proof for the sake of brevity). That is, even though $R_{explore}$ is less likely to be in state $J$ at any given time than $R_{exploit}$ is, $R_{explore}$ is still more likely to produce the *first J* because of its higher switching rate.

In summary, this section provides a clear picture of the relative merits of probability curve analysis and $EWT$ analysis. Probability curves provide insight into the dynamic non-linear interactions of GAFO behavior, but are not good predictors of traditional measures of GAFO performance. $EWT$s, on the other hand, collapse all of this behavior into a single figure of merit which is directly related to the usual notions of GAFO performance.

### 6.3    Analyzing GAFO *EWT*s

If *EWT* is a useful figure of merit, then it is important to understand how various features of GAFO situations affect *EWT*. Characterizing these effects will in turn provide insights (and make predictions) about how to improve GAFO performance. We present some preliminary results in this section.

#### 6.3.1    The Importance of Exploration for GAFOs

Finding a balance between exploration and exploitation has been an important theme of GA research from the very beginning. Achieving such a balance, however, is difficult since it is a complex non-linear function of selection, representation, operators, and fitness landscape. One of the frequent empirical observations is that GAFO performance can be improved by using higher mutation rates and more disruptive crossover operators (e.g., uniform crossover) than traditional analysis suggests. The preceding section indicates why: *EWT* measures of performance encourage more exploration than measures involving maximizing total (or average) payoff.

The previous $R_{explore}$-$R_{exploit}$ example provides an intuitive illustration of how too much exploitation is bad for *EWT*s. Table 5, given earlier, provided a more concrete example: for a fixed mutation rate of $u = 0.1$, adding crossover consistently improved *EWT*, but in all cases these "traditional" settings were outperformed by random search. Our intuition was that, for these simple 2-bit problems, the optimal exploration/exploitation ratio was much higher than we might expect, but that this ratio should decrease as a function of $l$.

To test this hypothesis, we used *EWT* analysis to estimate the "optimal" mutation rate (in the sense of minimizing *EWT*) for a variety of situations involving the fitness function $f(y) = integer(y) + 1$. We kept $n = 2$ and $\chi = 1.0$, but allowed $l$ to range from 2 to 5. We then estimated the optimal mutation rate by calculating $EWT(J)$ for every $\mu$ from 0.01 to 0.99, in increments of 0.01. Table 7 gives the optimum $\mu$ for each $l$.

| $l$ | 2 | 3 | 4 | 5 |
|---|---|---|---|---|
| optimal $\mu$ | 0.68 | 0.54 | 0.44 | 0.36 |
| *EWT* of GA with optimal $\mu$ | 1.19 | 3.25 | 7.18 | 14.52 |
| *EWT* of RAND ($\mu$=0.5) | 1.29 | 3.26 | 7.25 | 15.25 |

Table 7: Optimum $\mu$ for $EWT(J)$ as $l$ increases.

As expected, the advantage of high mutation rates falls off quickly as a function of increasing $l$. Notice also that with these "optimal" mutation rates, the GA is now slightly better than random search, but accomplishes this by using much higher levels of mutation than are typically used. This raises the interesting, but unconfirmed conjecture, that these optimal mutation rates will approach the traditional $1/l$ heuristic setting as $l$ increases.

The optimal mutation rates in table 7 that are greater than 0.50 are a bit surprising at first. With $\mu = 1.0$ we are essentially complementing each string in the population. For very small problems there exists a reasonable chance that the complement of the solution will appear in an early generation. Hence, a complement operator can improve *EWT*s.

As $l$ increases, this effect quickly starts to diminish, although interestingly, a complement operator can also be quite effective for certain classes of deceptive problems.

### 6.3.2  Interacting Effects of Crossover and Mutation

One can also use these models to analyze the interacting effects of crossover and mutation on *EWT*s. Table 8 summarizes a simple example using fitness function $f(y) = integer(y) + 1$ with $n = 5$ and $l = 2$:

| $\mu$ | $\chi = 0.0$ | $\chi = 1.0$ |
|-------|-------|-------|
| 0.5 | 0.31 | 0.31 |
| 0.1 | 0.71 | 0.52 |
| 0.01 | 5.07 | 2.65 |

Table 8: Effect on $EWT(J)$ of $\chi$ as $\mu$ decreases.

Note how crossover becomes increasingly important as $\mu$ decreases. However, for these small 2-bit problems, crossover is unable to increase exploration enough to maintain or improve on the *EWT* values obtained at higher mutation rates. Although we have not had time to verify it, we would expect to see a more dominant role for crossover as $l$ increases.

### 6.3.3  Effects of Scaling

A well-known property of proportional selection is its sensitivity to simple linear scaling of the fitness function. If we present a GA with two unknown functions $f$ and $g = f + 100$, the GA will generally converge more rapidly on $f$ than on $g$. This is easily shown using *EWT* analysis Table 9 illustrates this by duplicating the analysis in table 8 with only one change: the original fitness function $f$ is now $g(y) = f(y) + 100$.

| $\mu$ | $\chi = 0.0$ | $\chi = 1.0$ |
|-------|-------|-------|
| 0.5 | 0.31 | 0.31 |
| 0.1 | 0.92 | 0.71 |
| 0.01 | 9.52 | 6.25 |

Table 9: Effect of scaling on $EWT(J)$.

Compared with table 8, this situation is clearly more difficult as measured by *EWT* and illustrates why most GAFOs which use proportional selection also use some form of dynamic fitness scaling in order to "normalize" selection pressure.

### 6.3.4    Effects of Building Blocks

One can also study the effects of "building blocks" on *EWT*. To illustrate, we duplicated the analysis of table 8 with only one change: the fitness value of $f$ ("01") was increased by 1. Since the optimum string is "11", the idea was to equally reward both "01" and "10" and set the stage for crossover. Table 10 summarized the results.

| $\mu$ | $\chi = 0.0$ | $\chi = 1.0$ |
|---|---|---|
| 0.5 | 0.31 | 0.31 |
| 0.1 | 0.69 | 0.50 |
| 0.01 | 5.01 | 2.45 |

Table 10: Effect of building blocks on $EWT(J)$.

Clearly, as the mutation rates decrease and crossover plays a more dominant role, rewarding good building blocks uniformly improves *EWT* (in comparison with table 8). In this particular example the improvements are quite small and one might be tempted to question their statistical significance. However, recall that this is not data derived from empirical averages. These are exact values (subject to rounding errors) computed directly from the theory.


## 7   Summary and Discussion

This paper describes our initial exploration of transient Markov chain analysis as the basis for a stronger GAFO theory. Although closed form analysis is difficult in general, useful insights can be obtained by means of both visual and computational exploration of the transient behavior of the models. We are quite pleased with the initial progress and are optimistic of the future potential of this approach.

There are clearly a number of concerns, primary of which is the scalability of the results. So far, we have observed fairly consistent results as we increase both string length and population size. However, much more work is required to scale up to more realistic values of $n$ and $l$.

There are a variety of directions we are exploring. There are many other visualization techniques which have the potential for further elucidation of these models. In addition to expected waiting times, the variance of the waiting times is an important measure which can also be derived from the models. It is also possible to study the effects of other operators (e.g., uniform crossover) and other GA features such as population size, rank selection, and so on.

It would also be nice to see how well fitness correlation (Manderick et al., 1991), which takes into account aspects of the fitness function, representation, and the genetic operators, predicts *EWT* performance.

An interesting future possibility would be to create Markov models of other evolutionary algorithms and standard hill climbers, and then allow a GA to find those problems that are easy for GAs and hard for hillclimbers (or vice versa), using the *EWT* performance measure!

## Acknowledgements

We would like to thank Dr. Daniel Carr for suggesting visualization techniques, and Dr. Marty Fischer for suggestions on Markov Chain analysis.

## References

Davis, T. E., & Principe, J. C. (1991) A simulated annealing like convergence theory for the simple genetic algorithm. *Proceedings of the 4th International Conference on Genetic Algorithms*, San Diego, 174-181.

De Jong, K. A. (1992) GAs are not function optimizers. *Proceedings of the Foundations of Genetic Algorithms Workshop*. Vail, CO: Morgan Kaufmann.

De Jong, K. A. (1975) *An analysis of the behavior of a class of genetic adaptive systems.* Doctoral Thesis, Department of Computer and Communication Sciences. University of Michigan, Ann Arbor.

Goldberg, D. E. (1987) Simple genetic algorithms and the minimal, deceptive problem. Chapter 6 in *Genetic Algorithms and Simulated Annealing*, Lawrence Davis (ed.), Morgan Kaufmann.

Goldberg, D. E., & Segrest, P., (1987) Finite Markov chain analysis of genetic algorithms. *Proceedings of the 2nd International Conference on Genetic Algorithms*, Cambridge, 1-8.

Holland, J. H. (1975) *Adaptation in natural and artificial systems.* Ann Arbor, Michigan: The University of Michigan Press.

Horn, J. (1993) Finite Markov chain analysis of genetic algorithms with niching. *Proceedings of the 5th International Conference on Genetic Algorithms*, San Mateo, CA: Morgan Kaufmann, 110-117.

Horn, J., Goldberg, D. E., & Deb, K., (1994) Implicit niching in a learning classifier system: nature's way. *Evolutionary Computation*, Volume 2, #1, 37-66.

Juliany, J., & Vose, M. D., (1994) The genetic algorithm fractal. To appear in *Evolutionary Computation*, Volume 2, #1.

Manderick, B., de Weger, M., & Spiessens, P., (1991) The genetic algorithm and the structure of the fitness landscape. *Proceedings of the 4th International Conference on Genetic Algorithms*, San Diego, 143-150.

Mafoud, S. (1993) Finite Markov chain models of an alternative selection strategy for the genetic algorithm. *Complex Systems*, 7 (2), 155-170.

Nix, A. E., & Vose, M. D., (1992) Modelling genetic algorithms with Markov chains. *Annals of Mathematics and Artificial Intelligence* #5, 79 - 88.

Rudolph, G. (1994) Massively parallel simulated annealing and its relation to evolutionary algorithms. *Evolutionary Computation*, Volume 1, #4.

Suzuki, J. (1993) A Markov chain analysis on a genetic algorithm. *Proceedings of the 5th International Conference on Genetic Algorithms*, Urbana-Champaign, 146-153.

Vose, M. (1992) Modeling simple genetic algorithms. *Proceedings of the Foundations of Genetic Algorithms Workshop*, Vail, CO: Morgan Kaufmann, 63-74.

Whitley, D. (1992) An executable model of a simple genetic algorithm, *Proceedings of the Foundations of Genetic Algorithms Workshop*, Vail, CO: Morgan Kaufmann, 45-62.

Winston, W. (1991) Operations Research: Applications and Algorithms, 2nd Edition, PWS-Kent Publishing Company, Boston MA.

# Predictive Models Using Fitness Distributions of Genetic Operators


**John J. Grefenstette**
Navy Center for Artificial Intelligence
Code 5514
Naval Research Laboratory
Washington, DC 20375-5337
E-mail: GREF@AIC.NRL.NAVY.MIL


## Abstract


An important goal of the theory of genetic algorithms is to build predictive models of how well genetic algorithms are expected to perform, given a representation, a fitness landscape, and a set of genetic operators. This paper attempts to provide pieces of such a theory, in the form of tools that predict the behavior of genetic algorithms based on assumptions concerning the *fitness distribution* of genetic operators. The fitness distribution of an operator describes the distribution of fitness values of individuals resulting from an operator application as a function of the fitness of the original individual. It is shown that in some cases, the mean of the fitness distribution for genetic operators may be described by simple functions of the fitness of the parents. For these cases, predictive models of population fitness can be derived.


## 1  INTRODUCTION

The term *genetic algorithm* refers to a large class of algorithms that differ in a number of important design parameters, including the representation, the reproduction policy, and the genetic operators. One goal of the foundations of genetic algorithms is to understand the relationships between the performance of genetic algorithms and the design parameters of the algorithm. This paper attempts to make some progress by relating the performance of the algorithm to certain abstract properties of the genetic operators. We develop some tools that predict the behavior of genetic algorithms based on assumptions concerning the *fitness distribution* of genetic operators. The fitness distribution of an operator describes the distribution of fitness values of the individuals that result from an operator application as a function of the fitness of the original individual. When more fully developed, this analysis could be used to guide a user in exploring the space of representations and genetic operators, as shown in Figure 1.

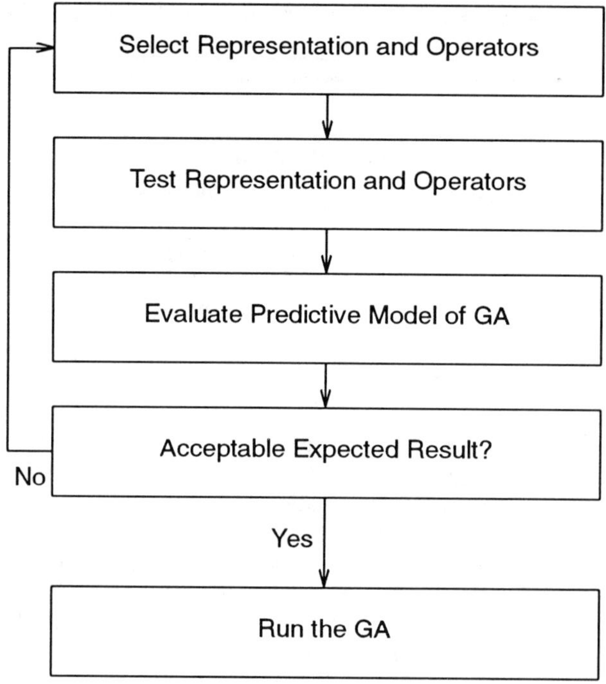


Figure 1: Predicting GA Performance

Throughout this paper, we treat genetic algorithms as heuristic function optimization routines (GAFO's, see De Jong (1992)). We focus on predictions about the mean population fitness, so we will not be concerned with questions about whether a genetic algorithm reaches the global optimum except in the indirect sense that the population average is a lower bound on the best value found by the genetic algorithm.

The genetic algorithm considered is a generational genetic algorithm, using proportional selection, and one or more operators such as crossover and mutation. We assume a large, finite population. For the most part, we will not be concerned with details about the genetic operators; it is hoped that the methods presented can be applied to any genetic operator. The restriction to proportional selection and generational reproduction is for convenience; future work could extend this method to other styles of genetic algorithms.

This work is closely related to several other recent efforts to derive predictive models based on statistical features of genetic operators. Kauffman (1989) describes a family of fitness landscapes for which he provides an analysis of how *rugged* the landscape is. Based on Kaufman's work, Manderick, de Weger and Spiessens (1991) show examples of strong relationships between overall performance of genetic algorithms and statistical features of the fitness landscape. Baeck (1992, 1995) analyzes the convergence rate of simple genetic algorithms, based on probabilities that mutation produces a superior individual. Muehlenbein and Schlierkamp-Voosen (1993) provide a predictive model for a "breeder" genetic algorithm. Altenberg (1994, 1995) provides a generalized mathematical framework for these ideas.

This paper develops a general predictive model for the population fitness based on correlations between the fitness of the parents and the fitness of the offspring. We focus on some alternatives for measuring the suitability of a given representation and operator set for a given problem. We abstract away most of the details of particular landscapes and genetic operators with the hope of making the model generally applicable to unknown functions.

The remainder of the paper is organized as follows: Section 2 introduces the key quantities to be used in building predictive models of convergence. Section 3 defines the central notion of the paper, the fitness distribution of a genetic operator. Preliminary data is provided that suggests that it is often possible to find simple relationships between the fitness of the parents and the expected fitness of the offspring. Section 4 gives a predictive model of convergence, based on assumptions of a linear relationship between the mean of the fitness distribution and the fitness of the parent. Section 5 extends the analysis to selection methods that include scaling. Section 6 presents a sample application of the approach to predict the performance of actual genetic algorithms. Section 7 discusses directions for extending this approach further.

## 2  PREDICTIVE MODELS OF POPULATION FITNESS

We are primarily concerned with deriving predictive models for the performance of genetic algorithms (Holland, 1975). This paper focuses on deriving "equations of motion" for the mean population fitness. A fundamental quantity for this purpose is called the *response to selection* (Muehlenbein and Schlierkamp-Voosen, 1993), defined as

$$R(t+1) = M(t+1) - M(t) \tag{1}$$

where $M(t)$ is the mean fitness[1] of the population at time $t$. The definition of $M(t)$ is

$$M(t) = \frac{1}{N}\sum_{i=1}^{N} f(x_i, t) \tag{2}$$

---

[1] Unless otherwise noted, fitness will be considered identical to the user-defined objective function, and is intended to be maximized by the genetic algorithm.

where $N$ is the population size and $f(x_i,t)$ is the fitness of the $i^{th}$ element of the population at time $t$. While our methods are equivalent to computing the response to selection, we will compute the expected mean fitness in the next generation directly, using the formula:

$$M(t+1) = \frac{1}{N}\sum_{i=1}^{N} C(x_i,t)D(x_i,t)$$

where $M(t)$ is the mean fitness of population at time $t$, $C(x,t)$ number of offspring of $x$ at time $t$, and $D(x,t)$ is the average (absolute) fitness of offspring of $x$ at time $t$. For now, we are make the simplifying assumption that $C$ and $D$ are statistically independent random variables. This assumption is safe for standard mutation operators, since the absolute fitness of the offspring of an individual under mutation is independent of the relative fitness, which determines the number of offspring. However, this independence assumption need not hold in general for crossover operators, since both the number of offspring and the fitness of the offspring of crossover depend on the rest of the current population. A future study will examine this assumption in more detail.[2] Treating $C$ and $D$ as independent random variables, we have:

$$E[M(t+1)] = \frac{1}{N}\sum_{i=1}^{N} E[C(x_i,t)]\,E[D(x_i,t)] \tag{3}$$

By iterating Eq. (3), we can produce predictions about the progress of the mean population fitness.

This paper deals exclusively with genetic algorithms that use proportional selection (possibly with scaling). For proportional reproduction, we have:

$$E[C(x_i,t)] = \frac{f(x_i,t)}{M(t)} \tag{4}$$

The remainder of the paper explores the impact of the final term above, $E[D(x,t)]$, the expected fitness of an individual's offspring.


## 3   FITNESS DISTRIBUTIONS OF GENETIC OPERATORS

One way to get a handle on the expected fitness of an individual's offspring is to observe that

$$E[D(x,t)] = \sum_{op} p_{op}\, E[D_{op}(f(x,t))] \tag{5}$$

where $p_{op}$ is the probability of applying operator $op$ and $E[D_{op}(y)]$ is the expected fitness of applying operator $op$ to an individual[3] with fitness $y$. This leads to the central

---

[2] See (Altenberg, 1995) for a discussion that removes this assumption.

[3] Here we are assuming that the genetic algorithm applies exactly one operator to each offspring, and that the operator probabilities sum to 1. For this purpose it is convenient to treat *cloning*, i.e., copying without applying mutation or crossover, as a distinct operator.

question in this paper:

*What is the expected effect of a genetic operator, as a function of the fitness of the original structure?*

Each $k$-ary genetic operator can be associated with an *operator mapping:*

$$Op : X^k \rightarrow X \tag{6}$$

from $k$-tuples of parents to offspring, where $X$ represents the universe of individuals. The mapping is typically one-to-many, since operators are typically stochastic. For example, a given mutation operator may produce a number of different offspring by mutating different randomly selecting positions within the parent, or crossover may produce different offspring by selecting different random crossover points. Operators that produce more than one offspring can also be be viewed as inducing a one-to-many mapping.

Each operator mapping also induces a mapping in the range, which we call the *fitness distribution* of the operator:

$$FD_{op}(F_p) = Prob\,(F_c = \text{fitness of offspring} \mid \text{parents have mean fitness } F_p) \tag{7}$$

That is, the fitness distribution of an operator $FD_{op}$ is the family of probability distributions of the fitness of the offspring, indexed by the mean fitness of the parents. While the distributions in $FD_{op}$ may be quite complex, it may be possible to learn something by estimating important features of those distributions, such as the mean or variance. In the remainder of this paper, we will focus on the mean of the fitness distribution (or $MFD$ ), as a function of the fitness of the operand.

We begin by examining the fitness distributions of simple genetic operators on some sample problems. All functions in the test suite use a binary representation. The sample problems include forms of the De Jong test suite:

$f_1$ (100 bits) is a simple 10-dimensional parabola.

$f_2$ (24 bits) is a 2-dimensional Rosenbrock saddle function.

$f_3$ (50 bits) is a 5-dimensional unimodal step function.

$f_4$ (240 bits) is a 30-dimensional quadratic function with Gaussian noise.

$f_5$ (34 bits) is the 2-dimensional Shekel's foxhole function, a highly multi-modal landscape..

In addition, our test suite includes:

$f_6$ (100 bits) is a form of multimodal Rastrigin function considered by Muehlenbein and Schlierkamp-Voosen (1993):

$$f_6(x) = 1.0 - (nA + \sum_{i=1}^{n} (x_i^2 - A\,\cos(2\pi x_i)))\,/\,B\,;$$

where $-5.12 \leq x_i < 5.12$ in increments of 0.01 (i.e., 10 bits per $x_i$), and $n=10$. The constants $A$ and $B$ were chosen to produce a minimum near 0.0 and a maximum near 1.0.

$f_7$ (55 bits) encodes a 55-bit Boolean satisfiability problem from De Jong and Spears (1989). This function has a large number of local optima, and many non-linear interactions among the genes.

All functions in the test suite are scaled to return a value between 0.0 and 1.0, and all to be maximized.

There are at least two issues that we expect these preliminary experiments to illuminate. First, is it possible to describe the correlation between the mean fitness of the offspring and the mean fitness of the parents of a genetic operator by a relatively simple function? Second, is it reasonable to assume that the fitness distribution of an operator is uniform across the entire space? If it is, then it would be possible to measure it prior to running a genetic algorithm by applying the operator to randomly generated points. We first examine mutation on the sample problems.

## 3.1    Mutation

We wish to examine the relationships between the fitness of the parent and the fitness of the offspring. We begin by taking static measurements of mutation operators in order to measure the effect of mutation rate. By *static measurements*, we refer to measurements taken independently of the genetic algorithm. We took static measurements of the fitness distribution of mutation on the sample problems as follows: For each of 100 randomly generated parents, we applied the mutation operator 30 times, and recorded the fitness of each offspring. We grouped the data into 100 bins defined by the fitness of the parents, with each bin covering 1% of the total fitness range for the function. For each non-empty bin, we computed the mean fitness of the parents and the mean and variance of the fitness of the offspring. Figure 2 shows the fitness of the offspring, as a function of the parent, for mutation rate[4] of 0.01 on the 10-dimensional quadratic function $f_1$. The circles represent the mean fitness of the offspring, and the error bars represent one standard deviation in the fitness of the offspring.

Noting an apparently linear correlation between the fitness of the parent and the mean fitness of the offspring, we computed a least squares regression between these quantities, with the result shown in the Table 1 for all test functions. In all cases, we found that the operator's MFD could be described very accurately with a linear function of the parent's fitness.

### 3.1.1    Effects of Mutation Rate

Assuming that the fitness of the offspring is linearly relating to the fitnss of the parent under the mutation operator, we next explore how the relationship changes as a function of the mutation rate. Figures 3 and 4 illustrate typical results on the function $f_1$. As the mutation increases, the slope of the MFD decreases, and the intercept increases toward

---

[4] The *mutation rate* is the probability of randomly resetting each bit.

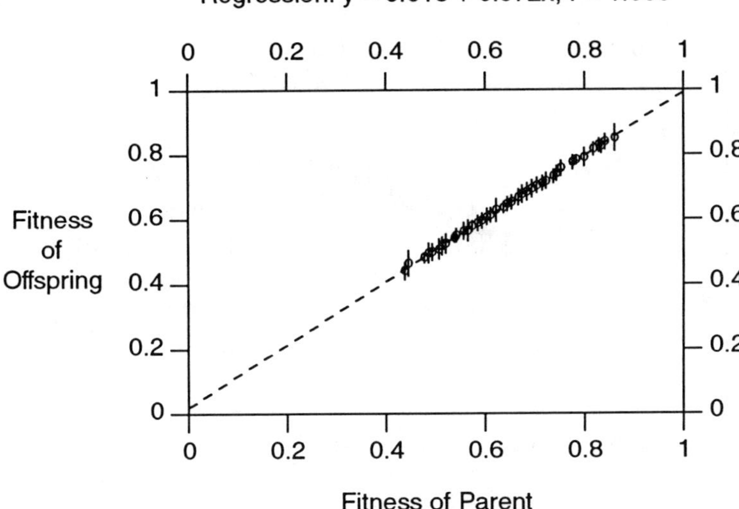



Figure 2: Static Estimates for Mutation (0.01) on $f_1$

**Table 1:**  Static Estimates of MFD for Mutation (0.01)

| Function | Regression Line | Corr. Coeff. |
|:---:|:---|:---:|
| $f_1$ | y = 0.018 + 0.972x | 1.000 |
| $f_2$ | y = 0.000 + 1.000x | 0.998 |
| $f_3$ | y = 0.008 + 0.986x | 1.000 |
| $f_4$ | y = 0.023 + 0.971x | 1.000 |
| $f_5$ | y = 0.002 + 0.949x | 0.998 |
| $f_6$ | y = 0.024 + 0.950x | 0.999 |
| $f_7$ | y = 0.003 + 0.988x | 0.999 |

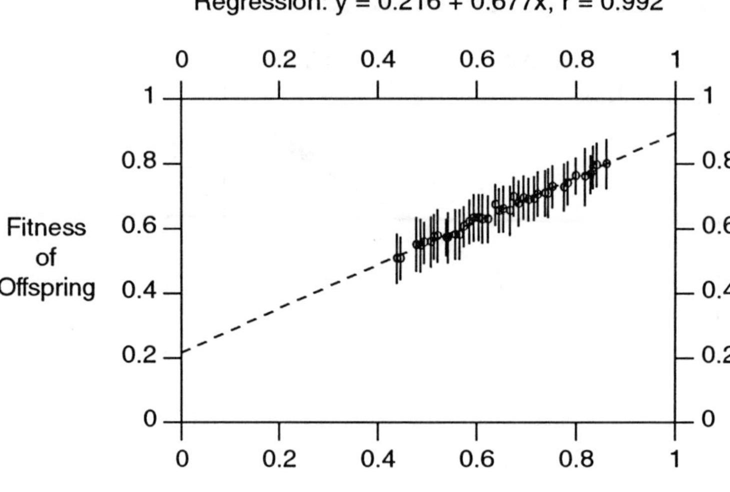



Figure 3:  Static Estimates for Mutation (0.10) on $f_1$

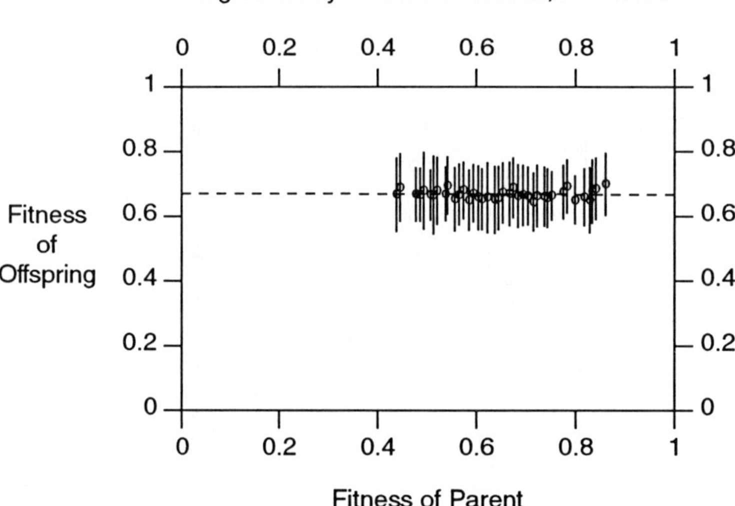



Figure 4: Static Estimates for Mutation (0.50) on $f_1$

the mean fitness of the entire search space.  Table 2 shows the results of increasing the mutation rate to 0.1 for all test functions.

**Table 2:**  Static Estimates of MFD for Mutation (0.10)

| Function | Regression Line | Corr. Coeff. |
|:---:|:---:|:---:|
| $f_1$ | y = 0.216 + 0.677x | 0.992 |
| $f_2$ | y = 0.302 + 0.658x | 0.980 |
| $f_3$ | y = 0.091 + 0.820x | 0.999 |
| $f_4$ | y = 0.256 + 0.682x | 0.996 |
| $f_5$ | y = 0.048 + 0.422x | 0.937 |
| $f_6$ | y = 0.202 + 0.564x | 0.983 |
| $f_7$ | y = 0.050 + 0.800x | 0.997 |

In all cases, as the mutation rate increases, the slope of the MFD decreases.  This pattern is very intuitive -- more mutation means that the fitness offspring is less similar to the fitness of the parent, and more similar to the overall mean fitness for the entire space.

### 3.1.2    Static vs. Dynamic Estimates

There are two limitations to taking a random sample of points in order to estimate features of the fitness distribution.  First, for many problems of interest, random generation is unlikely to produce points with high fitness values.  Second, a random sample of points may not give representative statistics for the fitness distributions that occur in the sample of points that evolve during the genetic algorithm.  To address these issues, we performed a dynamic measurement of the operator fitness distribution by running a genetic algorithm on the sample functions for 100 generations, with population size 1000.  During each 10th generation, 10 population elements were picked at random, and the mutation operator was applied 30 times.  The outcomes of the mutations were kept separate from the genetic algorithm to keep from influencing the search.  Comparing Figure 5 with Figure 3 shows that the dynamic measurements closely agree with the static measurements for $f_1$.

Figures 6 and 7 illustrate the general agreement between dynamic estimates and static estimates for the more complex foxhole function, $f_5$.  The results for all test functions are shown in Tables 3 and 4.  In all cases, very good linear models of fitness distribution were found.  While not identical to the static measurements, the dynamic measurements are generally very similar.  The trend toward lower slope with increasing mutation rate is consistent in both static and dynamic measurements.

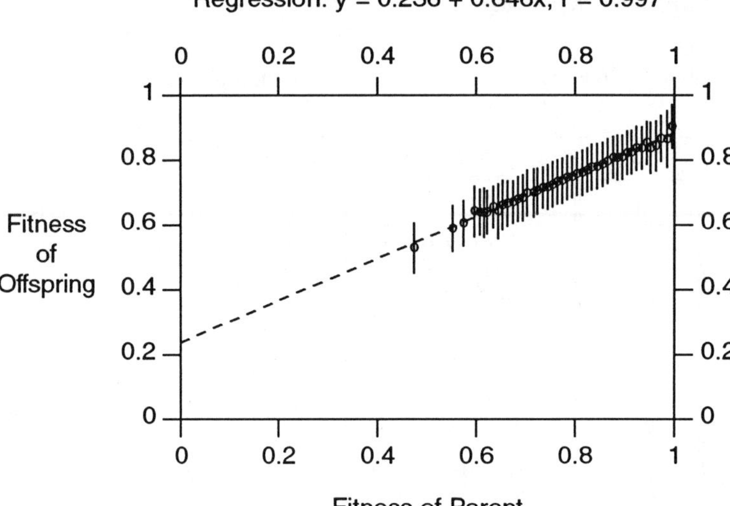



Figure 5:  Dynamic Estimates for Mutation (0.10) on $f_1$

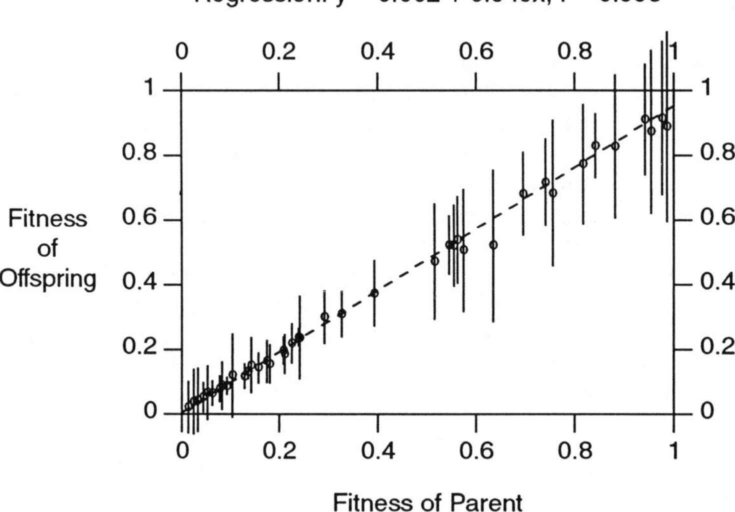



Figure 6:  Static Estimates for Mutation (0.01) on $f_5$

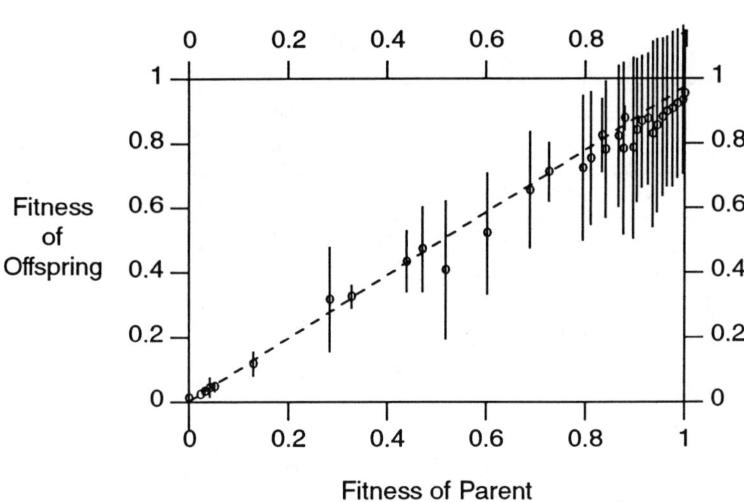



Figure 7:  Dynamic Estimates for Mutation (0.01) on $f_5$

**Table 3:**  Dynamic Estimates of MFD for Mutation (0.01)

| Function | Regression Line | Corr. Coeff. |
|----------|-----------------|--------------|
| $f_1$ | y = 0.017 + 0.972x | 1.000 |
| $f_2$ | y = 0.004 + 0.996x | 0.999 |
| $f_3$ | y = 0.011 + 0.978x | 1.000 |
| $f_4$ | y = 0.030 + 0.963x | 1.000 |
| $f_5$ | y = 0.001 + 0.972x | 0.996 |
| $f_6$ | y = 0.023 + 0.952x | 1.000 |
| $f_7$ | y = 0.008 + 0.972x | 1.000 |

**Table 4:** Dynamic Estimates of MFD for Mutation (0.10)

| Function | Regression Line | Corr. Coeff. |
|:---:|:---:|:---:|
| $f_1$ | y = 0.236 + 0.646x | 0.997 |
| $f_2$ | y = 0.300 + 0.670x | 0.977 |
| $f_3$ | y = 0.100 + 0.800x | 0.998 |
| $f_4$ | y = 0.298 + 0.629x | 0.999 |
| $f_5$ | y = 0.029 + 0.428x | 0.905 |
| $f_6$ | y = 0.206 + 0.566x | 0.993 |
| $f_7$ | y = 0.075 + 0.730x | 0.992 |

In summary, the preliminary data appears to support the assumption of a linear correlation between the fitness of the parent and the mean fitness of the offspring for mutation operators. The difference between static and dynamic measurements of fitness distributions appears to be small. However, our current studies have not addressed the issue of how fitness distribution may change over time during a genetic algorithm. This issue needs to be addressed in further studies. We now turn to crossover.

## 3.2  Crossover

We performed both static and dynamic measurement experiments for 2-point crossover on the sample functions. The method was similar to the method for mutation except that, since crossover is a binary operator, we compare the fitness of the result with the mean fitness of the two parents. The motivation for assuming a linear relationship between the fitness of the offspring and the mean fitness of the parents is that a linear relationship allows us to treat a $k$-ary operator as if it were a unary operator, with the fitness change in the offspring being "charged" equally to all parents. That is,

$$E[D(y_1, \cdots, y_k)] = a + b \left( \sum_{i=1}^{k} y_i / k \right) = \left( \sum_{i=1}^{k} a + b \, y_i \right) / k \tag{8}$$

This will simplify our later analysis.

The results of the preliminary experiments are shown in Figures 8-11 for two of the test functions, and in Tables 5 and 6 for all test functions.

In general, the relationship between the mean fitness of the offspring and the mean fitness of the parents appears to be more complex for crossover than for mutation. For any given mean parental fitness, the variance in the fitness of the offspring are typically much higher than for mutation. In addition, the linear correlation between the mean fitness of the parents and the mean fitness of the offspring is weaker than for mutation.

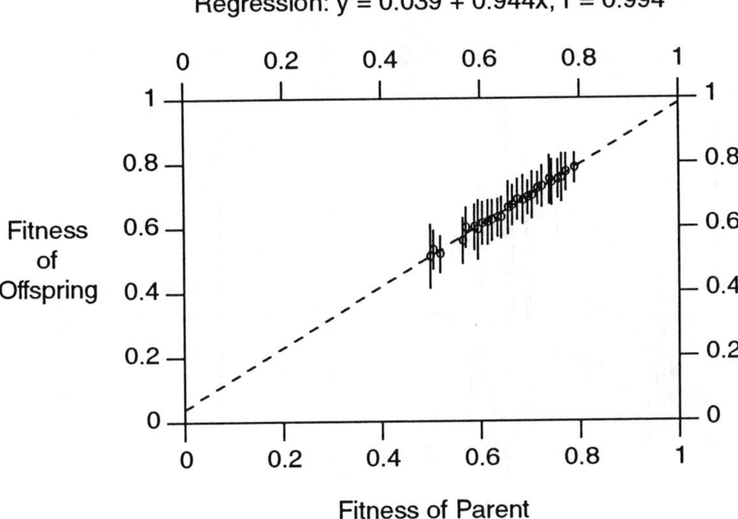


Figure 8:  Static Estimates for 2pt on $f_1$

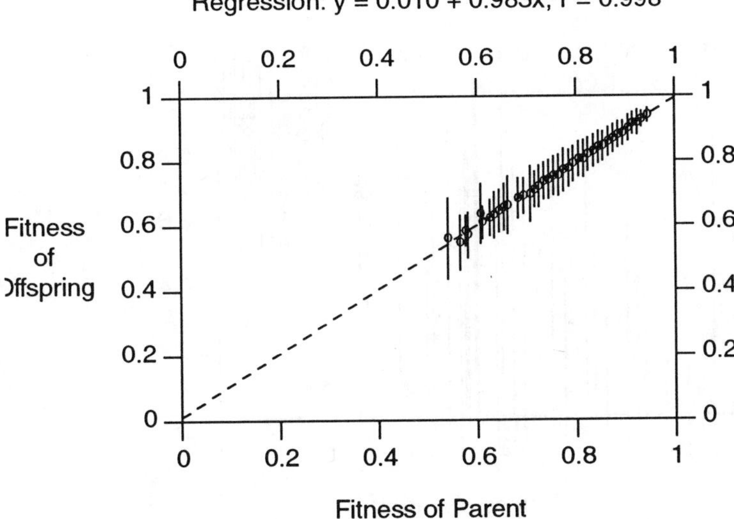


Figure 9:  Dynamic Estimates for 2pt on $f_1$

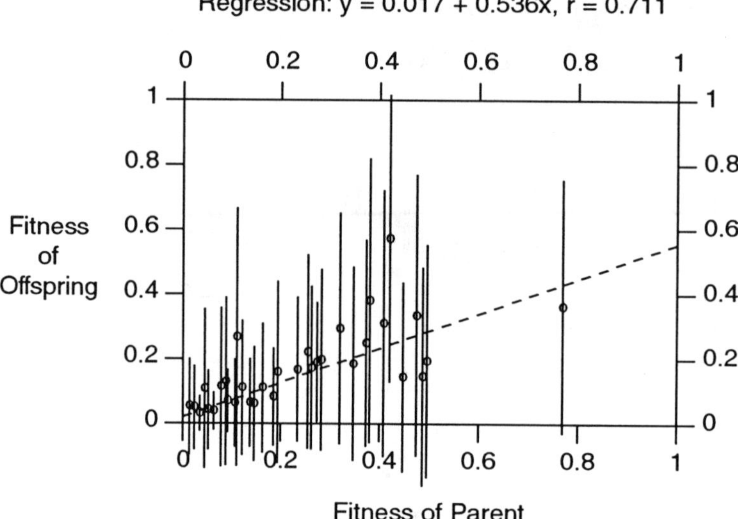

Figure 10:  Static Estimates for 2pt on $f_5$

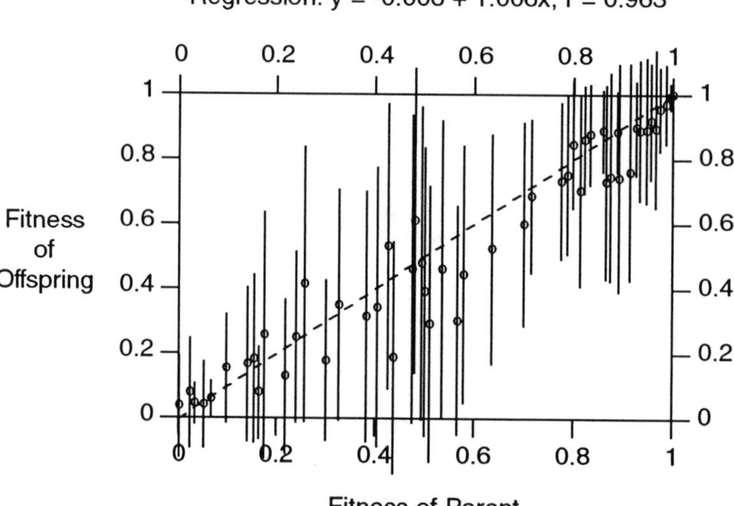

Figure 11:  Dynamic Estimates for 2pt on $f_5$

**Table 5:**  Static Estimates of MFD for 2-point Crossover

| Function | Regression Line | Corr. Coeff. |
|:---:|:---:|:---:|
| $f_1$ | y = 0.039 + 0.944x | 0.994 |
| $f_2$ | y = 0.173 + 0.804x | 0.949 |
| $f_3$ | y = -0.004 + 1.006x | 0.994 |
| $f_4$ | y = 0.018 + 0.974x | 0.997 |
| $f_5$ | y = 0.017 + 0.536x | 0.711 |
| $f_6$ | y = 0.041 + 0.919x | 0.998 |
| $f_7$ | y = 0.009 + 0.963x | 0.993 |

**Table 6:**  Dynamic Estimates of MFD for 2-point Crossover

| Function | Regression Line | Corr. Coeff. |
|:---:|:---:|:---:|
| $f_1$ | y = 0.010 + 0.983x | 0.998 |
| $f_2$ | y = 0.306 + 0.682x | 0.927 |
| $f_3$ | y = 0.000 + 1.000x | 0.999 |
| $f_4$ | y = 0.022 + 0.973x | 0.998 |
| $f_5$ | y = -0.006 + 1.006x | 0.963 |
| $f_6$ | y = 0.008 + 0.980x | 0.999 |
| $f_7$ | y = 0.007 + 0.987x | 0.999 |

Generally, there are greater differences between the static estimates and the dynamic estimates for crossover than for mutation. Future studies will investigate these non-linear effects in more detail. However, a linear relationship appears to provide at least a first order approximation in many cases.

## 4 PREDICTIVE MODEL BASED ON LINEAR FITNESS DISTRIBUTIONS

Given the preliminary data, it seems reasonable to begin by analyzing the general class of genetic operators with linear MFD, i.e.,

$$E[D(x_i,t)] = a + b f(x_i,t) \tag{9}$$

for some constants $a$ and $b$. In other words, the expected fitness of the offspring of $x$ is a linear function of the fitness of the parent $x$. Note that this formula can be used to describe the combined effect of any number of genetic operators, as long as each has a linear MFD. For example, suppose one has several genetic operators, each with a linear MFD. Then

$$E[D(x,t)] = \sum_{op} p_{op} E[D_{op}(f(x,t))] \tag{10}$$

$$= \sum_{op} p_{op}(a_{op} + b_{op}f(x,t))$$

$$= \sum_{op} p_{op}a_{op} + (\sum_{op} p_{op}b_{op})f(x,t)$$

Letting $a = \sum_{op} p_{op}a_{op}$ and $b = \sum_{op} p_{op}b_{op}$, we get Eq. (9).

For example, if the effect of crossover is described by $E[D_c(x)] = 0.001 + 0.8f(x)$, and the effect of mutation is $E[D_m(x)] = 0.01 + 0.9f(x)$, and crossover probability is $p_c = 0.90$, and mutation probability is $p_m = 0.10$, then the overall effect would be

$$E[D(x)] = (0.9*0.001+0.1*0.01) + (0.9*0.8+0.1*0.9)f(x) = 0.0019 + 0.81f(x)$$

For linear MFDs, the expected fitness in the next population fitness can be derived using Eq. (3):

$$E[M(t+1)] = \frac{1}{N}\sum \frac{f(x_i,t)}{M(t)}(a + b f(x_i,t)) \tag{11}$$

We define

$$SQ(t) = \sum_{i=0}^{N} f(x_i,t)^2 \tag{12}$$

and

$$V(t) = \frac{1}{N}SQ(t) - M(t)^2 \tag{13}$$

That is, V(t) is the standard (biased) estimate of the fitness variance in the population at time $t$. Using these definitions on Eq. (11) yields

$$E[M(t+1)] = a + \frac{bSQ(t)}{NM(t)}$$

$$= a + \frac{bV(t)}{M(t)} + bM(t) \tag{14}$$

or

$$R(t+1) = a + \frac{bV(t)}{M(t)} - (1-b)M(t) \tag{15}$$

Some important special cases can now be examined.

**Case 1:** $b = 0$. In this case, the expected fitness of the result of a genetic operator is independent of the fitness of the parent, and has expected value $a$. In this case, the model predicts that $E[M(t)] = a$ and $R(t) = 0$ for all $t$. This case can arise with a certain unfortunate choices of representation and operators. There are not many examples of this in the literature, but a hypothetical example might be a genetic algorithm that uses a simple cut-and-splice crossover operator on a permutation representation, along with a repair scheme that blindly maps the result to a legal permutation. Such an operator might result in essentially random offspring in large permutation spaces. In this case, the performance of the genetic algorithm is the same a random search.

**Case 2:** $a = 0$, $b = 1$. In this case, the expected fitness of the result of a genetic operator is the same as the fitness of the original parent. This case applies to the trivial genetic algorithm with no genetic operators, but it may also apply in other cases as well. Eq. (15) becomes

$$R(t+1) = \frac{V(t)}{M(t)} \tag{16}$$

This result has some interesting implications. First, it agrees with our intuition that if there is no fitness variance in the population at time $t$, and the genetic operators do not produce any fitness variation (on average), then the expected fitness improvement is zero. On the other hand, if the fitness variance is large, and the genetic operators are at least neutral with respect to fitness, then we expect a correspondingly large improvement in the population fitness. Eq. (16) also implies that, as the population average fitness rises over time, smaller improvements result from a fixed level of fitness variation. This is related to the well known *scaling problem* (Grefenstette, 1986). For example, if the population fitness variance is fixed, $V(t) = v^*$ for some constant $v^*$, then the expected learning curve of population fitness is described by $E[M(t)] = M(0) + v^* log(t+1)$.

**Case 3:** $a > 0$, $0 < b < 1$. This case applies to operators that are likely to improve individuals with low fitness and to harm individuals with high fitness. For example, many mutation operators in the preliminary experiments seem to fit this pattern. Specifically, if the fitness of an individual is less than $c = a/(1-b)$, then the operator is likely to improve the offspring. If the fitness of an individual is greater than $c$, then the operator is likely to reduce the fitness of the offspring. Unlike the previous case, this case predicts that at some point, $R(t)$ becomes 0, i.e., no further improvement in the population fitness is expected.  This point can be derived as follows:

$$R(t+1) = 0$$

$$a + \frac{bV(t)}{M(t)} - (1-b)M(t) = 0$$

when

$$M(t) = \frac{a \pm \sqrt{a^2 - 4b(b-1)V(t)}}{2(1-b)} \qquad (17)$$

Let's examine the behavior of this case using parameter values that are typical of the test functions.  We let $a = 0.05$ and $b = 0.9$, giving $c = 0.5$.  That is, individuals with fitness less 0.5 can be expected to produce improved offspring and individuals with fitness greater than 0.5 can be expected to produce offspring with lower fitness.  Eq. (17) says that the population average fitness reaches a plateau at a level that varies with $V(t)$.  As Figure 12 shows, for constant values of $V$ the level of the plateau for $M(t)$ increases as a function of $V$, as we might expect.

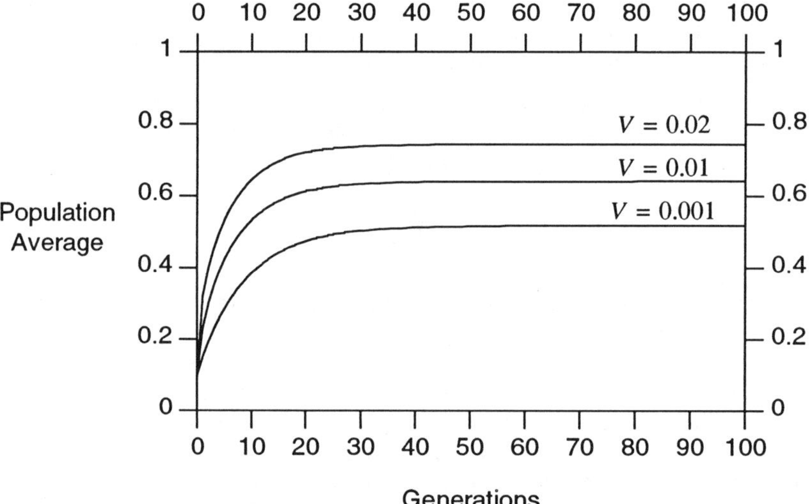


Figure 12:  Predicted Fitness as a Function of Population Variance

Looking again at Eq. (17), we see that as $b$ approaches 1, $R(t+1)$ is positive for larger values of $t$.  Thus the value of $b$ can be used as a measure of the appropriateness of a representation.  Poorly chosen representations are likely to have small values of $b$, meaning that the fitness of the offspring are nearly independent of the fitness of the parent.  Eq. (17) shows that as $b$ approaches 0, $R(t+1)$ approaches 0 when the mean population fitness reaches approximately $M(t) = a$.  In this case, the predicted effect would be a very early stagnation of the search. These observations allow us to make reasonable first-order predictions about the performance of the genetic algorithm (using pure proportional selection) as long as we can measure $a$, $b$, and $V(t)$.

## 5   SCALING

One way that practitioners have addressed the problem of reduced selection pressure indicated by Eq. (14) is by *scaling* the fitness function over time. That is, instead of using the raw objective function value $f(x)$ as the fitness for the purpose of selection, one uses a transformed value such as

$$f_s(x) = f(x) - B(t) \tag{18}$$

where $B(t)$ is a *baseline* that usually increases over time. The baseline might be defined with respect to the worst fitness observed over some period of time, or might track the mean of the variance of the population fitness. Let's examine the effects of scaling on our model.

In fitness scaling with proportional selection, we have

$$E[M(t+1)] = \frac{1}{N} \sum \frac{f(x_i,t) - B(t)}{M(t) - B(t)} (a + b f(x_i,t)) \tag{19}$$

Using Eqs. (13) and (14), this becomes:

$$E[M(t+1)] = a + \frac{b}{M(t) - B(t)} (V(t) - B(t)M(t) + M(t)^2) \tag{20}$$

which reduces to Eq. (14) when $B(t)=0$. As a simple case to analyze, suppose we define the baseline as $B(t) = cM(t)$ for some constant $c$, $0 < c < 1$. Assuming that all members of the population have fitness of at least $cM(t)$, Eq. (20) becomes

$$E[M(t+1)] = a + \frac{b}{(1-c)} \frac{V(t)}{M(t)} + bM(t) \tag{21}$$

Comparing this result with Eq. (14), we see that scaling causes the population fitness to increase more rapidly as $c$ approaches 1, as expected.

## 6   APPLYING THE MODEL

We are now in a position to apply some of the above results to model the behavior of a real genetic algorithm. We illustrate the method on function $f_7$ because it has a high degree of non-linear interactions among the genes and may therefore be most representative of many difficult real-world problems. The design parameters of the genetic algorithms were: population size = 100, probability of crossover = 0.6, probability of mutation = 0.04, proportional selection with scaling baseline = $0.5M(t)$. To be consistent with the model assumption, mutation was applied to an individual only if crossover was not applied. For those individuals to whom mutation was applied, the rate at which bits were reset was 0.01. The genetic algorithm was run ten times for 50

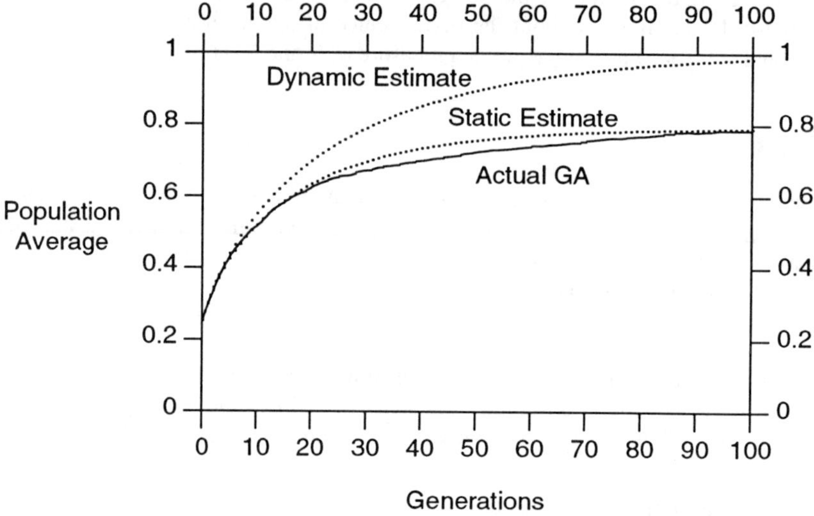


Figure 13: Predicted vs. Actual Population Fitness on $f_7$

generations, with the average population fitness over the ten runs plotted as the solid line in Figure 13.

Two predictive models were constructed, one based on static estimates and one based on dynamic estimates. For the first model, the parameters required by Eq. (21) were taken from Table 1 for mutation on $f_7$ and from Table 5 for crossover. These parameters are combined as described in Section 4 to get: $a = 0.4*0.003+0.6*0.009 = 0.0066$, and $b = 0.4*0.988+0.6*0.963 = 0.973$. The value for $c = 0.5$ corresponds to the baseline update policy. For the second model the parameters were taken from the Tables 3 and 6 showing the dynamic estimates for $a$ and $b$, and then combined as above. The value for the population variance $V(t) = 0.006$ was based on the variance shown in the first generation. The lower dotted line in Fig. 12 represents the predicted population fitness based on the static estimates. The upper dotted line represents the predicted population fitness based on the dynamic estimates.

In this case, the predictions for the population fitness based on the static estimates agree very well with the observed values for the first 100 generations. The dynamic estimates for this problem appear to be a bit high. This may reflect a tendency of the dynamic measurements to be more highly influenced by the fitness correlations pertaining to high fitness individuals. On other functions, the static estimates for the model parameters do not yield such an accurate prediction.

Future work will consider several possible approaches for improving the long-term accuracy of the predictive model. First, it may be inappropriate to use fixed linear models of the fitness distributions. It is more likely that the efficacy of the operators changes over time. Fortunately, all of the analysis above works just as well if we replace the constants $a$ and $b$ by $a(t)$ and $b(t)$. However, further studies are needed to obtain time-varying formulas for these parameters. Another area that needs attention, as noted above, is the analysis of the variance in the population fitness of genetic algorithms. In the above experiment we assumed a fixed value for the variance, but in reality the population variance changes over time. The model needs to be expanded to include formulas for changing population variance. Such refinements may eventually produce models that can predict the expected performance of a genetic algorithm, without running the algorithm. In any case, we expect that further analysis of why these simple models fail will provide new insights into the dynamic behavior of genetic algorithms.

## 7  SUMMARY

We have begun to develop some tools for predicting the performance of genetic algorithms by focusing on the fitness distribution of operators. Some of the current limitations of the approach have been mentioned above. For many combinations of fitness landscapes and genetic operators, the mapping between the mean fitness of the parents and the mean fitness of the offspring is unlikely to be linear. In fact, in some sense, the most interesting problems are those for which crossover produces decidedly non-linear results. Obviously, additional analytic tools are needed for more complex fitness distributions. Despite the evidence from the simple functions considered here, it is also likely that in general the dynamic fitness distribution may be arbitrarily different from the static distribution obtained by random sampling. That is, genetic operators might perform very differently on the individuals generated by the genetic algorithm than they perform on randomly selected structures. Some aspects of this phenomenon may be easy to handle. For example, one might reasonably assume that binary genetic operators such as crossover will typically have operands that are structurally similar in the later stages of the search. In this case, it might be possible to estimate the dynamic fitness distributions later in the search by generating a random sample of similar structures.

This paper focuses mainly on the approach shown in Figure 1, in which we want to decide whether a given representation is likely to perform well prior to running the genetic algorithm. Another approach would be to apply these methods dynamically, as shown in Figure 14. In this mode the genetic algorithm would be augmented by a *monitor* that predicts the future progress of the algorithm based on the most recent estimates of operator fitness distributions and terminates the algorithm once the point of diminishing returns has arrived. The lack of good stopping rules is a major deficiency in genetic algorithms, and this approach would fill that gap.

Despite the obvious need for more work, two advantages of the overall approach outlined here should be stressed. First, it does not require any explicit assumptions about the representation used by the genetic algorithm. Instead, the representation comes into play only indirectly, via the effects of the genetic operators. Consequently, these techniques can be applied to genetic algorithms using representations other than binary strings, such as real-value vectors, permutation representations, rule-based

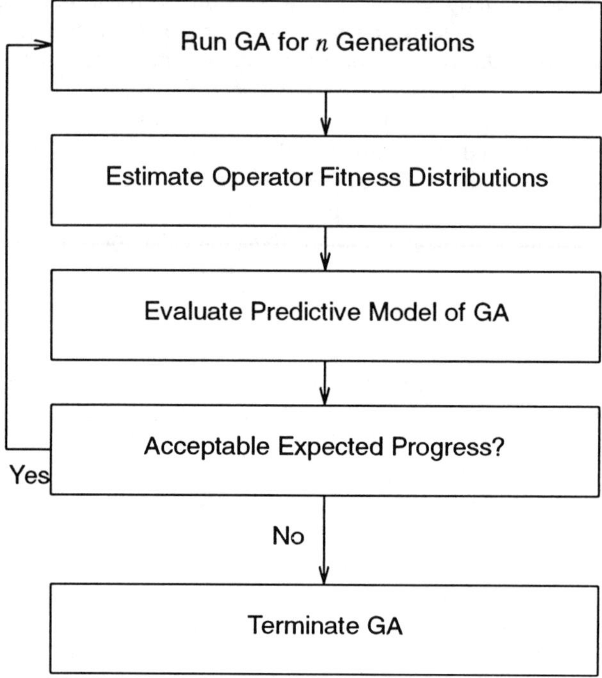



Figure 14: Dynamically Predicting GA Performance

representations or logical representations (e.g., genetic programming). Second, these methods could be used to provide a quantitative explanation for why a given representation/operator combination might fail. For example, if the fitness distribution of an operator were shown to be independent of the parent's fitness, then our model predicts failure.

Finally, assuming that these models can be successfully refined for generational genetic algorithms, an important next step would be to extend this approach to genetic algorithms that use other selection algorithms, such as rank-based selection or truncation selection. Incremental genetic algorithms could also benefit by this method of analysis. This paper has considered the simplest cases only, but the others do not appear to be fundamentally intractable. Further developments that include other forms of genetic algorithms will be presented in future reports.

## Acknowledgements

The author expresses thanks to the reviewers for comments that improved the clarity of this paper.

## REFERENCES


Altenberg, L. (1994). The evolution of evolvability in genetic programming. In *Advances in Genetic Programming,* (K. E. Kinnear, Ed.). MIT Press.

Altenberg, L. (1995). The Schema Theorem and Price's Theorem. In *Foundations of Genetic Algorithms 3*, D. Whitley (Ed.). San Mateo, CA: Morgan Kaufmann.

Baeck, T. (1992). The interaction of mutation rate, selection, and self-adaptation with a genetic algorithm. In *Parallel Problem Solving from Nature 2*, R. Maenner and B. Manderick (Eds.), Elsevier.

Baeck, T. (1995). Order statistics for convergence velocity analysis in evolutionary algorithms. In *Foundations of Genetic Algorithms 3*, D. Whitley (Ed.). San Mateo, CA: Morgan Kaufmann.

De Jong, K. A. (1993). Genetic algorithms are NOT function optimizers. In *Foundations of Genetic Algorithms 2*, D. Whitley (Ed.). San Mateo, CA: Morgan Kaufmann.

De Jong, K. A. and W. M. Spears (1989). Using genetic algorithms to solve NP-complete problems. *Proceedings of the Third International Conference on Genetic Algorithms,* San Mateo, CA: Morgan Kaufmann, 124-132.

Grefenstette, J. J. (1986). Optimization of control parameters for genetic algorithms. *IEEE Transactions on Systems, Man and Cybernetics 16(1),* 122-128.

Holland, J. H. (1975). *Adaptation in natural and artificial systems.* University of Michigan Press, Ann Arbor.

Kauffman, S. A. (1989). Adaptation on rugged fitness landscapes. In *Lecture Notes on Complexity,* D. Stein (Ed.), Addison Wesley, 527-618.

Manderick, B., de Weger, M. and P. Spiessens (1991). The genetic algorithm and the structure of the fitness landscape. *Proceedings of the Fourth International Conference on Genetic Algorithms,* San Mateo, CA: Morgan Kaufmann, 143-150.

Muehlenbein, H. and D. Schlierkamp-Voosen (1993). Predictive models for the breeder genetic algorithm. *Evolutionary Computation 1(1),* 25-49.

# Modeling Simple Genetic Algorithms for Permutation Problems

**Darrell Whitley and Nam-Wook Yoo**
Computer Science Department
Colorado State University
Fort Collins, CO 80523
whitley@cs.colostate.edu

## Abstract

An exact model of a simple genetic algorithm is developed for permutation based representations. Permutation based representations are used for scheduling problems and combinatorial problems such as the Traveling Salesman Problem. A remapping function is developed to remap the model to all permutations in the search space. The mixing matrices for various permutation based operators are also developed.

## 1   INTRODUCTION

Several exact models of simple genetic algorithms have been introduced that assume the genetic algorithm is processing binary strings. In this paper we develop exact models of the simple genetic algorithm when specialized recombination operators are applied to problems which are encoded as permutations. Kargupta, Deb and Goldberg (1992) refer to this class of genetic algorithms as *ordering genetic algorithms.* Permutation encoded problems are often used to represent scheduling problems and classic combinatorial optimization problems such as the Traveling Salesman Problem.

Kargupta, Deb and Goldberg (1992) explore how ordering problems can be deceptive–that is, how ordering problems can mislead a genetic algorithm. The notion of studying "deception" has received some criticism because deception is usually defined statically using properties that characterize the function, instead of being defined dynamically with respect to both the function and how the genetic algorithm behaves when processing the function (Grefenstette, 1993). The goal here is not to debate the importance of deception, but rather to provide tools which can be used to dynamically study "ordering genetic algorithms." This will also allow us to evaluate a genetic algorithm dynamically when processing functions that are identified as deceptive from a static point of view.

Another potential use of these models is to aid in the development of new permutation operators. Construction of new operators up to this point has been largely ad hoc, with little in the way of rigorous analysis to determine how a new operator will behave on a particular type of problem. The model introduced here can be used to study the interaction between specific operators and specific types of problems. We have developed the mixing matrix needed to describe four general types of permutation crossover operators. These include Order Crossover 1, Order Crossover 2, Position Crossover and Partially Mapped Crossover (PMX).

## 2   EXACT MODELS FOR SGAs

Goldberg (1987) developed the first dynamic models of the genetic algorithm for 2 bit strings. Bridges and Goldberg (1987) generalized this model to look at arbitrary individual strings and schemata for simple genetic algorithms (SGAs). Whitley et al. (1993; 1992) further generalized the Bridges and Goldberg model to provide a complete model of how all strings in the search space are processed by a simple genetic algorithm using selection and crossover. Vose and Liepins (1991) independently introduced another exact model which also includes the effects of mutation. All of these models were developed using infinite population assumptions.

The following notation is based on Vose and Liepins. The vector $p^t \epsilon \Re$ is defined such that the $k$ th component of the vector is equal to the proportional representation of string $k$ at generation $t$. The vector $s^t \epsilon \Re$ represents the $t$ th generation of the genetic algorithm and the $i$ th component of $s^t$ is the probability that the string represented by $i$ is selected for the gene pool. Thus, $s_0^t$ represents the proportional representation of string 0 in the population at generation t *after* selection has occurred, but before recombination is applied. Likewise, $p_0^t$ represents the proportional representation of string 0 (i.e., the string of all zeros) at generation t *before* selection occurs. Finally, let $r_{i,j}(k)$ be the probability that string $k$ results from the recombination of strings i and j. Now, using $\mathcal{E}$ to denote expectation,

$$\mathcal{E} \, p_k^{t+1} = \sum_{i,j} \, s_i^t \, s_j^t \, r_{i,j}(k). \tag{1}$$

To further generalize this model, a mixing matrix $M$ is constructed where the $i,j$th entry $m_{i,j} = r_{i,j}(0)$. Here $M$ is built by assuming that each recombination generates a single offspring. The calculation of the change in represention for string $k = 0$ is now given by

$$\mathcal{E} \, p_0^{t+1} \;=\; \sum_{i,j} s_i^t s_j^t r_{i,j}(0) \;=\; s^T M s \tag{2}$$

where $T$ denotes transpose. Note that this computation gives the expected representation of a single string, 0, in the next genetic population. Vose and Liepins also formalize the notion that when processing binary strings, bitwise exclusive-or (denoted $\oplus$) can be used to access various probabilities from the recombination function $r$. Specifically,

$$r_{i,j}(k) = r_{i,j}(k \oplus 0) = r_{i \oplus k, j \oplus k}(0). \tag{3}$$

This implies that the mixing matrix $M$, which is defined such that entry $m_{i,j} = r_{i,j}(0)$, can provide mixing information for any string $k$ just by changing how $M$ is accessed. By reorganizing the components of the vector $s$ the mixing matrix $M$ can yield information about the probability $r_{i,j}(k)$. A permutation function, $\sigma$, is defined as follows:

$$\sigma_j < s_0, ..., s_{N-1} >^T \; = \; < s_{j \oplus 0}, ..., s_{j \oplus (N-1)} >^T \tag{4}$$

where the vectors are treated as columns and N is the size of the search space. The computation

$$(\sigma_q \; s^t)^T M (\sigma_q \; s^t) = p_q^{t+1} \tag{5}$$

thus reorganizes $s$ with respect to string $q$ and produces the expected representation of string q at generation $t+1$. A general operator $\mathcal{M}$ can now be defined over $s$ which remaps $s^T M s$ to cover all strings in the search space:

$$\mathcal{M}(s) = < (\sigma_0 \; s)^T M (\sigma_0 \; s), ..., (\sigma_{N-1} \; s)^T M (\sigma_{N-1} \; s) >^T . \tag{6}$$

Recall that $s$ carries fitness information such that it corresponds to the intermediate phase of the population (after selection, but before recombination) as the genetic algorithm progresses from generation $t$ to $t+1$. Thus, to complete the cycle and reach a point at which the Vose and Liepins models can be executed in an iterative fashion, fitness information is introduced. A fitness matrix $F$ is defined such that fitness information is stored along the diagonal; the $i, i$ th element is given by $f(i)$ where $f$ is the fitness function.

Following Vose and Wright (1994):

$$s^{t+1} = (F p^{t+1}) / (1^T F p^{t+1}) \tag{7}$$

since

$$F p^{t+1} = < f_0 p_0^{t+1}, f_1 p_1^{t+1}, \ldots, f_{n-1} p_{n-1}^{t+1} > \tag{8}$$

and

$$1^T F p^{t+1} = f_0 p_0^{t+1} + f_1 p_1^{t+1} + \ldots + f_{n-1} p_{n-1}^{t+1} \tag{9}$$

is the population average, which implies $\sum_j s_j = 1$.

Whitley (1994) provides a more tutorial level introduction to these models.

## 3  EXACT MODELS FOR PERMUTATIONS

The Vose and Liepins model will be used as the basis for developing models of the simple genetic algorithm that process permutation based encodings. In developing these models for permutation encodings we consider two problems. First, a different transformation of the $s$ vector is required. Second, a concise way of developing the mixing matrix for various permutation based operators is possible (but not required).

The transformation of the $s$ vector for binary strings can be viewed in two ways. First, applying exclusive-or to the strings rotates the hypercube. Second, applying exclusive-or to the binary representations of the indices of the $s$ vector reorders the elements of the $s$ vector. For permutations, an analogous transform is possible.

## 3.1  THE MAPPING FUNCTION

In order to calculate the expected representation for all strings representing permutations, a mapping function is needed that allows one to access the probability of recombining string $i$ and $j$ and obtaining an arbitrary string $k$. For example, the remapping function denoted @ should function as follows:

$$r_{3421,1342}(3124) = r_{3421@3124,1342@3124}(1234).$$

This mapping can be achieved by simple element substitution. First, the function r can be generalized as follows:

$$r_{3421,1342}(3124) = r_{wzyx,xwzy}(wxyz)$$

where w, x, y and z are variables representing the elements of the permutation (e.g., w=3, x=1, y=2, z=4). If $wxyz$ now represents the canonically ordered permutation 1234,

$$r_{wzyx,xwzy}(wxyz) = r_{1432,2143}(1234) = r_{3421@3124,1342@3124}(1234)$$

The computation $Y = A@X$ behaves as follows. Let any permutation X be represented by $x_1x_2x_3, \ldots, x_n$. Then $a_1a_2a_3, \ldots, a_n @ x_1x_2x_3, \ldots, x_n$ yields $Y = y_1y_2y_3, \ldots, y_n$ where $y_i = j$ when $a_i = x_j$. Thus, (3421@3124) yields (1432) since $(a_1 = 3 = x_1) \Rightarrow (y_1 = 1)$. Next, $(a_2 = 4 = x_4) \Rightarrow (y_2 = 4)$, $(a_3 = 2 = x_3) \Rightarrow (y_3 = 3)$ and $(a_4 = 1 = x_2) \Rightarrow (y_4 = 2)$. This mapping function is analogous to the bitwise addition (mod 2) used to reorder the vector $s$ for binary strings. However, note that $A@X \neq X@A$. Furthermore, for permutation recombination operators it is *not necessarily true* that $r_{i,j} = r_{j,i}$.

## 3.2  CHOOSING A CANONICAL ORDERING

The actual ordering of the permutations in terms of the canonical form for $s$ can be arbitrarily chosen as long as it matches the mixing matrix. An ordering is chosen for the basis of a recursive function which provides a one-to-one invertible mapping between the permutation strings and a set of indices for the representation vectors $p$ and $s$ as well as the mixing matrix $M$.

Choose some ordering of the permutation elements which is defined to be sorted. Sort and index the N elements $(N \geq 1)$ of the permutation from 1 to N. The permutation corresponding to integer X (where $0 \leq X < N!$) is determined by the following algorithm that creates a permutation by picking elements from a list maintained in sorted order.

1. Set C = N; Set K = X;

2. If K = 0, pick all remaining elements in the sorted permutation in the order of appearance and stop.

3. IF $K < (C - 1)!$ pick the first element of the sorted list and GOTO 5. Otherwise, Continue.

4. Find $Y$ such that $Y - 1((C - 1)!) \leq K < Y((C - 1)!)$. The $Y^{th}$ element of the sort list is the next element of the permutation. $K = K - (Y - 1)((C - 1)!)$.

5. Delete the chosen element from the sorted list and reindex the remaining elements; C = C-1; GOTO 2.

The convertion from a permutation to an index merely inverts this process. For permutations of length three this generates the following ordering:

```
X = 0 indexes 123        X = 3 indexes 231
X = 1 indexes 132        X = 4 indexes 312
X = 2 indexes 213        X = 5 indexes 321
```

Having defined the canonical form of $s$ and a mapping function for reordering $s$, the only remaining task is to define the function $r_{i,j}(0)$ with respect to permutations for a specific operator. Permutation 0 in this case represents the standard form of the permutation, $123\ldots N$, which has its elements sorted from 1 to N.

## 3.3  THE MIXING MATRIX FOR ORDER CROSSOVER 1

The Order Crossover 1 recombination operator was first introduced by Dave Davis (1985). A related form, known as "C1," was also introduced by Reeves (1993). One variant of the operator can be described as follows.

Pick two strings to recombine. Label one parent the *cut string* and the other the *filler string*. Pick a contiguous section out of the cut string which is directly copied to the offspring. We will refer to the contiguous section of cut string as the "crossover section." The crossover section is placed in the offspring in the same absolute position it occupied in the cut string. Next, inherit those elements from filler string which are not in the crossover section from the cut string. These elements are inherited from the filler string based on relative order. For simplity we assume that relative order is determined starting at the beginning of the filler string. A "filler-block" is constructed from string 2 by deleting those elements that appear in the crossover section of string 1; this maintains these elements in the same relative order observed in string 2. (If a starting point other than the start of the string is chosen to determine relative order, a simple shift of the filler string can be done.)

The following is an example of Order Crossover 1. (Upper and lower case distinguish between parent 1 and parent 2.)

```
String 1:  A B C D E F G H I    crossover-section  _ _ C D E F _ _ _

String 2:  h d a e i c f b g    filler-block   h a i b g

Offspring:  b g C D E F h a i
```

Note that the filler block has no absolute order. The offspring is constructed by adding elements from the filler block to the crossover section of the cut string. The first element of the filler-block is added at the end of the crossover section, with the other elements being added in relative order. When the end of the string is reached, the process wraps around to complete the construction of the offspring.

We have explored many approaches to construct the mixing matrix for this operator. The following is the most efficient algorithm we have found. This method performs an O(N) calculation for each entry in the mixing matrix, where N is the number of elements in the permutation. The mixing matrix has $(N!)^2$ elements, so the construction of the entire mixing matrix has complexity $O(N(N!)^2)$. We first assign a unique number to each element in a permutation. The permutation with index 0 is represented by (1, 2, 3, ..., N). For illustration it is also sometimes convenient to represent this permutation as (A B C .... $\Omega$). Each entry $m_{i,j}$ of the mixing matrix is the probability of recombining permutation $i$ as the cutting string and $j$ as the filler string and obtaining the permutation with index 0.

This means that all possible crossover sections that can be used to produce permutation 0 must have exactly the same subsequence of elements in exactly the same absolute position as permutation 0. We will refer to these special crossover sections as "cutting sections." Thus the string H G C D E F A B has a one possible cutting section (_ _ C D E F _ _). The string (A B D C E F H G) has two possible cutting sections:

$$\text{(A B \_ \_ \_ \_ \_ \_)} \quad \text{and} \quad \text{(\_ \_ \_ \_ E F \_ \_)}.$$

Cutting sections are maximal by definition. If possible crossover sections include

$$\text{(\_ \_ \_ \_ E F \_ \_)}, \quad \text{(\_ \_ \_ D E F \_ \_)} \quad \text{and} \quad \text{(\_ \_ C D E F \_ \_)},$$

then only the last of these three is defined as the cutting section. The other substrings are possible crossover sections within that cutting section.

Besides the cutting section, two additional data structures defined with respect to a specific cutting section are needed to concisely calculate the probability of constructing permutation 0. The *minimal filler block* contains exactly those elements not in the cutting section, and thus the elements appear in the relative order required to construct permutation 0. Thus, once a specific cutting section is determined, the *miminal* filler block is also determined. One can then check to see if the filler string $j$ contains the required minimal filler block.

For a specific string j, *if there is no appropriate minimal filler block for a specific cutting section, then there is no appropriate filler block for any subsection of that cutting section,* since the filler block for an subsection of the maximal cutting section must contain as a subsequence the minimal filler block for the maximal cutting section. If no minimal filler block exists for a specific cutting section, then that cutting section cannot be used to generate permutation 0 (i.e., it generates permutation 0 with probability 0).

Not all subsections of a cutting section can be viable crossover sections, however, since not all subsections of a cutting section will yield permutation 0 when recombination occurs. To determine which subsection of a cutting section will produce permutation 0, one must define the *maximal filler block*. The *maximal filler block* is constructed from the minimal filler block. Let $x_q$ be the $q^{th}$ element of permutation zero and the first element of the minimal filler block. If element $x_{q-1}$ in permutation zero appears to the left of element $x_q$ in the filler string, it may be appended to the front of the current filler block. The process is then repeated with respect to $x_{q'}$ (the new first element of the enlarged filler block) and $x_{q'-1}$. The left expansion of the filler block stops when the leftward scan of the filler string fails to find the next element $x_{q'-1}$ to the left of the current $x_{q'}$ in the filler block. This same process is then applied to the right. Let $x_k$ be the $k^{th}$ element of permutation zero and the last element of the minimal filler block. If element $x_{k+1}$ appears to the right of element $x_k$ in the filler string, it is appended to the end of the current filler block and becomes the new end element $x_{k'}$. Building then continues to the right. This construction process yield the *maximal filler block*.

The following examples illustrate these principles. If cut string $i$ is H G C D E F A B with a cutting section (_ _ C D E F _ _), then filler string $j$ must have the minimal filler block (G H A B). Assume string $j$ is the permutation (F D G H E A B C). Now scanning to the left in string $j$ from G, we search for F, which appears and is added to the minimal filler block. This process now continues, searching to the left of F to find E, the next adjacent element to the left in permuation 0. The process stops when the next element is not found. The same process is applied to the right starting with element B. In this case, C appears to the right, and is added to the expanding filler block. The process then terminates. The resulting maximal filler block is (F G H A B C).

Those elements that appear in both the cutting section and the maximal filler block may optionally be included in either the crossover section or the filler block during recombination. Thus, in the previous example D and E must appear in the crossover section, but F and C can appear in either the filler block or the crossover section. Thus, all possible viable crossover sections that yield permutation 0 include (C D E), (C D E F), (D E F) and (D E).

The preceding rules apply only when string $i$ is not itself a copy of permutation 0. Special rules are required to construct the minimal filler section when $i$ is a copy of permutation 0.

For string $i = 0$ the entire string is the cutting section and there is no well defined minimal filler block. In this case filler blocks are defined with respect to element 1 and element N of string $i = 0$.

If element 1 appears before element N in string $j$ then exactly two possible filler blocks must be considered. A minimal filler block is initialized with element 1. The maximal filler block is now expanded by scanning right in filler string $j$ from element 1 and adding element to the right to construct the maximal filler block. A second minimal filler block is initialized with element N. The filler block is now expanded by scanning left in filler string $j$ and adding elements to the left in the expanding filler block.

For example, string $i$ is permuation 0, here represented by (A B C D E F) and string $j$ is (C E D A F B). A is to the left of F (i.e., element 1 appears before element N) and one of the maximal filler blocks with respect to A is (A B) with corresponding possible crossover sections of (C D E F) and (B C D E F) from string $i$. (We assume crossover never copies string $i$ completely.) The maximal filler block with respect to F from string $j$ is (E F).

If element 1 appears *after* element N in string $j$, only a single maximal filler block exists, but two minimal filler blocks exist: (1) and (N). Nevertheless the maximal filler block is constructed by initializing a string with (N 1); this string is expanded on both the left and right. This produces a single maximal filler block of the general form (N-X,...,N-1, N, 1, 2, ..., Y). If string $j$ is a shifted version of permutation zero, the entire string $j$ will constitute the filler section.

Having defined how to calculate the cutting section, the minimal filler block and the maximal filler block, we show how to calculate the probability of crossover. The two directed acyclic graphs shown in Figure 1 illustrate the relationship between cutting sections and filler blocks, as well as the effects of recombination (see the examples of recombination discussed below). Each node in a graph represents a cutting section and the associated minimal filler block. The exception is the root node, which has only a cutting section, and the last row of the graph, which represents special filler sections that are shifted versions of permutation 0 (e.g.,

2341, 3412, 4123). As described here, recombination does not occur at the root of the graph, or in the last row of the graph. All valid crossover sites have both a cutting section and a filler block. The cutting sections are represented by templates such as *23*, which indicate that the elements 2 and 3 occur in the absolute positions 2 and 3. The corresponding minimal filler block in this case is 41##. This is a relative order representation, introduced by Goldberg (1985; 1989) to describe relative order schemata. In this case, 41## indicates that 4 appears before 1, but it does not indicate the absolute positions at which 4 and 1 occur.

Possible viable crossover sections are found by identifying a particular cutting section and the maximal filler block associated with filler string $j$. This is performed as follows. Find the cutting section in the graph; next find the maximal filler section in the graph. Expand the graph down from the cutting section and up from the maximal filler section. All nodes in the intersection of these expansions are viable crossover sites. Count the number of viable crossover sites for all possible cutting sections. Assuming one cannot select all of cutting string $i$ to be the crossover section (i.e., the roots of the graphs in Figure 1 are not valid cutting sections), then the total number of crossover sites for this operator is $\binom{N+1}{2} - 1$. Thus, if M is the number of nodes in the intersection of the expansion associated with the cutting sections of cutting string $i$ and the maximal filler sections of filler string $j$, then the probability of producing permutation 0 when recombining $i$ and $j$ is given by $\frac{M}{\binom{N+1}{2}-1}$.

The top graph in Figure 1 illustrates how crossover nodes are identified when the cutting section is 12**, the associated minimal filler block is 34##, and the maximal filler block is 234#. (The cutting string $i$ in this case must be 1243, but the filler string $j$ could be 2134 or 2314.) A cone is projected downward from 123* and up from 234#; the intersection of these two cones indicates that there are two possible crossover sections: either 1*** or 12**. The bottom graph in figure 1 assumes the cutting section is 1234 and the maximal filler block is 3412.

One anomally occurs when both parents are permutation 0 (e.g. $i = j = 0$). In this case 1234 appears as a filler section twice in the last row of the graph. In this case, cones are projected up from both positions.

The construction of cutting sections and filler blocks can be done in O(N) time, since this requires scanning only strings $i$ and $j$.

### 3.4   AN EXAMPLE COMPUTATION

The computation for $s^T M s$ for an SGA using Order Crossover 1 to process a permutation of three elements is as follows.

$$p_0^{t+1} = [s_0, s_1, s_2, s_3, s_4, s_5] \begin{bmatrix} .8 & .6 & .6 & .8 & .8 & .6 \\ .2 & 0 & .2 & .2 & 0 & 0 \\ .2 & .2 & 0 & 0 & .2 & 0 \\ 0 & 0 & 0 & 0 & 0 & 0 \\ 0 & 0 & 0 & 0 & 0 & 0 \\ 0 & 0 & 0 & .2 & .2 & .2 \end{bmatrix} \begin{bmatrix} s_0 \\ s_1 \\ s_2 \\ s_3 \\ s_4 \\ s_5 \end{bmatrix} \qquad (10)$$

Note that the sum of the probabilites must equal to N!, where N is the number of elements in the permutation (in this case, N = 3 and N! = 6.) When all sources of string gains and

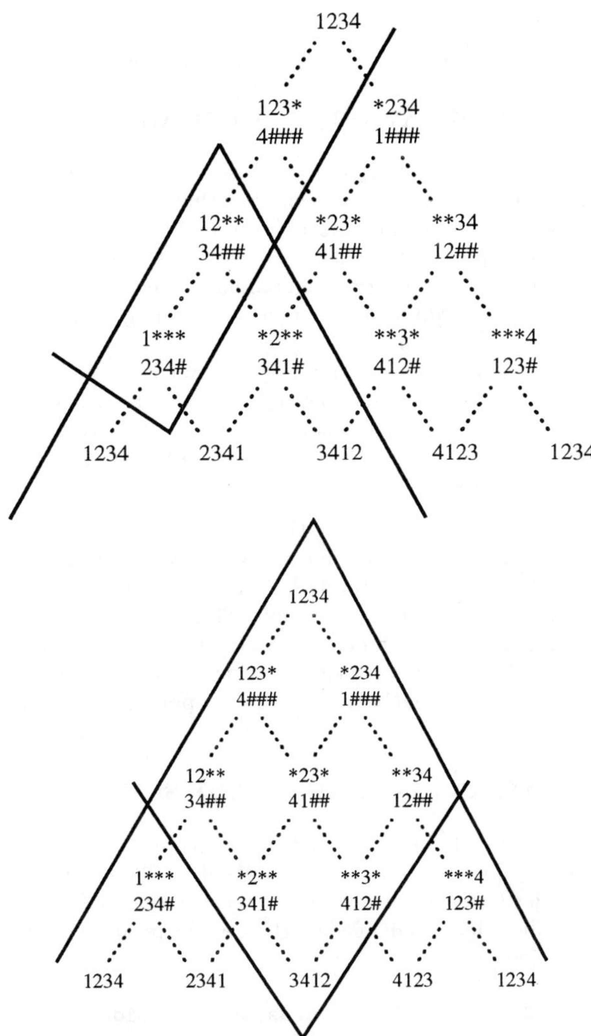

Figure 1: These graphs model the cutting sections and filler blocks associated with the "C1" variant of the order crossover 1 recombination operator. At each node in the graph, the top string represents a cutting section and the bottom string the associated minimal filler block. For a specific instance of recombination, however, the cutting section and the maximal filler block are located. All intermediate nodes represent a single unique and valid way of doing recombination that produces permutation 0.

losses are exhaustively enumerated by hand the calculation of the expected value of $p_0^{t+1}$ results in the same value. In both cases, we obtain:

$$p_0^{t+1} = s_0(.8(s_0 + s_1 + s_2 + s_3 + s_4) + .6s_5) + .4s_1s_2 + .2(s_1s_3 + s_2s_4 + s_5s_3 + s_5s_4 + s_5s_5). \quad (11)$$

### 3.5  CONVERGENCE BEHAVIOR AND THE MIXING MATRIX

The diagonal of the mixing matrix for Order Crossover 1 (as defined in Section 3.3) has an entry in column 1 and column 6. This implies that recombining permutation 0 with permutation 0 does not always yield permutation 0; in 20% of all cases it yields the inverse of permutation 0. (If permutation 0 is 1234, its inverse is 4321). Normally, for binary representations without mutation, the matrix diagonal has value 1.0 at $m_{1,1}$ and is 0 elsewhere. As discussed by Vose and Wright (1994) matrices with diagonals with 1.0 at $m_{1,1}$ and 0 elsewhere result in convergence where were the SGA model converges to a corner of the simplex; in other words, it will converge to a population composed of a single string. When mutation is turned on the SGA model converges to a point inside the simplex (i.e., the population converges in the sense that it is composed of a relatively stable combination of strings). Also, the addition of mutation results in a distribution of different values along the diagonal of the mixing matrix.

Our experiments show that this variant of Davis' crossover operator converges inside the simplex. It cannot converge to a population composed entirely of 1234, for example, because recombination continues to generate copies of 4321. Subsequent mixing of the strings 1234 and 4321 results in a relatively diverse population. Thus, this crossover operator has a built-in mutation effect; when identical parents are recombined an offspring that is the inverse of the parents is produced with a 20% probability. This effect is also somewhat adaptive since identical parents would be more likely to occur as the population begins to lose its genetic diversity.

### 3.6  ANOTHER VARIANT OF ORDER CROSSOVER 1

As defined Order Crossover 1 functions such that recombination of permutation 0 with permutation 0 does not always produce permutation 0. This can be corrected by using another variant of Order Crossover 1, where the relative order of the elements in the filler string (and hence the filler block) is defined starting at the position where the cutting section ends in parent $i$. For example,

```
String 1:  A B . C D E F . G H I    crossover-section  _ _ C D E F _ _ _

String 2:  h d . a e i c . f b g

           which can be shifted to yield  f b g h d a e i c
           with filler-block   b g h a i

Offspring:  a i C D E F b g h
```

The dots in this example represent the crossover points associated with the crossover section. Using this variant of Order Crossover 1, the mixing matrix becomes:

$$\begin{bmatrix} 1.0 & .6 & .6 & .4 & 1.0 & .6 \\ .2 & 0 & 0 & 0 & .2 & .2 \\ .2 & .2 & 0 & 0 & .2 & 0 \\ 0 & 0 & 0 & 0 & 0 & 0 \\ 0 & 0 & 0 & 0 & 0 & 0 \\ .2 & 0 & .2 & 0 & .2 & 0 \end{bmatrix} \tag{12}$$

This matrix can be compared to the matrix given in equation (10). Note that the sum of probabilities over any single row does not change since the relevant cutting sections do not change. The probabilities are redistributed over the columns, however, since in effect the filler strings are being shifted before filler-blocks are calculated.

In this case the diagonal has $m_{1,1} = 1.0$ and the diagonal is 0 elsewhere. Using this mixing matrix, the population converges to a corner of the simplex; final populations are filled with identical copies of the same string. This variant of Davis' crossover operator is used in subsequent experiments in this paper in order to allow better comparison with other operators.

## 3.7  EXPRESSING $M$ AS A SYMMETRIC MATRIX

These matrices can also be expressed in a symmetric form, where each entry $m_{i,j}$ is based on the assumption that either $i$ or $j$ can be randomly assigned as the cut and filler strings. The symmetric matrix $M'$ is related to the nonsymmetric matrix M as follows.

$$M' = (M + M^T)/2.$$

## 3.8  PMX, ORDER CROSSOVER 2 AND POSITION CROSSOVER

The following subsections offer descriptions of PMX, as well as Syswerda's (1991) Order Crossover 2 and Position Crossover. A proof is also given that shows that Order Crossover 2 and Position Crossover produce identical results in expectation.

The methods that we have developed to generate mixing matrices for these operators are not given in detail. Rather the operators are described in such a way as to highlight those features of the operators that are relevant to generating the corresponding mixing matrices.

### 3.8.1  PARTIALLY MAPPED CROSSOVER (PMX)

Goldberg and Lingle (1985) introduced the Partially Mapped Crossover operator (PMX). Given two parents, one is choosen as Parent 1. As with Davis' crossover operator, two crossover sites are selected and all of the elements in Parent 1 between the crossover sites are directly copied to the offspring. This means that the notion of a cutting section can still be applied to the PMX operator. The "top bar" in the following illustration shows the elements that are to be copied from Parent 1 to the offspring.

```
                    _____
Parent 1:  A B C D E F G    =>    Offspring: _ _ C D E _ _
Parent 2:  C F E B A D G
```

The inheritance of elements from Parent 2 is more complicated than in Davis' Order Crossover 1 operator.

PMX attempts to match the elements in Parent 2 (P2) between the crossover point in the following way. If element $P2_i$ (where index $i$ is within the crossover region) has already been copied to the offspring, take no action. Thus, in the above example, element E in Parent 2 requires no processing. If element $P2_i$ in Parent 2 has not already been copied to the offspring, then find $P1_i = P2_j$; if position $j$ has not been filled then let the offspring at $j$ (denoted $OS_j$) be assigned element $P2_i$. (I.e., if $OS_j$ is unassigned and $P1_i = P2_j$, then $OS_j = P2_i$.) Thus, in the preceeding example, B in Parent 2 is in the same position as D in Parent 1. Thus, find D in Parent 2 and copy B to the offspring in the corresponding position. This yields:

```
Offspring:      _ _ C D E B _
```

A problem occurs when we try to place element A in the offspring. Element A in Parent 2 maps to element E in Parent 1; E falls in position 3 in Parent 2, but position 3 has already been filled in the offspring. The position in the offspring is filled by C, so we now find element C in Parent 2. The position is unoccupied in the offspring, so element A is placed in the offspring at the position occupied by C in Parent 2. This yields:

```
Offspring:     A _ C D E B _
```

All of the elements in Parent 1 and Parent 2 that fall within the crossover section have now been placed in the offspring. The remaining elements can be placed by directly copying their positions from Parent 2. This now yields:

```
Offspring:     A F C D E B G
```

This yields two principles that simplify the construction of the mixing matrix. First, the elements occurring in selected positions in Parent 1 must directly generate elements of $S_0$. Second, elements that do not appear in the selected positions in either Parent 1 or Parent 2 are directly copied from Parent 2, and hence must also directly correspond to elements of $S_0$. Meeting these two restrictions is a prerequiste to generating the string $S_0$. Note that the "cutting" sections for Parent 1 strings are identical to the cutting sections defined under Davis' operator.

The mixing matrix for the permutation of three elements using PMX is as follows:

$$
\begin{bmatrix}
1.0 & .8 & .8 & .4 & .4 & .8 \\
.2 & 0 & .2 & 0 & 0 & .2 \\
.2 & .2 & 0 & 0 & 0 & .2 \\
0 & 0 & 0 & 0 & 0 & 0 \\
0 & 0 & 0 & 0 & 0 & 0 \\
.2 & .2 & .2 & 0 & 0 & 0
\end{bmatrix}
\tag{13}
$$

## 3.9  ORDER AND POSITION CROSSOVER

Syswerda's (1991) Order Crossover 2 and Position Crossover is different from either PMX or Davis' Order Crossover in that there is no contiguous block which is directly passed to the offspring. Instead several elements are randomly selected by absolute position.

The Order Crossover 2 operator starts by selecting K random positions in Parent 2. The corresponding elements from Parent 2 are then located in Parent 1 and reordered so that they appear in the same relative order as they appear in Parent 2. Elements in Parent 1 that do not correspond to selected elements in Parent 2 are passed directly to the offspring.

```
          Parent 1:   A B C D E F G
          Parent 2:   C F E B A D G
Selected Elements:      *   * *
```

The selected elements in Parent 2 are F, B and A. Thus, the relevant elements are reordered in Parent 1.

```
   Reorder  A B _ _ _ F _  from Parent 1 yields:  F B _ _ _ A _.
```

All other elements are copied directly from Parent 1.

```
 (F B _ _ _ A _)  combined with (_ _ C D E _ G)  yields:  F B C D E A G
```

## 3.10  AN ALTERNATIVE APROACH

For purposes of constructing the mixing matrix, Syswerda's Order Crossover 2 operator can be described in an alternative fashion. Pick the (L-K) elements from Parent 1 which are to be directly copied to the offspring:

```
      _ _ C D E _ G
```

Then scan Parent 2 from left to right; place each element which does not yet appear in the offspring in the next available position.

```
 # # C D E # G  =>  F # C D E # G =>   F B C D E # G  =>  F B C D E A G
```

Syswerda calls this second operator POSITION crossover, and treats it as a distinct crossover operator.

Lemma: Order Crossover and Position Crossover are identical in expectation (and hence produce identical mixing matrices) when Order crossover selects K positions and Position crossover selects L-K positions.

Proof:

Assume there is one way to produce a target string S by recombining 2 parents. Given a pair of strings which can be recombined to produce string S, the probability of selecting the K key positions using Order Crossover 2 required to produce a specific string S is $(1/\binom{L}{K})$, while for Position Crossover, the probability of picking the L-K key elements that will produce exactly the same effect is $(1/\binom{L}{L-K})$. Since $\binom{L}{K} = \binom{L}{L-K}$ the probabilities are identical.

Now assume there are R unique ways to recombine two strings to produce a target string S. The probabilities for each unique recombination event are equal as shown by the argument in the preceeding paragraph. Thus the sum of the probabilities for the various ways of ways of doing recombination are equivalent for Order Crossover 2 and Position Crossover.

QED.

Note that the Position Crossover operator is similar to Davis' Order Crossover, except that the elements that are directly copied to the offspring are randomly selected rather than being selected as a contigous block. Thus the "cutting sections" are different in this case. The following matrix assumes that the number of elements that are swapped under recombination is chosen randomly.

The mixing matrix for Order Crossover 2 for permutations composed of three elements is

$$\begin{bmatrix} 1.0 & .833 & .833 & .666 & .666 & .5 \\ .166 & 0 & .166 & .166 & 0 & 0 \\ .166 & .166 & 0 & & .166 & 0 \\ 0 & 0 & 0 & 0 & 0 & 0 \\ 0 & 0 & 0 & 0 & 0 & 0 \\ .166 & .166 & .166 & 0 & 0 & 0 \end{bmatrix} \tag{14}$$

## 3.11   BUILDING THE MIXING MATRIX

For all three operators (Order-1, PMX and Order-2/Position) it is easy to specify the relevant subblocks from Parent 1 that are required to produce the permutation string $S_0$. Elements are directly copied from Parent 1 in all three cases. Thus, for Parent 1, the only viable crossovers are those that copy elements from Parent 1 that directly correspond to elements in permutation $S_0$.

As with Davis' Order Crossover operator, we have found direct and efficient ways to generate crossover probabilities. Nevertheless, the efficiency with which mixing matrices are created is not extremely critical. These matrices need only be computed once. Thus, the one time cost of generating the appropriate matrix for a given operator and a permutation of L elements is minor compared to the cost of actually running the resulting models. This implies that in general exhaustive methods that look at all possible ways of doing recombination over all pairs of strings can be used to generate the mixing matrix as opposed to developing algorithms that exactly indentify pairs of strings that yield permutation 0 (as well as the corresponding probability) when recombined.

## 4   AN EXAMINATION OF SPECIFIC PROBLEMS

Kargupta, Deb and Goldberg (1992) introduce 2 problems designed to mislead a simple genetic algorithm. One of the problems, here denoted *Func-ABS*, is designed to be a "deceptive" absolute ordering problem. The other function, here denoted *Func-R1*, is designed to be a "deceptive" relative ordering problem. The functions are as follows.

```
Func-R1:  A RELATIVE ORDER DECEPTIVE PROBLEM
=======================================================

    f(1234) = 4.0        f(2314) = 1.2        f(3412) = 2.2
    f(1243) = 1.1        f(2341) = 1.5        f(3421) = 3.2
    f(1324) = 1.1        f(2413) = 2.4        f(4123) = 2.1
    f(1342) = 1.2        f(2431) = 1.2        f(4132) = 1.2
    f(1423) = 1.2        f(3124) = 1.2        f(4213) = 1.2
    f(1432) = 1.1        f(3142) = 2.2        f(4231) = 1.1
    f(2134) = 1.1        f(3214) = 1.1        f(4312) = 2.4
    f(2143) = 2.4        f(3241) = 1.2        f(4321) = 2.4


    Func-ABS:  AN ABSOLUTE ORDER DECEPTIVE PROBLEM
=======================================================

    f(1234) = 4.0        f(2314) = 2.0        f(3412) = 2.6
    f(1243) = 1.8        f(2341) = 2.6        f(3421) = 3.3
    f(1324) = 1.8        f(2413) = 2.6        f(4123) = 2.6
    f(1342) = 2.0        f(2431) = 2.0        f(4132) = 2.0
    f(1423) = 2.0        f(3124) = 2.0        f(4213) = 2.0
    f(1432) = 1.8        f(3142) = 2.6        f(4231) = 1.8
    f(2134) = 1.8        f(3214) = 1.8        f(4312) = 2.6
    f(2143) = 2.6        f(3241) = 2.0        f(4321) = 2.6
```

Figure 2 shows the results of executing the simple genetic algorithm model using both Davis' operator and PMX. Both operators appear to solve the functions *Func-ABS* and *Func-R1* successfully. However, for both functions PMX requires several generations before it can resolve the competition between the strings 1234 and 3421. Even if the population is infinitely large, 3421 dominates 1234 during the early generations. For finite populations genetic drift during the first 10 to 20 generations could create a bias toward 3421. This is particularly true for function *Func-ABS*. In general, it also appears that Davis' crossover operator is better able to propagate the optimal solution than PMX.

These results, unfortunately, are not directly comparable to the work of Kargupta et al. (1992). In order to directly test a simple genetic algorithm they concatenated eight identical size-four subproblems to create a 32 element permutation. Furthermore, the elements of the subproblems were loosely shuffled so that the defining length of each subproblem was six. Finally, because recombination on a permutation of 32 elements does not necessarily preserve the constitute subblocks of permutations, partial evaluation of incomplete subblocks was necessary. These changes very much alterred the evaluations of the individual subproblems.

One striking characteristic of the problems defined by Kargupta et al. is that the second best string in the space is 3421. By analogy with the principle of deception for binary strings, one would assume the second best point in the search space would be a focal point for the deception. Intuitively, misleading problems might be designed so that the search is directly toward 4321 when the optimum is at 1234. First, 4321 is the inverse of 1234; second, 4321 is most different from 1234 by several different measures.

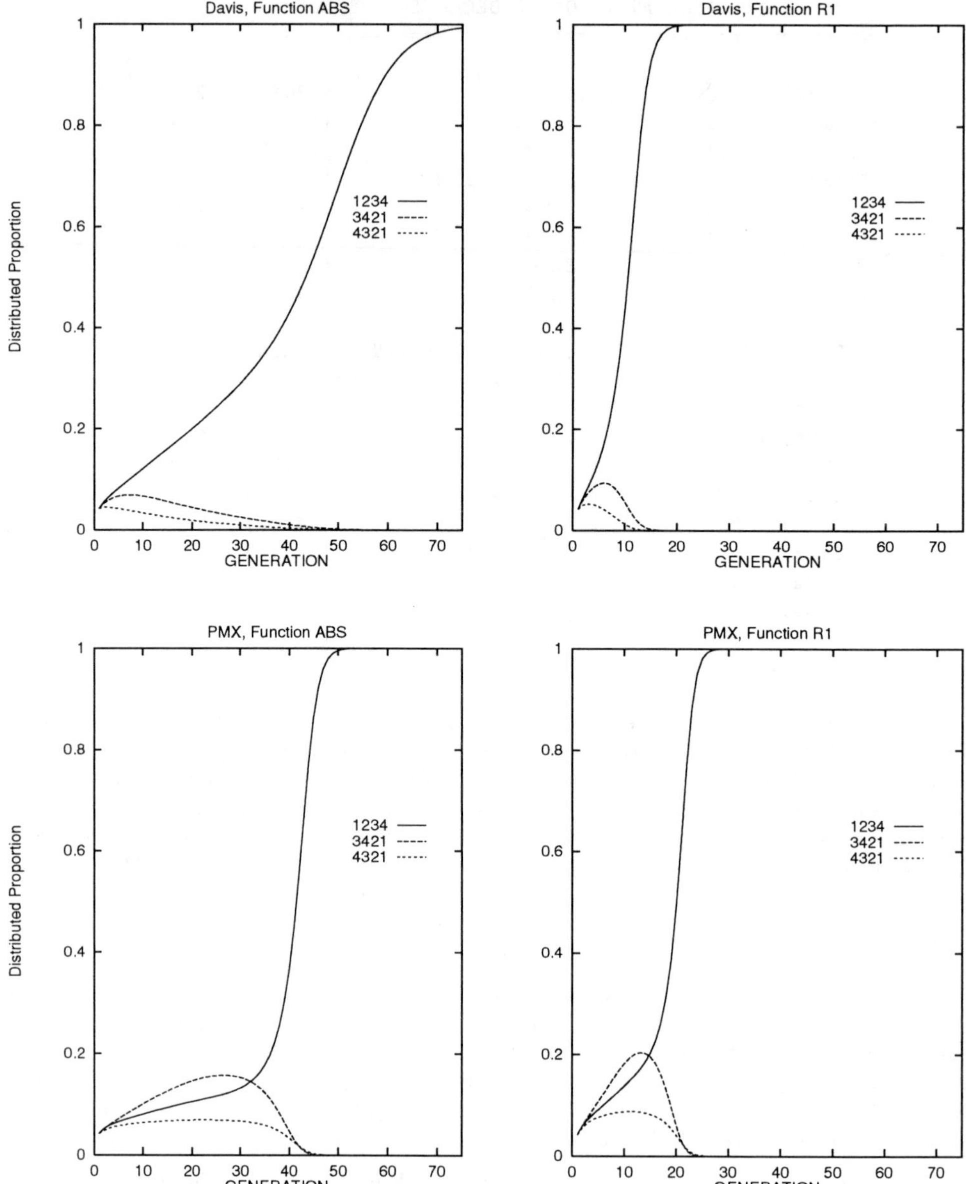



Figure 2: Four figures showing the behavior of a simple genetic algorithm on 2 different functions using 2 different operators.

## 4.1   ANOTHER MISLEADING FUNCTION

The following function, *Func-R2*, was created by exploiting a pattern that emerges as a permutation is mapped from a permutation to an integer using the algorithm in Section 3.2. The pattern, along with the integer index, is illustrated in the following definition of Func-R2.

```
Func-R2:   A MISLEADING RELATIVE ORDER PROBLEM
=====================================================

     0.   f(1234) = 40        12.  f(3124) = 14
     1.   f(1243) = 10        13.  f(3142) = 16
     2.   f(1324) = 12        14.  f(3214) = 18
     3.   f(1342) = 14        15.  f(3241) = 20
     4.   f(1423) = 18        16.  f(3412) = 22
     5.   f(1432) = 30        17.  f(3421) = 34

     6.   f(2134) = 12        18.  f(4123) = 16
     7.   f(2143) = 14        19.  f(4132) = 18
     8.   f(2314) = 16        20.  f(4213) = 20
     9.   f(2341) = 18        21.  f(4231) = 22
    10.   f(2413) = 20        22.  f(4312) = 24
    11.   f(2431) = 32        23.  f(4321) = 36
```

Note that all permutations starting with 1 are first, followed by all permutations starting with 2, and so on in numeric order. The last permutation starting with 1 (i.e., permutation 5) is such that all other elements are reversed compared to the permutation 0. Thus, 1234 and 1432 are maximally different in terms of their relative order except for having 1 as an initial element. (Note that in terms of absolute position, however, 1234 and 1432 share 2 elements.) This suggests that as one progresses through a subset of permutations that begin with a specific element that as the index increases the permutations are moving farther away from 1234 in terms of relative order information. This leads to the somewhat intuitive definition of *Func-R2*, with 4321 being the second best string in the search space. Figure 3 shows that both Davis' operator and PMX result in convergence for *Func-R2* to the population composed entirely of string 4321.

We next attempted to formalize the idea behind the creation of *Func-F2* and to define a new function *Func-F3*. We define a relative order matrix that has a "1" bit in position (X,Y) if row element X appears before column element Y in a permutation. (Note that the indices of the matrix are fixed. Any standard order will work; we use 1234.) The matrix thus yields a unique binary representation for each permutation. Also note that the diagonal is always 0s and that the upper and lower triangle are binary complements; thus, either one uniquely defines a permutation. This representation also allows us to define the Hamming distance between two permutations P1 and P2; this is denoted by HD(index(P1),index(P2)), where the permutations are represented by their integer index. As shown in the following examples, the Hamming distance is computed with respect to the lower triangle.

```
                    1 2 3 4
                   ---------
              1 | 0 1 1 1
   1 2 3 4    2 | 0 0 1 1            HD(0,0) = 0
              3 | 0 0 0 1
              4 | 0 0 0 0


                    1 2 3 4
                   ---------
              1 | 0 0 0 0
   2 4 3 1    2 | 1 0 1 1            HD(0,11) = 4
              3 | 1 0 0 0
              4 | 1 0 1 0


                    1 2 3 4
                   ---------
              1 | 0 0 0 0
   3 4 2 1    2 | 1 0 0 0            HD(0,17) = 5
              3 | 1 1 0 1
              4 | 1 1 0 0


                    1 2 3 4
                   ---------
              1 | 0 0 0 0
   4 3 2 1    2 | 1 0 0 0            HD(0,23) = 6
              3 | 1 1 0 0
              4 | 1 1 1 0
```

This representation has its problems. Certain binary strings are undefined, since $2^{(N^2)} > N!$. For example, consider the following upper triangle.

```
        1 1 1
          0 1
            0
```

Element 1 occurs before 2, 3 and 4, which poses no problem. But 2 occurs after 3, 2 occurs before 4, but 4 occurs after 3. Using $>$ to denote relative order, this implies a nonexistant ordering such that:

$$3 > 2 > 4 \quad \text{but} \quad 4 > 3.$$

Thus, not all matrices correspond to permutations. Nevertheless, the binary representation does afford a metric in the form of Hamming distance and suggests an alternative way of constructing deceptive problems.

Once a binary representation exists several methods for constructing deceptive problems
could be employed. We use principles similar to those for designing deceptive trap functions
of unitation proposed by Deb and Goldberg (1992). In this case the value of the string is the
Hamming distance between the relative order matrix for the string that is being evaluated
and the string 1234; this is also just the number of bits that occur in the permutation's
binary representation taken from the lower triangle of the relative order matrix in column
order. The string 1234 is then assigned the value f(4321) + 1. Since the relative order
matrix for 4321 has the largest Hamming distance away from 1234, this means that 4321
has the second best evaluation and 1234 will be the global optimum.

The following table defines function *Func-R3* and gives the index of the string, the string
itself, its the corresponding binary lower triangle respresentation and its evaluation.

```
      Func-R3:   A MISLEADING RELATIVE ORDER TRAP FUNCTION
      ================================================================
      Index String Binary Value        Index String  Binary  Value
      ================================================================
        0.    1234  000000   7          12.   3124   010100    2
        1.    1243  000001   1          13.   3142   010110    3
        2.    1324  000100   1          14.   3214   110100    3
        3.    1342  000110   2          15.   3241   111100    4
        4.    1423  000011   2          16.   3412   011110    4
        5.    1432  000111   3          17.   3421   111110    5

        6.    2134  100000   1          18.   4123   001011    3
        7.    2143  100001   2          19.   4132   001111    4
        8.    2314  110000   2          20.   4213   101011    4
        9.    2341  111000   3          21.   4231   111011    5
       10.    2413  101001   3          22.   4312   011111    5
       11.    2431  111001   4          23.   4321   111111    6
```

As figure 3 shows, Davis' operator strongly converges to 1234 while PMX converges to 4321
for *Func-R3*. However, simple experimentation shows that results very similar to those
produced for *Func-R2* can be acheived by simply adjusting the evaluation of string 1234.
As the fitness value for permutation 1234 is reduced from 7.0 to below 6.4, the resulting
graphs look almost identical to the results shown for *Func-R2*. At f(1234) = 6.5 the SGA
using Davis' operator converges to 4321, but when f(1234) = 6.6, it converges to 1234.
Further experimentation shows that PMX undergoes a similar transition between f(1234) =
7.1 and f(1234) = 7.2.

These results suggest that, like binary deceptive functions, the "deceptiveness" of these
problems depends in part on the magnitude of the isolated global optimum compared to the
other strings in the space. These results also illustrate that deceptiveness is not an inherent
characteristic of the function, but rather defines a relationship between a function and a
particular algorithm. What is "deceptive" for one instanciation of a genetic algorithm may
be easy for a hill-climber or a different variant of genetic algorithm. In this case, changing
recombination operators changes the dynamical behavior of the Simple Genetic Algorithm.

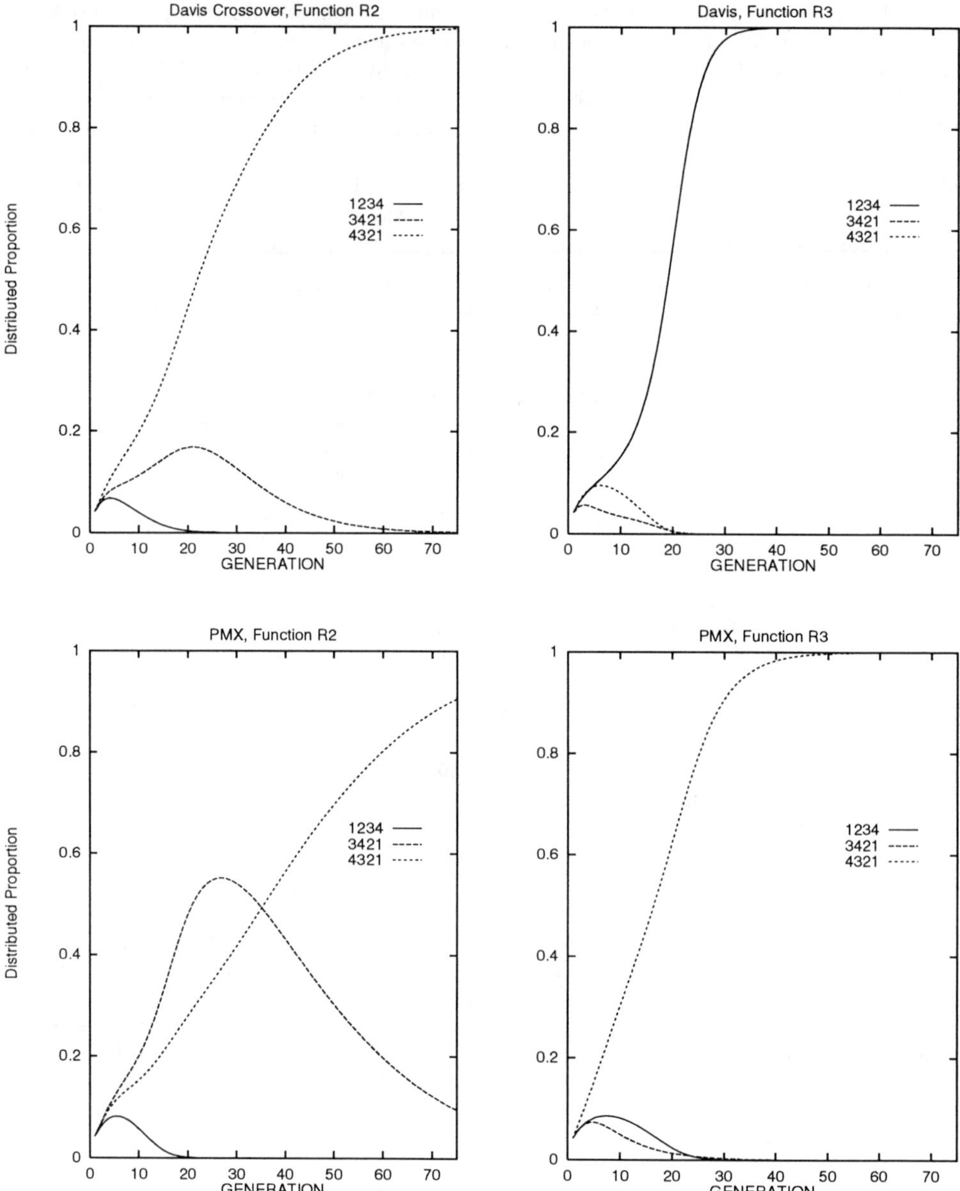



Figure 3: Four figures showing the behavior of a simple genetic algorithm on 2 different functions using Davis' recombination operator versus PMX.

## 5  CONCLUSIONS

In this paper we have described a general way to remap the selection vector $s$ for permutations. In subsequent work with Michael Vose not presented in the current paper, the correctness of these results have been proven. These results depend on the fact that the recombination process can be rewritten in a symbolic form such that a form of variable substitution can be used to remap the symbolic form to each individual string in the search space (as is the case for the scheme given in Section 3.1). Given such a symbolic form, it is possible to reorder the $s$ vector so as to remap and thus generalize the $s^T M s$ computation to cover all strings in the search space.

This paper also introduces a scheme for indexing permutation and developed methods for concisely calculating the entries in the mixing matrix for a variant of Davis' Order Crossover 1 operator. We also looked at the mixing matrix for a variant of Order Crossover 1 which uses a different notion of relative order when defining the filler block. We have also developed methods to calculate the mixing matrix for Syswerda's Order Crossover 2 as well as for Goldberg's PMX operator. In general, however, exhaustive enumeration is the most simple way to generate the mixing matrix; the cost of generating the mixing matrix is small compared to the cost of executing the resulting model and the mixing matrix need only be generated once. This paper also has shown that the mixing matrix for Syswerda's Position Crossover operator is identical to the mixing matrix for Syswerda's Order Crossover 2 operator.

These results now set the stage for a more complete analysis regarding the behavior of simple genetic algorithms applied to ordering problems. These tools should also be useful when designing new operators for relative order problems.

The results presented in this paper also suggest that our understanding of what schemata are important for different types of representations such as permutations is still very limited. The tools developed in this paper should provide a means of looking at relative order schemata in more detail and allow more detailed analyses of how those schemata are dynamically processed by a simple genetic algorithm.

### Acknowledgements

Thanks to Michael Vose for his work on the correctness of the symbolic representation of the permutation encoding. Thanks to John Dzubera for his comments on a draft of this paper. This work was supported in part by NSF grant IRI9312748.

### References

Bridges, C. and Goldberg, D. (1987) An analysis of reproduction and crossover in a binary-coded genetic Algorithm. *Proc. 2nd International Conf. on Genetic Algorithms and Their Applications.* J. Grefenstette, ed. Lawrence Erlbaum.

Davis, L. (1985) Applying Adaptive Algorithms to Epistatic Domains. *Proc. International Joint Conf. on Artificial Intelligence.*

Deb, K. and Goldberg, D. (1993) Analyzing Deception in Trap Functions. *Foundations of Genetic Algorithms -2-.* D. Whitley, ed. Morgan Kaufmann.

Goldberg, D. (1987) Simple Genetic Algorithms and the Minimal, Deceptive Problem. In,

*Genetic Algorithms and Simulated Annealing,* L. Davis, ed., Pitman.

Goldberg, D. (1989) *Genetic Algorithms in Search, Optimization and Machine Learning.* Reading, MA: Addison-Wesley.

Goldberg, D. and Lingle, R. Jr., (1985) Alleles, Loci, and the Traveling Salesman Problem. *Proc. 1st International Conf. on Genetic Algorithms and Their Applications.* J. Grefenstette, ed. Lawrence Erlbaum.

Grefenstette, J. (1993) Deception Considered Harmful. *Foundations of Genetic Algorithms -2-.* D. Whitley, ed. Morgan Kaufmann.

Kargupta, H., Deb, K. and Goldberg, D. (1992) Ordering Genetic Algorithms and Deception. Parallel Problems Solving from Nature, 2. R. Manner and B. Manderick (eds). Elsevier Science Pubs. pp: 47-56.

C. Reeves, 1993 A genetic algorithm for flowshop sequencing. To appear: *Computers and Ops. Res.*

Syswerda, G. (1991) Schedule Optimization Using Genetic Algorithms. *Handbook of Genetic Algorithms.* L. Davis, ed. Van Nostrand Reinhold.

Vose, M. and Liepins, G., (1991) Punctuated Equilibria in Genetic Search. *Complex Systems* 5:31-44.

Vose, M. and Wright, A., (1994) Simple Genetic Algorithms with Linear Fitness. unpublished manuscript.

Vose, M. and Wright, A., (1995) Stability of Vertex Fixed Points and Applications *Foundations of Genetic Algorithms -3-.* D. Whitley and M. Vose, eds. Morgan Kaufmann.

Whitley, D., (1993) An Executable Model of a Simple Genetic Algorithm. *Foundations of Genetic Algorithms -2-.* D. Whitley, ed. Morgan Kaufmann.

Whitley, D. (1994) A Genetic Algorithm Tutorial. *Statistic and Computing,* 4:65-85.

Whitley, D., Das, R., and Crabb, C. (1992) Tracking Primary Hyperplane Competitors During Genetic Search. *Annals of Mathematics and Artificial Intelligence.* 6:367-388.

# Population Size and Genetic Drift in Fitness Sharing

**Samir W. Mahfoud**
Department of Computer Science
University of Illinois at Urbana-Champaign
1304 West Springfield Avenue
Urbana, IL 61801
mahfoud@gal4.ge.uiuc.edu

## Abstract

Sharing methods promote the formation and maintenance of stable subpopulations or *niches* in genetic algorithms. This paper derives, for various models of sharing, lower bounds on the population size required to maintain, with probability $\gamma$, a fixed number of desired niches. It also derives expressions for the expected time to disappearance of a desired niche, and relates disappearance time to population size. Models are presented of sharing under selection, and sharing under both selection and crossover. Some models assume that all niches are equivalent with respect to fitness. Others allow niches to differ with respect to fitness. Models of selection are applicable to GAs with sharing in which crossover is insignificantly disruptive. All models are applicable to GAs with sharing that incorporate low levels of mutation. GAs with sharing are run on seven test problems in optimization and classification, using population sizes derived from the models.

## 1   INTRODUCTION

The simple genetic algorithm (GA), when confronted with a problem having multiple solutions, will converge, in the best case, to a population containing only one of those solutions (Goldberg & Segrest, 1987). This behavior prompted the development of GAs capable of forming and maintaining stable subpopulations or *niches*. GAs that employ *niching methods* are capable of locating multiple solutions within a single population.

One niching method that has proven effective is *fitness sharing* (*sharing* for short) (Goldberg & Richardson, 1987). Sharing derates the fitnesses of population elements according to the number of individuals in a niche, so that the population ends up distributed across multiple niches. However, *genetic drift* due to variance in the selection process limits the number of niches that can be maintained. (Genetic drift can be defined as the fluctuation of subsolution frequencies, caused by noise in the selection process.)

The most effective method of combating genetic drift is to raise the population size to a level sufficient to protect the desired niches. Hence population sizing is a central issue in fitness sharing, and more generally, in the study of niching methods and traditional GAs.

The remainder of this paper will review sharing, introduce the models to be used and their associated assumptions, analyze genetic drift under sharing, and use the genetic drift results to size populations. More specifically, the paper will derive expressions for the expected time to disappearance, or *drift time*, of a desired niche, and use these expressions to bound, under the various models, the minimal population size required to maintain, with probability $\gamma$, a fixed number of desired niches. The paper's first models are of sharing with only selection, but are applicable to problems in which crossover and mutation are minimally disruptive. Subsequent models incorporate sharing under both selection and crossover. All models are applicable to typical GAs with sharing that employ small rates of mutation. Theoretically derived population sizes are tested through multiple runs, on seven test problems in optimization and classification, of a GA with sharing.

## 2   FITNESS SHARING

Fitness sharing was introduced by Goldberg and Richardson (1987) as the "method of sharing functions". Sharing derates each population element's fitness by an amount related to the number of similar individuals in the population. Specifically, an element's *shared fitness*, $f'$, is equal to its prior fitness $f$ divided by its *niche count*. An individual's niche count is the sum of *sharing function* ($sh$) values between itself and each individual in the population (including itself). The shared fitness of a population element $i$ is given by the following equation:

$$f'(i) = \frac{f(i)}{\sum_{j=1}^{n} sh(d(i,j))} \ .$$  (1)

The sharing function $sh$ is a function of the distance $d$ between two population elements; it returns a '1' if the elements are identical, a '0' if they cross some threshold of dissimilarity, and an intermediate value for intermediate levels of similarity. The threshold of dissimilarity is specified by a constant, $\sigma_{share}$; if the distance between two population elements is greater than or equal to $\sigma_{share}$, they do not affect each other's shared fitness. Most commonly-used sharing functions are of the form

$$sh(d) = \begin{cases} 1 - \left(\frac{d}{\sigma_{share}}\right)^{\alpha}, & \text{if } d < \sigma_{share} \ ; \\ 0 \ , & \text{otherwise} \ . \end{cases}$$  (2)

In the above equation, $\alpha$ is a constant (typically set to 1.0) used to regulate the shape of the sharing function. Both genotypic and phenotypic distance measures can be employed; the appropriate choice depends upon the problem being solved.

Sharing can be implemented using any selection method. Stochastic remainder selection (Baker, 1987; Goldberg, 1989) has often been combined with sharing. Roulette-wheel selection (RWS) (Goldberg, 1989) is a simpler method. Tournament selection is another possibility, but special provisions must be made to promote stability. Oei, Goldberg, and

Chang (1991) combine sharing with binary tournament selection, calculating shared fitnesses with respect to the new population as it is being filled. Another possible selection scheme for sharing is stochastic universal selection (SUS) (Baker, 1987), which is known for its high stability.

We model sharing with roulette-wheel selection in the remainder of this paper, primarily because RWS lends itself well to the type of analysis we perform. Since RWS is the least stable of commonly used proportionate-selection schemes, bounds on drift time and population size computed using models of sharing with RWS can also serve as bounds for sharing under more stable selection methods.

## 3  MODELLING FRAMEWORK

The models of this paper make use of a few definitions and simplifying assumptions. These definitions and assumptions allow extraction of the major behavioral characteristics of sharing. As demonstrated in later simulations, the predictive value of the models is not diminished by their assumptions; the models would in fact not be possible without these assumptions.

The preliminary models of this study assume that all niches are equivalent with respect to fitness. Subsequent models allow niches to differ with respect to fitness. Some models are for sharing under selection alone. Other models are for sharing with selection and crossover.

### 3.1  EQUIVALENCE CLASSES

The first definition involves partitioning the search space into equivalence classes that correspond to niches. This study emphasizes locating multiple peaks of an objective function. Therefore, we partition the search space into a number of equivalence classes equal to the number of local maxima in the search space. Each class contains all elements within its corresponding maximum's *basin of attraction*.

We will define a local maximum's basin of attraction using the common notion of hillclimbing under an appropriately defined neighborhood operator. A point is in the basin of attraction of a local maximum if it would hillclimb to that maximum under a given neighborhood operator and deterministic hillclimbing algorithm. We make the hillclimbing algorithm deterministic so that it enforces a tie-breaking procedure, and so that the possibility of a point hillclimbing to two different peaks, given two different runs, is zero.

The best neighborhood operator for a particular problem is problem-dependent. Examples of neighborhoods are epsilon-neighborhoods in multi-dimensional, real-valued variable spaces, and 1-bit Hamming neighborhoods. As an example, if $N$ is defined as a neighborhood of $\pm\epsilon$ in the phenotype, and if the phenotype contains only one variable, then points which lie under a peak will be in the basin of attraction of that peak. We assume an appropriate neighborhood operator for each problem.

Using the partitioning above, the objective of the GA with sharing is to locate and maintain $c$ equivalence classes. (We freely interchange the terms, peak, class, and niche.) We index these $c$ classes from 0 to $c-1$ and, at a given time, denote the number of population elements belonging to each class as $I_0, \ldots, I_{c-1}$ respectively ($\sum_{i=0}^{c-1} I_i = n$).

## 3.2  REPRESENTATIVE FITNESSES

We assume that each class $i$ has a *representative fitness* $f_i$, which we define to be the height of the corresponding peak. Our models assume that for each class $i$, all elements of that class have identical fitness $f_i$. This assumption becomes increasingly valid as runs approach equilibrium; from a maintenance standpoint, we are most interested in an algorithm's behavior at equilibrium. It is possible to relax this assumption so that $f_i$ is the mean fitness of class $i$'s elements, each class has a certain variance in the fitness of its elements, and fitnesses are distributed according to some predefined distribution (Deb, 1989). This would incorporate an additional source of noise into the model — internal class fitness variance. However, as demonstrated in this study, our assumption of identical fitnesses within a class buys a more powerful model, where power is measured by predictive rather than descriptive value.

We also require that for all $i$, $f_i \geq 0$. This requirement of positive fitnesses is already enforced for many GAs. Where objective functions can take on negative values, some appropriate scaling mechanism must be used to make $f$ a positive function.

## 3.3  DESIRABLE PEAKS

Our preliminary models assume that of the $c$ peaks, we are interested in locating all of them. Later, more general models assume we wish to locate at least $b$ of the $c$ highest maxima. We implement the latter models as follows. First we assign a fitness threshold. Maxima with fitnesses below the threshold are considered undesirable; maxima with fitnesses above the threshold, desirable. We let $b$ be the number of desirable maxima, and $c$ be the total number of maxima. The niching method's challenge is to locate the desirable peaks in the presence of possibly many more, undesirable peaks.

## 3.4  MAINTENANCE OF CLASSES

Our models operate from the standpoint of class maintenance rather than class formation — of maintaining niches in a quasi-equilibrium in the population. Therefore, we assume that all desired classes are initially represented in the population. (At time or generation $t = 0$, for all desired classes $i$, $I_i > 0$.) Note that this is a requirement for our models — not for our actual GAs. If class formation is successful in a GA with sharing, then as the GA approaches equilibrium, the maintenance assumption becomes increasingly valid.

The process of locating a local maximum is addressed in the standard GA literature for unimodal function optimization. The population size required to locate a single peak is a signal-to-noise issue both within and across schemata (Goldberg, Deb, & Clark, 1992). The process of both locating and maintaining peaks can incorporate estimates based upon both signal-to-noise and class maintenance considerations. We expect that for most multimodal optimization problems of interest, class maintenance requirements will override signal-to-noise requirements. (This has been the case in all experiments conducted to date.) We utilize this rule-of-thumb due both to successful experimentation and to the intuitive notion that the multimodality dimension of problem hardness will cause significantly more trouble for a niching GA than will the location of any single peak. If, as expected, class maintenance requirements subsume class formation requirements, then a population size sufficient to maintain a number of classes will also be sufficient to form them.

## 3.5   MUTATION REMOVED

A key simplifying assumption of our framework is the removal of mutation, the GA's local neighborhood operator. We assume, as many authors have previously pointed out, that mutation in combination with selection has a hillclimbing effect, regardless of whether we define classes based on Hamming neighborhoods or phenotypic epsilon-neighborhoods. This should roughly be the case for most commonly used representations. Since our framework incorporates a hillclimbing algorithm that puts equivalence classes in a one-to-one correspondence with local maxima, adding small rates of mutation to a GA should keep its behavior within the scope of our models.

In multimodal function optimization, we are interested primarily in the peaks under which niched-selection and crossover deposit points. The selection-plus-crossover algorithm has done its job if it deposits in a desirable distribution. We assume that selection-plus-mutation or some other type of genetic hillclimbing can move a point to the top of a peak once the point has been successfully deposited.

Note that we are not ignoring mutation, just separating it out. We can hence concentrate on more germane aspects of multimodal function optimization in our models — locating peaks via niched-selection and crossover — and ignore the variation about local points in the search space (typically variation *within* each equivalence classes) induced by mutation. Some of our later simulations incorporate mutation with little effect on the model. Note that sharing's restorative pressure compensates for the occasional mutation that strays from its original niche.

## 3.6   CROSSOVER

We will not assume a particular type of crossover for our framework. Instead, individual models can, given the class membership of both elements undergoing a cross and also given the details of the crossover operator, assign probabilities that the offspring will be members of various of the $c$ classes.

One assumption that will not vary throughout this study is that crossing two elements of the same class will yield two offspring of that class. This is generally accurate for the partitions of this study, and is universally accurate under standard crossover operators for other useful partitions such as schema-based partitions. Radcliffe (1993) calls this requirement *respect*. He says that the presence of respect allows a GA to "converge upon good formae [equivalence classes]".

Preliminary models assume no crossover in order to isolate selection. These models nevertheless have predictive value for GAs with sharing and crossover (and mutation), on problems in which crossover's disruptive effects are negligible. (Sharing's restorative pressure compensates for any minor disruptions.) More advanced models incorporate crossover. Actual runs of GAs with crossover, throughout this study, make use of single-point crossover.

## 3.7   PERFECT DISCRIMINATION

We make the additional assumption that all classes are fully distinguishable via the proper setting of $\sigma_{share}$ or via a similar technique. This is equivalent to Horn's (1993) assumption of non-overlapping niches, also known as *perfect discrimination* or *perfect sharing*. Let $A$

and $B$ be arbitrary equivalence classes under our framework, and let $a$, $b$, $a_1$, and $a_2$ be arbitrary elements of the solution space. If $a \in A$ and $b \in B$ ($B \neq A$), then $sh(d(a,b)) = sh(d(b,a)) = 0$.

Since under our framework all elements of a class have identical fitness, the elements within a class contribute 100% to each other's fitness. Therefore if $a_1 \in A$ and $a_2 \in A$, then $sh(d(a_1, a_2)) = sh(d(a_2, a_1)) = 1$. Note that if niches were allowed to overlap, then neighboring niches would partially contribute to the fitnesses of each other's elements, and elements within a niche would not fully contribute to each other's fitnesses.

We expect our models to be applicable to both cases with non-overlapping niches and with small overlaps among niches. This is not a significant restriction, since sharing is most effective in cases of no overlap. As the amount of overlap increases, the effectiveness of sharing diminishes. Note that niches need not be equidistant or spaced in any particular way.

## 4  GENETIC DRIFT UNDER SHARING

This section first analyzes and illustrates sharing's distributional properties from the perspective of our modelling framework. It examines the likelihood that sharing loses important solutions, and derives closed-form expressions for the expected time to disappearance of a class. This time to disappearance or *drift time* is related to the population size $n$, number of classes $c$, and relative class fitnesses (which we designate using ratio $r$). We illustrate, both theoretically and empirically, the drift time of sharing.

### 4.1  DISTRIBUTIONAL PROPERTIES

Sharing is able to operate within any GA selection scheme. We model sharing with roulette-wheel selection, with the understanding that since RWS is the noisiest of commonly used proportionate-selection schemes, our models will bound the behavior of sharing under noise-reduced, proportionate-selection schemes such as stochastic remainder selection and stochastic universal selection. Specifically, we expect bounds on quantities such as drift time and population size, computed using RWS, to also serve as bounds for less noisy, proportionate-selection schemes. RWS not only gives us bounding behavior, but also offers the advantage of simplicity, making our modelling task a more promising venture.

#### 4.1.1  ROULETTE-WHEEL SELECTION

Before examining sharing with roulette-wheel selection, we first look at RWS in isolation. Under RWS, in any given trial, the probability of selecting some element of an arbitrary class $i$, $P_s(i)$, is proportional to fitness:

$$P_s(i) \;=\; \frac{I_i f_i}{\sum_{j=0}^{c-1} I_j f_j} \; . \tag{3}$$

Note that $\sum_{i=0}^{c-1} P_s(i) = 1$.

Employing the formulas for the mean and variance of the binomial distribution for $I_i$, the expected number of population elements in Class $i$ after one generation ($n$ Bernoulli trials) is

$$\mu_i \;=\; n\, P_s(i) \; , \tag{4}$$

with variance,

$$\sigma_i^2 \; = \; n \, P_s(i) \, (1 - P_s(i)) \; . \tag{5}$$

The above results tell us a great deal about the behavior of a GA that runs RWS. The distribution at time $t + 1$ of population elements among classes depends both upon the distribution at time $t$ and the relative fitnesses of the classes. Given multiple classes of identical fitness, where one class has become more frequent than the others, there is no restoration — the expected number of each class in a given generation is the same as the actual number of each in the previous generation. (If all $f_i$ are the same, Equations 3 and 4 tell us, respectively, that for all $i$, $P_s(i) = I_i/n$ and $\mu_i = I_i$.) This lack of restorative pressure, in combination with the significant variance of RWS and finite population size, leads to the eventual disappearance of all but one class (Goldberg & Segrest, 1987). Given classes of nonuniform fitness, the highest-fit class is expected to take over the entire population: a rough estimate of takeover time can be obtained by iterating Equation 4 for the fittest class $i$ until $\mu_i \geq n$.

### 4.1.2  SHARING WITH ROULETTE-WHEEL SELECTION

Let us now add fitness sharing to roulette-wheel selection. Shared fitness, denoted by $f'$, for an arbitrary class $i$, is given by $f'_i = f_i/I_i \quad (I_i \neq 0)$. Substitution into Equation 3 yields

$$P_s(i) \; = \; \frac{I_i f'_i}{\sum_{j=0}^{c-1} I_j f'_j} \; = \; \frac{f_i}{\sum_{j=0}^{c-1} f_j} \; . \tag{6}$$

The mean and variance for the number of population elements in Class $i$ after one generation ($n$ Bernoulli trials) are given in the following two equations:

$$\mu_i \; = \; n \, P_s(i) \; ; \tag{7}$$

$$\sigma_i^2 \; = \; n \, P_s(i) \, (1 - P_s(i)) \; . \tag{8}$$

Two special cases of Equation 6 are of interest. For $c$ classes of identical fitness ($f_0 = f_1 = \ldots = f_{c-1}$),

$$\forall_i \; P_S(i) \; = \; \frac{f_i}{\sum_{j=0}^{c-1} f_j} \; = \; \frac{1}{c} \; . \tag{9}$$

For two classes ($c = 2$), $A$ and $B$,

$$P_s(A) \; = \; \frac{I_A f'_A}{I_A f'_A + I_B f'_B} \; = \; \frac{f_A}{f_A + f_B} \; = \; \frac{r}{r+1} \; , \tag{10}$$

where $r = f_A/f_B$.

For sharing with roulette-wheel selection, the expected distribution and its variance are independent of the starting distribution (since the $I_i$ terms drop out of Equation 6); they depend only upon relative class fitnesses. This explains the *restorative pressure* inherent in sharing methods, where classes that contain other than their share of population elements can expect to be restored to the proper number in one generation. This restorative pressure keeps drift from becoming an overwhelming factor, since unlike RWS alone, RWS with sharing does not give stochastic fluctuations the opportunity to accumulate over multiple generations. A related beneficial property of sharing, uncovered by the above model, is that no greater threat exists of a class becoming extinct when it has only one representative in the population than when it has many.

The independence of successive generations under this sharing model allows us to perform further algebraic derivations of properties of sharing such as drift time and population size. Because of this independence, sharing, unlike the simple GA, is not a Markov chain. (A Markov chain is a sequence of trials in which the outcome of a trial depends only upon the outcome of the previous trial.) Horn (1993) discovered this non-Markov property of sharing when the column entries of his transition matrix for "perfect sharing" turned out to be identical. Horn's observation, along with the results presented in this study, suggest that Markov chains may be unnecessarily complex for modelling sharing.

Given classes of nonuniform fitness, the least fit class will not disappear if sharing is employed, unless its expected number of individuals is small enough to be overcome by noise. Deb (1989) noted that genotypic sharing sometimes loses peaks of relatively low fitness. He attributed this loss to the noisy discrimination of genotypic sharing: the setting of $\sigma_{share}$ must take into account distances between peaks, as well as relative class fitnesses. Specifically, to maintain the lower of peaks $i$ and $j$, the following $\sigma_{share}$ is required:

$$\sigma_{share} \leq \frac{d(i,j)}{1 - r_{i,j}} \; , \tag{11}$$

where $d(i,j)$ is the Hamming distance between the maxima of peaks $i$ and $j$, and $r_{i,j} = \min(f_i/f_j, f_j/f_i)$. For $r_{i,j} = 1$, any $\sigma_{share}$ is sufficient to maintain both peaks.

Note that Deb's calculation does not take population size into account. This suggests that another factor might also be at work in genotypic as well as phenotypic sharing: genetic drift due to the relative insignificance of lower peaks. Examples of this type of genetic drift follow. The perfect discrimination assumption of our models allows us to ignore the problem Deb encountered.

### 4.1.3   EXPERIMENTAL VERIFICATION

We now illustrate some of the previously derived distributional properties. Figures 1 and 2 show the expected distribution after one generation and its standard deviation, for RWS alone and sharing with RWS, given a population of size 32. Figure 1 is for two classes of equal fitness; Figure 2, two classes of unequal fitness. The two figures illustrate the previously stated concept, that for RWS, the expected distribution is a function of the prior distribution; with sharing added, however, the expected distribution becomes independent of the prior distribution.

Figures 3 and 4 compare sample runs of both algorithms to expected behavior. In particular, runs of RWS and sharing with RWS proceed for 100 generations, on the simple two-class optimization problems, $f_B = f_A = 1$ and $f_B = 4f_A = 4$. These are one-bit problems in which the '0' genotype corresponds to Class $A$; the '1', to Class $B$. The representative fitnesses of the two classes, $A$ and $B$, are designated $f_A$ and $f_B$, respectively. The initial class distribution in both sample runs is uniform. Other GA parameters are $n = 32$, $p_c = p_m = 0$, and $\sigma_{share} = 0.5$.

In Figure 3, where both classes are of equal fitness, under RWS, as expected, genetic drift allows Class $A$ to eventually take over the whole population. (Class $A$ is just as likely to disappear, allowing Class $B$ to take over the entire population.) RWS's high variance and lack of restorative pressure cause the GA to wander aimlessly in both directions, until Class $B$ loses all its elements. Sharing, since it incorporates RWS, also exhibits similar fluctuations, this time about the mean value of 16 elements per class. Sharing's restorative

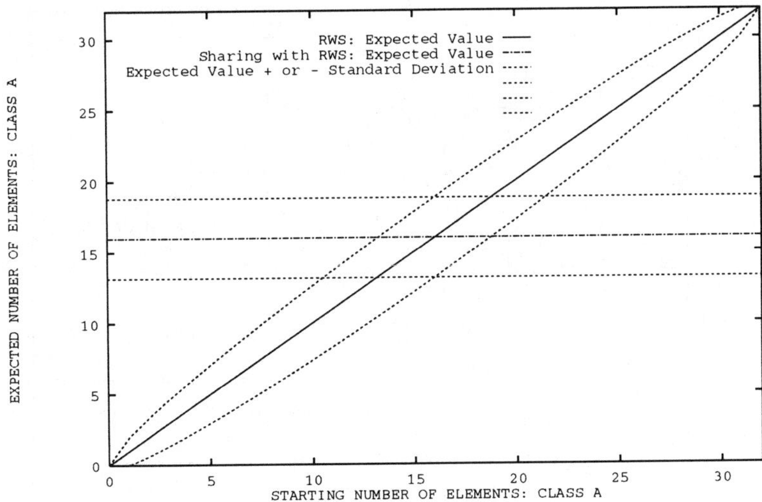

Figure 1: The mean and standard deviation of the expected number of elements in a class after a generation, are given for RWS alone, and sharing with RWS. Model parameters are $n = 32$, $c = 2$, and $f_B = f_A$. The curves are calculated from Equations 4, 5, 7, and 8.

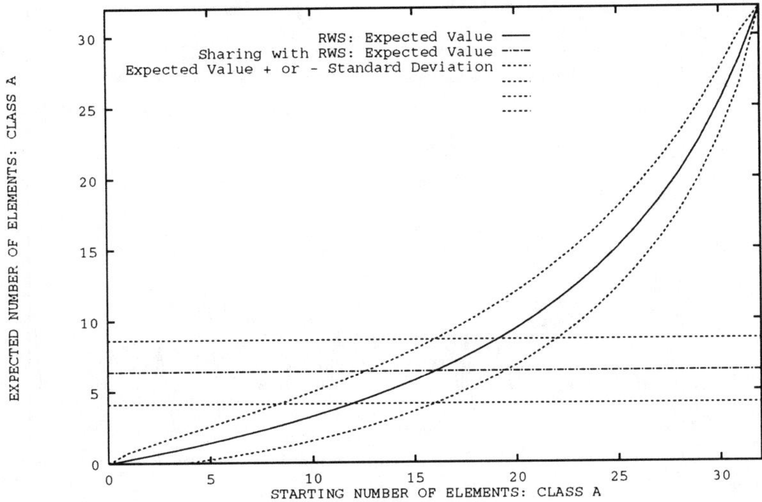

Figure 2: The mean and standard deviation of the expected number of elements in a class after a generation, are given for RWS alone, and sharing with RWS. Model parameters are $n = 32$, $c = 2$, and $f_B = 4f_A$. The curves are calculated from Equations 4, 5, 7, and 8.

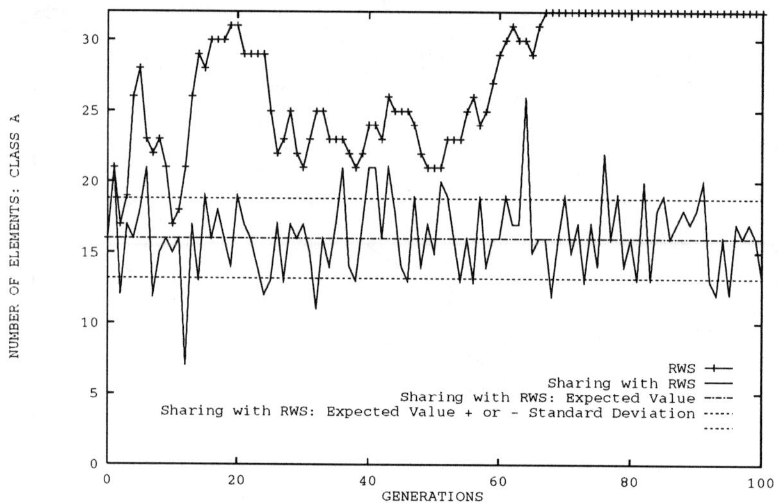

Figure 3: Sample runs of RWS, and sharing with RWS, are compared to the expectation and standard deviation for sharing with RWS, computed from Equations 7 and 8. Parameters are $n = 32$, $c = 2$, $f_B = f_A$, $p_c = p_m = 0$, and $\sigma_{share} = 0.5$.

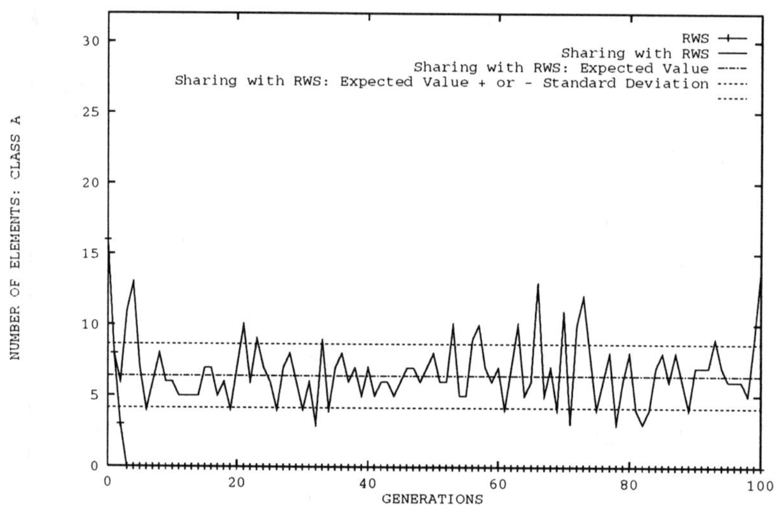

Figure 4: Sample runs of RWS, and sharing with RWS, are compared to the expectation and standard deviation for sharing with RWS, computed from Equations 7 and 8. Parameters are $n = 32$, $c = 2$, $f_B = 4f_A$, $p_c = p_m = 0$, and $\sigma_{share} = 0.5$.

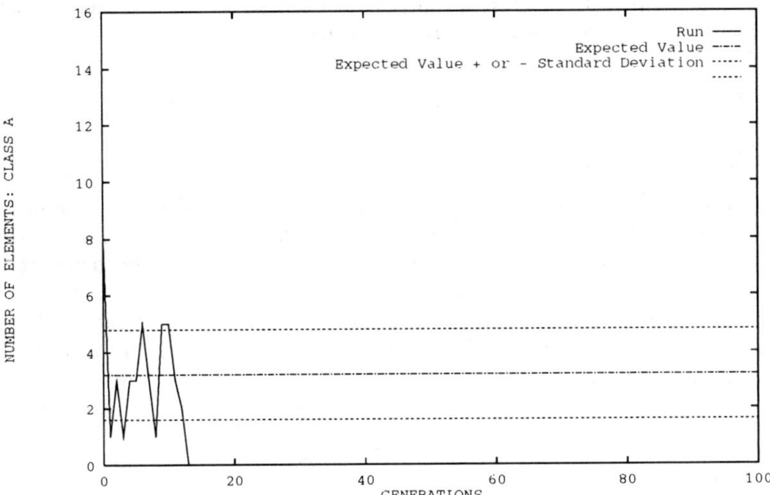


Figure 5: A sample run of sharing with RWS is compared to the expectation and standard deviation for sharing with RWS, computed from Equations 7 and 8. Parameters are $n = 16$, $c = 2$, $f_B = 4f_A$, $p_c = p_m = 0$, and $\sigma_{share} = 0.5$.

pressure, however, maintains both classes in equal proportions on the average, for the full 100 generations.

In Figure 4, selection pressure causes Class $A$, the weaker of the two, to disappear rapidly under RWS (by generation 3). When sharing is added, Class $A$ is maintained in proportion to its relative fitness, with some fluctuation about the expected niche size of 6.4. At times, the number of elements in Class $A$ fluctuates dangerously close to zero. This suggests that sharing with RWS, although more stable than RWS alone, is not immune from genetic drift.

Figure 5 verifies the above suspicion. On the one-bit, two-class problem $f_B = 4f_A = 4$, when population size is cut in half to $n = 16$, expected niche size also drops by half, down to 3.2. Sharing with RWS allows the stronger Class $B$ to take over the entire population after the fatal fluctuation in generation 12. (Again, $p_c = p_m = 0$ and $\sigma_{share} = .5$.) This proves the earlier conjecture, that given perfect discrimination between peaks, lower peaks may still disappear due to genetic drift. The next section examines the exact point at which a class can be expected to disappear and this point's relation to population size.

## 4.2   LOSS PROBABILITIES

We now bound the probability of losing a class in a single generation. Equation 6 gives the probability $P_s(i)$ of selecting some element of an arbitrary class $i$ in one trial of sharing with RWS (one spin of the roulette wheel using shared fitnesses). The probability of selecting some element outside Class $i$ is $1 - P_s(i)$. After a full generation, the probability of losing all elements of Class $i$ is simply the probability of selecting all $n$ elements from outside Class $i$:

$(1 - P_s(i))^n$. Since any of the $c$ classes can potentially lose all its elements, the probability $X$ of one or more classes disappearing after one generation is

$$X \leq \sum_{i=0}^{c-1}(1 - P_s(i))^n \ . \qquad (0 < X < 1) \qquad (12)$$

The probability of maintaining all classes for a generation is $1 - X$.

The above expression is an inequality because the probabilities of intersection of loss events are not subtracted off (e.g., for a three-class problem, the probability of losing both Class 1 and Class 2 would be included twice in the above summation). When the distribution of class selection probabilities does not stray too far from uniform, and when $n \gg c$, intersection terms are insignificant, and the inequality (12) can be treated as an equation. For example, consider the $c = 3$ case, where classes are of uniform fitness. We perform the full calculation, subtracting off intersections:

$$X \ = \ 3(1 - \frac{1}{3})^n - 3(\frac{1}{3})^n \ . \qquad (13)$$

Simplification yields

$$X \ = \ \frac{2^n - 1}{3^{n-1}} \ = \ \frac{2^n}{3^{n-1}} - \frac{1}{3^{n-1}} \ . \qquad (14)$$

This differs in only an exponentially decreasing increment from the bound derived from (12):

$$X \ \leq \ \frac{2^n}{3^{n-1}} \ . \qquad (15)$$

In fact, for $n = 32$, the bound is indistinguishable from the exact quantity up to the 15th decimal place.

In realistic optimization problems, we will not be interested in locating peaks that are of low fitness; hence we will have near-uniformity. (Extraneous, lower-fitness peaks will be modelled later, separate from the $c$ desired classes.) In addition, maintaining $c$ peaks typically requires $n$ to be some multiple of $c$; hence $n \gg c$. We can tell if either condition is severely violated, because the above summation will approach or exceed 1.0, leading to a useless probability bound.

For the special case where all classes have identical fitness ($\forall_i \ P_s(i) = 1/c$), we obtain

$$X \ \leq \ c(1 - \frac{1}{c})^n \ . \qquad (16)$$

Note that the right-hand side of the above expression has two useful forms:

$$c(1 - \frac{1}{c})^n \ = \ \frac{(c-1)^n}{c^{n-1}} \ . \qquad (17)$$

We can calculate the conditions under which (16) gives a useful estimate for $X$. Since all classes are of identical fitness, the near-uniformity condition is satisfied. That leaves the condition $n \gg c$. How much greater than $c$ must n be? Starting with the inequality,

$$c(1 - \frac{1}{c})^n \ < \ 1 \ , \qquad (18)$$

with a little manipulation we obtain

$$n \ \ln(1 - \frac{1}{c}) \ < \ -\ln c \ . \qquad (19)$$

Using approximation (89) of the appendix to simplify the above left-hand side, yields

$$n > c \ln c \ .$$  (20)

Therefore, (16) gives a useful bound for $X$ for values of $n$ greater than $c \ln c$, with increasing utility for larger $n$, relative to $c \ln c$.

For the special case of two classes ($c = 2$), $A$ and $B$, the calculation of $X$ is exact, since it is not possible to lose both classes:

$$X = \frac{r^n + 1}{(r + 1)^n} \ ,$$  (21)

where $r = f_A / f_B$.

## 4.3  LOSS DISTRIBUTION

We have set the groundwork for computing the expected time to extinction of one of the $c$ classes. We have already bounded the probability of extinction occurring in a single generation. Since successive trials are independent in our sharing model, the expected extinction time is straightforward to compute.

Each generation, at least one class disappears from the population with probability $X$. This probability of disappearance remains constant from generation to generation, until a loss actually occurs. Therefore, the loss of one or more classes can be treated as a binomial event, occurring with probability of "success" $X$, with the stipulation that once a success occurs, $X$ is no longer valid. Since we are not interested in repeated successes, but only in strings of failures followed by a success, this limitation will have no effect.

We now examine the time required to lose at least one class. Recall our prior assumption that all classes are initially represented in the population. This assumption tells us that the probability of losing one or more classes after exactly 0 generations is 0; the probability of losing one or more classes after exactly one generation is $X$; after exactly two generations, $(1 - X)X$; after exactly $G$ generations, $(1 - X)^{G-1}X$, which is simply the probability of $G - 1$ "failures" to lose a class, followed by a "success". Treating the number of generations $L$ required to lose at least one class as a random variable, yields the *loss distribution*:

$$P(L = G) = (1 - X)^{G-1}X \ . \qquad (1 \leq G < \infty)$$  (22)

Figure 6 shows the loss distribution for two classes of equal fitness under a population of size $n = 8$. Note that the loss distribution is a *geometric distribution* (Freund & Walpole, 1980).

The expected number of generations required to lose at least one class is the mean of the geometric (loss) distribution,

$$\mu_L = \frac{1}{X} \ .$$  (23)

The derivation of Equation 23 is presented in the appendix. Equation 23 is intuitively what one would expect, the inverse of the single generation loss probability. The variance in the expected number of generations to loss is the variance of the geometric (loss) distribution,

$$\sigma_L^2 = \frac{1 - X}{X^2} = \mu_L^2 - \mu_L \ .$$  (24)

The derivation of Equation 24 is also presented in the appendix.

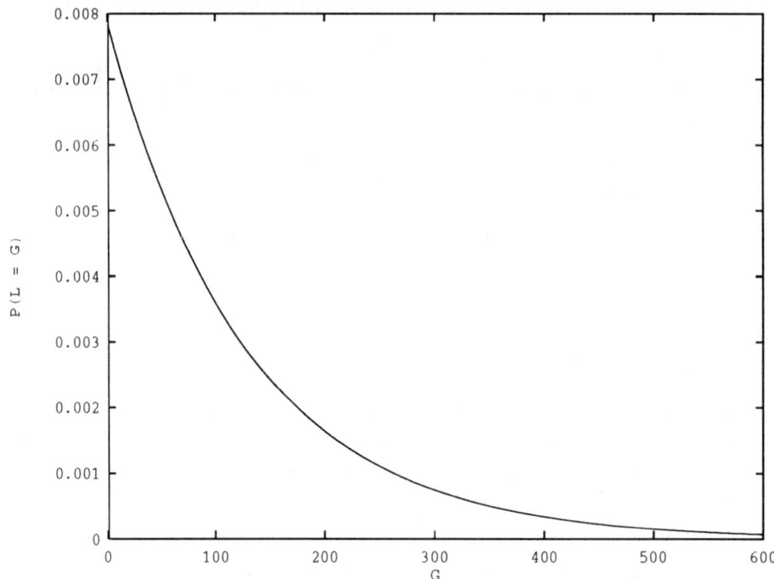

Figure 6: The loss distribution of Equation 22 is shown for $c = 2$, $n = 8$, and $f_B = f_A$.

From summing values of the loss distribution from 1 to $G$ generations, we obtain $P(L \leq G)$, the probability of losing, in $G$ generations or fewer, all elements of one or more of the $c$ classes. (All classes are being tried simultaneously.)

$$P(L \leq G) \;=\; \sum_{i=1}^{G}(1 - X)^{i-1}X \;=\; X\sum_{i=0}^{G-1}(1 - X)^i \;. \tag{25}$$

$X$ is independent of $i$, and $0.0 < X < 1.0$. This *cumulative loss distribution* is shown in Figure 7 for the case of $c = 2$, $n = 8$, and $f_B = f_A$. Using the formula for the partial sum of a geometric series (Equation 85 of the appendix) yields

$$P(L \leq G) \;=\; X\frac{1 - (1 - X)^G}{1 - (1 - X)} \;=\; 1 - (1 - X)^G \;. \tag{26}$$

Thus the probability $\gamma$ of maintaining all $c$ classes for at least $G$ generations is given by

$$\gamma \;=\; 1 - P(L \leq G) \;=\; (1 - X)^G \;. \tag{27}$$

Taking the $G^{\text{th}}$ root of both sides allows us to solve for $X$, resulting in the following generally applicable equation for sharing:

$$X \;=\; 1 - \gamma^{\frac{1}{G}} \;. \tag{28}$$

## 4.4   DRIFT TIME

Figure 8 shows, for $c = 2$, two fitness ratios, and various population sizes, the expectation and standard deviation in the number of generations to loss of a class. Curves above and

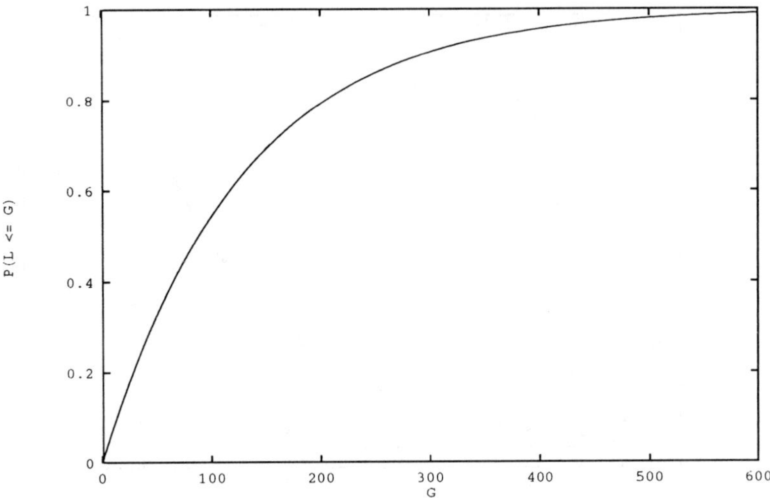

Figure 7: The cumulative loss distribution of Equation 26 is shown for $c = 2$, $n = 8$, and $f_B = f_A$.

below the mean curve indicate a range of one standard deviation from the mean. Note that the lower curve, $\mu_L - \sigma_L$, converges to .5 . This is because

$$\lim_{n \to \infty} \sqrt{\mu_L^2 - \mu_L} \;=\; \mu_L - .5 \;\; . \tag{29}$$

Even for very small $n$, $\sigma_L \approx \mu_L - .5$. The fact that one standard deviation in the downward direction takes us close to zero does not mean that typical runs, regardless of population size, will lose a class immediately: the standard deviation does not tell us everything about the loss distribution. Because of infinite potential upward deviation in the expected number of generations to loss, and limited potential downward deviation, we can decrease the probability of a run losing a class to as close to zero as we desire. This is accomplished by raising $n$, and will be detailed in the upcoming section on population sizing.

Figure 9 shows, for multiple classes of uniform fitness, a lower bound on the expected number of generations to loss of at least one class, as a function of $c$ and $n$. The bound is obtained by substituting the right-hand side of (16) into Equation 23. This bound shows that drift time is roughly an exponential function of $n$ but a rapidly decreasing function of $c$. This is evident if we employ a large-$c$ approximation (Equation 90 of the appendix):

$$\mu_L \;=\; \frac{1}{X} \;\approx\; \frac{1}{c(1 - \frac{1}{c})^n} \;\approx\; \frac{e^{n/c}}{c} \;\; . \tag{30}$$

For the special case of $c = 2$, we can compare our derived drift time with Horn's (1993) graph, drawn using a Markov chain model of sharing. Horn graphs the expected number of generations to loss of a class in the one-bit, two-class, "perfect sharing" case. We obtain

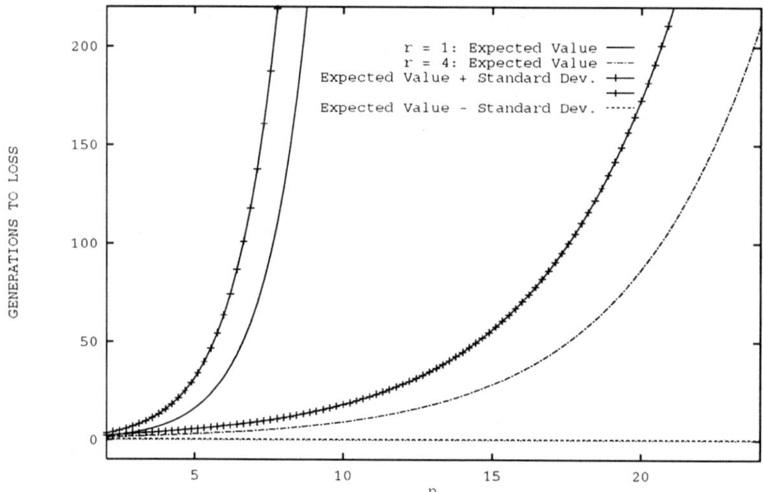


Figure 8: $\mu_L \pm \sigma_L$, calculated from (23) and (24) is shown for increasing $n$, with $c = 2$ and $r = f_A/f_B$.

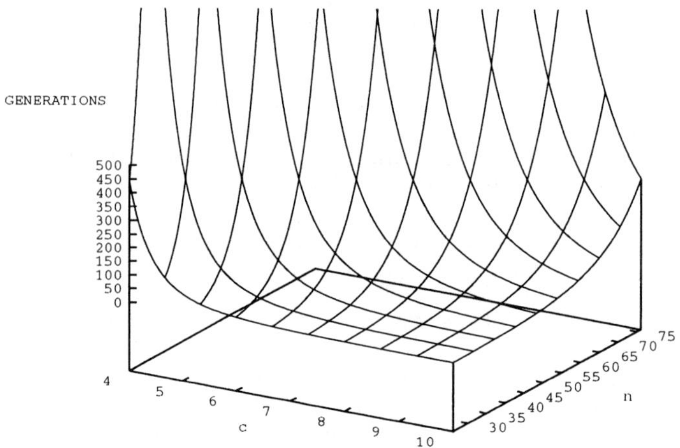


Figure 9: A lower bound on expected drift time, calculated from (16) and (23), is shown as a function of $c$ and $n$, for multiple classes of uniform fitness.

Table 1: Mean drift times $\bar{x}$ for 5000 runs of sharing with RWS are compared with expected drift times $\mu_L$ from the sharing model, for $c = 2$, and two different fitness ratios. A 95% confidence interval for $\mu_L$ is calculated from $\bar{x}$. Sample standard deviation is $s$, and the model's standard deviation is $\sigma_L$. For the actual GA, $p_c = p_m = 0$ and $\sigma_{share} = .5$. All drift time statistics are in generations.

| $n$ | $\bar{x}$ | $\mu_L$ | $\mu_L$: 95% C.I. | $s$ | $\sigma_L$ |
|---|---|---|---|---|---|
| | | | $f_B = f_A$ | | |
| 2 | 2.00 | 2.00 | $(1.96, 2.04)$ | 1.42 | 1.41 |
| 4 | 8.04 | 8.00 | $(7.83, 8.25)$ | 7.46 | 7.48 |
| 6 | 32.47 | 32.00 | $(31.60, 33.34)$ | 32.02 | 31.50 |
| 8 | 129.18 | 128.00 | $(125.65, 132.71)$ | 125.66 | 127.50 |
| 10 | 516.23 | 512.00 | $(502.05, 530.41)$ | 512.43 | 511.50 |
| | | | $f_B = 4f_A$ | | |
| 2 | 1.46 | 1.47 | $(1.44, 1.48)$ | 0.82 | 0.83 |
| 4 | 2.41 | 2.43 | $(2.36, 2.46)$ | 1.82 | 1.86 |
| 6 | 3.80 | 3.81 | $(3.71, 3.89)$ | 3.22 | 3.27 |
| 8 | 6.03 | 5.96 | $(5.88, 6.18)$ | 5.42 | 5.44 |
| 10 | 9.47 | 9.31 | $(9.23, 9.71)$ | 8.85 | 8.80 |
| 12 | 14.50 | 14.55 | $(14.11, 14.89)$ | 14.07 | 14.04 |
| 14 | 23.01 | 22.74 | $(22.39, 23.63)$ | 22.84 | 22.23 |
| 16 | 35.42 | 35.53 | $(34.45, 36.39)$ | 34.58 | 35.03 |
| 18 | 55.83 | 55.51 | $(54.31, 57.35)$ | 55.80 | 55.01 |
| 20 | 86.17 | 86.74 | $(83.78, 88.56)$ | 86.59 | 86.24 |
| 22 | 134.89 | 135.53 | $(131.15, 138.63)$ | 135.86 | 135.03 |
| 24 | 215.33 | 211.76 | $(209.47, 221.19)$ | 217.80 | 211.26 |

an expression for this quantity by substituting the right-hand side of Equation 21 into Equation 23:

$$\mu_L = \frac{(r+1)^n}{r^n + 1} \ , \tag{31}$$

where $r$ is the fitness ratio of the two classes. For two classes of equal fitness ($r = 1$), Equation 31 reduces to $\mu_L = 2^{n-1}$. Horn concludes from his graph that drift time is an exponential function of $n$. This is verified by the above equation as follows. Without loss of generality, assume that $0 < r \leq 1$. The denominator of Equation 31 will be in the interval $(1, 2]$, but the numerator will grow exponentially at a rate of $(1+r)^n$. However, our equation predicts that growth is not as exponential as depicted in Horn's graph. This is because the graph is off by a factor of $n$ due to a failure to divide by $n$ (J. Horn, personal communication, June, 1993).

Table 1 compares the sharing-with-RWS model to statistics from 5000 runs on the one-bit, two-class functions defined earlier ($f_B = f_A$ and $f_B = 4f_A$). The table gives 95% confidence intervals for the expected drift time, given the average drift time over 5000 runs. All runs use uniform initialization. For both functions, experimental results at various $n$ with $p_c = p_m = 0$ and $\sigma_{share} = .5$ correspond nearly perfectly with derived results.

Compare Table 1's expected drift time for $f_B = 4f_A$ using $n = 16$, with the earlier runs

Table 2: For fixed $n = 32$, $c$ is varied, and the $f_i$ are uniform. The estimator $\hat{\mu}_L$ (computed from lower bound (23)) for expected drift time in sharing is compared with the sample mean $\bar{x}$ from 5000 runs of sharing with RWS ($p_c = p_m = 0$; $\sigma share = .5$). All drift time statistics are in generations. Sample standard deviation is $s$.

| $c$ | $\bar{x}$ | $\hat{\mu}_L$ | % Error | $s$ |
|---|---|---|---|---|
| 12 | 1.74 | 1.35 | 22.41% | 1.15 |
| 11 | 2.28 | 1.92 | 15.79% | 1.68 |
| 10 | 3.27 | 2.91 | 11.01% | 2.70 |
| 9 | 5.10 | 4.82 | 5.49% | 4.61 |
| 8 | 9.19 | 8.97 | 2.39% | 9.04 |
| 7 | 19.75 | 19.82 | 0.35% | 18.96 |
| 6 | 57.93 | 56.97 | 1.66% | 58.97 |
| 5 | 256.94 | 252.44 | 1.75% | 252.90 |

from Figures 4 and 5. The table explains why the $n = 16$ run drifted but the $n = 32$ run did not: $n = 32$ requires an average of 1262.18 generations to drift, but we only ran it for 100; $n = 16$, on the other hand, requires only 35.53 generations on the average.

The final simulations of this section test bounds (16) and (20). We fix $n$ at 32 and vary $c$, employing starting distributions as close to uniform as possible. (Sometimes $n$ is not evenly divisible by $c$.) Class fitnesses are uniform ($\forall_{i,j} \; f_i = f_j$), and the GA (RWS plus sharing) employs a five-bit encoding in which each possible string is a class. However, only $c$ of the 32 possible classes are placed into the initial population. Since crossover and mutation are turned off ($p_c = p_m = 0$), only those $c$ classes will be present in subsequent populations. Using (20) to calculate at which $c$ our bound becomes useless, $13 \ln 13 = 33.34 > n$, but $12 \ln 12 = 29.82 < n$: the maximum useful $c$ for $n = 32$ is 12. To verify, if we substitute $c = 13$ and $n = 32$ into the right hand side of (16), we obtain $X \leq 1.0036$, an illegally high probability. Substituting $c = 12$ and $n = 32$, on the other hand, yields $X \leq .7412$. We perform 5000 runs at each $c$ and employ $\sigma_{share} = .5$ in the GA. Results are shown in Table 2.

As $c$ decreases relative to $n$, accuracy of the computed bound increases. Note that even for the maximal $c = 12$, the bound is only off by 22.41%. To solve real problems, we will be using a $c$ to $n$ ratio higher than that for even the $c = 5$ case in Table 2, which has only 1.75% error. Note that the computed sample mean contains slight sampling error which, as $c$ decreases (to seven or less), begins to overshadow the bounding error. We do not give drift times for $2 \leq c \leq 4$ because of prohibitive run times for 5000 runs. For $c = 2$, as noted earlier, the calculated drift time would be exact and was previously given in Equation 31. For $c = 3$, the calculated drift time would be nearly exact, indistinguishable from the exact value up to the 10th significant digit. (An expression for the exact drift time can be obtained from Equations 14 and 23.) We expect that the $c = 4$ bound would also be extremely accurate.

# 5   POPULATION SIZE: SELECTION ONLY; ALL CLASSES DESIRABLE

The most effective method of combating genetic drift is to raise the population size to a level sufficient to protect the desired niches. Hence population sizing is a central issue in fitness sharing, and more generally, in the study of niching methods and traditional GAs. In fact, in most GAs, population size is the single, most critical parameter. This section uses the prior genetic drift results to derive bounds on minimum required population sizes for sharing. Specifically, this section derives, for three related models of sharing, bounds on the population size required to maintain, with probability $\gamma$, a fixed number of niches. The first model assumes all niches are equivalent with respect to fitness. The next two models allow niches to differ with respect to fitness. The models of this section do not consider the effects of crossover. These models still have predictive value for GAs with sharing and crossover (and mutation), however, on problems in which crossover and mutation are minimally disruptive. (Sharing's restorative pressure will compensate for any minor disruptions.) To verify this, we run GAs with sharing, RWS, and even crossover and mutation, on seven test problems of varying difficulty in optimization and classification, using population sizes derived from the models.

A sufficiently large population will ensure that the GA with sharing maintains, with confidence $\gamma$, all desired classes for a sufficient number of generations $G$ — that genetic drift and other disruptive forces do not eliminate any class. Substituting the right-hand side of Equation 28 into (12) yields the following general relationship for sharing under RWS:

$$1 - \gamma^{\frac{1}{G}} \leq \sum_{i=0}^{c-1}(1 - P_S(i))^n \; . \tag{32}$$

From (32), we can obtain bounds on $n$, for $c$ classes of identical fitness, and for $c$ classes of arbitrary fitness. It is important to keep in mind that $n$ in the above equation represents the minimum population size required to maintain $c$ classes for at least $G$ generations with probability of at least $\gamma$. If we call the actual population size that the GA employs $n'$, then any $n' \geq n$ will be sufficient to maintain $c$ classes for at least $G$ generations with probability of at least $\gamma$. We call $n$ the *minimum required population size* and $n'$ the *actual population size*.

In practice, we will not be able to obtain an exact $n$ except in the $c = 2$ case. However, we can derive upper bounds on $n$ that also serve as lower bounds on $n'$. The relationship among $n$, $n'$, and the derived population size bound is

$$n \leq \textit{population size bound} \leq n' \; . \tag{33}$$

## 5.1   CLASSES OF IDENTICAL FITNESS

For $c$ classes of equal fitness, for all classes $i$, $P_S(i) = 1/c$ (from Equation 9). Substituting $1/c$ for $P_S(i)$ in (32) and solving for $n$, yields

$$n \leq \frac{\ln \frac{1-\gamma^{\frac{1}{G}}}{c}}{\ln \frac{c-1}{c}} \leq n' \; . \tag{34}$$

The middle term of the above expression is our desired population size bound. We verify this as follows. Inequality (12) tells us that the more trials per generation the GA performs (the higher the actual population size), the smaller the probability $X$ that one or more classes disappear after one generation. Equation 27 tells us that the smaller $X$ is, the higher the probability $\gamma$ that all $c$ classes will be maintained for at least $G$ generations. Therefore, a larger population will yield a higher $\gamma$. Hence, any $n' \geq n$ in (34) will maintain, with probability of at least $\gamma$, $c$ classes of equal fitness for at least $G$ generations.

For large $c$, the bound in (34) can be simplified using approximation (89) of the appendix as follows:

$$\frac{\ln \frac{1-\gamma^{\frac{1}{G}}}{c}}{\ln \frac{c-1}{c}} \approx c\left[-\ln\left(\frac{1-\gamma^{\frac{1}{G}}}{c}\right)\right] \, . \tag{35}$$

This simplification is good for all but the smallest $c$. Either bound in (35) can also serve as a population sizing tool for $c$ classes of nearly uniform fitness. In practice, the actual population size we employ will be one of the bounds in (35), rounded up to the nearest even integer.

For two classes of equal fitness, we can derive an exact expression for required population size, that corresponds to the bound in (34) with $c = 2$:

$$n = 1 - \frac{\ln(1-\gamma^{\frac{1}{G}})}{\ln 2} \approx 1 - 1.4427\ln(1 - \gamma^{\frac{1}{G}}) \, . \tag{36}$$

## 5.2   CLASSES OF ARBITRARY FITNESS: DERIVATION I

In the general case, inequality (32) can not be solved symbolically for $n$. However, one can obtain a lower bound for $n'$, at or above which, one is guaranteed with confidence of at least $\gamma$, to maintain $c$ classes for at least $G$ generations. The representative fitness $f_{min}$ of the least-fit peak is at least some percentage, specified by $r$, of the representative fitness $f_{max}$ of the globally optimal peak. The user need only specify this minimum-to-maximum fitness ratio of the desired peaks, $r = f_{min}/f_{max}$ $(0.0 < r \leq 1.0)$. For instance, $r = .8$ would model the maintenance of $c$ peaks, where the fitnesses of all peaks are within 80% of the fitness of the highest peak. This model allows population sizing in the presence of sketchy or partial information about the heights of peaks in the fitness landscape. The derivation proceeds as follows:

$$\forall_i \; P_s(i) = \frac{f_i}{\sum_{j=0}^{c-1} f_j} = \frac{\frac{f_i}{f_{max}}}{\sum_{j=0}^{c-1} \frac{f_j}{f_{max}}} \; ; \tag{37}$$

$$\forall_i \; P_s(i) \geq \frac{\frac{f_{min}}{f_{max}}}{\sum_{j=0}^{c-1} \frac{f_{max}}{f_{max}}} \; ; \tag{38}$$

$$\forall_i \; P_s(i) \geq \frac{r}{c} \; ; \tag{39}$$

$$\sum_{i=0}^{c-1}(1 - P_s(i))^n \leq \sum_{i=0}^{c-1}(1 - \frac{r}{c})^n \; ; \tag{40}$$

$$\sum_{i=0}^{c-1}(1 - P_s(i))^n \leq c(1 - \frac{r}{c})^n \, . \tag{41}$$

Substituting the left-hand side of (32) into inequality (41) yields

$$1 - \gamma^{\frac{1}{G}} \leq c(1 - \frac{r}{c})^n \, . \tag{42}$$

Solving for $n$ once again yields a lower bound for $n'$:

$$n \;\leq\; \frac{\ln \frac{1-\gamma^{\frac{1}{G}}}{c}}{\ln \frac{c-r}{c}} \;\leq\; n' \;. \tag{43}$$

For large $c$, the above bound can be simplified using approximation (89) as follows:

$$\frac{\ln \frac{1-\gamma^{\frac{1}{G}}}{c}}{\ln \frac{c-r}{c}} \;\approx\; \frac{c}{r}\left[-\ln\left(\frac{1-\gamma^{\frac{1}{G}}}{c}\right)\right] \;. \tag{44}$$

Note the similarity between the derived population size bounds in (35) and (44). In fact, substituting fitness ratio $r = 1$ into (44) yields the bounds of (35).

## 5.3   CLASSES OF ARBITRARY FITNESS: DERIVATION II

The fact that required experimental population sizes were in many cases much lower than those derived from (43) prompted the search for a tighter bound. We examine at which $f_i$ the right-hand side of (12) is maximal. Maximizing the right-hand side of (12) is equivalent to maximizing the following sum given $f_{min}$ and $f_{max}$, under the constraints that for all classes $k \in [0, c-1]$, $f_{min} \leq f_k \leq f_{max}$:

$$\sum_{i=0}^{c-1}(1 - \frac{f_i}{\sum_{j=0}^{c-1} f_j})^n \;. \tag{45}$$

We can prove that the maximum value of (45) is a tighter bound as follows. First, note that for all $f_i$ and $f_j$ in $[f_{min}, f_{max}]$,

$$X \;\leq\; \sum_{i=0}^{c-1}(1 - \frac{\frac{f_i}{f_{max}}}{\sum_{j=0}^{c-1} \frac{f_j}{f_{max}}})^n \;\leq\; (1 - \frac{\frac{f_{min}}{f_{max}}}{\sum_{j=0}^{c-1} \frac{f_{max}}{f_{max}}})^n \;. \tag{46}$$

Therefore,

$$X \;\leq\; \sum_{i=0}^{c-1}(1 - \frac{f_i}{\sum_{j=0}^{c-1} f_j})^n \;\leq\; c(1 - \frac{r}{c})^n \;, \tag{47}$$

proving that (45) is at least as close to $X$ as the right-hand side of (42). It follows that (45) will also yield a tighter bound on $n$.

Assuming $c$ is an even number, we observe that the maximum for (45) occurs when half of the $f_i$ are at $f_{max}$ and half are at $f_{min}$. Hence, a better upper bound on $n$ (and lower bound on $n'$) is the solution to the inequality,

$$1 - \gamma^{\frac{1}{G}} \;\leq\; \frac{c}{2}\left[(1 - \frac{2r}{c(r+1)})^n + (1 - \frac{2}{c(r+1)})^n\right] \;. \tag{48}$$

While one can not solve symbolically for $n$, one can easily obtain numeric solutions given $\gamma$, $G$, $c$, and $r$, via Newton's method. As in Derivation I, given $c$ classes of identical fitness ($r = 1$), (48) reduces to (34).

Figures 10–12 show the lower bound for $n'$ as a function of $c$, $r$, and $\gamma$, respectively, with other parameters fixed. Note in Figure 10 that with $r$, $\gamma$, and $G$ fixed, the bound for $n'$ is

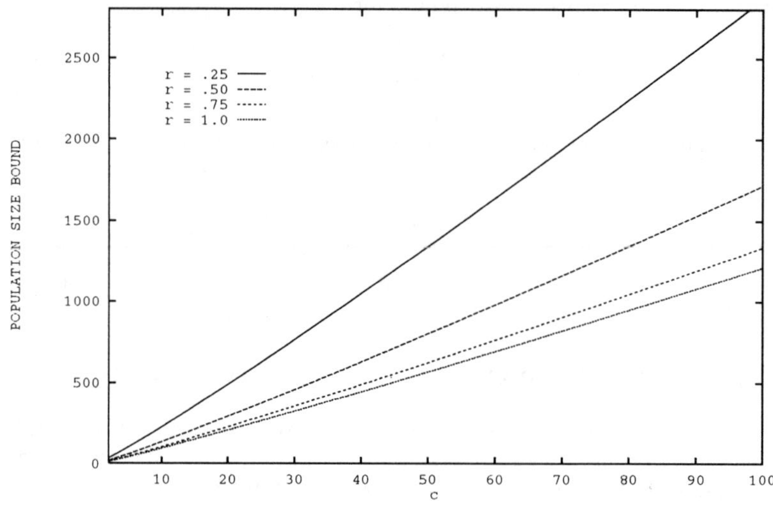

Figure 10: The population size bound from (48) is shown as a function of $c$, at various $r$, for $\gamma = .95$ and $G = 100$.

a slightly superlinear function of $c$. We can derive the form of this relationship between $n$ and $c$ from the right-hand side of (44) as follows:

$$\frac{c}{r}\left[-\ln\left(\frac{1-\gamma^{\frac{1}{G}}}{c}\right)\right] \;=\; \frac{c}{r}\left[-\ln(1-\gamma^{\frac{1}{G}})+\ln c\right] \;=\; k_1 c[k_2 + \ln c] \;, \qquad (49)$$

where $k_1 = 1/r$ and $k_2 = -\ln(1-\gamma^{\frac{1}{G}})$. Therefore,

$$n' \;\geq\; k_1 c(k_2 + \ln c) \;, \qquad (50)$$

where $k_1$ and $k_2$ are positive constants. For $r = 1$, the form reduces to

$$n' \;\geq\; c(k_2 + \ln c) \;. \qquad (51)$$

## 5.4 EXPERIMENTAL VERIFICATION

We now examine the accuracy of the theoretical results on seven test problems of increasing difficulty. In all seven problems, the goal is to locate all peaks. The following parameters and conditions are enforced in all runs of sharing with RWS. Populations are randomly initialized; GAs run for a fixed number of generations $G = 100$; the sharing constant is $\alpha = 1.0$. Population sizes are derived from an appropriate model, indicated in the accompanying text. We perform a number of runs on each test function. Where indicated, we employ crossover and mutation, in addition to sharing with RWS. The results are summarized in Table 3.

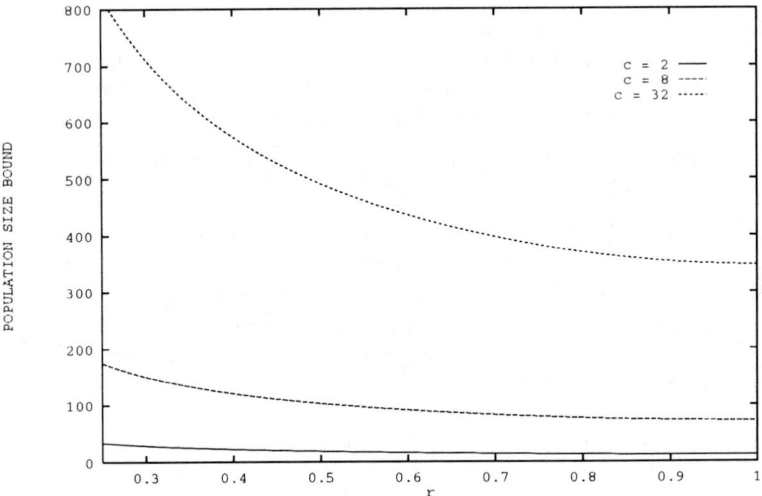

Figure 11: The population size bound from (48) is shown as a function of $r$, at various $c$, for $\gamma = .95$ and $G = 100$.

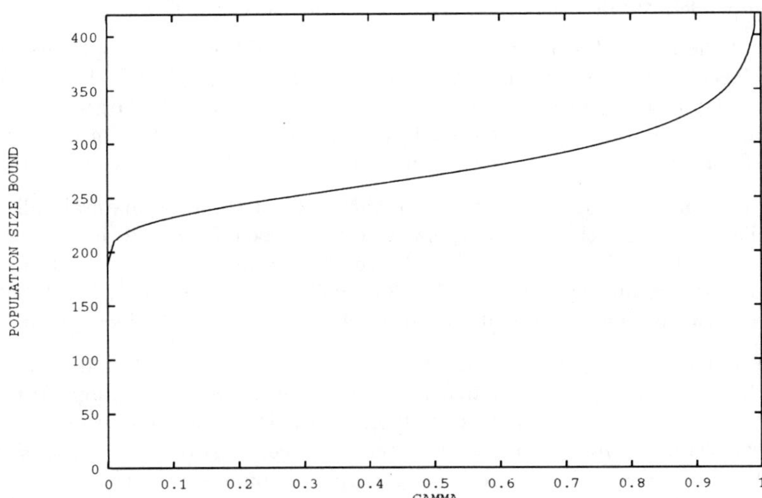

Figure 12: The population size bound from (34) is shown as a function of $\gamma$, for $c = 32$, $r = 1$, and $G = 100$.

Table 3: This table displays the minimum percentage $\gamma$ of runs we expect to maintain all $c$ classes, versus the actual percentage from runs of the GA with sharing. Results are given for seven different test problems. For each problem, the actual population size employed $n'$ comes from an appropriate population sizing formula, and $G = 100$.

| Problem | $\gamma$ | Experimental % | $c$ | $n'$ | Runs | $p_c$ | $p_m$ |
|---------|----------|----------------|-----|------|------|-------|-------|
| C-2     | 95%      | 95%            | 2   | 12   | 5000 | 0.0   | 0.00  |
| C-32    | 75%      | 91%            | 32  | 300  | 100  | 0.0   | 0.00  |
| M1      | 90%      | 95%            | 5   | 44   | 100  | 0.9   | 0.01  |
| M2      | 90%      | 95%            | 5   | 94   | 100  | 0.9   | 0.01  |
| M3      | 95%      | 100%           | 25  | 266  | 100  | 1.0   | 0.00  |
| PAR-5   | 95%      | 99%            | 16  | 166  | 100  | 1.0   | 0.00  |
| PAR-10  | 95%      | 100%           | 512 | 7074 | 15   | 1.0   | 0.00  |

To begin, we run a GA with sharing and RWS, 5000 times on the 1-bit, two-class problem, $f_0 = f_1 = 1$ ($f_i$ is the representative fitness of Class $i$). We call this problem $C\text{-}2$ ; $C\text{-}2$ is the simplest possible two-class problem. We start with this problem to verify the accuracy of the two-class population-sizing equation (36), in the absence of extraneous forces. We record the percentage of runs that maintain the two classes for the full 100 generations. Our population sizing equation, with $\gamma = .95$ and $G = 100$, tells us to use a population size of at least 11.93. We employ $n' = 12$. Note that the population sizing equation for the two-class case is exact, rather than a bound. Out of 5000 runs, using $\sigma_{share} = .5$ (perfect discrimination) and $p_c = p_m = 0$, 4748 (95%) maintain both classes for the duration of the run. This obviously compares very favorably with the expected 95% .

Next, we test the multi-class population-sizing formula (35) on a 5-bit, 32-class problem in which each genotype is a class, and for all classes $i$, $f_i = 1.0$. We call this problem $C\text{-}32$. This time we try a confidence level of $\gamma = .75$. Substitution into the large-$c$ approximation of (35) yields a population size bound of 298.18. Running the GA 100 times using $n' = 300$, $p_c = p_m = 0$, and $\sigma_{share} = .5$, 91% of the runs maintain all 32 classes to generation 100.

Note that a significantly larger percentage (than 75%) of the runs maintain all 32 classes on $C\text{-}32$. The reason for this is that although (35) is exact for $c = 2$, it is a lower bound for $c > 2$, and additional confidence is purchased cheaply in terms of population size: from (35), at least 90% confidence requires $n' = 332$; 95%, $n' = 354$; and 99%, $n' = 406$. This relationship between $\gamma$ and the population size bound was previously displayed in Figure 12.

The third problem $M1$, displayed in Figure 13, is a five-peak sine function from Deb's (1989) study, in which all peaks are of uniform height and are spaced evenly throughout the interval $[0, 1]$. The single variable is encoded using 30 bits. Utilizing parameters similar to Deb's, we run a GA with sharing, $p_c = .9$, $p_m = .01$, phenotypic comparison, and $\sigma_{share} = .1$, for 100 runs of 100 generations each. We once again employ population-sizing formula (35), since we expect disruption due to crossover and mutation, and the noise introduced by slightly overlapping niches, to be minimal. Substituting $\gamma = .9$, $G = 100$, and $c = 5$ into (35), we obtain a population size bound of 42.33. (Deb used a population size of 100.) Despite the addition of crossover and mutation, and the slightly imperfect comparison resulting from slightly overlapping niches, with $n' = 44$, 95% of the runs find all classes and maintain them for 100 generations. This is 5% better than the prespecified 90% confidence level.

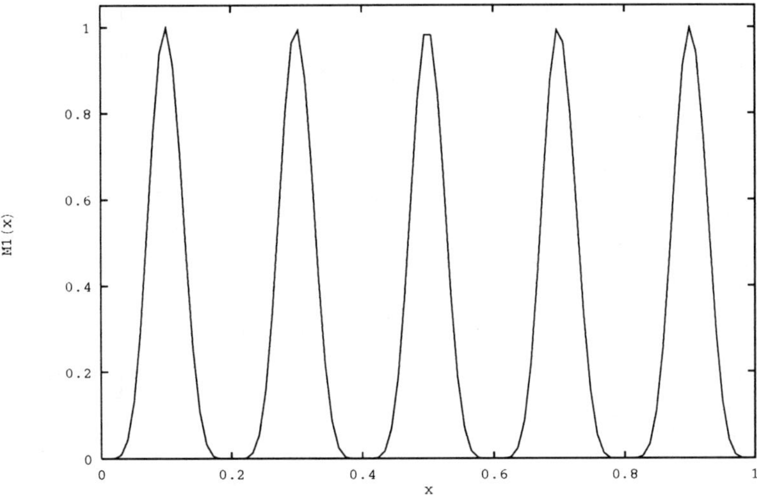

Figure 13: Test function *M1* is displayed.

The fourth problem *M2*, displayed in Figure 14, is Deb's (1989) five-peak sine function in which peaks are of nonuniform height, but are spaced evenly throughout the interval $[0, 1]$; the shortest peak is of height .25; the tallest, 1.0. Using the same parameters as we did on *M1* ($p_c = .9$, $p_m = .01$, $\sigma_{share} = .1$, phenotypic comparison; $c = 5$, $\gamma = .9$, $G = 100$), but with $r = .25$, the population-sizing formula (48) yields a recommended population size of 94. (Formula (43) yields a recommended population size of 170; Deb used a population size of 100.) For 100 runs under a population of size 94, 95% of the runs converge. This is once again 5% better than the prespecified 90% confidence level. Note that for both *M1* and *M2*, we are able to undercut Deb's population size of 100, with at least 90% confidence that our runs will converge. The population sizing formulas we employ explain Deb's success in locating and maintaining the five peaks using a population size of 100.

The fifth problem *M3*, from De Jong's (1975) thesis, is a negated and translated version of Shekel's foxholes problem. *M3*, displayed in Figure 15, is a two-dimensional problem with 25 peaks, ranging in height from 476 to 500. We employ a 34-bit encoding, 17 bits for each dimension. We run a GA with sharing, $p_c = 1.0$, $p_m = 0.0$, phenotypic comparison, and $\sigma_{share} = 11$; we perform 100 runs. Once again, we expect the disruption due to crossover and the noise due to overlapping niches to be minimal. We employ sizing formula (48), with $\gamma = .95$, $G = 100$, $c = 25$, and $r = .95$. This gives us a recommended population size of 266. (De Jong employed a population size of 50, but was searching for only one peak.) All 100 runs locate the 25 peaks, once again surpassing the preset confidence level.

The last two problems of this section, *PAR-5* and *PAR-10*, are covering problems. Given a set of positive and negative training examples, the objective is to find a concept description that includes all of the positive examples, but none of the negative examples. We map this to a multimodal optimization problem by using the full population as a disjunctive-normal-form

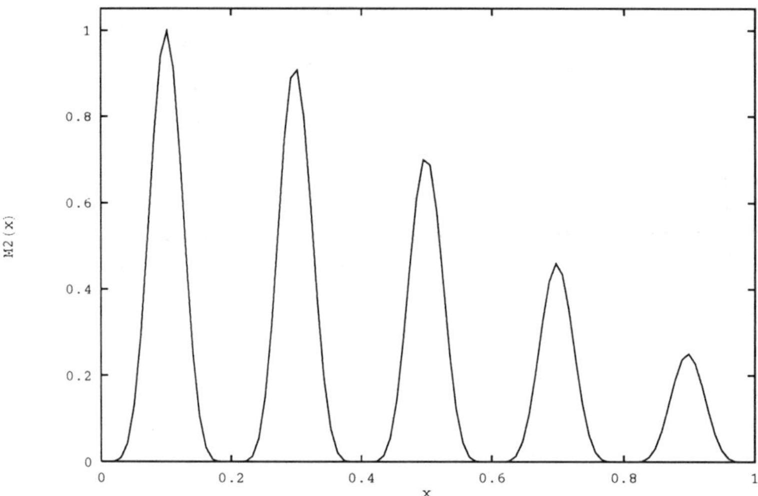

Figure 14: Test function *M2* is displayed.

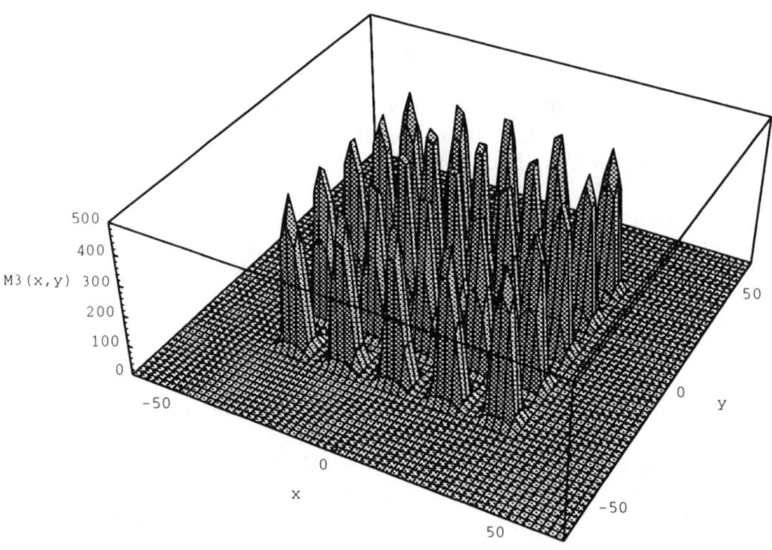

Figure 15: Test function *M3* is displayed.

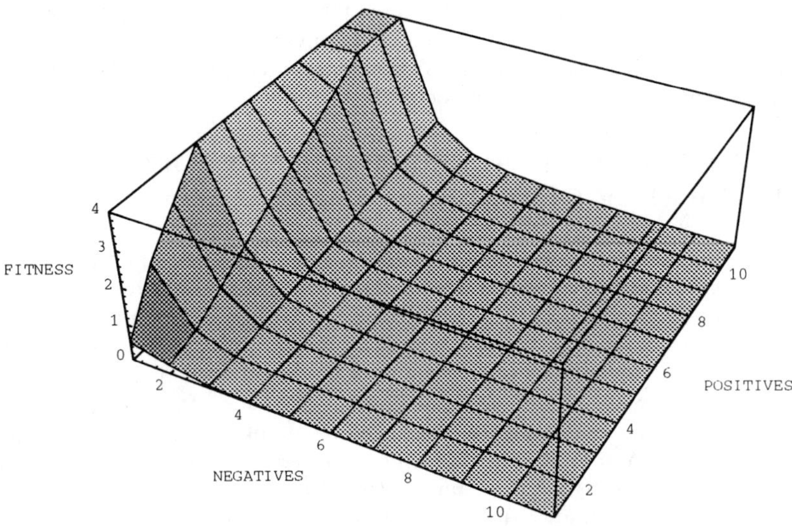


Figure 16: This function assigns fitness to a classification rule based upon the number of positive and negative examples that the rule covers. The function is used for problems *PAR-5* and *PAR-10*.

concept description, and letting each population element represent a disjunct. We use the function shown in Figure 16 to assign fitnesses to individual disjuncts (population elements), based on the number of positive and negative examples a disjunct covers. In general, higher fitnesses are assigned for covering positive examples; lower fitnesses for negative examples. Note that the fitness function in Figure 16 is not shown over the usual variable space (the variable space in this case is of high dimensionality), but over the space defined by both the number of positive examples covered by the disjunct, and the number of negative examples covered by the disjunct. Individuals in the population are represented by a concatenation of two-bit values that represent boolean variables. A '00' value corresponds to a '0' bit; '11', to a '1' bit; '01' and '10', to a wildcard (a don't care symbol).

*PAR-5* and *PAR-10* are both boolean, odd-parity problems. This means that if an odd number of variables are "on", the example is positive; if an even number of variables are "on", the example is negative. *PAR-5* is a five-bit (five-variable) parity problem; *PAR-10* is a ten-bit (ten-variable) parity problem. The solution to *PAR-5* requires the location and maintenance of 16 disjuncts ($c = 16$); the solution to PAR-10 requires the location and maintenance of 512 disjuncts ($c = 512$). Since all classes are of equivalent fitness and since we expect operator disruption and other sources of noise to be minimal, we employ population-sizing formula (35) with $\gamma = .95$ and $G = 100$. According to (35), *PAR-5* requires a population size of at least 166; *PAR-10*, at least 7074.

We run sharing with RWS, $p_c = 1.0$, $p_m = 0.0$, genotypic comparison, and $\sigma_{share} = 3.5$. To get the GA to completely converge after application of sharing, a bitclimber (with a neighborhood size of one bit) runs after the GA has completed its 100 generations. On *PAR-5*, 99 out of 100 runs converge to the correct final concept (a population containing 16 unique disjuncts). On *PAR-10*, all fifteen runs converge to the correct final concept (a population containing 512 unique disjuncts). On the parity problems, the number of runs converging again exceeds the preset confidence level.

## 6  POPULATION SIZE: SELECTION ONLY; DESIRABLE AND UNDESIRABLE CLASSES

In many problems that one encounters, it is costly or impractical to find all peaks. In the worst case, given a massively multimodal problem, enumerating the local optima may be of the same order of complexity as enumerating the entire search space (Horn & Goldberg, in press). In the case that one does not wish to locate all peaks, one is almost always interested in locating the highest peaks. This section concentrates upon the solution of this general class of problems. Like earlier, we assume the existence of $c$ local optima. However, instead of wanting to locate all optima, we are interested in locating at least the $b$ highest maxima, where $b \leq c$. Assuming no tiebreaking is necessary, we call the $b$ highest maxima *desirable* peaks and the $c - b$ lowest maxima *undesirable* or *extraneous* peaks. (If tiebreaking is necessary, some peaks will have the option of being either desirable or undesirable.)

Let us index the $b$ desirable classes from 0 to $b - 1$, and the $c - b$ undesirable classes from $b$ to $c - 1$. We can rewrite Equation 6 to separate the summation of desirable and undesirable classes:

$$P_s(i) \;=\; \frac{f_i}{\sum_{j=0}^{b-1} f_j + \sum_{j=b}^{c-1} f_j} \; . \tag{52}$$

Since we do not care if any of the extraneous classes disappear, we can rewrite expression (12) as a summation over just the desirable classes. Hence, the probability $X$ of one or more desirable classes disappearing after one generation, becomes

$$X \;\leq\; \sum_{i=0}^{b-1} (1 - P_s(i))^n \; . \qquad (0 < X < 1) \tag{53}$$

The loss distribution and cumulative loss distribution remain the same as previously calculated in Equations 22 and 25. Therefore, Equation 28 also still holds. Substituting the right-hand side of Equation 28 for $X$ in (53) yields the following relationship for sharing under RWS:

$$1 - \gamma^{\frac{1}{G}} \;\leq\; \sum_{i=0}^{b-1} (1 - P_S(i))^n \; . \tag{54}$$

From (54), we can once again obtain bounds on $n$. We proceed immediately to the most general case, $c$ classes of arbitrary fitness. We relate the minimum population size required to maintain at least the $b$ best classes for at least $G$ generations with probability of at least $\gamma$, to $n$ and $n'$.

In order to examine at which $f_i$ the right-hand side of (53) is maximal, we first make a few definitions. Let $f_{max}$ be the fitness of the global maximum or maxima; let $f_{min}$ be the fitness of the least-fit desirable class or classes; let $f_{extra}$ be the fitness of the most-fit extraneous class or classes. The following ordering holds: $f_{extra} \leq f_{min} \leq f_{max}$. We define the following ratios: $r = f_{min}/f_{max}$ and $r' = f_{extra}/f_{max}$. Note that $r' \leq r$. We would like to maximize the following sum:

$$\sum_{i=0}^{b-1}(1 - \frac{f_i}{\sum_{j=0}^{b-1} f_j + \sum_{j=b}^{c-1} f_j})^n \quad . \tag{55}$$

The above sum is maximized when the expression $\sum_{j=b}^{c-1} f_j$ is maximal, which occurs when for all extraneous classes $j$, $f_j = f_{extra}$. Letting $s$ be the number of extraneous classes ($s = c - b$), the maximization of the above sum reduces to the maximization of

$$\sum_{i=0}^{b-1}(1 - \frac{f_i}{\sum_{j=0}^{b-1} f_j + s f_{extra}})^n \quad . \tag{56}$$

Assuming $b$ is an even number, the maximum for (56) occurs when half of the $f_i$ are at $f_{max}$ and half are at $f_{min}$. Substituting half $f_{max}$ and half $f_{min}$ yields the following expression for the maximum:

$$\frac{b}{2}\left[(1 - \frac{f_{min}}{\frac{b}{2}(f_{max} + f_{min}) + s f_{extra}})^n + (1 - \frac{f_{max}}{\frac{b}{2}(f_{max} + f_{min}) + s f_{extra}})^n\right] \quad . \tag{57}$$

Simplification yields a lower bound on $n'$, the solution to the inequality,

$$1 - \gamma^{\frac{1}{G}} \leq \frac{b}{2}\left[(1 - \frac{2r}{b(r+1) + 2r's})^n + (1 - \frac{2}{b(r+1) + 2r's})^n\right] \quad . \tag{58}$$

Given $\gamma$, $G$, $b$, $s$, $r$, and $r'$, one can easily obtain numerical bounds for $n$ and $n'$ via Newton's method. To make matters simpler, one could substitute for both $r$ and $r'$ an intermediate value that denotes a threshold between desirable fitness ratios and undesirable fitness ratios. Given $c = b + s$ desirable classes of identical fitness ($r = r' = 1$), (58) reduces to (34).

We test population sizing formula (58) on a constructed 8-bit problem. In the problem we construct, each of the 256 individual solutions is in a separate class ($c = 256$). We designate four solutions — 00111111, 01111111, 10111111, and 11111111 — as desirable, and assign them fitnesses of 4.0. We designate the other 252 classes as undesirable and assign them fitnesses of 1.0. Formula (58), with $b = 4$, $s = 252$, $r = 1$, $r' = .25$, $G = 100$, and $\gamma = .90$, recommends a population size of 550. This is a considerable savings over the population size of 7488 recommended by prior formula (48) that assumes we want to maintain all 256 classes. We perform 90 runs of a GA with sharing, RWS, and genotypic comparison, employing $n' = 550$, $p_c = 1.0$, $p_m = 0.0$, $\sigma_{share} = .5$, and $\alpha = 1.0$. 100% of the runs locate all four desired optima and maintain them to generation 100. Once again, population sizing according to our model exceeds the prespecified confidence level, in this case of 90%.

# 7  POPULATION SIZE; SELECTION PLUS CROSSOVER

The sharing models developed in the previous sections bound the behavior of a full GA with sharing on problems in which crossover and other operators are not overly disruptive. This section incorporates crossover into the modelling. The incorporation of crossover provides a template for incorporating various sources of noise, such as mutation.

Recall that $P_s(i)$ is the probability of selecting some element of an arbitrary class $i$, in one trial of sharing with RWS. Let $j$ be an arbitrary class. In two consecutive trials of sharing with RWS, the probability of selecting some element of $i$, followed by some element of $j$ (in that order) is $P_s(i)P_s(j)$. We use the following notation to indicate the probability of producing one Class $k$ and one Class $l$ element by crossing a Class $i$ element (the first parent) with a Class $j$ element (the second parent):

$$p(i \times j \Rightarrow \{k, l\}) \ . \tag{59}$$

Given an arbitrary class $A$, the probability of producing either one or two Class $A$ elements by crossing a Class $i$ element (first parent) with a Class $j$ element (second parent) is

$$p(i \times j \Rightarrow \{A, A\}) + \sum_{k=0, k \neq A}^{c-1} p(i \times j \Rightarrow \{A, k\}) \ . \tag{60}$$

The probability of not producing any Class $A$ elements in such a cross is

$$Y(i, j, A) \ = \ 1 - p(i \times j \Rightarrow \{A, A\}) - \sum_{k=0, k \neq A}^{c-1} p(i \times j \Rightarrow \{A, k\}) \ . \tag{61}$$

The probability of selecting an element of Class $i$ followed by an element of Class $j$ (in that order), and after applying crossover with probability $p_c$, obtaining two elements from outside Class $A$, is

$$P_s(i)P_s(j)\left[ p_c \ Y(i, j, A) + (1 - p_c)(1 - P_s(A))^2 \right] \ . \tag{62}$$

After the combined operation of selecting two elements (via sharing with RWS) and crossing them with probability $p_c$, the probability of not producing any Class $A$ elements is

$$\sum_{i=0}^{c-1} \sum_{j=0}^{c-1} \left[ p_c \ P_s(i)P_s(j) \ Y(i, j, A) + (1 - p_c)P_s(i)P_s(j)(1 - P_s(A))^2 \right] \ . \tag{63}$$

Simplification yields

$$(1 - p_c)(1 - P_s(A))^2 + p_c \sum_{i=0}^{c-1} \sum_{j=0}^{c-1} P_s(i)P_s(j) \ Y(i, j, A) \ . \tag{64}$$

Substituting back the expression for $Y(i, j, A)$, the probability of not having any Class $A$ elements in the population after one generation ($n/2$ of the operations in (64)) is

$$\left[ (1 - p_c)(1 - P_s(A))^2 + p_c \right.$$
$$- p_c \sum_{i=0}^{c-1} \sum_{j=0}^{c-1} P_s(i)P_s(j) \ p(i \times j \Rightarrow \{A, A\})$$
$$\left. - p_c \sum_{i=0}^{c-1} \sum_{j=0}^{c-1} P_s(i)P_s(j) \sum_{k=0, k \neq A}^{c-1} p(i \times j \Rightarrow \{A, k\}) \right]^{n/2} \ . \tag{65}$$

Since any of the $c$ classes can potentially lose all its elements, the probability $X$ of one or more classes disappearing after one generation is

$$X \le \sum_{m=0}^{c-1} \left[ (1 - p_c)(1 - P_s(m))^2 + p_c \right.$$

$$- p_c \sum_{i=0}^{c-1} \sum_{j=0}^{c-1} P_s(i)P_s(j)\, p(i \times j \Rightarrow \{m, m\})$$

$$\left. - p_c \sum_{i=0}^{c-1} \sum_{j=0}^{c-1} \sum_{k=0, k \ne m}^{c-1} P_s(i)P_s(j)\, p(i \times j \Rightarrow \{m, k\}) \right]^{n/2}. \qquad (66)$$

The probability of maintaining all classes for a generation is $1 - X$. The above inequality takes into account gains as well as losses of class elements.

We now consider crosses through which we can produce either one or two elements of an arbitrary class $A$. We partition all such crosses into the following six cases:

1. $A \times A \Rightarrow \{A, A\}$ ,
2. $A \times \textit{non-A} \Rightarrow \{A, A\}$ ,
3. $\textit{non-A} \times \textit{non-A} \Rightarrow \{A, A\}$ ,
4. $A \times A \Rightarrow \{A, \textit{non-A}\}$ ,
5. $A \times \textit{non-A} \Rightarrow \{A, \textit{non-A}\}$ , and
6. $\textit{non-A} \times \textit{non-A} \Rightarrow \{A, \textit{non-A}\}$ .

We will now eliminate less significant terms from expression (66). Note that the inequality still holds after elimination of these terms. First, we assume that crossing two elements from the same class always produces two elements of that class. Therefore, the right-hand side of Case 1 has probability 1, given the left-hand side, allowing us to eliminate Case 4 (whose right-hand side has probability 0). In other words, $p(i \times j \Rightarrow \{m, m\}) = 1$ if $i = m$ and $j = m$; 0, otherwise. Cases 2, 3, and 6 involve gaining elements of classes. We will assume such gains are negligible (leaving Case 5 as the only remaining case of interest). Therefore, $p(i \times j \Rightarrow \{m, k\}) = 0$ if $i \ne m$ and $j \ne m$. We can now rewrite (66) as

$$X \le \sum_{m=0}^{c-1} \left[ (1 - p_c)(1 - P_s(m))^2 + p_c - p_c(P_s(m))^2 \right.$$

$$\left. - 2p_c \sum_{j=0, j \ne m}^{c-1} \sum_{k=0, k \ne m}^{c-1} P_s(m)P_s(j)\, p(\textit{cross}(m, j) \Rightarrow \{m, k\}) \right]^{n/2}. \qquad (67)$$

We use the notation $\textit{cross}(m, j)$ in place of $m \times j$ to indicate that order no longer matters; our crossover operator is symmetric. We are now concerned with the probability of losing an element of Class $m$ via crossover with an element of a different class. For all classes $a \ne m$, in a cross between elements of Classes $a$ and $m$, the probability of producing one Class $m$ element is greater than or equal to the probability that crossover does not disrupt $m$. In other words, disruptions happen more frequently than actual losses, because losses are caused only by disruptions, but not every disruption leads to a loss. (A class may be regained after a disruptive cross.)

$$\forall_{a \ne m} \sum_{k=0, k \ne m}^{c-1} p(\textit{cross}(m, a) \Rightarrow \{m, k\}) \ge (1 - p_d(m)) , \qquad (68)$$

where $p_d(m)$ is the probability that crossover disrupts $m$. The above bound yields a further simplification:

$$X \le \sum_{m=0}^{c-1} \Big[ (1 - p_c)(1 - P_s(m))^2 + p_c(1 - (P_s(m))^2) - 2p_c(1 - p_d(m))P_s(m)(1 - P_s(m)) \Big]^{n/2} . \tag{69}$$

Note that with $p_c = 0$, or $\forall_m \, p_d(m) = 0$, (69) simplifies to the previously derived expression (12) for selection alone. Note also that under full crossover ($p_c = 1$), the first term drops out of the above expression. Under full disruption ($\forall_m \, p_d(m) = 1$), the third term drops out; under full disruption, in order for a class to survive to the next generation, either at least one cross must occur within the elements of that class, or the class must be passed through at least once without crossover. For schema-based class definitions, $p_d(m) = \delta(m)/(l-1)$ for single-point crossover, and $p_d(m) = 1 - .5^{o(m)}$ for uniform crossover, where $\delta$ is the defining length and $o$ is the order of a schema, using the standard definitions (Goldberg, 1989).

The previously derived Equation 28, $X = 1 - \gamma^{\frac{1}{G}}$, also holds for sharing with crossover. Therefore,

$$1 - \gamma^{\frac{1}{G}} \le \sum_{m=0}^{c-1} \Big[ (1 - p_c)(1 - P_s(m))^2 + p_c(1 - (P_s(m))^2) - 2p_c(1 - p_d(m))P_s(m)(1 - P_s(m)) \Big]^{n/2} . \tag{70}$$

From (70), we can once again obtain bounds on $n$ and $n'$. We give the derivations in the following sections for two cases. In the first case, we assume that all classes are desirable and that we have $c$ classes of identical fitness. The second, more general case, models both desirable and undesirable classes of arbitrary fitness. In the remainder of this paper, we assume that disruption probabilities for all classes can be bounded by a maximal disruption probability $p_d$. The inequality (70) still holds if we substitute $p_d$ for all $p_d(m)$.

## 7.1  ALL CLASSES DESIRABLE; IDENTICAL FITNESSES

For $c$ classes of identical fitness,

$$1 - \gamma^{\frac{1}{G}} \le c \Big[ (1 - p_c)(1 - \frac{1}{c})^2 + p_c(1 - \frac{1}{c^2}) - 2p_c(1 - p_d)\frac{1}{c}(1 - \frac{1}{c}) \Big]^{n/2} . \tag{71}$$

Solving for $n$ gives an overestimate for the minimum population size required to maintain, with probability $\gamma$, $c$ classes of identical fitness for at least $G$ generations:

$$n \le \frac{2 \ln \frac{1 - \gamma^{\frac{1}{G}}}{c}}{\ln \big[ (1 - p_c)(1 - \frac{1}{c})^2 + p_c(1 - \frac{1}{c^2}) - 2p_c(1 - p_d)\frac{1}{c}(1 - \frac{1}{c}) \big]} \le n' . \tag{72}$$

Figure 17 shows bounded population size as a function of $c$, at various $p_d$, with other parameters fixed ($\gamma = .95$, $G = 100$, $p_c = 1.0$). Note that even with full crossover, the slightly superlinear relationship is maintained between the population size bound and $c$. Note also that population size at first increases slowly as the probability of disruption increases. However, the rate of increase quickens as $p_d$ approaches 1. It is illuminating to

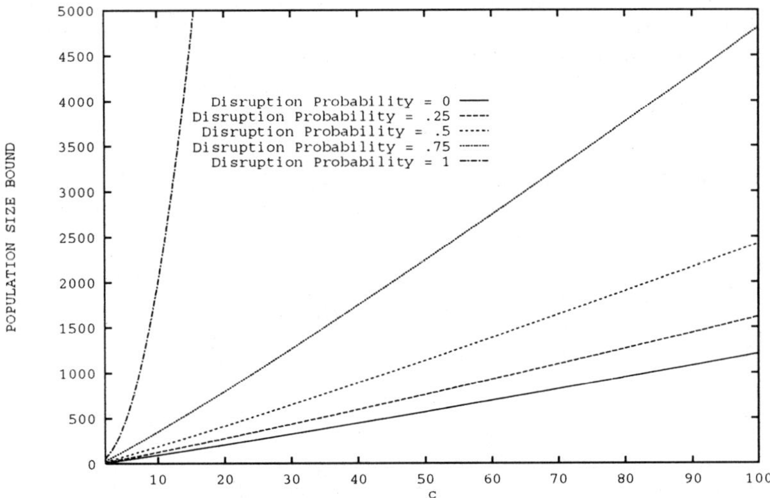



Figure 17: The population size bound of (72) is shown as a function of $c$, at various disruption probabilities $p_d$, with $\gamma = .95$, $G = 100$, and $p_c = 1.0$, for classes of identical fitness.

compare the bounds on $X$ (calculated from (69)) at two extremes, $p_d = 0$ and $p_d = 1$, for $c$ classes of identical fitness, with $p_c = 1$. At $p_d = 0$,

$$X \leq c(1 - \frac{1}{c})^n \ . \tag{73}$$

At $p_d = 1$,

$$X \leq c(1 - \frac{1}{c^2})^{n/2} \ . \tag{74}$$

## 7.2   DESIRABLE AND UNDESIRABLE CLASSES; ARBITRARY FITNESSES

Our starting point is the summation in (70), over $b$ desirable classes, with $p_d$ substituted for $p_d(m)$:

$$1 - \gamma^{\frac{1}{G}} \ \leq \ \sum_{m=0}^{b-1} \Big[ (1 - p_c)(1 - P_s(m))^2 + p_c(1 - (P_s(m))^2)$$
$$- 2p_c(1 - p_d)P_s(m)(1 - P_s(m)) \Big]^{n/2} \ , \tag{75}$$

where, as before,

$$P_s(m) \ = \ \frac{f_m}{\sum_{j=0}^{b-1} f_j + \sum_{j=b}^{c-1} f_j} \ , \tag{76}$$

and the $b$ desirable classes are indexed from 0 to $b - 1$; the $c - b$ undesirable classes, from $b$ to $c - 1$.

As in the previous section, we maximize the right-hand side of (75) over the $P_s(m)$. This maximization is accomplished when we minimize all $P_s(m)$. Like last time, this task reduces to the simultaneous minimization, for all desired $m$, of

$$\frac{f_m}{\sum_{j=0}^{b-1} f_j + s f_{extra}} \,, \tag{77}$$

where $s$ is the number of extraneous peaks and $f_{extra}$ is the fitness of the fittest extraneous peak. This minimum occurs when half of the $f_m$ for the $b$ desired peaks are at $f_{min}$ and half are at $f_{max}$. For the half at $f_{min}$,

$$U = P_s(min) = \frac{f_{min}}{\frac{b}{2}(f_{max} + f_{min}) + s f_{extra}} = \frac{2r}{b(r+1) + 2r's} \,, \tag{78}$$

where $r = f_{min}/f_{max}$, and $r' = f_{extra}/f_{max}$. For the half at $f_{max}$,

$$V = P_s(max) = \frac{f_{max}}{\frac{b}{2}(f_{max} + f_{min}) + s f_{extra}} = \frac{2}{b(r+1) + 2r's} \,. \tag{79}$$

A lower bound on $n'$ comes from the solution to the inequality,

$$1 - \gamma^{\frac{1}{G}} \leq \frac{b}{2}\left[(1-p_c)(1-U)^2 + p_c(1-U^2) - 2p_c(1-p_d)U(1-U)\right]^{n/2} +$$
$$\frac{b}{2}\left[(1-p_c)(1-V)^2 + p_c(1-V^2) - 2p_c(1-p_d)V(1-V)\right]^{n/2} \,. \tag{80}$$

Given $\gamma$, $G$, $b$, $s$, $p_c$, $p_d$, $r$, and $r'$, one can obtain numerical bounds for $n$ and $n'$ via Newton's method. Again, one could substitute an intermediate threshold $r''$ for both $r$ and $r'$.

Figure 18 illustrates the effect of varying $p_c$ when disruption is maximal ($p_d = 1.0$). In this worst-case scenario, crossover is always destructive, never constructing any desirable solutions. Population size bounds are derived from expression (80), using $\gamma = .95$, $G = 100$, $r'' = 1.0$, $b = 32$, and $s \doteq 1000$. As the figure shows, given high disruption, required population size increases exponentially as $p_c$ approaches 1. A crossover probability of $p_c = .6$ requires a population size of roughly $28,500$; $p_c = .7$, $38,000$; $p_c = .8$, $57,000$; $p_c = .9$, $113,000$; and $p_c = 1.0$, $23,500,000$. The model tells us to stay away from crossover probabilities close to 1.0. Of course, one should not make $p_c$ too low, to avoid stifling exploration and the location of niches.

## 8   EXTENSIONS

There are numerous promising extensions to the research presented in this paper. We briefly mention some of the possibilities.

We have modelled the major forces in GAs that incorporate fitness sharing: selection, sharing, and crossover. In order to apply a sharing model to problem-solving, one must have a method of setting that model's parameters. The most general model of this paper, corresponding to expression (80), requires eight parameters: $\gamma$, $G$, $b$, $s$, $p_c$, $p_d$, $r$, and $r'$. The parameter $\gamma$ is easy to set: the user merely specifies a minimum level of confidence, such as 95%, that he/she would like to have in the model's predicted values. The number of generations $G$ is also easy to set. GA theory tells us that the minimum number of generations should be of the order of some multiple of $\log n$, or alternatively, $\log l$, where $l$

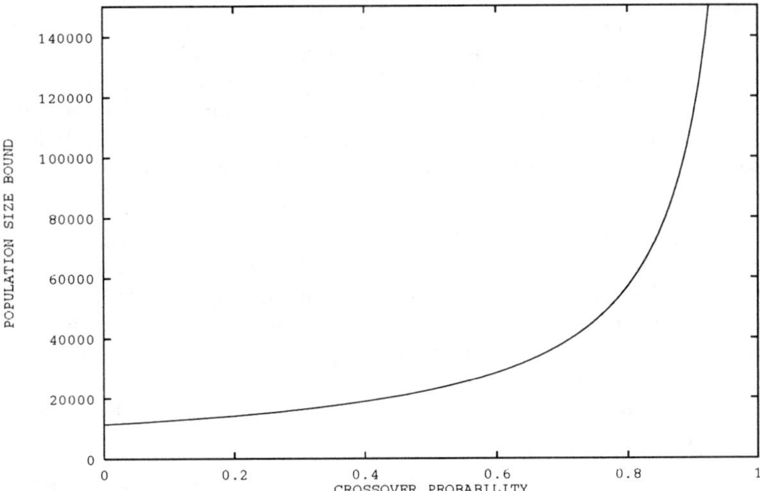


Figure 18: The population size bound of (80) is shown as a function of $p_c$, for $\gamma = .95$, $G = 100$, $p_d = 1.0$, $r'' = 1.0$, $b = 32$, and $s = 1000$.

is the string length. The user can set $G$ to some arbitrary value greater than the number of generations the GA will run. We have been using $G = 100$; GAs with sharing take nowhere near 100 generations to finish running. The models are not sensitive to increases in $G$.

A user can set the parameter $b$ by specifying the minimum number of sufficiently diverse solutions the GA is to return. Of course, if the fitness landscape does not contain $b$ peaks, sharing will be unable to find $b$ peaks. A user can set $r$ and $r'$ by substituting a parameter $r''$ for both $r$ and $r'$, where $r' \leq r'' \leq r$; $r''$ indicates a desired quality of solution. The user can specify that the GA return at least $b$ diverse solutions, all of which are within $100 \times r''$ percent of the quality or fitness of the global optimum or optima.

The modelling parameter $p_d$ can be set in several ways. One can assume minimal disruption and set it to zero, as we did in the models that ignore crossover. Alternatively, one can assume the worst and set it to one, in which case $p_c$ should be set to a value less than one to allow at least some solutions to pass through from generation to generation, undisrupted. The effect of intermediate values of $p_d$ was shown in Figure 17.

The user should set $p_c$ to whatever value of $p_c$ is to be used in the GA. We recommend using a value of less than 1.0 on real-world problems, because if good solutions and subsolutions are susceptible to disruption, we would like many of them to be passed through untouched from generation to generation. Values of $p_c$ between .6 and .9 are most common in the GA literature. Figure 18 gave some insight into why these may be popular values.

The modelling parameter that might give the user the most trouble is $s$, the number of extraneous peaks in the landscape. One approach to setting this parameter, given an unknown fitness landscape, is to attempt overestimation. This is equivalent to simply choosing a large number for $s$. Problem-specific information can be used whenever available. If none is immediately available, one approach to obtaining some is dynamic estimation. From prior runs or from early generations, one might be able to gain some idea of the number of peaks in the search space. Another approach would be to run hillclimbers from each point within several randomly chosen neighborhoods, and to count the number of unique solutions returned. From this sample, one could make a rough estimate of the modality of the search space. Methods for estimating the number of peaks in the fitness landscape deserve further research.

One can model minor forces in GAs that incorporate sharing, in much the same way we added crossover. Minor forces should produce low levels of noise and can be modelled, like crossover, as potential disruptors. Mutation, for instance, can be modelled in much the same way it is incorporated into the schema theorem. The probability that mutation disrupts schema $H$ is $(1 - p_m)^{o(H)}$. Whether or not class definitions correspond to schema definitions, we expect that mutation will disrupt a class very rarely, assuming that the usual low levels of mutation are employed. Higher mutation probabilities can be incorporated into the model if one can estimate the probability of mutation disrupting a class.

If sampling is employed in the computation of shared fitnesses, it would be useful to model the additional noise introduced by sampling, in order to determine the minimal required sample size. Goldberg and Richardson (1987) suggest that to compute an individual's niche count (sum of sharing function values between it and all population elements), $k$ samples of the population be taken, where $k \ll n$. They call the mean sharing function value for the sample $\mu_i$, and set niche count equal to $(n - 1)\mu_i + 1$. The '1' subtracted and added is for the individual itself, since all individuals share fully with themselves. We did not employ sampling in this paper.

Another useful extension of this study would be to model class formation as well as maintenance. We have already modelled the effects of higher crossover rates. Considering the constructive as well as the destructive effects of crossover would perhaps yield an optimal crossover probability for sharing. As mentioned earlier, niche formation is an issue of signal-to-noise within each niche (Goldberg, Deb, & Clark, 1992). It has been the case in practice that inter-niche population sizing considerations (niche maintenance) override intra-niche considerations (niche formation). This has allowed a population that is sized to maintain niches, more than enough elements to form the niches. However, this may not be the case for some problems. A potential combined method is to size populations using both approaches, and to employ the maximum recommended population size, perhaps adjusted upwards by a constant to account for interactions.

We have so far used RWS exclusively in our models of sharing, with the understanding that computed bounds will also apply to sharing under any of the more-stable, fitness-proportionate selection schemes. (We in fact recommend the use of stochastic universal selection for actual applications of sharing.) One could attempt to locate tighter bounds by modelling individual proportionate-selection schemes that are less noisy than RWS.

It is possible to allow flexibility in the definition of a class's representative fitness. Deb (1989), for instance, represented the mean and variance of fitnesses among the individuals clustered atop each peak. We have chosen not to do this in order to preserve the independence of successive trials. However, a hybrid model may be possible in which successive trials are still independent, but class fitnesses are fuzzy rather than definite, and are modelled as sources of noise.

One final possibility is to model overlapping niches. Horn (1993) did this in his Markov chain model, but limited his attention to 1-bit problems. We chose not to model overlapping niches because our models are already predictive in cases of minor overlap, because the effectiveness of sharing diminishes as overlap increases, and to preserve the independence of successive generations. Again, we could preserve the independence assumption by modelling overlap as a source of disruption or noise.

## 9  CONCLUSION

This study has derived lower bounds on drift time and population size for sharing with roulette-wheel selection, both with and without crossover. Because roulette-wheel selection has the highest variance among commonly used proportionate-selection methods, the bounds also apply to sharing under more-stable selection schemes, such as stochastic remainder selection and stochastic universal selection. This study's derivations are based upon models of fitness sharing that are built from the perspective of niche maintenance. The models yield insights into behavioral characteristics of GAs that incorporate fitness sharing.

Several of the models of this study were tested by running GAs with sharing, using population sizes derived from the models. On all test problems, the number of runs locating and maintaining all classes surpassed the confidence level provided to the model. The models were predictive, even on problems with small disruptions and low noise-levels introduced by crossover, mutation, and overlapping niches.

**Acknowledgments**

Support is provided by NSF Grant ECS-9022007, US Army Contract DASG60-90-C-0153, AFOSR Grant F49620-94-1-0103, and the UIUC Department of General Engineering. The author thanks David Goldberg for much valuable discussion and insight related to this work, and the FOGA attendees and reviewers for their helpful comments.

**References**

Baker (1987). Reducing bias and inefficiency in the selection algorithm. *Genetic algorithms and their applications: Proceedings of the Second International Conference on Genetic Algorithms*, 14–21.

De Jong, K. A. (1975). An analysis of the behavior of a class of genetic adaptive systems. (Doctoral dissertation, University of Michigan). *Dissertation Abstracts International, 36*(10), 5140B. (University Microfilms No. 76-9381).

Deb, K. (1989). *Genetic algorithms in multimodal function optimization* (Masters Thesis and TCGA Report 89002). Tuscaloosa: University of Alabama, The Clearinghouse for Genetic Algorithms.

Freund, J. E., & Walpole, R. E. (1980). *Mathematical statistics*. Englewood Cliffs, NJ: Prentice Hall.

Goldberg, D. E. (1989). *Genetic algorithms in search, optimization, and machine learning*. Reading, MA: Addison-Wesley.

Goldberg, D. E., Deb, K., & Clark, J. H. (1992). Genetic algorithms, noise, and the sizing of populations. *Complex Systems, 6*, 333–362.

Goldberg, D. E., & Richardson, J. J. (1987). Genetic algorithms with sharing for multimodal function optimization. *Genetic algorithms and their applications: Proceedings of the Second International Conference on Genetic Algorithms*, 41–49.

Goldberg, D. E., & Segrest, P. (1987). Finite Markov chain analysis of genetic algorithms. *Genetic algorithms and their applications: Proceedings of the Second International Conference on Genetic Algorithms*, 1–8.

Horn, J. (1993). Finite Markov chain analysis of genetic algorithms with niching. *Proceedings of the Fifth International Conference on Genetic Algorithms*, 110–117.

Horn, J. & Goldberg, D. E. (in press). Genetic algorithm difficulty and the modality of fitness landscapes. *Foundations of genetic algorithms, 3*.

Oei, C. K., Goldberg, D. E., & Chang, S. J. (1991). *Tournament selection, niching, and the preservation of diversity* (IlliGAL Report 91011). Urbana: University of Illinois, Illinois Genetic Algorithms Laboratory.

Radcliffe, N. J. (1993). Genetic Set Recombination. In D. Whitley, (Ed.), *Foundations of genetic algorithms, 2* (pp. 203–219). San Mateo: Morgan Kaufmann.

### Appendix

The mean $\mu_L$ of the geometric (loss) distribution is the expected value of the random variable $L$ given by:

$$\mu_L = \sum_L L \cdot P(L) = \sum_{i=1}^{\infty} iX(1-X)^{i-1} = \frac{X}{1-X} \sum_{i=1}^{\infty} i(1-X)^i \ . \tag{81}$$

By Equation 86,

$$\mu_L = \frac{X}{1-X} \frac{1-X}{(1-(1-X))^2} = \frac{1}{X} \ . \tag{82}$$

The variance $\sigma_L^2$ of the geometric (loss) distribution is the second moment about the mean of the random variable $L$:

$$\sigma_L^2 = \sum_L (L - \mu_L)^2 \cdot P(L) \tag{83}$$

$$= \sum_{i=1}^{\infty} (i - \frac{1}{X})^2 X(1-X)^{i-1}$$

$$= \frac{X}{1-X} \sum_{i=1}^{\infty} (i^2 - \frac{2i}{X} + \frac{1}{X^2})(1-X)^i$$

$$= \frac{X}{1-X} \left[ \left( \sum_{i=1}^{\infty} i^2 (1-X)^i \right) - \frac{2}{X} \left( \sum_{i=1}^{\infty} i(1-X)^i \right) + \frac{1}{X^2} \left( \sum_{i=1}^{\infty} (1-X)^i \right) \right] \ .$$

Summing the infinite series above, according to Equations 86–88 yields:

$$\sigma_L^2 = \frac{X}{1-X}\left[\frac{(1-X)(1+1-X)}{(1-(1-X))^3} - \frac{2}{X}\frac{1-X}{(1-(1-X))^2} + \frac{1}{X^2}\left(\frac{1}{1-(1-X)} - 1\right)\right]$$

$$= \frac{1-X}{X^2} .$$

$$\hspace{12cm}(84)$$

$$\sum_{i=0}^{k} x^i = \frac{1-x^{k+1}}{1-x} \qquad (0.0 < x < 1.0) \hspace{3cm}(85)$$

$$\sum_{i=0}^{\infty} x^i = \frac{1}{1-x} \qquad (0.0 < x < 1.0) \hspace{3cm}(86)$$

$$\sum_{i=0}^{\infty} i x^i = \frac{x}{(1-x)^2} \qquad (0.0 < x < 1.0) \hspace{3cm}(87)$$

$$\sum_{i=0}^{\infty} i^2 x^i = \frac{x(1+x)}{(1-x)^3} \qquad (0.0 < x < 1.0) \hspace{3cm}(88)$$

$$\lim_{\epsilon \to 0} \ln(1-\epsilon) = -\epsilon \qquad (-\ln(1-\epsilon) > \epsilon) \hspace{3cm}(89)$$

$$\lim_{b \to \infty} (1 - \frac{a}{b})^c = e^{-\frac{ac}{b}} \hspace{4cm}(90)$$

# An Approach to the Study of Sensitivity for a Class of Genetic Algorithms

**Márton E. Balázs***
Babeş-Bolyai University
Department of Mathematics and Informatics
str. M. Kogălniceanu 1, 3400 Cluj
Romania

## Abstract

This paper defines a notion of sensitivity to the convexity of the fitness function used for the class of genetic algorithms using proportional selection and gives some results relative to this notion. The basic idea is that the convexity of the fitness function influences the selective pressure, a property which has been successfully used in genetic algorithms using fitness scaling but without a theoretical foundation. The results in the paper are extensions of the work of Grefenstette and Baker (Grefenstette and Baker, 1989) and of the results of the author (Balázs, 1993b and Balázs, 1994).

## 1   INTRODUCTION

In (Balázs, 1993b) we presented a preliminary version of our results concerning the study of sensitivity for a class of genetic algorithms to the convexity of the fitness functions used. This research was suggested by the paper of Grefenstette and Baker (Grefenstette and Baker, 1989) where they showed the impact of the fitness functions on the behaviour of genetic algorithms. In the present paper we give further results on this topic.

Section 2 gives a short presentation of the results in (Grefenstette and Baker, 1989) concerning genetic algorithms using a monotonic selection algorithm and a monotonic fitness function. In Section 3 we prove some results concerning genetic algorithms using uniform selection and convex or concave fitness functions. Based on these results in Section 4 definitions of sensitivity for the considered class of genetic algorithms is given, together with

---

*Presently at Worcester Polytechnic Institute, Dept. of Computer Science, 100 Institute Rd, Worcester, MA 01609

suffucient conditions for this property of a genetic algorithm. Finally Section 5 gives means to compare the sensitivity of genetic algorithms of the same class and shows how experimental observations on the behaviour of some genetic algorithms can be explained in terms of the results obtained. The final section draws some short conclusions on the paper and points out the direction for the future work on the topic.

## 2 GENETIC ALGORITHMS USING A MONOTONIC SELECTION ALGORITHM AND A MONOTONIC FITNESS FUNCTION

Selection is probably the most important step in a genetic algorithm because it determines which individuals will contribute (and to what amount) to the creation of a new population. As such the nature of the *selection method* used greatly influences the behaviour of a genetic algorithm. As in (Grefenstette and Baker, 1989) we shall consider selection to be partitioned into two steps:

1. the *selection algorithm*, which assigns to each individual $x$ in the population $P(t)$ a real number $tsr(x, t)$ called its *target sampling rate*;

2. the *sampling algorithm*, which given the target sampling rate for each individual in $P(t)$ bulids a new population $P(t+1)$ by creating copies of individuals depending on their target sampling rates.

In the present paper we shall concentrate on the selection algorithm, considering (as in (Grefenstette and Baker, 1989)) that an optimal sampling algorithm is given. Thus we shall study methods for computing the target sampling rate for an individual as well as the effect of such methods on the allocation of trials to hyperplanes. This latter will be characterized for a given hyperplane $H$, at a moment $t$ by the *target sampling rate of the hyperplane $H$* defined by

$$tsr(H, t) = \sum_{x \in H} \frac{tsr(x, t)}{n(H, t)},$$

where $n(H, t)$ denotes the number of representatives of hyperplane $H$ in $P(t)$.

For an optimization problem formulated in terms of an objective function $f$ the target sampling rate for an individual $x$ at moment $t$ is given as a composition of two functions: a *selection function* and a *fitness function*, that is

$$tsr(x, t) = s(u(x, t), t).$$

The best known selection algorithm is *proportional selection* defined by

$$tsr(x, t) = \frac{u(x, t)}{\overline{u}(t)},$$

where $\overline{u}(t)$ denotes the average fitness of the individuals in the population at moment $t$. The first characterization of genetic algorithms given by Holland in (Holland, 1992) is based on proportional selection.

In situations when the objective function is to be minimized and/or it can take on negative values the fitness function is usually obtained by a transformation of the objective function $u(x,t) = k(f(x),t)$ such that

(i) $u(x,t) \geq 0$ for all $x$ and $t$;

(ii) for any (fixed) $t$ and for all $x_1, x_2 \epsilon P(t)$ such that $f(x_1) \leq f(x_2)$ the following holds:

- $u(x_1,t) \leq u(x_2,t)$ if $f$ is to be maximized;

- $u(x_1,t) \geq u(x_2,t)$ if $f$ is to be minimized.

These would suggest that the only reason for introducing the fitness function is to transform every optimization problem into a maximization problem. However we shall see later in this paper that the choice of the fitness function greatly influences the behaviour of a genetic algorithm.

In the rest of this paper we shall put one more condition on the fitness function, namely that for any (fixed) $t$ and any $x \epsilon P(t)$

$$0 \leq u(x,t) \leq 1,$$

such that if $f(x_m)$ is the worst objective function value for elements in $P(t)^1$, then $u(x_m,t) = 0$, respectively if $f(x_M)$ is the best objective function value in $p(t)$, then $u(x_M,t) = 1$. Note that this condition is added only to keep our discussion simple, and the only effect it can have is on the values produced as entries for the sampling algorithm, but this can be corrected by a linear transformation on $u$.

In the following we shall omit the parameter $t$ whenever our discussion refers to a certain (fixed) population. We shall use the full notations each time when the value of $t$ is relevant.

Grefenstette and Baker (1989) showed that even for very simple fitness functions (linear ones) the interpretation of Holland's Schema Theorem is not clear. According to them this problem is due to the fact that the theorem refers to the fitness function, which is a design parameter of the genetic algorithm, instead of giving a characterization in terms of the objective function. They suggest that characterization of genetic algorithms should state "`how the space defined by the objective function is searched by the genetic algorithm`".

In the rest of this section we give a short presentation of the results in (Grefenstette and Baker, 1989). To make the discussion simple in the following we shall consider (without loss of generality) that $f$ is to be maximized.

**Definition 2.1.** A fitness function $u$ is *monotonic* if the following condition holds:
$$u(x) \leq u(y) \text{ iff } f(x) \leq f(y).$$

*Note 2.1.* As shown in (Grefenstette and Baker, 1989) the class of monotonic fitness functions includes many frequently used fitness functions, thus it constitutes a natural object of study.

**Definition 2.2.** A selection algorithm is *monotonic* if at any moment $t$ it assigns target

---

[1]i.e. the lowest in the case of a maximization problem, respectively the highest in the case of a minimization problem

sampling rates to individuals such that
$$tsr(x) \leq tsr(y) \text{ iff } u(x) \leq u(y).$$

*Note 2.2.*  Proportional selection, selection by ranking, as well as many other selection algorithms frequently used in practice are monotonic.

The results presented in the following will refer to genetic algorithms using a monotonic selection algorithm and a monotonic fitness function. To give the central characterization of this section one more definition is needed.

**Definition 2.3.**  Given the population $P(t)$ we say that the hyperplane $H_1$ is dominated by the hyperplane $H_2$ in $P(t)$ and denote it by $H_1 \leq_{D,t} H_2$ if

$$\max\{f(x) \mid x \epsilon H_1 \cap P(t)\} \leq \min\{f(x) \mid x \epsilon H_2 \cap P(t)\}.$$

Now we can give the following result((Grefenstette and Baker, 1989)):

**Theorem 2.1.**  In any genetic algorithm using a monotonic selection algorithm and a monotonic fitness function, for any hyperplanes $H_1, H_2$ in $P(t)$

$$H_1 \leq_{D,t} H_2 \Rightarrow tsr(H_1) \leq tsr(H_2).$$

The proof of the theorem is based on the above definitions and is straightforward.

This theorem, although it gives a weaker characterization of the considered class of genetic algorithms then the Schema Theorem does, is more appealing because it is formulated in terms of the objective function.

A more general characterization of the considered class of genetic algorithms can be given based on the following definition:

**Definition 2.4.**  A hyperplane $H_1$ is *completely dominated* by another hyperplane $H_2$, and is denoted by $H_1 \leq_D H_2$ if

$$\max\{f(x) \mid x \epsilon H_1\} \leq \min\{f(x) \mid x \epsilon H_2\}.$$

The following corollary holds:

**Corollary 2.1.**  In any genetic algorithm using a monotonic selection algorithm and a monotonic fitness function, for any hyperplabnes $H_1$ and $H_2$

$$H_1 \leq_D H_2 \Rightarrow \forall(t)tsr(H_1, t) \leq tsr(H_2, t).$$

This result states that under the given condition $H_2$ grows at least as fast as $H_1$ does in any generation, in any genetic algoritm of the considered class.

In the end of their paper Grefenstette and Baker suggest the search for conditions which allow characterizations of the sensitivity of selection algorithms. The next section we lay the basis for the discussion of sensitivity.

## 3  GENETIC ALGORITHMS USING PROPORTIONAL SELECTION AND THE CONVEXITY OF FITNESS FUNCTIONS

In the previous section a characterization of genetic algorithms using a monotonic selection algorithm and a monotonic fitness function was given. This covers a broad class of genetic algorithms used in practice. However these results can neither give bounds on the growth of the number of representatives of hyperplanes, nor capture sensitivity aspects of genetic algorithms.

We claim that one possible reason for these deficiencies is that in the class considered some selection algorithms may "work against" some qualities of certain fitness functions, a fact which is not captured by the given characterizations. To illustrate this let us consider that our problem is to maximize the function $f_0$. Let $m_0 = \min\{f_0(x) \mid P(t)\}$ and $M_0 = \max\{f_0(x) \mid P(t)\}$ for a certain $t$, and suppose that $0 < m_0 < M_0$. Let us further consider the fitness function $u_0$ given by

$$u_0(x) = \ln(\frac{f(x) - m_0}{M_0 - m_0} \cdot (e - 1) + 1),$$

which is similar to $u(x) = b - log(f(x))$ considered in (Grefenstette and Baker, 1989).

This fitness function has some nice properties which make it appealing, such as

a. it reduces the danger of premature convergence by damping out differences between large values of $f(x)$;

b. it exaggerates differences between small values of $f(x)$ which has the effect of making the algorithm "sensitive" to small differences between low valued individuals.

Since $u_0$ is monotonic, for a genetic algorithm using a monotonic selection algorithm and $u_0$ as fitness function we can apply Theorem 2.1. However there are monotonic selection algorithms which void the mentioned qualities of $u_0$. Let the target sampling rate of an individual $x$ be defined by

$$tsr(x) = \frac{(e^{u(x)} - 1)\frac{M_0 - m_0}{e - 1} + m_0}{\mu}$$

where $\mu$ is the mean value of the function values for the individuals in $P(t)$. Obviously this selection algorithm is monotonic, and thus it satisfies the condition of Theorem 2.1. Substituting $u_0$ for $u$ we obtain

$$tsr_o(x) = \frac{f(x)}{\mu(t)}$$

which means a target sampling rate proportional to the function value. Thus the genetic algorithm using $tsr_0$ as selection algorithm uses a proportional selection which lacks the mentioned properties.

For the reason mentioned and illustrated above we shall discuss properties of the kind listed for $u_0$ for a narrower class of genetic algorithms, the ones using proportional selection. Obviously this selection algorithm is monotonic and in addition it has the following property:

For any hyperplane $H$, at any moment $t$

$$tsr(H) = \sum_{x \epsilon H} \frac{tsr(x)}{n(H)} = \sum_{x \epsilon H} \frac{u(x)}{\overline{u} \cdot n(H)} = \frac{u(H)}{\overline{u}}$$

where $u(H)$ is the average fitness of the representatives of $H$ in $P(t)$. We shall call such a generic algorithm *Proportional Selection Genetic Algorithm* (PSGA).

*Note 3.1.* Obviously all the results in the previous section are valid for PSGA's using a monotonic fitness function.

Let us now try to give a characterization of PSGA's using a monotonic fitness function with properties similar to those of $u_0$ above. In order to do this we need some more definitions.

First recall that given a real-valued function $g : D(\subseteq \Re) \to \Re$ the divided difference of $g$ with respect to the points $x, y \epsilon D$ is defined by

$$[x, y; g] = \frac{g(x) - g(y)}{x - y}.$$

Divided differences of higher order are defined recursively, e.g. the divided difference of $g$ with respect to the points $x, y, z \epsilon D$ is defined as

$$[x, y, z; g] = \frac{[x, y; g] - [y, z; g]}{x - z}.$$

**Definition 3.1.** We say that $u$ is a *convex fitness function* if for any individuals $x_1$, $x_2$ and $x_3$ in the domain of $f$

$$[f(x_1), f(x_2), f(x_3); u] \geq 0$$

where $[x,y,z;h]$ denotes the second order divided difference of the function $h$ in the points $x$, $y$ and $z$.

The fitness function $u$ is said to be *concave* if for any individuals $x_1$, $x_2$ and $x_3$ in the domain of $f$

$$[f(x_1), f(x_2), f(x_3); u] \leq 0.$$

The following two theorems give a property of PSGA's using a monotonic and convex, respectively concave fitness functions, which makes them interesting from the point of view of study of sensitivity.

**Theorem 3.1.** For a PSGA using a monotonic and convex fitness function $u$, for any $x_1$, $x_2$ and $x_3$ in $P(t)$ such that $f(x_1) < f(x_2) < f(x_3)$

$$f(x_3) - f(x_2) \geq f(x_2) - f(x_1) \Rightarrow tsr(x_3) - tsr(x_2) \geq tsr(x_2) - tsr(x_1).$$

The corresponding result for concave fitness functions is given by

**Theorem 3.2.** For a PSGA using a monotonic and concave fitness function $u$, for any $x_1$, $x_2$ and $x_3$ in $P(t)$ such that $f(x_1) < f(x_2) < f(x_3)$

$$f(x_3) - f(x_2) \leq f(x_2) - f(x_1) \Rightarrow tsr(x_3, t) - tsr(x_2, t) \leq tsr(x_2, t) - tsr(x_1, t).$$

Since the proofs of the two theorems are absolutely analogous we shall only give the proof for the second one.

*Proof.* (Theorem 3.2.) Since $u$ is concave, we have

$$[f(x_1), f(x_2), f(x_3); u] \leq 0$$

which by the definition of the divided difference is

$$\frac{\frac{u(x_3)-u(x_2)}{f(x_3)-f(x_2)} - \frac{u(x_2)-u(x_1)}{f(x_2)-f(x_1)}}{f(x_3) - f(x_1)} \leq 0.$$

Using the hypothesis that $f(x_1) < f(x_2) < f(x_3)$ we obtain

$$\frac{u(x_3) - u(x_2)}{f(x_3) - f(x_2)} \leq \frac{u(x_2) - u(x_1)}{f(x_2) - f(x_1)},$$

which is equivalent to

$$u(x_3) - u(x_2) \leq (u(x_2) - u(x_1))\frac{f(x_3) - f(x_2)}{f(x_2) - f(x_1)}.$$

The condition $f(x_3) - f(x_2) \leq f(x_2) - f(x_1)$ means that

$$(0 <)\frac{f(x_3) - f(x_2)}{f(x_2) - f(x_1)} \leq 1,$$

by which the previous inequality becomes

$$u(x_3) - u(x_2) \leq u(x_2) - u(x_1).$$

Dividing this latter inequality by $\bar{u}$ we obtain

$$tsr(x_3) - tsr(x_2) \leq tsr(x_2) - tsr(x_1),$$

which completes the proof. $\square$

Although these results are more general the following two corollaries explain better the importance of the above theorems.

**Corollary 3.1.** For a PSGA using a monotonic and convex fitness function $u$, for any $x_1$, $x_2$ and $x_3$ in $P(t)$ such that $f(x_1) < f(x_2) < f(x_3)$ and $f(x_3) - f(x_2) = f(x_2) - f(x_1)$

$$tsr(x_3) - tsr(x_2) \geq tsr(x_2) - tsr(x_1).$$

**Corollary 3.2.** For a PSGA using a monotonic and concave fitness function $u$, for any $x_1$, $x_2$ and $x_3$ in $P(t)$ such that $f(x_1) < f(x_2) < f(x_3)$ and $f(x_3) - f(x_2) = f(x_2) - f(x_1)$

$$tsr(x_3) - tsr(x_2) \leq tsr(x_2) - tsr(x_1).$$

The proofs of these two corollaries are identical to those of the corresponding two theorems by noting that $f(x_3) - f(x_2) = f(x_2) - f(x_1)$ implies

$$\frac{f(x_3) - f(x_2)}{f(x_2) - f(x_1)} = 1$$

The first corollary states that in a PSGA using a monotonic and convex fitness function the *distinction between two individuals*, made by their target sampling rates is the greater the higher their objective values are. Stated otherwise, such an algorithm strongly favors the individuals with higher objective values.

On the other hand the second corollary states that a PSGA using a monotonic and concave fitness function damps out the differences between large objective values (exactly as $u_0$ did).

Although it is not relevant for the further discussions on sensitivity, let us give a characterization of how the convexity (concavity) of the fitness function used influences the allocation of trials to hyperplanes by a PSGA.

We shall only give the result and make the corresponding proof for concave fitness functions, the ones for the convex case being absolutely analogous.

We have the following theorem:

**Theorem 3.3.** In a PSGA using a monotonic and concave fitness function for any hyperplanes $H_1$, $H_2$ and $H_3$ represented in $P(t)$ such that $H_1 <_{D,t} H_2 <_{D,t} H_3$ and $f(x_3) - f(x_2) \leq f(x_2) - f(x_1)$ for all $x_1 \epsilon H_1$, $x_2 \epsilon H_2$ and $x_3 \epsilon H_3$

$$tsr(H_3) - tsr(H_2) \leq tsr(H_2) - tsr(H_1).$$

*Proof.* Let $x_i^{min}$ denote an individual such that $f(x_i^{min}) = \min\{f(x) \mid x \epsilon H_i \cap P(t)\}$ for $i = 1, 2, 3$ and $x_i^{max}$ an individual such that $f(x_i^{max}) = \max\{f(x) \mid x \epsilon H_i \cap P(t)\}$ for $i = 1, 2, 3$.

Using these notations the inequality $f(x_3) - f(x_2) \leq f(x_2) - f(x_1)$ in the hypothesis of the theorem implies

$$f(x_3^{max}) - f(x_2^{min}) \leq f(x_2^{min}) - f(x_1^{max}),$$

which by Theorem 3.2. gives

$$u(x_3^{max}) - u(x_2^{min}) \le u(x_2^{min}) - u(x_1^{max}).$$

This is equivalent to

$$\sum_{i=1}^{n(H_3)} \frac{u(x_3^{max})}{n(H_3)} - \sum_{i=1}^{n(H_2)} \frac{u(x_2^{min})}{n(H_2)} \le \sum_{i=1}^{n(H_2)} \frac{u(x_2^{min})}{n(H_2)} - \sum_{i=1}^{n(H_1)} \frac{u(x_1^{max})}{n(H_1)}.$$

Since $u$ is monotonic we have

$$\sum_{i=1}^{n(H_3)} \frac{u(x)}{n(H_3)} - \sum_{i=1}^{n(H_2)} \frac{u(x)}{n(H_2)} \le \sum_{i=1}^{n(H_2)} \frac{u(x)}{n(H_2)} - \sum_{i=1}^{n(H_1)} \frac{u(x)}{n(H_1)},$$

that is

$$u(H_3) - u(H_2) \le u(H_2) - u(H_1),$$

which divided by $\bar{u}(> 0)$ gives

$$tsr(H_3) - tsr(H_2) \le tsr(H_2) - tsr(H_1).$$

Thus our proof is complete. $\square$

***Note 3.2.*** We can make similar notes concerning the behaviour of PSGA's using monotonic and convex (concave) fitness functions relative to the allocation of hyperplanes as we did after Corollary 3.1. and Corollary 3.2.

In the following section we shall use these results to study some sensitivity properties of PSGA's.

## 4  SENSITIVITY OF A PSGA TO THE CONVEXITY OF THE USED FITNESS FUNCTION

In this section we shall introduce a concept of sensitivity which will make it possible to describe the behaviour of certain PSGA's. Let us first give an intuitive description of what we shall mean by "sensitivity" of a PSGA.

Selection in genetic algorithms is done based on the comparison of the objective function values of individuals in a population. However the distinction between individuals is not directly based on their objective function values but is made via their target sampling rate. As we have seen in Section 2 this is a composition of two functions. In the case of PSGA's one of these function (the selection algorithm) is fixed. It should be intuitively clear that by changing the fitness function one can influence the way a PSGA distinguishes between individuals (this fact has actually been recognized and used in various applications by the means of parametrized fitness functions). In the following we shall try to give a means to measure the way a PSGA distinguishes between individuals (sensitivity) and prove some results on how some characteristics of fitness functions influence this property of the algorithm.

**Definition 4.1.** In a genetic algorithm using a selection algorithm defined by *tsr*, by the *absolute distance* of two individuals $x_1$ and $x_2$ in $P(t)$, denotes the distance between their target sampling rates, i.e.

$$\delta_{tsr}(x_1, x_2) = \mid tsr(x_1) - tsr(x_2) \mid .$$

We define the *relative distance* of the two individuals by

$$\rho_{tsr}(x_1, x_2) = \frac{\delta_{tsr}(x_1, x_2)}{\mid f(x_1) - f(x_2) \mid}$$

In the following while speaking about a single algorithm we shall omit the subscript *tsr*.

With this notion we can give a first definition concerning sensitivity.

**Definition 4.2.** Let us consider a genetic algorithm and let $x_1, x_2, x_3$ and $x_4$ be individuals in some population $P(t)$. We say that the genetic algorithm makes a *stronger (weaker) distinction* between $x_3$ and $x_4$ than between $x_1$ and $x_2$ if

$$\rho(x_3, x_4) \geq \rho(x_1, x_2).$$

Similarly the genetic algorithm makes a *weaker distinction* between $x_3$ and $x_4$ than between $x_1$ and $x_2$ if

$$\rho(x_3, x_4) \leq \rho(x_1, x_2).$$

This definition captures how the selection in a genetic algorithms is influenced by the differences between objective function values.

Let us now see how the convexity (concavity) of a fitness function influences the distinction made by a PSGA between individuals·in a population. To simplify the discussion we shall prove the following lemma:

**Lema 4.1.** If a fitness function is convex (concave) then it is monotonic.

*Proof.* We first consider the proof for the convex case. We have to prove that if a fitness function $u$ is convex then for any $x$ and $y$ in $P(t)$

$$u(x) \leq u(y) \Leftrightarrow f(x) \leq f(y).$$

Let $x_m$ denote an element in $P(t)$ such that $f(x_m) = \min\{f(x) \mid x \epsilon P(t)\}$ and let us assume that $x$ and $y$ are two individuals in $P(t)$ such that $f(x_m) < f(x) < f(y)$. By the definition of convexity we have

$$[f(x_m), f(x), f(y); u] \geq 0,$$

that is

$$\frac{\frac{u(x_m)-u(x)}{f(x_m)-f(x)} - \frac{u(x)-u(y)}{f(x)-f(y)}}{f(x_m)-f(y)} \geq 0.$$

By the condition imposed on fitness functions in Section $2^2$ $u(x_m) = 0$, which together with our hypothesis $f(x_m) < f(x) < f(y)$ makes the previous inequality equivalent to

$$u(x) - u(y) \leq (f(x) - f(y)) \cdot \frac{-u(x)}{f(x_m)-f(x)}.$$

But the right side of this inequality represents a negative number, which means

$$u(x) \leq u(y).$$

The inverse implication is absolute identical except for the rearrangement of the inequation. Thus our proof for the convex case is complete.

For the concave case the proof is similar, except only for that the third individual considered for building the divided difference will be an $x_M$ such that $f(x_M) = \max\{f(x) \mid x \epsilon P(t)\}$. Now the proof of the lemma is complete. $\square$

*Note 4.1.* The above lemma gives us in the following the possibility to use "convex (concave) fitness function" instead of "monotonic and convex (concave) fitness function".

Let us now give definitions of two types of sensitivity for genetic algorithms.

**Definition 4.3.**  We say that a genetic algorithm is *high-value sensitive* if for any $x_1, x_2, x_3 \epsilon P(t)$ such that $f(x_1) < f(x_2) < f(x_3)$ it makes a stronger distiction between $x_2$ and $x_3$ than between $x_1$ and $x_2$, i.e.

$$\rho(x_2, x_3) \geq \rho(x_1, x_2).$$

Similarly we say that a genetic algorithm is *low-value sensitive* if for any $x_1, x_2, x_3 \epsilon P(t)$ such that $f(x_1) < f(x_2) < f(x_3)$ it makes a weaker distiction between $x_2$ and $x_3$ than between $x_1$ and $x_2$, i.e.

$$\rho(x_2, x_3) \leq \rho(x_1, x_2).$$

By this definition we call high-value sensitive those genetic algorithms which make a stronger distinction in favor of individuals with higher objective function values, while low-value sensitive will be those genetic algorithms which distingush more strongly between individuals having low objective function values.

**Theorem 4.1.** A PSGA using a convex fitness function is high-value sensitive.

**Theorem 4.2.** A PSGA using a concave fitness function is high-value sensitive.

*Proof.* We only give the proof for Theorem 4.1 (i.e. the convex case), the one for Theorem 4.2 being similar.

---

[2] i.e. that the value of the fitness function corresponding to the "worst" objective function value is 0.

Let $x_1$, $x_2$ and $x_3$ be three individuals in $P(t)$ such that $f(x_1) < f(x_2) < f(x_3)$. The convexity of the fitness function (let it be $u$) means

$$\frac{\frac{u(x_3)-u(x_2)}{f(x_3)-f(x_2)} - \frac{u(x_2)-u(x_2)}{f(x_2)-f(x_1)}}{f(x_3) - f(x_1)} \geq 0,$$

which by the hypothesis is equivalent to

$$\frac{u(x_3) - u(x_2)}{f(x_3) - f(x_2)} - \frac{u(x_2) - u(x_2)}{f(x_2) - f(x_1)} \geq 0.$$

Dividing this inequality by $\bar{u}$ ve have

$$\frac{tsr(x_3) - tsr(x_2)}{f(x_3) - f(x_2)} - \frac{tsr(x_2) - tsr(x_2)}{f(x_2) - f(x_1)} \geq 0,$$

and this is exactly what we wanted to prove, i.e.

$$\rho(x_2, x_3) \geq (\leq)\rho(x_1, x_2).$$

$\square$

This theorem explains us the behaviour in selection of a certain class of genetic algorithms (PSGA's). It makes clear for instance what makes a PSGA using fitness function $u_0$ defined in Section 3 have the listed properties. More precisely, the function $u : [m_0, M_0] \rightarrow [0, 1]$ defined by

$$u(t) = \ln(\frac{t - m_0}{M_0 - m_0} \cdot (e - 1) + 1)$$

is twice (in fact infinite times) derivable on $(m_0, M_0)$ and has its second order derivative negative for all $t\epsilon(m_0, M_0)$, i.e. is concave (in analytical sense). But this means that its second order divided difference is negative for any three points in its domain and so for any three distinct values of the objective function. According to the above theorem this means that a PSGA using $u_0$ as fitness is low-value sensitive.

Let us consider another example. Filipič (1992) described a GA application where the fitness function used was similar to the following (except that he defined it for a minimization problem):

$$u_k(x) = \left( \frac{f(x) - f_{min}}{f_{max} - f_{min}} \right)^{1/k},$$

where $f_{min}$ and $f_{max}$ are (estimated) lower, respectively upper bounds of the objective function $f$ and $k > 1$ is a parameter of the algorithm. He (correctly) noted that by using this fitness functions "...only the best solutions ... receive distinguished high fitness values." Following the same reasoning as above we can easily show that the considered fitness function is convex (for any $k > 1$) which, by Theorem 4.1 explains the behaviour noted by Filipič (1992).

However the above conclusion is not the only reason for which we chose the latter example. The note made in (Filipic, 1992) concerning the effect of the fitness function $u_k$ on the behaviour of the genetic algorithm also has a first part, namely "Increasing $k$, while $k > 1$, causes a wider and wider range of high cost solutions[3] to be assigned low fitness...". What is interesting about this note is that it gives (even if just qualitatively) a comparison between the effect of several fitness functions ("...more and more..."). In the next section we shall try to formally capture this phenomenon by defining a way to compare the effects of two different fitness functions of a certain class on the behaviour of a PSGA.

## 5   COMPARING THE SENSITIVITIES OF PSGA -S

As we did throughout this paper in this section too we shall only concentrate on a certain class of fitness functions. Let us start by defining the class to be considered.

**Definition 5.1.** We say that a fitness function is **uniform** if it is either convex or concave.

In the following we shall only consider PSGA's using a uniform fitness function. We call such a genetic algorithm **Uniform** PSGA (UPSGA).

We shall now define an ordering relation over the class of UPSGA's which allows comparing two such algorithms with respect to their sensitivity.

**Definition 5.2.** Let $A_1$ and $A_2$ two UPSGA's using the fitness functions $u_1$ and $u_2$ respectively. We say that $A_1$ is **less sensitive** than $A_2$ and denote this relation by $A_1 \leq_S A_2$ if for any population $P(t)$ and any individuals $x_1$, $x_2$ and $x_3$ in $P(t)$ such that $f(x_1) < f(x_2) < f(x_3)$

$$\rho_{tsr_1}(x_2, x_3) - \rho_{tsr_1}(x_1, x_2) \leq \rho_{tsr_2}(x_2, x_3) - \rho_{tsr_2}(x_1, x_2).$$

We also say that $A_2$ is **more sensitive** than $A_1$.

Put in words this definition says that a UPSGA is more sensitive than another one if it makes a stronger distinction between higher objective function values than the second one.

The central theorem of this section gives a sufficient condition for an UPSGA to be more sensitive than another.

**Theorem 5.1.** Let $A_1$ and $A_2$ be two UPSGA's using the fitness functions $u_1$ and $u_2$ respectively. If for any population $P(t)$ and any individuals $x_1$, $x_2$ and $x_3$ in $P(t)$ such that $f(x_1) < f(x_2) < f(x_3)$ the inequality

$$[f(x_1), f(x_2), f(x_3); u_1] \leq [f(x_1), f(x_2), f(x_3); u_2]$$

is true, then $A_1 \leq_S A_2$.

To prove this theorem we shall first prove the following lemma:

**Lemma 5.1.** Let $A_1$ and $A_2$ two UPSGA's using the fitness functions $u_1$ and $u_2$ respectively. If for any population $P(t)$ and any individuals $x_1$, $x_2$ and $x_3$ in $P(t)$ such that $f(x_1) < f(x_2) < f(x_3)$ the inequality

---

[3]Remember that the problem there was to minimize a function.

$$[f(x_1), f(x_2), f(x_3); u_1] \le [f(x_1), f(x_2), f(x_3); u_2]$$

is true, then $u_1(x) \ge u_2(x)$ for all $x \epsilon P(t)$.

*Proof.* Let (as in the case of the Lemma 4.1.) $x_m$ denote a member of $P(t)$ such that $f(x_m) = \min\{f(x) \mid x \epsilon P(t)\}$ and $x_M$ a member of $P(t)$ such that $f(x_M) = \max\{f(x) \mid x \epsilon P(t)\}$. By our conditions on fitness functions $u_1(x_m) = u_2(x_m) = 0$ and $u_1(x_M) = u_2(x_M) = 1$ . Let further $x$ be a members of $P(t)$ such that $f(x_m) < f(x) < f(x_M)$. By the hypothesis we have

$$[f(x_m), f(x), f(x_M); u_1] \le [f(x_m), f(x), f(x_M); u_2],$$

which, by the above assumptions implies

$$\frac{1 - u_1(x)}{f(x_M) - f(x)} - \frac{u_1(x)}{f(x) - f(x_m)} \le \frac{1 - u_2(x)}{f(x_M) - f(x)} - \frac{u_2(x)}{f(x) - f(x_m)}.$$

By rearranging this inequality we obtain

$$\frac{u_2(x) - u_1(x)}{f(x) - f(x_m)} + \frac{u_2(x) - u_1(x)}{f(x_M) - f(x)} \le 0,$$

that is

$$(u_2(x) - u_1(x))[\frac{1}{f(x) - f(x_m)} + \frac{1}{f(x_M) - f(x)}] \le 0.$$

But this inequality can only be true if

$$u_2(x) \le u_1(x).$$

Thus our proof is complete. $\square$

Let us now return to Theorem 5.1.

*Proof.* (Theorem 5.1.) Let $x_1$, $x_2$ and $x_3$ be three individuals in $P(t)$ such that $f(x_1) < f(x_2) < f(x_3)$. By the hypothesis of out theorem the inequality

$$[f(x_1), f(x_2), f(x_3); u_1] \le [f(x_1), f(x_2), f(x_3); u_2]$$

is true. By the definition of divided differences this means

$$\frac{u_1(x_3) - u_1(x_2)}{f(x_3) - f(x_2)} - \frac{u_1(x_2) - u_1(x_1)}{f(x_2) - f(x_1)} \le \frac{u_2(x_3) - u_2(x_2)}{f(x_3) - f(x_2)} - \frac{u_2(x_2) - u_2(x_1)}{f(x_2) - f(x_1)}.$$

This is equivalent to

$$\overline{u}_1 \cdot \left[ \frac{tsr_1(x_3) - tsr_1(x_2)}{f(x_3) - f(x_2)} - \frac{tsr_1(x_2) - tsr_1(x_1)}{f(x_2) - f(x_1)} \right] \le$$

$$\le \overline{u}_2 \cdot \left[ \frac{tsr_2(x_3) - tsr_2(x_2)}{f(x_3) - f(x_2)} - \frac{tsr_2(x_2) - tsr_2(x_1)}{f(x_2) - f(x_1)} \right],$$

or, equivalently

$$\frac{tsr_1(x_3) - tsr_1(x_2)}{f(x_3) - f(x_2)} - \frac{tsr_1(x_2) - tsr_1(x_1)}{f(x_2) - f(x_1)} \le$$

$$\le \left[ \frac{tsr_2(x_3) - tsr_2(x_2)}{f(x_3) - f(x_2)} - \frac{tsr_2(x_2) - tsr_2(x_1)}{f(x_2) - f(x_1)} \right] \cdot \frac{\overline{u}_2}{\overline{u}_1}.$$

But by Lemma 5.1 $u_1(x) \ge u_2(x)$ for all $x \epsilon P(t)$, which implies $\overline{u}_1 \ge \overline{u}_2$, or equivalently $\overline{u}_2 / \overline{u}_1 \le 1$. By this the previuos inequality implies

$$A_1 \le_S A_2,$$

and our proof is complete. $\square$

Put into words, Theorem 5.1 means that for genetic algorithms with proportional selection using uniform fitness functions, the "more convex" the fitness function, the more sensitive the algorithms are to high objective function values.

Let us now return to the fitness function $u_k(k > 1)$ defined in the previous section. Actually this is a family of fitness functions defined by the parameter $k$. Let $k_1$ and $k_2$ be two real numbers such that $1 < k_1 < k_2$. It can be easily shown that $u_{k_1}''(t) < u_{k_2}''(t)$ for all $t \epsilon (f_{min}, f_{max})$ which implies that the same relation holds between the second order divided differences for any three elements of the same segment[4]. This latter means that the condition of Theorem 5.1 is fulfilled and thus the UPSGA using $u_{k_1}$ as fitness function is more sensitive then the one using $u_{k_2}$. This conclusion explains the second note on the fitness functions $u_k$ quoted from (Filipič, 1992).

## 6  CONCLUSIONS

In this paper we introduced ways to study the sensitivity of a class of genetic algorithms. The results presented explain the behaviour in selection of these algorithms and gives theoretical justification for some qualities of certain fitness functions recognized by several authors as well as for the success of using scaling methods for fitness functions.

In (Balázs, 1993b) we also showed that for UPSGA's a lower bound on the growth of the number of representatives of hyperplanes can be given.

Our further work in this direction will concern the study of scaling of fitness functions for a UPSGA. Some preliminary results on this are given in (Balázs, 1994).

---

[4] $u''(t)$ denotes the second order derivative of the function $u$ in $t$.

## References

Balázs, M.E. (1993a) On an Experiment Using Genetic Algorithms for Solving Equations, *submitted to Studia Universitatis Babeş-Bolyai.*

Balázs, M.E. (1993b) On a Class of Fitness Functions for Genetic Algorithms Using Proportional Selection, *submitted to Revue d'Analyse Numerique et de Théorie de l'Approximation.*

Balázs, M.E. (1994) Genetic Algorithms and Applications, *PhD Thesis*, Babeş-Bolyai University, Cluj.

Filipič, B. (1992) Enhancing Genetic Search to Schedule a Production Unit, Proc. ECAI'92 Neumann, B. Ed., John Wiley & So.

Goldberg, D. (1989) Genetic Algorithms in Search, Optimization and Machine Learning, *Addison-Wesley.*

Grefenstette, J.J. and Baker,J.E. (1989) How Genetic Algorithms Work: A Critical Look at Implicit Parallelism, *Proceedings of ICGA'89*, Ed. Schaffer.

Holland, J.H., (1975) Adaptation in Natural and Artificial Systems, *Ann Arbor: The University of Michigan Press.*

# PART 3

# FITNESS LANDSCAPES AND GENETIC OPERATORS

# Genetic Algorithm Difficulty and the Modality of Fitness Landscapes

**Jeffrey Horn**[*] **and David E. Goldberg**[†]
Illinois Genetic Algorithms Laboratory
University of Illinois at Urbana-Champaign
117 Transportation Building
104 South Mathews Avenue
Urbana, IL 61801-2996

## Abstract

We assume that the modality (i.e., number of local optima) of a fitness landscape is related to the difficulty of finding the best point on that landscape by evolutionary computation (e.g., hillclimbers and genetic algorithms (GAs)). We first examine the limits of modality by constructing a unimodal function and a maximally multimodal function. At such extremes our intuition breaks down. A fitness landscape consisting entirely of a single hill leading to the global optimum proves to be harder for hillclimbers than GAs. A provably maximally multimodal function, in which half the points in the search space are local optima, can be easier than the unimodal, single hill problem for both hillclimbers and GAs. Exploring the more realistic intermediate range between the extremes of modality, we construct local optima with varying degrees of "attraction" to our evolutionary algorithms. Most work on optima and their basins of attraction has focused on hills and hillclimbers, while some research has explored attraction for the GA's crossover operator. We extend the latter results by defining and implementing *maximal* partial deception in problems with $k$ arbitrarily placed global optima. This allows us to create functions, such as the *minimum distance* function $f_{mdG}$, with $k$ isolated global optima and multiple local optima attractive to both crossover and hillclimbers. The function $f_{mdG}$ seems to be a powerful new tool for generalizing deception and relating hillclimbers (and Hamming space) to GAs and crossover.

---

[*]Department of Computer Science, internet e-mail: jeffhorn@uiuc.edu
[†]Department of General Engineering, internet e-mail: deg@uiuc.edu

## 1   INTRODUCTION

Genetic algorithms (GAs) are robust adaptive systems that have been applied successfully to hard optimization problems, both artificial and real world. Yet GAs do fail. When and why do they fail? The question of what makes a problem hard for a GA has received a good deal of attention – and some controversy – as of late. The controversy is largely a tempest in a teapot. If we are ever to understand how hard a problem GAs can solve, how quickly, and with what reliability, we must get our hands around what "hard" is. Goldberg (1993) suggests several quasi-separable dimensions of GA problem difficulty:

- Isolation

- Misleadingness

- Noise

- Multimodality

- Crosstalk

Important progress has been made (Goldberg, 1994) in understanding the role of each of these facets of difficulty. Example work includes the study of deception (the combination of solution isolation and suboptimum misleadingness) by Whitley (1991), Goldberg (1989b, 1989c, 1991) and others. Rudnick and Goldberg (1991), Goldberg and Rudnick (1991), Goldberg, Deb, and Clark (1992) and Kargupta and Goldberg (1994), among others, try to quantify and bound both deterministic and stochastic noise introduced by GA operators and the fitness function itself. Goldberg, Deb, and Horn (1992) introduce *massively* multimodal functions, and Kargupta and Goldberg (1994) look at crosstalk. These and other studies have yielded important insights and practical prescriptions, but a significant amount of work remains.

Some have suggested that we first create a full-fledged *description* of problem difficulty, with all the notation necessary to be complete and exact, but complex systems understanding is not achieved via this route (Goldberg, 1993, 1994). The more usual method is to design or *prescribe* problems that maximally but boundedly challenge a GA along one or more dimensions of problem difficulty. The work presented here continues largely in that vein by investigating deception and modality jointly. We believe that work like this ultimately will be assembled to form a rough patchquilt of models and metrics that help us quantify and analyze how hard a problem is for a particular GA.

## 2   PRELIMINARIES: LANDSCAPES AND OPTIMA

We make use of the paradigm of a *fitness landscape* (Wright, 1988), which we define here as a search space $S$, a metric $d$, and scalar fitness function $f$ defined over elements $s$ of $S$. Assuming the goal is to maximize fitness, we can imagine the globally best solutions (the global optima, or "globals") as "peaks" in the search space. For the purposes of this paper, we define local optimality as follows. We first assume a non-negative-real valued, scalar fitness function $f(s)$ over fixed length $\ell$-bit binary strings $s$, $f(s) \in \Re \geq 0$. Without loss of generality, we assume $f$ is to be maximized. A *local optimum* in a discrete search space $S$ is a point, or region, with fitness function value strictly greater than those of *all* of its nearest neighbors. By "region" we mean a set of interconnected points of equal fitness.

That is, we treat as a single optimum the set of points related by the transitive closure of the nearest-neighbor relation such that all points are of equal fitness[1]. This definition allows us to include flat plateaus and ridges as single optima, and to treat a flat fitness function as having no local optima. The "nearest neighbor" relation assumes a metric on the search space, call it $d$, where $d(s_1, s_2) \in \Re \geq 0$ is the metric's distance between points $s_1$ and $s_2$. Then the nearest neighbors of a point $s'$ are all points $s \in S, s \neq s'$ such that $d(s', s) \leq k$, for some neighborhood radius $k$. In this paper we use only *Hamming distance* (number of bit positions at which two binary strings differ) as the metric[2], and assume $k = 1$. Thus a point $s$ (or connected region of equal fitness) with fitness $f(s)$ greater than that of all its immediate neighbors (strings differing from $s$ in only one bit position) is a local optimum.

# 3  MINIMUM MODALITY CAN BE HARD

At one extreme of the modality spectrum we have unimodality. Unimodal functions have only one local optimum, which is therefore the global optimum. It is well-known that such problems can be hard when the optimum is isolated, with little or no information available elsewhere in the search space. Such isolated peaks on otherwise flat fitness landscapes have been called *needle-in-a-haystack* (NIAH) problems (Goldberg, 1989a), and are clearly solvable only by enumeration of the space. But if we decrease the isolation of the single optimum, increase the size of its basin of attraction, and add information to larger portions of the search space, intuition tells us that the search should become easier and shorter than enumeration. In particular, if we make the entire search space a single hill, where every point is on a path to the global optimum, even simple evolutionary algorithms, such as a 1-bit hillclimber, should quickly optimize the function. But Horn, Goldberg, and Deb (1994) show otherwise.

## 3.1  CONSTRUCTION OF THE LONG PATH

Horn, Goldberg, and Deb (1994) construct two different functions of $\ell$-bit strings in which all points are on the path to the only optimum, but in which path length grows exponentially in $\ell$. Thus even a 1-bit hillclimber is guaranteed not only to find the global optimum but to make constant progress toward it. However, for reasonably large $\ell$ ($> 90$, for example), the hillclimber, and many other local searchers, effectively will never converge to the global. Below we summarize one of the two constructions from (Horn, Goldberg, & Deb, 1994), namely the Root2path.

We choose a stepsize $k = 1$ to illustrate the construction of the Root2path. Each point on the path must be exactly $k = 1$ bit different from the point behind it and the point ahead of it on the path, while also being at least $k + 1 = 2$ bits away from any other point on the path.

The construction of the path is intuitive. If we have a Root2path $P_\ell$ of dimension $\ell$ ($=$ number of bits), we can basically double it by moving up two dimensions to ($\ell + 2$) as follows. Let $P_\ell$ be a list of binary strings representing consecutive steps on the path (e.g.,

---

[1] The requirement for equality could be relaxed to allow for fitnesses within some $\delta$ of the globally optimal fitness.

[2] A recurring theme of this paper is the demonstration that Hamming distance among optima, and the shape of the Hamming space landscape in general, are quite important to GA search by crossover, contrary to recent discussions in the GA community.

$P_4 = \{0000, 0001, 0011, ...\}$). Make two copies of $P_\ell$, say copy00 and copy11. Add "00" to the beginning of each string (point) in copy00, and add "11" to each point in copy11[3]. Now each point in copy00 is at least two bits different from all points in copy11. Also, copy00 and copy11 are both paths of stepsize one and of dimension $\ell + 2$. Furthermore, the endpoint of copy00 and the endpoint of copy11 differ only in their first two bit positions ("00" versus "11"). By adding a "bridge" point that is the same as the endpoint of copy00 but with "01" in the first two bit positions, we can connect the end of copy00 and the end of copy11[4]. Reversing the list in copy11, we concatenate copy00, the bridge point, and Reverse[copy11] to create the Root2path $P_{\ell+2}$ of dimension $\ell + 2$, with length essentially twice that of $P_\ell$:

$$|P_{\ell+2}| = 2|P_\ell| + 1. \tag{1}$$

For the dimensions in between the doublings, $P_{\ell+1}$, we can simply use the path $P_\ell$ by adding a "0" to each point in $P_\ell$. If $|P_\ell|$ is exponentional in $\ell$, then $|P_{\ell+1}|$ is exponential in $\ell + 1$.

For the base case, we use the first dimension $\ell = 1$. Here we have only two points in the search space: 0 and 1. We put them both on the Root2path for $\ell = 1$. Thus, $P_1 = \{0, 1\}$, where 0 is the beginning and 1 is the end (i.e., the global optimum).

So with every other incremental increase in dimension $\ell$, we have an effective doubling of the path length. We can solve the recurrence relation in Equation 1 exactly, but it is clear that the path length increases in proportion to $2^{\ell/2}$ or $(\sqrt{2})^\ell$. Thus the path length grows exponentially in $\ell$ with base $\approx 1.414$, although it is an ever-decreasing fraction of the space[5].

We make one end of the path the global optimum, and adjust the fitnesses of the rest of the path so that fitness decreases as we move along the path away from the global optimum and towards the beginning of the path. If we choose the all zeroes point to be the beginning of the path (rather than the end), we can easily make the rest of the search space (all points not on the path) lead to the beginning of the path. We do this by setting the fitness of offpath points to some increasing function of the number of zeros (*nilness*) in the string, such as $f(s) = f(0000...0) - u(s)$. Here $f(0000...0)$ is the fitness at the beginning of the path[6] and $u(s)$ is the *unitation* (number of ones) of string $s$.

Horn, Goldberg, and Deb (1994) also show how to extend this construction to create paths of stepsize $k > 1$, where nonconsecutive points on the path are separated by at least $k + 1$ bits. Paths constructed this way are of order $O(2^{\ell/(k+1)})$ steps in length, which is exponential in $\ell$ for fixed $k$. They then show empirically that various types of one-bit hillclimbers do indeed take exponential time, in expectation, to climb such paths[7].

---

[3]Thus the point "1001" in $P_\ell$ would become the point "001001" in copy00 and "111001" in copy11.

[4]Alternatively, we can connect the beginning of copy00 to the beginning of copy11.

[5]Thus for large $\ell$, the path itself is essentially a NIAH, with a vanishing probability of a random starting point "landing" anywhere on or near the path.

[6]Horn, Goldberg, and Deb (1994) call the offpath points with their nilness function the *nilness slope*. Together the *path* plus the *slope* form the single *hill* that fills the entire search space.

[7]The problem of finding a maximally long path with minimal separation has some history, and is known as the "snake-in-the-box" problem, or the design of distance preserving codes, in the literature on combinatorics (Preparata, 1974). Maximizing the length of paths with $k$-bits of separation is an open problem, even for $k = 1$. However, upper bounds have been found that are $< O(2^\ell)$. Thus the longest paths we can ever find will be $O(2^{\ell/c})$ for some constant $c \geq 1$. For the Root2path, $c = 2$ for $k = 1$. Horn, Goldberg, and Deb (1994) suggest the Fibonacci path, which yields a $c = 1/Log_2\Phi \approx 1.44042$ when $k = 1$, where $\Phi$ is the golden ratio.

## 3.2   VISUALIZATION IN TWO DIMENSIONS

We try to visualize a long path in two dimensions in Figure 1, top. Here the fitness is a function of the integers $x$ and $y$: $f_{lp}(x, y)$, for the "long path" function. As with the Root2path and Fibonacci paths constructed in (Horn, Goldberg, & Deb, 1994), the two dimensional spiral path is generated by induction on the size of the search space, in this case $s^2$. Here $s$ is the integer range over which $x$ and $y$ each vary. For the base case $s = 1$, the single point is the global optimum, with fitness 1, and is the only point on the path. Informally, the inductive step is to take a path of dimension $s$, add a ring (or rather, square) of points around the outside, each with fitness 0, then add another ring of points and add them to the path, incrementing the fitness of every point on the $s$-dimensional path by the number of new path points added. This gives us a long path of dimension $s + 2$. In other words, every other increment of $s$ adds another ring to the spiral and pushes up the old, inner spiral to maintain the slope up to the global at the center. Thus the construction of the two dimensional spiral path has the same inductive form as those of binary-space long paths. However, in two dimensions we can actually put half the search space on the spiraling path to achieve path lengths of $O(|\text{search space}|)$. Again, we can separate non-adjacent points on the two dimensional spiral path by any number $k$ of steps[8] by simply adding rings to the spiral every $k$ increments of $s$ instead of every other increment.

## 3.3   EMPIRICAL RESULTS

The long path problem is clearly and demonstrably difficult for local searchers (that is, algorithms that search small neighborhoods with high probability, and larger neighborhoods with vanishingly small probability). Such algorithms include hillclimbers and the GA's mutation operator. Apparently, however, such long path problems are amenable to GA crossover. It is obvious from their inductive construction that these paths have structure. The same basic subsequences of steps are used over and over again on larger scales, resulting in fractal self-similarity. Such structure might induce building blocks exploitable by crossover (Holland, 1992). In particular, patterns such as "00" and "11" are common to all points on the (binary-space) path, and are used over and over again in the construction of the path.

Although we have not yet performed a schema analysis (Bethke, 1981) of these functions[9], we have some preliminary empirical results (Horn, Goldberg, & Deb, 1994). These early results indicate that a GA with crossover alone ($p_m = 0$) outperforms $k = 1$ step hillclimbers (e.g., steepest ascent, next ascent) and several mutation algorithms (e.g., random mutation hillclimbing (RMHC)) by reaching the global optimum using several orders of magnitude fewer function evaluations. More testing and analysis are required, but if the GA is superior to hillclimbing (i.e., finds the global in $< O(2^{\ell/ck})$ time), then we have found a problem that distinguishes GAs from hillclimbers. Such a result might be of particular interest to those looking at when GAs outperform hillclimbers (Mitchell & Holland, 1993). One answer might be "on a hill".

Although GA crossover can outperform some simple hillclimbers on some long path problems, fairly large population sizes are apparently required for crossover to succeed. Horn, Goldberg, and Deb (1994) report reliable performance (in converging to the global optimum)

---

[8] We assume the *metropolitan* or *city-block* metric for this 2-D space.

[9] We assume familiarity with fundamental concepts of GA theory, such as building blocks and schema analysis, at least to the extent presented in (Goldberg, 1989a).

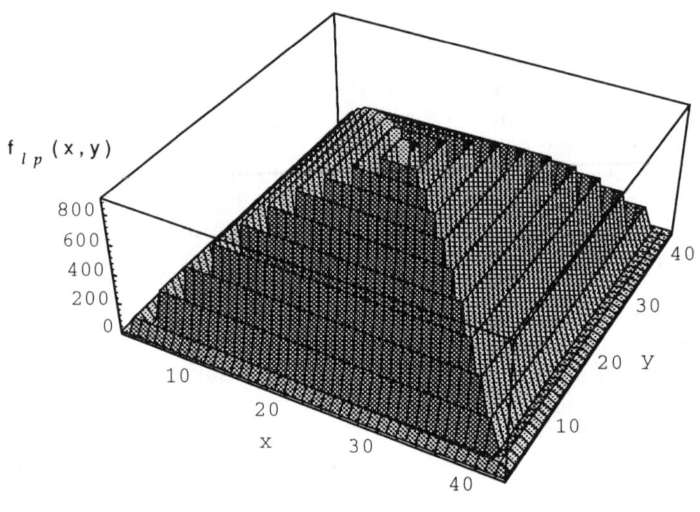

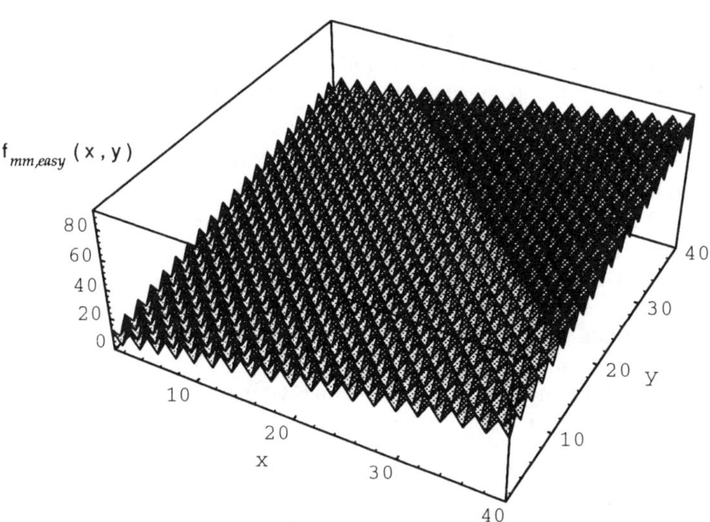

Figure 1: The two extremes of modality. *Top:* A unimodal problem, $f_{lp}(x, y)$, in which every point in the space is on an long path (growing exponentially in $x$ and $y$) to the global optimum. *Bottom:* A maximally multimodal function, $f_{mm,easy}(x, y)$ that is easy for a GA to optimize.

only with population sizes of $N = 4000, 5000$, and $6000$, on Root2path problem lengths of $\ell = 29, 39$, and $49$ respectively. As we show in the next section on "maximum modality", the GA does not optimize the long path problems reliably with small population sizes (e.g., $N = 300$).

The long path function is interesting also because it points out that the modality of a search space, if measured solely as the number of local optima, is at best a first order estimate of the amenability of the space to search by hillclimbers, mutation, or by evolutionary search algorithms in general.

## 4 MAXIMUM MODALITY CAN BE EASY

At the other extreme of the modality spectrum, what is the maximum number of local optima possible in a binary problem of size $\ell$-bits? We assume minimum radius (1-bit) peaks, so that our requirement for local optimality is minimal. That is, a point is a local optimum if and only if all adjacent points have inferior fitness values. We can calculate an upper bound on the number of such optima.

Let $p$ be the number of local "peaks". In an $\ell$-bit problem, each peak must have exactly $\ell$ immediate neighbors that are not local optima (call them "nonoptima"). Thus the number of adjacent pairs of optimum-nonoptimum is $p * \ell$. That is, for a problem to have $p$ local optima it must have $p * \ell$ different pairings of optima and adjacent nonoptima. There are exactly $2^\ell - p$ nonoptima. Each of these nonoptima can have at most $\ell$ adjacent optima. Thus an *upper* bound on the number of optimum-nonoptimum pairings is $(2^\ell - p) * \ell$. We can increase $p$ until the number of optimum-nonoptimum pairs equals the maximum: $p * \ell = (2^\ell - p) * \ell$. We derive $p = 2^{\ell-1}$, which is half the size of the search space[10]. This is an upper bound on the number of local optima.

Using the concept of unitation, we can construct a function with $2^{\ell-1}$ local optima, thus showing that our upper bound is indeed the exact maximum number of local optima. Ackley (1985, 1987a, 1987b) constructs such a "fine-grained local maxima" function, naming it the *porcupine function*. Although he neither claims nor shows that the porcupine function has the *maximum* number of local optima, Ackley does point out that it has "an exponential number of local maxima" (Ackley, 1987b). Here we construct a strictly non-negative variant of the porcupine function and prove that it does indeed contain $2^{\ell-1}$ local optima.

### 4.1 CONSTRUCTION

A *maximally multimodal* function $f_{mm}(s)$ of unitation assigns a high fitness to all bit strings $s$ of odd unitation, for example, and a low fitness to all strings of even unitation:

$$f_{mm}(s) = \begin{cases} 1 & \text{if } \mathrm{Odd}(u(s)) \\ 0 & \text{otherwise.} \end{cases} \tag{2}$$

Since all strings of odd unitation are separated from each other by strings of even unitation, odd unitation strings are indeed local optima. Strings of odd unitation occupy exactly half the search space[11].

---

[10]In other words, the number of optima cannot exceed the number of nonoptima.

[11]It is interesting to note that maximally multimodal functions, in which half the search space are local optima, do not have to be functions of unitation but must have all of their local optima

A maximally multimodal function has the maximum number of possible "attractors" on which a search algorithm might get stuck. But of course each optimum's basin of attraction is at a minimum size. To illustrate that massive multimodality *by itself* does not imply difficulty for GAs or hillclimbers in general, we can add a gentle slope to the function that leads quickly to the global optimum (all ones in this case)[12], as Ackley did in his porcupine function (Ackley, 1985, 1987a, 1987b):

$$f_{mm,easy}(s) = u(s) + 2 * f_{mm}(s). \tag{3}$$

The function $f_{mm,easy}(s)$ resembles a one-max function "with bumps". A hillclimber with a non-zero probability $p_{up2}$ of taking a step of size two or more bits uphill will climb to the global optimum in at most $\ell/p_{up2}$ steps[13]. For any $p_{up2}$ that decreases no faster than linearly in $\ell$, and in particular for a constant $p_{up2}$, the hillclimber will climb the hill in expected $O(\ell)$ steps[14].

## 4.2  SCHEMA ANALYSIS

A GA is also unlikely to have difficulty in quickly optimizing this function. In addition to being amenable to search by the GA's mutation operator, the function appears easy for crossover when we apply a static analysis of schema partitions. In every schema partition, the schema containing the global optimum (the all ones schema) must have a higher average fitness than all other schemata competing in that partition. To see why the all ones schema always wins, we first calculate the schema average fitness for any schema as a function of the schema's unitation (number of ones in the defined bits). In a partition of order $o$, the fitness of a schema $\hat{s}$ is equal to the unitation of the schema ($= u(\hat{s})$) plus the average unitation of the $(\ell - o)$ undefined bit positions ($= (\ell - o)/2$), plus twice the average contribution of $f_{mm}(s)$, the parity of unitation function, which will be $2 * 1/2$:

$$\bar{f}_{mm,easy}(\hat{s}) = u(\hat{s}) + (\ell - o)/2 + 1. \tag{4}$$

The schemata with highest unitation will always be the winners of their partition competitions.

The function $f_{mm,easy}(s)$ is also amenable to Walsh analysis (Bethke, 1981; Goldberg, 1989b), since it can be written as a summation of just a few Walsh functions. Using the notation of Goldberg (1989b), we note that for $f_{mm,easy}(s)$ all the Walsh coefficients $w_i$ of

---

be of the same parity (i.e., either odd or even). This result can be shown by induction: Choose a local optimum. It has either odd or even unitation. The nearest neighbors are not local optima and are all of the opposite parity of unitation from the chosen optimum. Their nearest neighbors in turn must be local optima (since the function maximizes the number of optimum-nonoptimum pairings) and must be of the same parity as the first chosen optimum, and so on.

[12] Here we assume that $\ell$ is odd. For even $\ell$, we should change $f_{mm}(s)$ to favor even unitation if we want the all ones string to be the global optimum.

[13] This is an upper bound on expectation: $E[t] \leq \ell/p_{up2}$, where $t$ is the number of steps taken to reach the global. Note that these calculations assume nothing about the average number of function evaluations (or time involved) in taking a single step.

[14] A hillclimber with a significant $p_{up2}$ is also expected to climb the Root2path in linear or constant time. However, Horn, Goldberg, and Deb (1994) also showed how to construct the *CubeRoot2path*, a long path for hillclimbers of step size 2. A hillclimber with significant $p_{up2}$ but near zero $p_{up3}$ (probability of taking a step size of three or more bits) will take an expected time exponential in $\ell$ to climb such a path. In other words, the intractability of the long path problem class, and the ease of the maximally multimodal (easy) problem, (for hillclimbers of stepsize $k$) both scale with increasing $k$.

all orders $i$ are zero, except for $w_0 = \ell/2 + 1$, $w_1' = -1/2$, and $w_\ell = -1$, where $w_1'$ stands for all of the order-1 Walsh coefficients, which are identically valued in a function of unitation. The fitness of a schema $\hat{s}$ with order $o < \ell$ is simply expressed:

$$\bar{f}_{mm,easy}(\hat{s}) = w_0 + u(\hat{s})(-w_1') = \ell/2 + 1 + \frac{u(\hat{s})}{2}. \tag{5}$$

Again it is clear that for all competition partitions the schemata with highest unitation will have the greatest schema average fitness, thus pointing the way to the global optimum (the all ones point).

## 4.3  VISUALIZATION IN TWO DIMENSIONS

Figure 1, bottom, is a visualization of a maximally multimodal function in two dimensions. Here the decision variables are the positive integers $x$ and $y$, and the fitness function is

$$f_{mm,easy}(x,y) = (x+y) + \begin{cases} 10 & \text{if Even}(x+y) \\ 0 & \text{otherwise.} \end{cases} \tag{6}$$

Just as in the case of binary strings, our 2-D formulation makes half the search space local optima while providing a constant gradient pointed straight at the global (for any $\geq$ 2-bit hillclimber) as well as plenty of schema information for crossover (at least for binary coded integers).

## 4.4  EMPIRICAL RESULTS

Empirical results confirm the prediction that a crossover-based GA will perform well on $f_{mm,easy}(s)$. (Here we switch back to the $\ell$-dimensional version of $f_{mm,easy}$ over binary strings $s$.) Table 1 summarizes a brief experiment in which we ran a GA with crossover alone (probability of mutation $p_m = 0$) on three different sizes ($\ell = 29, 39$ and $49$ bits) of both the long path problem $f_{lp}(s)$ and the maximally multimodal problem $f_{mm,easy}(s)$. The GA used in the experiment was a simple, generational GA with probability of (single point) crossover $p_c = 1.0$, (deterministic) binary tournament selection, and population size $N = 300$. For each problem type and size (e.g., 39-bit long path problem) we ran 40 trials (i.e., 40 different random initial populations). The long path problems were all Root2paths with step size $k = 1$ as specified (by pseudocode) in (Horn, Goldberg, & Deb, 1994). The maximally multimodal problem $f_{mm,easy}(s)$ used in the experiment is the same as that described in Equation 3 above. For each trial, the GA was run until the convergence criterion (uniform fitness of the population) was met. The final, converged population was then checked for the global optimum.

As Table 1 indicates, the GA performs much better on $f_{mm,easy}(s)$ than on $f_{lp}(s)$ for the three problem sizes shown. The GA with crossover alone cannot find reliably the end of the long path (i.e., the global optimum) for the larger problem sizes (i.e., $\ell = 39, 49$), except at higher population sizes (e.g., $N = 5000, 6000$) (Horn, Goldberg, & Deb, 1994). The relative ease with which the GA solves $f_{mm,easy}(s)$ is consistent with our analysis above, with Ackley's reported observations of GA performance on his porcupine function (Ackley, 1985, 1987a, 1987b), and with our intuitions based on knowledge of the problem's construction. The relative performance of GA crossover is certainly not predicted, however, by a simple count of local optima in the search space. The maximally multimodal function is interesting if only because it points out that the modality of a search space, if measured solely as the

Table 1: Unimodal versus Multimodal Problem Difficulty

| GA PERFORMANCE (**Long Path** vs. **Max. Multimodal**) | | |
|---|---|---|
| | *No. of Trials (of 40) Converging to Global* | |
| **problem type** | **problem size** | |
| | $\ell = 29$   $\ell = 39$   $\ell = 49$ | |
| Long Path (Root2path, $k = 1$) $f_{lp}$ | 5    2    0 | |
| Maximally Multimodal $f_{mm,easy}$ | 40   39   39 | |

number of local optima, is at best a first order estimate of GA difficulty (or difficulty for evolutionary search algorithms in general).

# 5 INTERMEDIATE MODALITY: LOCAL OPTIMA AND THEIR BASINS OF ATTRACTION

The results of the previous two sections remind us that the fitness landscapes of interest to us (i.e., those that challenge the GA in a realistic and general manner) have intermediate modality. But it is not clear how to add modality to the long path problem, or to reduce the modality of the maximally multimodal function. For example, we might be tempted to generalize the work on maximum modality by maximizing the number of optima that are $k$ or more bits apart (i.e., each optimum has a local neighborhood of radius $\geq (k-1)$ bits in which it is optimal). Unfortunately, calculating the maximum number of such optima for arbitrary $k$ is an open problem in coding theory known as *sphere packing* (Harary, Hayes, & Wu, 1988; MacWilliams & Sloane, 1977). We can calculate an upper bound by simply dividing the search space size, $2^{\ell}$, by the hypervolume of the *nonoverlapping* local neighborhoods of the optima, $\sum_{r=0}^{\lceil k/2 \rceil - 1} \binom{\ell}{r}$. But this results in a very loose upper bound, as evidenced by the simple case of $k = 2$ bit separation: the upper bound yields $2^{\ell}$ while we know that the actual maximum is half that[15].

## 5.1 BACKGROUND

Although *maximizing* the number of local optima with neighborhoods of radius $k$ is an open problem, work has proceeded along the lines of measuring and controlling the number of optima and their basins of attraction (or the "attractiveness" of the optima). Such work can be divided into two types: that which assumes hillclimbing attraction and that which assumes GA crossover attraction. That is, most papers analyzing local optima assume one type of algorithm or the other. We give some background on both approaches, but focus on GA crossover.

---

[15]It is interesting to note that sphere packing with radius $\lceil k/2 \rceil - 1$ also provides an upper bound (within a factor of two) on the path length of $(k-1)$-step long path problems, since nonconsecutive steps on the path must be at least $k$ bits apart. However, tighter upper bounds on $(k-1)$-step paths have been found (Preparata, 1974).

### 5.1.1  Hillclimbing Attraction

A number of recent papers define peaks (i.e., local optima together with their basins of attraction) in terms of hillclimbing. Goldberg (1991) formally defines basins of attraction to a point $x^*$ as all points $x$ such that a given hillclimber has a non-zero probability of climbing to within some $\epsilon$ of $x^*$ if started within some $\delta$-neighborhood of $x$. Jones and Rawlins (1993) introduce *reverse hillclimbing* and *probabilistic ascent* as techniques for defining the basin of attraction of a particular local optimum in a fitness landscape for hillclimbers with known probabilities of ascent. Mahfoud (1993) analyzes the performance of multimodal GAs on multi-niche problems, where each niche is a local optimum with a basin of attraction defined by the probability of a hillclimber reaching the local optimum from a point in the basin.

### 5.1.2  GA Attraction

The literature on the attraction of peaks and regions in the landscape to the GA's crossover operator is largely based on Holland's *schema theorem* (Holland, 1992) and schema average fitness calculations (Bethke, 1981). Goldberg (1987, 1989a, 1989b, 1989c) and later others (Whitley, 1991; Homaifar, Qi, & Frost, 1991; Deb, Horn, & Goldberg, 1993) defined and constructed deceptive landscapes, in which the GA should be attracted to suboptimal local optima and led away from the global optimum. Schema analysis has also been used to construct "GA-easy" functions (Wilson, 1991) which have large basins of attraction for the global optimum [16]. More recently, Mitchell and Holland (1993) have begun to weaken the GA-easy conditions by limiting the number and order of schema partitions leading toward the global[17].

We look to deception for guidelines on how to lead or mislead a GA both toward and away from multiple optima. Since a function with more than two global optima implies partial (and not full) deception[18], we first review and define partial deception.

### 5.1.3  Partial Deception Defined

One must be careful in defining partial deception. It is easy to weaken the requirements for full deception such that a GA can easily find the global optimum of some functions meeting those requirements. We briefly present the definitions we use in this paper.

A *deceptive attractor* (Whitley, 1991) is the suboptimal point $D$ toward which a GA is (mis)led. In a particular schema partition, the schema containing the deceptive attractor is called the *deceptive schema*, while the schemata containing the global optima are called the *global schemata*. In general, a *deceptive partition* is a partition in which the deceptive schema has a high (schema average) fitness and/or all of the global schemata have low fitness. The rather vague concept of deceptive schemata "beating" global schemata, in terms of schema average fitness, has been interpreted in several different ways by different researchers. Here we list three specific definitions of interest to us (the order of labeling has only chronological

---

[16]Like our maximally multimodal function, previous GA-easy functions contain local optima that can make the problem difficult for hillclimbing.

[17]It is interesting to note that according to our definition of local optimum, the Royal Road functions are unimodal.

[18]A function with more than one global optimum cannot be misleading in all $\ell$ of its order one partitions. Two (or more) distinct global optima must differ in at least one bit position. The order one schema partitions defined at each of those partitions must "point to" at least one of the globals.

meaning):

- **Type I deceptive** – global schemata lose to all other schemata (Bethke, 1981).
- **Type II deceptive** – deceptive schema wins over all other schemata (Goldberg, 1987).
- **Type III deceptive** – deceptive schema has higher fitness than all global schemata (Grefenstette, 1992).

It is not yet clear which, if any, of these definitions implies more difficulty for the GA on partially deceptive landscapes[19]. For fully deceptive functions, all partitions of order $< \ell$ are type II and III deceptive[20]. But in general (i.e., partial deception), deceptive and global schemata can be placed anywhere in the fitness ordering of a partition's schemata.

In the design of maximally misleading functions, our goal is to choose $D$ and define the landscape such that the GA converges to $D$ with high probability. We assume that we are given one or more globals (that is, their locations and perhaps their fitness value). In the case of a single global optimum $g$, the above definitions are sufficient to unambiguously identify a unique $D$, which is the complement of $g$ (Whitley, 1991). We can then construct *fully deceptive* functions in which the schema containing $D$ is the winner of *every* partition (i.e., types II and III deception) at every order up to the string length $\ell$ (Goldberg, 1989a, 1989b, 1990). Full deception is clearly maximally misleading to a GA. It is also clearly bimodal, with local optima[21] at $D$ and at $g$. To add more optima, and basins of GA attraction, we need to define partial deception.

Deception becomes a more practical tool of GA theory when it is embedded in fitness landscapes as *partial deception*. But at the moment, we can only define partial deception vaguely as less misleading than full deception and more misleading than GA-easy. Trying to order partially deceptive functions according to some scalar measure of deception is problematic. Goldberg recognized the need to generalize full deception and did so by defining *order k full deception* (Goldberg, 1991). Homaifar, Qi, and Frost (1991) call such limited deception *reduced order k deception*. Although it has gone by other names, this kind of partial deception is most widely known as *bounded deception*. A problem has bounded deception of order $k$ if and only if *all* partitions of order $(k-1)$ or less are deceptive [22]. Partitions of order $\geq k$ might or might not be deceptive. Thus for $k = \ell$, bounded deception is full deception. Goldberg, Deb, and Korb (1991) construct examples of boundedly deceptive problems by concatenating some number $m$ of fully deceptive subfunctions of length $\ell_s$ to get an $(m * \ell_s)$-bit function of order $\ell_s$ bounded deception. Such functions have $2^m$ local optima, one of which is global.

The order $k$ of bounded deception establishes a partial order over functions. We can safely say that a function of order $k$ bounded deception is at least as difficult for a GA as a function of order $k' < k$ bounded deception, all other problem dimensions (e.g., noise, crosstalk) being roughly equal.

---

[19]We do note, however, that types I and II deception conditions imply type III.

[20]Such partitions can also be considered type I deceptive (at least for some of the fully deceptive functions constructed in the literature) if we discount the global optimum from schema average fitness calculations, a modification suggested and justified later in this paper.

[21]Whitley (1991) proves that $D$ need not be a local optimum. But if it is not, then one of its immediate neighbors must be.

[22]Deceptive partition here means that the winner of a partition is the schema containing $D$, (i.e., type II deception).

Other attempts to define, quantify, or order the degree of partial deception have resulted in unnecessarily weakening the requirements for deception. For example, Grefenstette (1992) described an $\ell = 20$-bit function in which all partitions defined over the first ten bits lead toward the deceptive attractor (i.e., type II deception) and all partitions defined over the last ten bits lead toward the global optimum. "Despite this high level of Deception [*sic*]," this function was easily optimized by a GA with population size 200. However, as Goldberg pointed out with his analysis of a similarly constructed partially deceptive function (Goldberg, 1991), we do not want to call such problems highly deceptive. Any function with low order partitions that lead toward the global optimum (i.e., any function with building blocks) is amenable to GA search. Adding additional misleading bits does not necessarily make the problem any more deceptive, let alone "arbitrarily more Deceptive..." (Grefenstette, 1992), because the number of low order building blocks remains undiminished. A function of low order $k$ bounded deception is probably more difficult for a GA than Grefenstette's function with some arbitrarily large number of misleading bits, even though the boundedly deceptive problem will have fewer deceptive partitions overall[23].

The above example points out the importance of both number and *order* of deceptive partitions. As discussed above, order $k$ bounded deception only allows comparisons between functions with the same number of deceptive partitions, $\binom{\ell}{o}$, at each order $o < \min(k_1, k_2)$, where $k_i$ are the orders of bounded deception for two functions. Goldberg, Deb, and Horn found another way to construct and order partially deceptive functions without losing essential misleadingness (Goldberg, Deb, & Horn, 1992; Deb, Horn, & Goldberg, 1993). They constrain a "bipolar deceptive function" to be a function of *folded unitation* $u_{fld}(s)$, which is simply the number of ones minus the number of zeros: $u_{fld}(s) = u(s) - (\ell - u(s)) = 2\,u(s) - \ell$. This leads to a symmetric function of unitation, $f_{bip}(u_{fld}(s))$. Enforcing full deception in the composite function $f_{bip} \circ u_{fld}$ leads to two globals (all ones and all zeros) in the unfolded binary space of full strings (i.e., Hamming space), and $\binom{\ell}{\ell/2}$ deceptive attractors (all points consisting of half ones and half zeros, for even $\ell$). The symmetry of the function, induced by the folding, means that the single global optimum in the folded unitation space corresponds to two (complementary) global optima in Hamming space. The single deceptive attractor in the folded unitation space maps to many deceptive attractors in Hamming space.

Goldberg, Deb, and Horn show that the full deception enforced on the folded unitation function led to partitions in the unfolded function in which the schemata containing the *most* deceptive attractors won (type II deception). This occurs in all partitions where the schemata containing the globals (the global schemata) can be distinguished from the schemata containing the deceptive attractors. Thus, at order one, where the two schemata ...#1#... and ...#0#... compete, there is no possible distinction between the globals and the deceptive optima, and thus no preference between the schemata (i.e., they had equal fitness). But at order two, and above, the deceptive attractors can be distinguished, hence ...#01#... and ...#10#... beat ...#11#... and ...#00#... in all order two partitions.

Note that having two distinct globals precludes full deception and therefore requires some kind of partial deception at best (or worst!). By constraining the function to be of folded unitation, Goldberg, Deb, and Horn are able to make the overall function maximally deceptive by enforcing full deception in the folded function. They are then able to examine

---

[23]It is interesting to note that Grefenstette's (1992) function is not only unimodal by our definitions, but is also, like the long path problem, a single hill to the global optimum. All points in the search space lie on stepsize-1 paths to the global.

its implications in the unfolded space. The result is a function that has deceptive attractors located maximally far from *both* globals, and in which the deceptive schemata win in all partitions (type II), up to order $\ell$, in which it is possible to distinguish globals from deceptives.

## 5.2   MAXIMAL BI-GLOBAL DECEPTION

We first generalize the work of Goldberg, Deb, and Horn on bipolar deceptive functions to the case of bi-global deceptive functions. We do not assume a function of unitation, folded or not, nor do we assume bipolarity (i.e., where the two globals are full complements of each other). We only assume two globals arbitrarily placed in the space. Rather than first choosing the deceptive attractor, as is usually done, we will instead try to *maximize deception* and see what deceptive attractor emerges. We use such terms as "maximal deception" loosely at first, and define them rigorously later.

Let the two arbitrarily chosen globals in an $\ell$-bit problem be $G = \{g_1, g_2\}$, and let the distance between them be $d_G$ bits. How do we choose a deceptive attractor $D$ that maximizes deceptive partitions? An upper bound on the number of possibly deceptive partitions is the number of partitions in which we can *distinguish* $D$ from the $G$. We shall call these simply *resolvable partitions*. We now try to place $D$ so as to maximize the number of resolvable partitions at every order $o$.

We first note that there are $(\ell - d_G)$ bits in which the two globals agree. Intuitively, our deceptive attractor should disagree with both globals in these bit positions to maximize the number of resolvable partitions. For each of the $(\ell - d_G)$ bits of agreement between the globals, setting the corresponding bit position in $D$ to be the complement of the globals' bit setting gives one more bit position in which deceptive schemata can be distinguished from global schemata. Thus giving $D$ the complement of the $(\ell - d_G)$ global bit settings only increases the number of resolvable partitions at every order. We therefore assume such complementary bit settings for the $(\ell - d_G)$ bit positions of $D$ (in which $g_1$ and $g_2$ agree) and next consider only how to set the $d_G$ bit positions in which the globals disagree.

Let $d_1^D$ be the Hamming distance from $D$ to $g_1$. Then $d_G - d_1^D$ is the distance from $D$ to $g_2$. At any order $o$ schema partition there are $\binom{d_G}{o}$ partitions[24]. For exactly $\binom{d_1^D}{o}$ of these partitions, we cannot distinguish $D$ from $g_2$, since all $o$ defined bits are chosen from the $d_1^D$ bits that distinguish $D$ from $g_1$ and hence are positions at which $D$ and $g_2$ are in agreement. Similarly, there are exactly $\binom{d_G - d_1^D}{o}$ partitions in which we cannot distinguish $D$ from $g_1$. So the total number of resolvable partitions, $N_{rp}(o)$ at order $o$ is

$$N_{rp}(o) = \binom{d_G}{o} - \left[ \binom{d_1^D}{o} + \binom{d_G - d_1^D}{o} . \right] \tag{7}$$

To maximize $N_{rp}$ we must minimize the sum of the two binomial coefficients in the square brackets above. Since $\binom{d_1^D}{o}$ is a strictly increasing function of $d_1^D$, and $\binom{d_G - d_1^D}{o}$ is strictly decreasing in $d_1^D$, the minimum of their sum will occur when $d_1^D = d_G - d_1^D \Rightarrow d_1^D = d_G/2$, for even $d_G$, and $d_1^D = \lfloor d_G/2 \rfloor$ or $\lceil d_G/2 \rceil$, for odd $d_G$. That is, we will have the maximum possible number of resolvable partitions when we our deceptive attractor lies equally distant from $g_1$ and $g_2$, which means it is *maximally minimally distant* from $G$. Here we define

---

[24] We assume throughout this paper that $\binom{n}{m} = 0$ for $m > n$.

*minimal distance* from a point $D$ to a set $G$ of $k$ points as the minimum of the distances from $D$ to each point $g_i \in G$, $1 \le i \le k$. The *maximally minimally distant point* from a set $G$ is simply the point[25] in the space with the greatest minimal distance to $G$.

Note that we have maximized the resolvable partitions in the sense that we have the maximum number of resolvable partitions at every order. Assume that we can make all resolvable partitions deceptive, in at least one of the three senses defined earlier (we show that we can in the next section). We conjecture that a function $f_1$ with more deceptive partitions at every order $o < \ell$ than another function $f_2$ is more misleading to a GA, all other problem dimensions being roughly equal. Thus we are suggesting another relation that induces a partial ordering on the space of partially deceptive functions, just as Goldberg's bounded deception does. And just as bounded deception has full deception at the extreme, our ordering has a maximum for a given placement of globals. A *maximally* deceptive function has no fewer deceptive partitions at each order than any other deceptive function possible given the set of globals. When the global set consists of only one global, the maximally deceptive function is a fully deceptive function. Otherwise, it is partially deceptive[26].

## 5.3   A FUNCTION TO MEET THE BI-GLOBAL DECEPTIVE CONDITIONS

In the section above we showed that to maximize the number of resolvable partitions at every order in a bi-global problem, we should choose the deceptive attractor to be the point that is maximally minimally distant from the two globals. Such a result is meaningless if we cannot define a function that is actually misleading to a GA in those resolvable partitions. In other words, is it possible to make all the resolvable partitions deceptive? Or does this lead to too many constraints? In this section we construct a function that satisfies our deceptive conditions in all of the resolvable partitions.

### 5.3.1   Construction

The use of maximal minimal distance to $G$ in choosing our deceptive attractor suggests the use of such a function as the fitness function itself. That is, let the fitness of a point/string $s$ be its Hamming distance to the nearest global. Let us call such a minimum distance function simply $f_{md}(s)$:

$$f_{md}(s) = \min_{\forall g \in G} H(s, g), \tag{8}$$

where $H(s, g)$ is the Hamming distance from a point $s$ to the global $g$. At the globals themselves, of course, we substitute some globally optimal value $f_{max}$ to get a function of

---

[25]In the bi-global case there will always be $\binom{d_G}{d_G/2}$ such points for even $d_G$, and $2 * \binom{d_G}{\lfloor d_G/2 \rfloor}$ such points for odd $d_G$. For the purposes of this paper, we assume that when the maximally minimal distance criterion yields a *set* of points, then we arbitrarily choose a single deceptive attractor from that set. We could also choose the entire set or some subset to be the *set* of attractors. Our deception analyses and results would not change, and we would have multiple deceptive optima with increased "carrying capacity" for niched GAs (Goldberg, Deb, & Horn, 1992). But such considerations are beyond the scope of this paper.

[26]We note that the bipolar deceptive function (Goldberg, Deb, & Horn, 1992; Deb, Horn, & Goldberg, 1993) is also a maximally deceptive function by our definition above. And a maximally deceptive function for two ($k = 2$) bipolar globals, with the further restriction to symmetric or *folded* unitation, is *bipolar deceptive* according to (Goldberg, Deb, & Horn, 1992) and (Deb, Horn, & Goldberg, 1993).

minimum distance "plus globals":

$$f_{mdG}(s) = \begin{cases} f_{max} & \text{if } s \in G \\ f_{md}(s) & \text{otherwise,} \end{cases} \tag{9}$$

The min-dist function, with globals, $f_{mdG}(s)$, has some very interesting properties. Like trap and unitation functions, it is easy to define, is readily visualized, has mostly linear gradients, and is amenable to schema analysis.

Our first observation is that the max-min-dist deceptive attractor is clearly a local optimum of $f_{mdG}(s)$ and indeed must be the global optimum of $f_{md}(s)$. This is true by definition of $D$ as the point of *maximal* min-dist. To guarantee that $f_{max}$ is globally optimal, we could set $f_{max} = f_{md}(D) + 1$. Or, to avoid having to find $D$, we can simply let $f_{max} = \ell + 1$, which is guaranteed to be global since the greatest Hamming distance in an $\ell$-bit problem is $\ell$.

Another observation is that $f_{mdG}(s)$ essentially reduces to a simple trap function (Goldberg, Deb, & Clark, 1992; Deb & Goldberg, 1993, 1994) when $G$ contains a single global optimum. Similarly, when $G$ contains only two complementary strings, such as the all zeroes and all ones strings, $f_{mdG}(s)$ reduces to a *bipolar* deceptive trap function (Goldberg, Deb, & Horn, 1992; Deb, Horn, & Goldberg, 1993). For example, if we set $f_{max} = \ell + 1$ then the function

$$f_{mdG}^{trap}(s) = f_{mdG}(s) - 1 \tag{10}$$

might be called a *generalized, k-global trap function*. The function $f_{mdG}^{trap}(s)$ is zero-valued at all points adjacent to the global optima, as in other examples of trap functions. And if $\ell = 4$ and $G = \{1111\}$, $f_{mdG}^{trap}(s)$ is exactly the fully deceptive trap function given as function $f_4$ in (Goldberg, Deb, & Clark, 1992)[27].

A final observation is that $f_{mdG}(s)$ illustrates the separability of *misleadingness* and *isolation* as dimensions of problem difficulty. One can view the function $f_{md}(s)$ as providing the essential misleadingness of $f_{mdG}(s)$, while we could define a function

$$f_G(s) = \begin{cases} f_{max} & \text{if } s \in G \\ 0 & \text{otherwise} \end{cases} \tag{11}$$

that provides the isolation of the globals. The function $f_{mdG}(s) = f_{md}(s) + f_G(s)$ is then literally the additive combination of misleadingness and solution isolation.

### 5.3.2   Schema Analysis

Next we perform a modified schema analysis of $f_{mdG}(s)$ looking for deceptive partitions. Our modification to regular schema analysis is this: we ignore the global optima. That is, we assume their fitness is zero by simply analyzing $f_{md}(s)$ rather than $f_{mdG}(s)$. Adding the globally optimal values $f_{max}$ to our schema fitness calculations would complicate them. The only point of doing so would be to find constraints on $f_{max}$ in order to meet deception conditions on schema average fitnesses. We are not very interested in such constraints, since it really doesn't matter how large $f_{max}$ is, as long as it is globally optimal. The value of the global optima do not enter into the GA's schema processing until a global is found, at which time the search is over and we are no longer interested in GA schema processing. We are

---

[27]The function $f_{mdG}(s)$ also can be seen as a generalization of Whitley's fully deceptive function (Whitley, 1991) to multiple globals.

modeling GA performance in the *search* for global optima; that is, during the generations preceding the discovery of a global.

We begin our schema analysis by assuming two globals $g_1$ and $g_2$. As before, we ignore the bit positions in which $g_1$ and $g_2$ agree, since considering the fitness contributions of these bits does not change the ranking of schemata within a competition partition. To see why this is so, remember that the fitness of a schema $\hat{s}$ of $f_{md}(s)$ is the average distance to the nearest global over all strings instantiating $\hat{s}$. Thus the bit positions at which $g_1$ and $g_2$ agree always add the same amount to the average fitness of each schema within a particular partition, regardless of the schema.

We assume $\ell$ bit positions in which $g_1$ and $g_2$ differ. We now calculate exact schema average fitnesses for any schema in an order $o$ partition. Let $\hat{s}$ be a schema in the given order $o$ partition, and let $d_1^{\hat{s}}$ be the distance from $\hat{s}$ to global $g_1$, making $(o - d_1^{\hat{s}})$ the distance from $\hat{s}$ to $g_2$. (We define the distance from a schema $\hat{s}$ to a point, such as global $g_1$, to be the number of bit positions, over the $o$ defined bit positions in $\hat{s}$, in which $\hat{s}$ and $g_1$ differ. Note that $0 \leq d_1^{\hat{s}} \leq o$.)

To calculate the average fitness of $\hat{s}$ in $f_{md}(s)$, we add up the fitnesses of all strings contained in $\hat{s}$ and divide by the number of such strings:

$$\bar{f}_{md}(\hat{s}) = \frac{\sum_{s \in \hat{s}} f_{md}(s)}{2^{\ell - o}}. \tag{12}$$

We concentrate now on the sum in the numerator, since this will order the average fitnesses of schemata in the partition. The $2^{\ell - o}$ strings in the summation can be divided into two groups, those that are closest to $g_1$ and those that are closest to $g_2$. Let $d$ be the number of bit positions from the $\ell - o$ undefined bit positions at which a particular string $s$ disagrees with $g_1$. That is, the total distance from $s$ to $g_1$ is $d + d_1^{\hat{s}}$. When this total distance is less than half of $\ell$, then $s$ is closer to $g_1$ than to $g_2$, and the fitness of $s$ is its distance to $g_1$: $d + d_1^{\hat{s}}$. There are exactly $\binom{\ell - o}{d}$ strings in $\hat{s}$ that are $d$ bits different from $g_1$ in the $\ell - o$ undefined bits of the partition. Furthermore, $g_1$ will be the closest global to $s$ for $d = 0$ up to $d + d_1^{\hat{s}} = \lfloor \ell/2 \rfloor \Rightarrow d \leq \lfloor \ell/2 \rfloor - d_1^{\hat{s}}$. Thus the total contribution of strings near $g_1$ to the average fitness of $\hat{s}$ is

$$\sum_{d=0}^{\lfloor \ell/2 \rfloor - d_1^{\hat{s}}} (d + d_1^{\hat{s}})\binom{\ell - o}{d}. \tag{13}$$

We calculate a similar sum for the remaining points, which are all closer to $g_2$. These points have fitness $(\ell - (d + d_1^{\hat{s}}))$, which is their distance to $g_2$, and they occur when $(\lfloor \ell/2 \rfloor - d_1^{\hat{s}} + 1) \leq d \leq (\ell - o)$. Adding these two sums together, we get the exact schema average fitness of any schema $\hat{s}$ in an order $o$ partition of $f_{md}(s)$:

$$2^{\ell - o} \bar{f}_{md}(\hat{s}) = \sum_{d=0}^{\lfloor l/2 \rfloor - d_1^{\hat{s}}} (d + d_1^{\hat{s}})\binom{\ell - o}{d} + \sum_{d=\lfloor \ell/2 \rfloor - d_1^{\hat{s}} + 1}^{\ell - o} (\ell - d - d_1^{\hat{s}})\binom{\ell - o}{d}. \tag{14}$$

We can show that this sum increases as $d_1^{\hat{s}}$ approaches $d_1^{\hat{s}} = \lfloor o/2 \rfloor$ from $d_1^{\hat{s}} = 0$ and as it approaches $d_1^{\hat{s}} = \lceil o/2 \rceil$ from $d_1^{\hat{s}} = o$. Thus the more maximally minimally distant a *schema* is from the schemata containing the globals, the higher its average fitness. In particular, the maximum of $\bar{f}_{md}(\hat{s})$ occurs at $d_1^{\hat{s}} = \lceil o/2 \rceil$ and $d_1^{\hat{s}} = \lfloor o/2 \rfloor$.

This last result has several important implications for $f_{md}(s)$. First, it means that in all the resolvable partitions, the schema containing the deceptive attractor $D$ has greater average fitness than the schemata containing the globals. Since $f_{md}(s)$ maximizes the number of resolvable partitions at every order, it also therefore maximizes the number of partitions where the global schemata lose to the deceptive schema (type III deceptive partitions). Second, in all but the order one and order $\ell$ partitions, the global schemata lose to all other schemata[28]. Thus $f_{md}(s)$ is maximally deceptive according to type I partition deception.

Third, the above result implies that the winning schema (i.e., superior to all others) in every partition is the schema that is maximally minimally different from the global schemata. If the winning schema contains the deceptive attractor $D$, the partition is type II deceptive. How many type II deceptive partitions can a deceptive attractor possibly have, at a given order $o$? The analysis is similar to our previous analysis. Let $d_1^D$ be the distance from a deceptive attractor $D$ to global optimum $g_1$ with $\ell$-bits of separation between $g_1$ and $g_2$. Assume an even partition order $o$. We can choose half the order $o$ bit positions, from among the $d_1^D$ bit positions in which $D$ and $g_1$ differ, in exactly $\binom{d_1^D}{o/2}$ ways. We can choose the other $o/2$ bits, from among the $\ell - d_1^D$ bit positions that differ from $g_2$, in exactly $\binom{\ell - d_1^D}{o/2}$ ways. So there are $\binom{d_1^D}{o/2}\binom{\ell - d_1^D}{o/2}$ partitions of even order $o$ in which the deceptive schema wins. Similarly, for odd order $o$ partitions this number is $\binom{d_1^D}{\lfloor o/2 \rfloor}\binom{\ell - d_1^D}{\lceil o/2 \rceil} + \binom{d_1^D}{\lceil o/2 \rceil}\binom{\ell - d_1^D}{\lfloor o/2 \rfloor}$. It is clear that the number of type II deceptive partitions is maximized when $d_1^D = \ell - d_1^D$, $\Rightarrow d_1^D = \ell/2$ for even $\ell$ (and either of $\lfloor \ell/2 \rfloor$ or $\lceil \ell/2 \rceil$, for odd $\ell$). Thus the choice of $D$ as the deceptive attractor maximizes the number of type II deceptive partitions at every order. The function $f_{md}(s)$ is therefore maximally deceptive according to all three types of partition deception we defined.

## 5.4  GENERALIZATION TO $k$ GLOBALS

We would like to immediately generalize our results to the case of $k$ globals placed arbitrarily. That is, given any set $G$ of $k$ globals in an $\ell$-bit problem, we should place the deceptive attractor(s) at those points maximally minimally distant from the entire set $G$ in order to maximally mislead the GA. Unfortunately the analysis used above becomes much more complicated when applied to $k$ globals. With more than two globals we lose the symmetry of bit position agreement/disagreement (where agreement with $g_1$ at a position means disagreement with $g_2$ at that position, and where being $d_1^D$ bits away from $g_1$ means being $\ell - d_1^D$ bits away from $g_2$).

While we are continuing to explore the generalization to $k$ globals, we can present some intriguing initial results.

### 5.4.1  Visualization in Two Dimensions

It is instructive to visualize the spatial relationship of the deceptive attractor $D$ (the max-min-dist point) to the set $G$ of $k$ globals. We therefore return to our use of two dimensional analogues of our binary search spaces and functions. In Figure 2 we show $k = 5$ global optima located at grid positions $G = \{(7, 59), (5, 21), (30, 7), (62, 3), (62, 51)\}$. Here we assume two integer-valued decision variables $\{x, y\}$ each taking values in the range $(0..63)$. The maximally minimally distant point from $G$ is $D = (32, 39)$, as shown on the left of Figure 2.

---

[28]At order one (for the $\ell$ positions in which the globals differ) both competing schemata are global schemata.

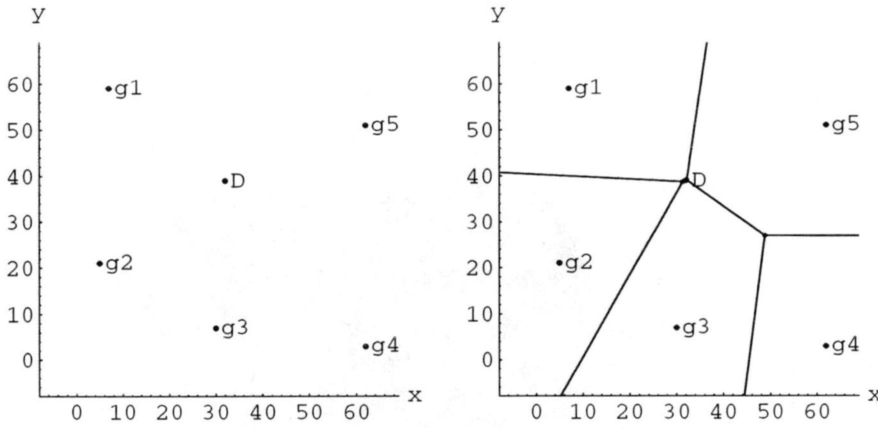

Figure 2: *Left:* A two dimensional problem with $k = 5$ globals at $G = \{(7, 59), (5, 21), (30, 7), (62, 3), (62, 51)\}$, and a maximally minimally distant point at $D = (32, 39)$. *Right:* The Voronoi diagram of the set $G$.

Interestingly, this point lies at the intersection of Voronoi lines in the Voronoi diagram of $G$, shown on the right of Figure 2. Since the lines in a Voronoi diagram divide the space into neighborhoods of elements of $G$ and their nearest neighbors (Conway & Sloane, 1993), and thus lie on points equidistant from the nearest two globals, $D$ must lie at an intersection of at least three Voronoi lines.

To better illustrate the relationship between the Voronoi diagram and our maximum minimum distance criterion, we redefine $f_{md}$ to be a function of integers $x$ and $y$ rather than of binary strings:

$$f_{md}(x, y) = \min_{\forall (x_g, y_g) \in G} \sqrt{(x_g - x)^2 + (y_g - y)^2}. \tag{15}$$

Noting that the maximum value is $f_{md}(D) \approx 32.0156$, we choose $f_{max}$ to be 34:

$$f_{mdG}(x, y) = \begin{cases} 34 & \text{if } (x, y) \in G \\ f_{md}(x, y) & \text{otherwise.} \end{cases} \tag{16}$$

We plot $f_{mdG}(x, y)$, at the top of Figure 3, for the five globals. We note how the ridges correspond to the lines of the Voronoi diagram, and how each local optimum (except the globals) occurs at intersections of such lines. By definition of $f_{md}(x, y)$ and Voronoi diagrams, this must be the case. Thus the min-dist function $f_{md}(x, y)$ leads to an interesting, rugged, multimodal landscape with apparent basins of attraction for hillclimbers. To see that there are indeed basins of attraction for the local optima, we plot the local gradients of $f_{md}(x, y)$ at the bottom of Figure 3. As expected, these gradients point away from the nearest globals and towards the nearest ridge. We would expect a simple hillclimber to follow the local gradients up to the nearest ridge and thence to a local optimum. Finally we note that the max-min-point $D$ seems to have the largest basin of attraction (of all optima shown) for a simple hillclimber.

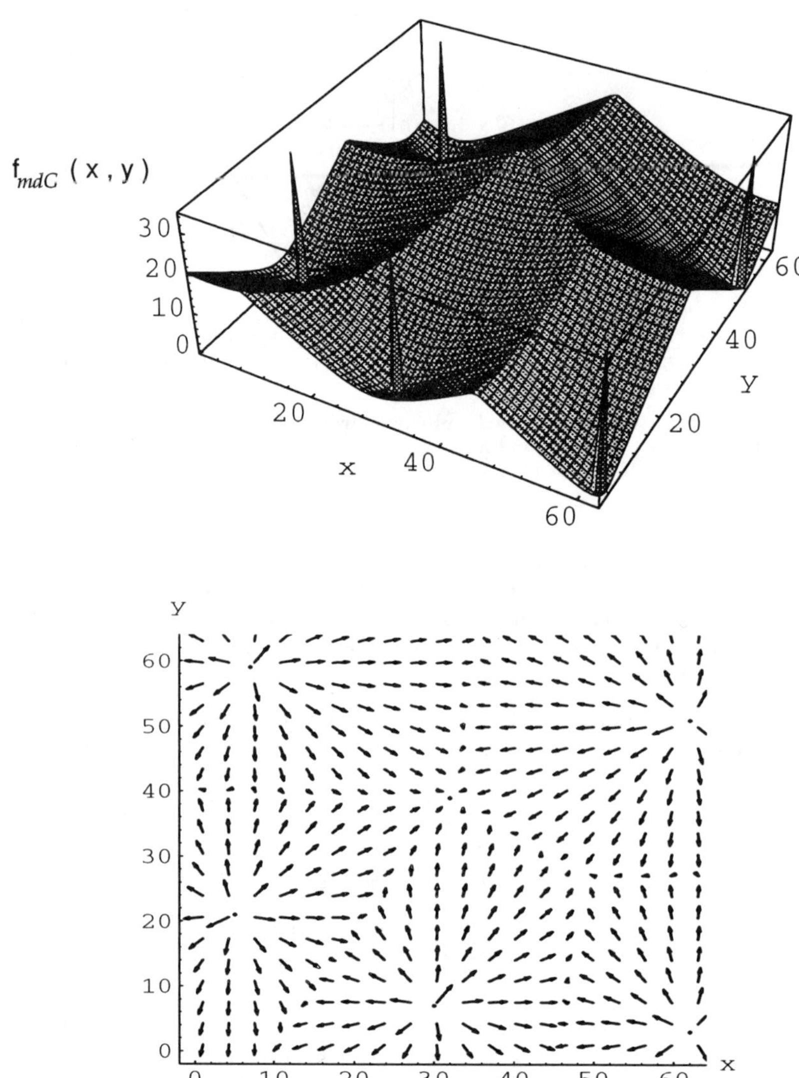

Figure 3: *Top:* A surface plot of $f_{mdG}(x, y)$. *Bottom:* This function is difficult for a hillclimber because all gradients lead away from the nearest global and, eventually, to a local optimum, as shown in this vector plot of $f_{mdG}(x, y)$.

### 5.4.2  Schema Analysis

Again, to be of interest in the study of GA difficulty and multimodality, the min-dist function $f_{mdG}(s)$ with $k$ globals must be misleading to the GA's crossover operator as well as to mutation. The schema analysis of $f_{mdG}(s)$ is complicated by the interactions of the multiple globals. We can however make a quick observation that indicates we are headed in the right direction (in order to make the GA head in the wrong direction!).

Assume any order $o$ resolvable partition in an $\ell$-bit problem with $k$ globals. Let $D$ be our choice of deceptive attractor. Let $\hat{s}_D$ be the schema containing the deceptive attractor and let $\hat{s}_i$ be the schema containing[29] global $g_i$, $1 \leq i \leq k$. We define $\vec{d^D} = \{d_1^D, d_2^D, ..., d_k^D\}$ to be the vector of distances from the deceptive schema $\hat{s}_D$ to each of the global schemata $\hat{s}_i$. Thus $d_i^D$, where $(0 \leq d_i^D \leq o)$, is the Hamming distance from $\hat{s}_D$ to $\hat{s}_i$, defined only over the $o$ fixed bit positions. We also define similar distance vectors for each of the global schemata $\hat{s}_i$: $\vec{d^i} = \{d_1^i, d_2^i, ..., d_k^i\}$, for $(i \in 1..k)$ where $d_j^i$ is the Hamming distance $(0 \leq d_j^i \leq o)$ between $\hat{s}_i$ and $\hat{s}_j$. Finally, for each possible setting $s$ of the $(\ell - o)$ bits undefined in this partition, we associate another vector of distances to the globals: $\vec{d_s} = \{d_1^s, d_2^s, ..., d_k^s\}$, where $d_i^s$ is the number of bits $(0 \leq d_i^s \leq \ell - o)$, in which $s$ differs from global $g_i$ over the $(\ell - o)$ bits undefined by the partition (but defined by $s$).

To calculate the average fitness of a global schema $\hat{s}_i$, we generate the $2^{\ell - o}$ substrings $s$ in the hyperplane defined by $\hat{s}_i$. For each $s$ we calculate its distance vector $\vec{d_s}$ and add to it the distance vector $\vec{d^i}$ for $\hat{s}_i$. We then take the minimum component of the vector resulting from this summation as the distance to the nearest global from $s$. Summing the minimum components of these summed distance vectors over all $s \in \hat{s}_i$ and dividing by $2^{\ell - o}$ gives the average schema fitness[30] $\bar{f}_{md}(\hat{s}_i)$. We calculate $\bar{f}_{md}(\hat{s}_D)$ similarly, using $\vec{d_s}$ and $\vec{d^D}$.

Now if $\vec{d^D} \geq \vec{d^i}$ in all components (that is $d_j^D \geq d_j^i$ , $\forall j \in 1..k$), for a particular global $g_i$, then clearly $\bar{f}_{md}(\hat{s}_D) > \bar{f}_{md}(\hat{s}_i)$, and the deceptive schema will beat the $i$th global schema. If $\vec{d^D}$ is superior (i.e., greater in all $k$ components) to all $k$ of the $\vec{d^i}$, then the deceptive schema will be superior to all the global schemata in that partition. Such a partition would thus be type III deceptive. To maximize the number of such partitions, we should try to increase the number of partitions in which the deceptive schema is as different as possible from all of the global schemata. Note that $\vec{d^D} \geq \vec{d^i}$ is only a *sufficient* condition for type III deception in a partition. Thus the number of partitions satisfying $\vec{d^D} \geq \vec{d^i}$ is only a lower bound on the number of type III deceptive partitions. However, this sufficient condition is met more often (i.e., at more partitions at every order) by the max-min-dist point $D$ than by any other string. This in turn suggests that the max-min-dist point $D$ will turn out to be the most attractive local optimum for GA crossover on the min-dist function with $k$ globals.

### 5.4.3  Empirical Results

To verify that $f_{mdG}(s)$ is misleading to a GA, in the sense that the GA will tend to converge to a deceptive local optimum rather than a member of the global set $G$, we perform an experiment on a constructed function. We employ the methodology presented in (Goldberg,

---

[29]Some schemata may contain more than one global. This does not affect our analysis.

[30]Note that we again use $f_{md}(s)$ for schema fitness calculations, rather than $f_{mdG}(s)$, effectively ignoring the globals.

Deb, & Clark, 1992) and used again in (Goldberg, Deb, & Horn, 1992) to construct an order-$\ell_s$ boundedly deceptive problem.

We first define a (partially) deceptive subfunction $f_s$ of length $\ell_s$ bits. We then concatenate $m$ identical copies of these subfunctions to form a length $\ell = m\ell_s$ problem $f$ that is a linear combination of the $m$ subfunctions. That is, the value of $f(s)$ is simply $\sum_{i=1}^{m} f_s(s_i)$, where $s_i$ is the $i^{th}$ substring of $\ell_s$ bits in string $s$. Thus the first subfunction is defined over the first $\ell_s$ bits, the second subfunction is defined over the next $\ell_s$ bits, and so on. Since each of the $m$ subfunctions is defined over groups of adjacent bits, the problem assumes a *tight* ordering of loci in the encoding. Because the problem is a linear combination of the (partially) deceptive subfunctions, deceptive schema partitions are *additive* across subfunction boundaries. That is, any deceptive partition from one copy of $f_s$ can be combined with any deceptive partitions from any other copies of $f_s$ to form a higher order deceptive partition of the larger function $f$. This means that the essential misleadingness of $f_s$ is preserved in $f$. However, the additive combination of the subfunctions also means that if the GA can solve *each* of the order-$\ell_s$ partitions corresponding to the $f_s$, then it can simply recombine those solutions (instances of the $k$ subfunction global optima) through crossover to find one of the $k^m$ global optimum of $f$.

Our subfunction $f_{md5G}(s_i)$ is a $k = 5$ global, $\ell_s = 10$-bit instance of the trap function version of $f_{mdG}^{trap}(s)$ given in Equation 10. We choose the five globals arbitrarily:

$$G = \{0000000000, 0010110001, 1101110011, 0101010010, 1000101111\}.$$

This fully defines the $2^{10} = 1024$ values of $f_{md5G}(s_i)$:

$$f_{md5G}(s_i) = \left\{ \begin{array}{ll} 10 & \text{if } s_i \in G \\ f_{md}(s_i) - 1 & \text{otherwise.} \end{array} \right. \tag{17}$$

We concatenate $m = 5$ copies of $f_{md5G}(s_i)$ to create an $\ell = 50$-bit problem $f_{5md5G}(s)$. Since $f_{5md5G}(s) = \sum_{i=1}^{5} f_{md5G}(s_i)$, where $s_i$ is the $i^{th}$ group of 10 bits in $s$, $f_{5md5G}(s)$ has $k^m = 5^5 = 3125$ global optima with fitness $f_{5md5G}^{max} = 5 * f_{md5G}(g \in G) = 5 * 10 = 50$. When we enumerate the 1024 values of $f_{md5G}(s_i)$ we find five deceptive local optima:

$$D = \{0111001101, 0111101100, 1011011100, 1110011100, 1111001100\},$$

each with fitness $f_{md5G}(d \in D) = 6 - 1 = 5$ since they are each exactly six bits different from the most similar global optimum. Thus $f_{5md5G}$ has $5^5 = 3125$ deceptive local optima of fitness $5 * 5 = 25$ (where all five copies of $f_{md5G}$ are converged to members of $D$). It also has $\binom{5}{1} * 5 * 5^4 = 15625$ local optima of fitness $10 + 4 * 5 = 30$ (where four copies of $f_{md5G}(s_i)$ have converged to members of $D$, and one has converged to a global optimum). In general $f_{5md5G}(s)$ has $\binom{5}{i} 5^i 5^{5-i}$ local optima, with fitness $10i + (5 - i)5$, in which exactly $i$ of the subfunctions are converged to members of $G$ and the rest are converged to members of $D$. Thus $f_{5md5G}(s)$ has a total of $100,000$ local optima, of which 3125 are global. Not only could we call $f_{5md5G}(s)$ *massively multimodal* (Goldberg, Horn, & Deb, 1992), but we could introduce the term *massively multiglobal* as well, since the number of global optima in functions like $f_{5md5G}(s)$ grows as $k^m$. Yet despite the large number of global optima, $f_{5md5G}(s)$ apparently is not as easy for the GA to solve as is a uniglobal function like $f_{mm,easy}$.

We run the same simple GA on $f$ as was described earlier in its application to $f_{mm,easy}$ and $f_{lp}$ (Table 1): a generational GA with deterministic binary tournament selection, single

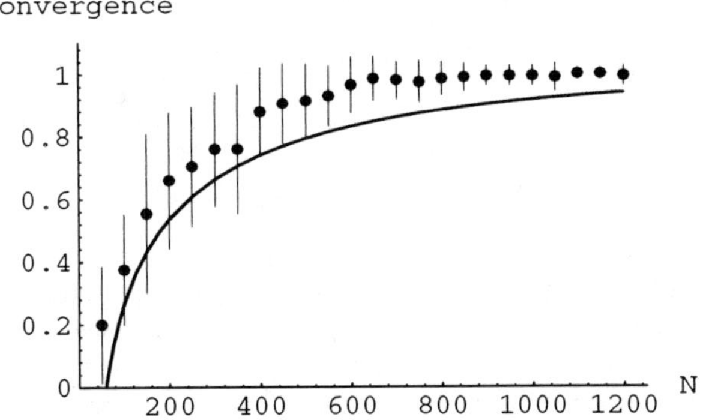



Figure 4: Predicted and actual GA performance on a boundedly, partially deceptive problem $f_{5md5G}(s)$. The plotted points are the average convergence values over 40 trials. Error bars extend one standard deviation above the mean, and one below. The solid line is the lower bound on expectation given by Goldberg, Deb, and Clark's (1992) population sizing equation. $N$ is population size.

point crossover with $p_c = 1.0$, and no mutation ($p_m = 0$). Here we run the GA at several different population sizes, using 40 different trials (different random initial populations) at each population size. For each trial we run the GA to convergence[31], and then measure the number of subfunctions optimized (i.e., number of subfunction global optima in an individual). Dividing the number of subfunctions optimized (zero to five) by five normalizes our convergence measure (zero to one).

We plot this convergence measure in Figure 4 for population sizes $N = 50$ to 1200, sampling every fifty generations. The plotted points track the mean convergence of each set of 40 trials, while the error bars extend one standard deviation above and one standard deviation below each plotted mean value. Figure 4 illustrates the difficulty of the problem for the GA with inadequate population size. A brief examination of the some of the final populations revealed that the GA usually converges to deceptive optima (members of $D$) when it fails to converge to a global optimum in a particular subfunction. With sufficient population sizes, however, the GA can overcome the partial deception of the $f_{md5G}(s_i)$ and reliably find a global optimum of $f_{5md5G}(s)$.

Clearly population sizing is critical to overcoming this type of bounded, maximal partial deception. We turn briefly to (Goldberg, Deb, & Clark, 1992) for some analytical guidance. The population sizing equations developed by Goldberg, Deb, and Clark (1992) can provide a lower bound on the expected performance of a simple GA on problems of bounded difficulty. Their framework is applied successfully to fully deceptive subfunctions in (Goldberg, Deb, & Clark, 1992), and to bipolar deceptive subfunctions in (Goldberg, Deb, & Horn, 1992). We apply it to our $k$-global, maximal partial deceptive subfunctions. The reader is referred to (Goldberg, Deb, & Clark, 1992) for guidance on applying the population sizing equations. Here we give only the problem specific parameters necessary to the equation.

One can extract from (Goldberg, Deb, & Clark, 1992) the expected convergence (normalized)

---

[31]Our convergence criterion was uniform fitness in the current population (i.e., minimum fitness equals maximum fitness in the population).

on a problem of bounded deception:

$$E[conv(N)] = 1 - e^{-g(N,d,\ell_s,\sigma_M^2)/2} \frac{1}{\sqrt{2\pi\, g(N,d,\ell_s,\sigma_M^2)}}, \tag{18}$$

where

$$g(N,d,\ell_s,\sigma_M^2) = \frac{nd^2}{2^{(\ell_s+1)}\sigma_M^2}, \tag{19}$$

$N$ is population size, $\ell_s$ is the length of the subfunction, and $d$ is the "signal" of the subfunction's global optima to be detected among the "noise" (variance) $\sigma_M^2$ of the entire function. For our functions $f_{md5G}(s_i)$ and $f_{5md5G}(s)$, $\ell_s = 10$, and the signal $d$ is simply the difference between the global fitness and the fitness of the nearest competitor (the deceptive optima): $d = 10 - 5 = 5$. Finally, $\sigma_M^2 = (m-1)\sigma_m^2$, where $m$ is the number of subfunctions and $\sigma_m^2$ is the variance in a single subfunction. For us $m = 5$. One can approximate $\sigma_m^2$ by sampling, but with only 1024 values in $f_{md5G}(s_i)$ we calculate it exactly as $\sigma_m^2 = 1.31095$, so that $\sigma_M^2 = (5-1) * 1.31095 = 5.2438$.

Plugging the above calculated values into Equation 18, we can plot the lower bound on expected convergence as the solid line in Figure 4. From this plot it appears that the population sizing equation provides an adequate lower bound on expected GA convergence on our multiglobal, multimodal, partially deceptive problem.

### 5.4.4   Extensions

Increasing the number of global optima $k$ in the subfunctions, and increasing the number $m$ of subfunctions, can lead to very high degrees of modality. For example, Goldberg, Deb, and Horn (1992) use five copies of their six bit bipolar deceptive function resulting in 32 global optima among over five million local optima. Five million is approximately 0.5% of the $2^{30}$ total size of the search space, and is thus within two orders of magnitude of the absolute maximum number of local optima (50%).

Adding global optima to the subfunction $f_{md5G}(s_i)$ (i.e., increasing $k$) should in general decrease the misleadingness of the problem. Thus a fully deceptive subfunction (e.g., a uniglobal trap function) should be more difficult to optimize (i.e., require larger population sizes) than a bi-global deceptive subfunction (e.g., a bipolar deceptive trap function), which should in turn be more difficult than a $k \geq 3$-global subfunction. Preliminary experiments indicate that this is the case. It would be interesting, however, to try to isolate the decrease in difficulty due to simply having more globals in the initial population (due to higher $k$) from the decrease in difficulty due to having fewer deceptive partitions at higher $k$, if indeed these two effects are separable.

The $f_{mdG}(s)$ function, although general with respect to the number and placement of globals, can be generalized further. We could make each global more attractive by simply increasing the radii $r_{g,i}$ of each global $g_i$. Thus $f_{md}(s)$ would be defined as before *outside* of the $r_{g,i}$-bit neighborhoods of each global. Within each neighborhood, however, the $f_{mdG}(s)$ could be a plateau of optimal fitness, or a hill leading to the global.

Finally, we note that the function $f_{md}$ is not analytic at the globals nor any of the points on the Voronoi lines. A differentiable version of $f_{md}$ could allow additional analysis (e.g., of the function's gradients, schema average fitnesses, etc.). Selecting the minimum (or maximum) distance from a set of distances can be done using the *maximum Holder norm*. Using any lower order (i.e., finite) Holder norm in place of the maximum (or *infinite order*) Holder norm yields a function $df_{md}$ that is differentiable everywhere and can be made arbitrarily close to $f_{md}$ by increasing the order of the norm. We use such a technique to quickly and easily generate the gradient plot in Figure 3, bottom, taking the derivative of an approximation to $f_{mdG}(x, y)$ using a finite order Holder norm for $f_{md}(x, y)$.

# 6  CONCLUSIONS

Modality by itself, if defined solely as the number of local optima, actually tells us little about the difficulty of searching a space. Similarly, full deception and GA-easiness in uni- or bimodal landscapes tell us only about the extreme boundaries of GA success and failure. But maximally deceptive multimodal functions allow us to embed deception in much more rugged and general landscapes, and to define arbitrarily sized and spaced local optima and their basins of attraction to a GA. These more realistic instances of deception illustrate the difficulty of generalizing simple approaches to solving *fully* deceptive problems, such as a complement operator (Grefenstette, 1992). The complement of the deceptive attractor in a fully deceptive problem is indeed the global optimum, but this does not hold in the more general case of partial deception. For example, in a bipolar deceptive problem the complement of every deceptive optimum is another deceptive optimum.

However, generalizing the definitions of full deception in order to characterize partial deception is tricky. It is all too easy to lose the essential quality of misleadingness. We have introduced a general method of relaxing the deception conditions that partially orders problem spaces according to GA misleadingness. We can now make more connections between crossover's search of hyperplanes and the population's movement over the fitness landscape. For example, in the past we have generally chosen the deceptive attractor $D$ first, and then defined deceptive partitions in terms of $D$. Here we saw how maximizing the number of deceptive partitions of all orders leads to a unique choice of deceptive local optimum, since the number of deceptive partitions increases with distance to the set of globals. Finally, we defined a simple, general, deceptive multimodal problem, the min-dist function, that seems to relate the attraction of crossover to interesting geometric features of the landscape, such as Voronoi diagrams and Delaunay triangularizations (Conway & Sloane, 1993), in addition to local optima, ridges, and the landscape's gradient field. We must define landscape characteristics important to crossover or we will continue to look at fitness surfaces from a hillclimber's rather limited point of view.

### Acknowledgments

We thank Georges R. Harik, Kaitlin Sherwood, Joseph C. Culberson, Terry Jones, and several anonymous referees for their comments and suggestions. The first author acknowledges support provided by NASA under Contract NGT-50873. The second author acknowledges support provided by AFOSR under Grant F49620-94-1-0103 and by the US Army under Contract DASG60-90-C-0153.

### References

Ackley, D. H. (1985). A connectionist algorithm for genetic search. In J. J. Grefenstette (Ed.), *Proceedings of an International Conference on Genetic Algorithms* (pp. 121–135). Hillsdale, NJ: Lawrence Erlbaum Associates, Publishers.

Ackley, D. H. (1987a). *A connectionist machine for genetic hillclimbing*. Boston: Kluwer Academic Publishers.

Ackley, D. H. (1987b). An empirical study of bit vector function optimization. In L. Davis (Ed.), *Genetic algorithms and simulated annealing* (pp. 170–204). London: Pitman Publishing.

Bethke, A. D. (1981). Genetic algorithms as function optimizers. (Doctoral dissertation, University of Michigan at Ann Arbor). *Dissertation Abstracts International*, **41**(9), 3503B. (University Microfilms No. 81-06101).

Conway, J. H., & Sloane, N. J. A. (1993). *Sphere packings, lattices, and groups* (2nd ed.). New York: Springer-Verlag.

Deb, K., & Goldberg, D. E. (1993). Analyzing deception in trap functions. In D. Whitley (Ed.), *Foundations of genetic algorithms 2*. San Mateo, CA: Morgan Kaufmann.

Deb, K., & Goldberg, D. E. (1994). Sufficient conditions for deceptive and easy binary functions. *Annals of Mathematics and Artificial Intelligence*, **10**(1994), 385–408.

Deb, K., Horn, J., & Goldberg, D. E. (1993). Multimodal deceptive functions. *Complex Systems*, **7**, 131–153.

Goldberg, D. E. (1987). Simple genetic algorithms and the minimal deceptive problem. In L. Davis (Ed.), *Genetic algorithms and simulated annealing* (pp. 74-88). London: Pitman Publishing.

Goldberg, D. E. (1989a). *Genetic algorithms in search, optimization, and machine learning*. Reading, MA: Addison–Wesley.

Goldberg, D. E. (1989b). Genetic algorithms and Walsh functions: part I, a gentle introduction. *Complex Systems*, **3**, 129–152.

Goldberg, D. E. (1989c). Genetic algorithms and Walsh functions: part II, deception and its analysis. *Complex Systems*, **3**, 153–171.

Goldberg, D. E. (1991). Construction of high-order deceptive functions using low-order Walsh coefficients. *Annals of Mathematics and Artificial Intelligence*, **5**, 35–48.

Goldberg, D. E. (1993, February). Making genetic algorithms fly: a lesson from the Wright brothers. *Advanced Technology for Developers*, **2**, 1–8.

Goldberg, D. E. (1994, March). Genetic and evolutionary algorithms come of age. *Communications of the Association for Computing Machinery*, **37**(3), 113–119.

Goldberg, D. E., Deb, K., & Clark, J. H. (1992). Genetic algorithms, noise, and the sizing of populations. *Complex Systems*, **6**, 333–362.

Goldberg, D. E., Deb, K., & Horn, J. (1992). Massive multimodality, deception, and genetic algorithms. In R. Männer, & B. Manderick (Ed.), *Parallel Problem Solving from Nature, 2* (pp. 37–46). Amsterdam: North-Holland.

Goldberg, D. E., Deb, K., & Korb, B. (1991). Don't worry, be messy. In R. K. Belew, & L. B. Booker (Ed.s), *Proceedings of the Fourth International Conference on Genetic Algorithms* (pp. 24–30). San Mateo, CA: Morgan Kaufmann.

Goldberg, D. E. & Rudnick, M. (1991). Genetic algorithms and the variance of fitness. *Complex Systems*, **5**, 266–278.

Grefenstette, J.J. (1992). Deception considered harmful. In L. D. Whitley (Ed.), *Foundations of Genetic Algorithms, 2* (pp. 75–91). San Mateo, CA: Morgan Kaufmann.

Harary, F., Hayes, J. P., & Wu, H-J. (1988). A survey of the theory of hypercube graphs. *Computational Mathematical Applications, 15*(4), 277–289.

Holland, J. H. (1992). *Adaptation in natural and artificial systems* (2nd ed.). Cambridge, MA: The MIT Press.

Homaifar, A., Qi, X., & Foster, J. (1991). Analysis and design of a general GA deceptive problem. In R. K. Belew, & L. B. Booker (Ed.s), *Proceedings of the Fourth International Conference on Genetic Algorithms* (pp. 196–203). San Mateo, CA: Morgan Kaufmann.

Horn, J., Goldberg, D. E., & Deb, K. (1994). Long path problems. In Y. Davidor, H.-P. Schwefel, & R. Männer (Ed.s), *Lecture Notes in Computer Science: Vol. 866. Parallel Problem Solving From nature – PPSN III* (pp. 149–158). Berlin: Springer-Verlag.

Jones, T., & Rawlins, G. J. E. (1993). Reverse hillclimbing, genetic algorithms and the busy beaver problem. In S. Forrest (Ed.), *Proceedings of the Fifth International Conference on Genetic Algorithms* (pp. 70–75). San Mateo, CA: Morgan Kaufmann.

Kargupta, H. & Goldberg, D. E. (1994). *Decision making in genetic algorithms: a signal-to-noise perspective* (IlliGAL Report No. 94004). Urbana-Champaign, IL: University of Illinois at Urbana-Champaign, Illinois Genetic Algorithms Laboratory, Department of General Engineering.

MacWilliams, F. J., & Sloane, N. J. A. (1977). *The Theory of Error Correcting Codes.* Amsterdam: North-Holland.

Mahfoud, S. W. (1993). Simple analytical models for genetic algorithms for multimodal function optimization. In S. Forrest (Ed.), *Proceedings of the Fifth International Conference on Genetic Algorithms* (p. 643). San Mateo, CA: Morgan Kaufmann.

Mitchell, M., Forrest, S., & Holland, J. H. (1991). The royal road for genetic algorithms: fitness landscapes and GA performance. In J. Varela, & P. Bourgine (Ed.s), *Toward a Practice of Autonomous Systems: Proceedings of the First European Conference on Artificial Life* (pp. 245–254). Cambridge, MA: The MIT Press.

Mitchell, M., & Holland, J. H. (1993). When will a genetic algorithm outperform a hill climbing? In S. Forrest (Ed.), *Proceedings of the Fifth International Conference on Genetic Algorithms* (p. 647). San Mateo, CA: Morgan Kaufmann.

Preparata, F. P. (1974, September). Difference-preserving codes. *IEEE Transactions on Information Theory (IT), 20*(5), 643–649.

Rudnick, M. & Goldberg, D. E. (1991). *Signal, noise, and genetic algorithms* (IlliGAL Report No. 91005). Urbana-Champaign, IL: University of Illinois at Urbana-Champaign, Illinois Genetic Algorithms Laboratory, Department of General Engineering.

Whitley, D. L. (1991). Fundamental principles of deception in genetic search. In G. J. E. Rawlins (Ed.), *Foundations of Genetic Algorithms* (pp. 221–241). San Mateo, CA: Morgan Kaufmann.

Wilson, S. W. (1991). GA-easy does not imply steepest-ascent optimizable. In R. K. Belew, & L. B. Booker (Ed.s), *Proceedings of the Fourth International Conference on Genetic Algorithms* (pp. 85–89). San Mateo, CA: Morgan Kaufmann.

Wright, S. (1988). Surfaces of selective value revisited. *American Naturalist, 131*, 115–123.

# Greedy Recombination and Genetic Search
# on the Space of Computer Programs

**Walter Alden Tackett**
University of Southern California[1]
email: order@netcom.com, tackett@enee.usc.edu
Snail mail: 298 4th Ave. Suite 400
San Francisco, CA 94118-2468 USA

## Abstract

Many natural organisms overproduce zygotes and subsequently decimate the ranks of offspring at some later stage of development. The basic purpose of this behavior is the reduction of parental resource investment in offspring which are less fit than others according to some metabolically cheap fitness measure. An important insight into this process is that for single-pair matings all offspring are products of the same parental genotypes: the selection taking place therefore seeks the most fit recombination of parental traits. This paper presents the Greedy Recombination operator $R_B(n)$ for genetic programming, which performs greedy selection among potential crossover sites of a mating pair. The properties of $R_B(n)$ are described both from a statistical standpoint and in terms of their effect upon search; comparisons are drawn to existing methods. We formulate the class of *constructional* problems, which allow precise control over the fitness structure in the space of expressions being searched. The constructional approach is used to create simple GP analogies of the "Royal Road" problems used to study classical GA. The effects of $R_B(n)$ upon search properties, fitness distributions, and genotypic variations are examined and contrasted with effects of selection and recombination methods.

## 1. Introduction

The production of a large number of offspring and their culling down to a smaller number of select individuals is common among living things. This phenomenon is known variously as soft selection, brood selection, spontaneous abortion, and a host of other terms depending upon the stage of development at which the culling of offspring takes place. The "bottom line" of this behavior in nature is the reduction of parental resource investment in offspring who are potentially less fit than others.

---

[1]This research was sponsored in part by the University of Southern California Zumberge Research and Initiation fund.

The means of culling offspring are widely varied, ranging from reabsorption of immature seeds by plants (Darwin 1876) to sibling and parental cannibalism among animals (Stearns 1987). In some cases the parent uses biochemical measurements to determine which offspring are chosen, while in others such as sibling-competition a more obvious form of tournament selection is at work. The net result is that the resources of the parent are expended only upon those offspring which tend to lie in the upper tail of the fitness distribution induced by the brood culling criteria.

The use of "Soft Brood Selection" in genetic programming was first proposed by Altenberg (1993; 1994), who conjectures that it should increase the upper and lower tails of the population fitness distribution. This is due to the effect of "constructional fitness," which describes the variation in fitness of subtrees, or subexpressions, as a function of the loci in which they are inserted under recombination. There are two implications of immediate interest for the work presented here: the first is that an increase in the fitness point spread is effectively an increase in fitness variance, which confers a continued evolvability upon the population according to Fisher's fundamental theorem of natural selection (Fisher 1958). The second is that Altenberg's analysis is based on the idea that a block of code only has a useful net effect when appearing in a specific context: this captures a critical property of computer programs. This paper presents an alternative but entirely compatible analysis based on search properties of the genetic method.

We present the *Greedy Recombination Operator* $R_B(n)$ for artificial genetic systems and demonstrate that the principles of reduction in parental resource investment and of improved search among recombined traits carry over from natural systems. For purposes of testing we present a class of problems borrowed from binary-string GA encodings which is new to the domain of genetic programming. In these "Constructional Problems" fitness is based strictly upon syntactic form of expressions rather than semantic evaluation. A particular target expression is assigned a "perfect" fitness, while those subexpressions resulting from its hierarchical decomposition comprise intermediate fitness values. If the intermediate fitness values increase monotonically with the complexity of subexpressions in the hierarchy then we call the resulting problem a "Royal Road" after (Forrest and Mitchell 1993). Alternatively, if some intermediate expressions have lower fitness than subexpressions which they contain, the resulting problem is designated a "Royal Road with potholes" (Holland 1994) which is similar to the deceptive functions described in (Goldberg 1989). These problems form a set of benchmarks used in comparing Greedy Recombination toother methods of selection and recombination. . A variety of measurements which track fitness moments, probability of success, and diversity, are introduced in support of the benchmarking process.

It is shown that improved performance can be achieved with significant reduction in CPU and memory requirements relative to standard GP due to reduced population size requirements. The fitness evaluation of brood members is performed with a "culling function" which is a subset of the fitness evaluation function for full-fledged population members. A significant result is that large reductions in the cost of the culling function produce small performance degradation of the population members. We conjecture that random recombination is likely to produce unfit code even when both parents are highly fit: even a simplistic culling function is beneficial since it will tend to discriminate between code which is "in the ballpark" and that which is not. We go on to discuss the important theoretical considerations which guide the construction of a quality measure for any fitness evaluation subset used in selecting among brood members.

## 2. Greedy Recombination Operator $R_B(n)$ for Genetic Programming

The term *Greedy Recombination* is adopted here in contrast to the term "Brood Selection" used in (Altenberg 1994) and (Tackett and Carmi 1994b). It is (arguably) a recombination operator which serves as a substitute for the "standard" genetic programming crossover operation defined in (Koza 1992). Thus the name is chosen so as not to be confused with *selection* operators such as the Steady-State method (Syswerda 1989; Whitley 1989). Readers familiar with Evolution Strategies (Bäck and Schwefel 1993) may draw a comparison between $R_B(n)$ and the $(\mu,\lambda)$-ES method. We will see in Section 3.3.2 that despite surface similarities there are significant differences between the methods which can in turn produce important differences in search properties.

Treated as a "black box," the *Greedy Recombination Operator* $R_B(n)$ produces two offspring from two parents as does standard crossover. Internally $R_B(n)$ is parameterized by the *brood size factor* n and the *culling function* $F_B$; whereas standard GP crossover recombines two parents to produce one pair of offspring, $R_B(n)$ produces a "brood" comprising n pairs of offspring and keeps only the best two individuals. The surviving members of the brood are selected according to fitness values assigned by the culling function $F_B$ which is in general different than the fitness function applied to the population.

$F_B$ can be much less costly than the fitness evaluation applied to population members and still retain the effectiveness of $R_B(n)$. This allows many brood members to be evaluated at a cost comparable to the evaluation of one "mature" population member, thereby *minimizing the investment of resources* in unfit populations members. Genetic programming under $R_B(n)$ can use a smaller population size than is necessary under standard crossover, and the CPU time which would otherwise be used to evaluate extra population members is instead spent on evaluation of large broods. The net result is an improvement in fitness of population members for equivalent CPU resources and reduced memory requirements. The Brood Recombination Operator can be stated in pseudocode form as follows:

**Algorithm $R_B(n)$:**
**Step 1.**    Select parents $P_1$ and $P_2$ *from the population per (Koza 1992)*
**Step 2.**    For $i = 1$ to n **perform crossover** *per (Koza 1992):*
**Step 2.1.**          **Randomly select crossover points** *(subtrees)* $S_{i1}$ *and* $S_{i2}$ *from* $P_1$ *and* $P_2$
**Step 2.2.**          **Exchange subtrees** $S_{i1}$ *and* $S_{i2}$ *to form brood offspring* $B_{i1}$ *and* $B_{i2}$
**Step 3.**    **Test the 2n members** *of the brood to determine fitness according to* $F_B$
**Step 4.**    **Sort the 2n members** *of the brood in order of fitness*
**Step 5.**    **Select offspring** *("Children")* $C_1$ *and* $C_2$ *which are fittest of the 2n brood members*
**Step 6.**    **Return** $C_1$ *and* $C_2$ *as the offspring produced by* $R_B(n)$

The procedure described above is similar to performing K-tournament selection with K = 2n among all possible successors which can be generated from a pair of individuals by the crossover operation (see Section 3.2). Because all members of the tournament are derived from the same parent genotypes, $R_B(n)$ is selecting among recombinations rather than selecting among individuals.

## 2.1. Reduced Investment of CPU and Memory Resources

Step 3 of algorithm $R_B(n)$ evaluates the fitness of the 2n brood members according to $F_B$. If $F_B$ is the same fitness measure used to evaluate the population at large then the cost of fitness evaluation, typically the bottleneck in most GP experiments, is multiplied by a factor of $n^2$. Clearly, this is not nature's model for brood selection: it is the analogy of letting each potential offspring lead a full mature life. For any complex task the random insertion of a subtree into a program which results from a single GP crossover operation will frequently result in nonsense code even when both parents are highly fit.  Therefore it is easy to imagine that for many problems fitness evaluation for population members may be quite costly while a criteria $F_B$ that discriminates between programs which are "in the ballpark" as opposed to being "totally bogus" may be quite cheap.  The quantitative approach we take is to parameterize the costs of greedy recombination in terms of CPU (time) and memory (space) resources relative to standard GP, where resource costs are defined as follows:

$C_p$ = CPU cost of evaluating a full-fledged population member;

$C_B$ = CPU cost of evaluating a brood member using $F_B$;

M  = Average "size" of population or brood member in memory.

Then we can define algorithm resource investment on a per-generation basis in terms of CPU and memory resource consumption:

*Time to create new population under standard GP  crossover:*
1.
$$T_1 = C_P N_1$$
*Space to create new population under standard GP crossover:*
2.
$$S_1 = M N_1$$
*Time to create new population under $R_B(n)$:*
3.
$$T_2 = C_P N_2 + n C_B N_2$$
*Space to create new population under $R_B(n)$:*
4.
$$S_2 = M(N_2 + 2n)$$

---

[2] Note that this comparison is made to the method of recombination proposed in (Koza 1992) which chooses two recombinations from a single pair of parents.  One could easily reformulate Koza's work to choose only a single offspring from each mating pair, and likewise choose n individual offspring from n parental pairings unde $R_B(n)$.

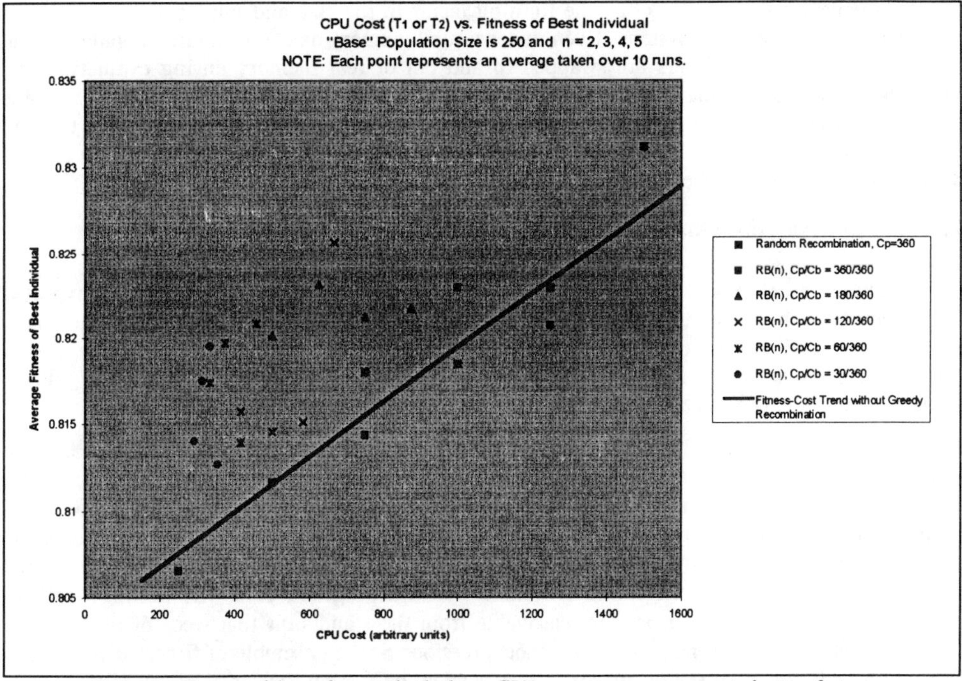



*Figure 1: Fitness of best-of-run individual vs. CPU resource use on an inductive feature-classification problem for a variety of recombination parameters (Tackett 1994). A trend line is fitted to five points which depict genetic programming with "standard"-i.e. random choice of-recombination insertion sites using population sizes of $N_1$ = 250, 500, 750, 1000, and 1250. Also shown are five families consisting of four points each, which use a population size of $N_2$ = 250 and culling functions $F_B$ having CPU costs $C_P/C_B$= 360/360, 180/360, 120/360, 60/360, and 30/360 relative to the fitness evaluation function which drives selection. The four different points in each family are generated by using different brood size factors n=2, 3, 4, and 5 which pick the best two recombinations out of 4, 6, 8, and 10 trials, respectively.*

The terms $N_1$ and $N_2$ in Equations 1-4 are the population sizes required to produce equivalently good results between standard GP and $R_B(n)$ respectively, and the cost of evaluating population fitness is included in the computation of $T_1$ and $T_2$. The goal of applying $R_B(n)$ is that such results can be achieved with $T_2 < T_1$ and $S_2 < S_1$ due to $N_2 < N_1$ and $C_B < C_P$. Note that the given formulae assume that crossover is the only reproduction operator, although it is easy to adapt them if there are other operators used. Figure 1 depicts typical resource vs. performance results for $R_B(n)$ against a difficult[3] induction problem, taken from (Tackett 1994). It can be seen from this plot that performance levels are achieved using $R_B(n)$ which require 50%-100% more computation when $R_B(n)$ is not used. Whereas savings of CPU resources is a relatively obvious

---

[3] Note that the problem shown is difficult in the sense of having a geometrically complex Bayesian discriminant in $\Re^2$. There is no a priori evidence that the search space it represents should be biased against or in favor of $R_B(n)$.

benefit, memory resources are often the limiting factor in the size and number of GP runs that can be achieved on a given system. Even under virtual memory machines a large population can cause "thrashing" as members are swapped in and out of real memory during evaluation and breeding. Therefore it may make sense in practice to apply $R_B(n)$ with $F_B$ the same as the population fitness function strictly as a memory-saving device. In that case the first term in Formula (3) can be omitted since the value produced by $F_B$ for each brood member can be re-used as the fitness rating for selection.

## 2.2. An Analytic Basis for Greedy Recombination

This section briefly presents a mathematical argument which illustrates the expected improvement in the ability to find ever-fitter offspring under $R_B(n)$. Section 3.2 will later show how similar predictions can be made from a different set of assumptions based on search properties. Here, a diagram of hypothetical fitness distributions of two subexpressions allows visualization of the process taking place.

We introduce the concept of the *canonical fitness* of expressions, which we will denote as $f_c(S,w)$. Canonical fitness refers not to a scalar fitness value, but rather to a probability distribution associated with the expression S. Specifically, $f_c(S,w)$ is the relative frequency with which S occurs within (all possible) programs that have fitness value w. This frequency is taken over the space of all programs P with size less than some fixed positive integer k. Size may be considered as the count of atomic functions and terminals within a program, or as the nesting depth of expressions (placing limits on size is reasonable from the standpoint that trees of infinite size cannot be evaluated). Over the set of all subexpressions S, the ensemble of fitness distributions $f_c(S,w)$ forms a canonical search space. It is dependent only upon the function set, terminal set, and fitness evaluation function: these are exactly the critical design elements in genetic programming.

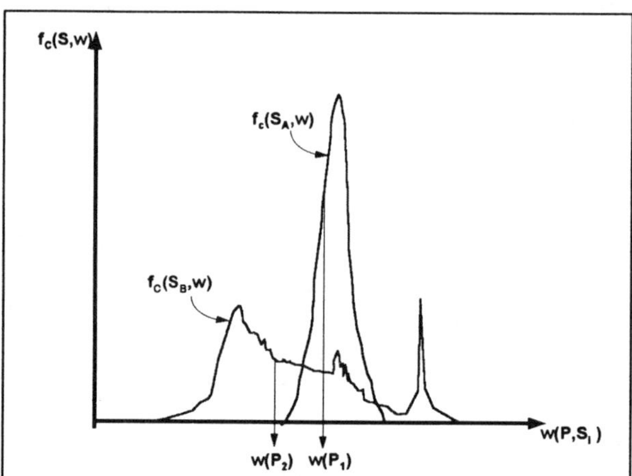


*Figure 2: Canonical fitness distribution $f_c(S,w)$ of two subexpressions $S_A$ and $S_B$. Fitness values of parent expressions $P_1$ and $P_2$ are points within these distributions.*

Figure 2 is a sketch which depicts the (hypothetical) canonical fitness distributions $f_c(S,w)$ for two expressions, $S_A$ and $S_B$: the x-axis is $w(\mathbf{P},S_i)_{i=\{A,B\}}$, the fitness of all programs which contain the subexpression $S_i$. The y-axis is the probability $f_c(S_i,w)$ that $S_i$ occurs in an expression with fitness w. A useful transformation of $f_c(S_i,w)$ is the probability density $F_c(S_i,w)$. It is the probability of finding a program containing $S_i$ which has fitness less than or equal to w:

5.
$$F_c(S_i,w) = \int_{-\infty}^{w} f_c(S_i,v)\, dv$$

Figure 2 provides some insights to the operation of $R_B(n)$. Consider that $S_A$ is the subexpression chosen from the *crossover point* of parent $P_1$ and inserted into the crossover point of parent $P_2$ to form offspring $B_{i1}$. Likewise, $S_B$ is the subexpression inserted from $P_2$ to $P_1$ to form $B_{i2}$. Thus $w(P_1)$ and $w(B_{i1})$ are both points in $f_c(S_A,w)$, while $w(P_2)$ and $w(B_{i2})$ are both points in $f_c(S_B,w)$: the production of offspring via crossover represents a traversal of the curve described by $f_c(S_i,w)$. Assuming that the same subexpression is not randomly drawn multiple times, $R_B(n)$ is sampling an ensemble of 2n distributions: n of these distributions are denoted $f_c(S_{i1},w)_{i=\{1,n\}}$ and have $S_{i1}\ \varepsilon$ $P_1$ in common; the other n distributions sampled are $f_c(S_{i2},w)$ where $S_{i2}\ \varepsilon\ P_2$. Price's covariance theorem (Price 1970; Altenberg 1994) shows that *evolvability* of a system, the ability of a population to continually improve, requires correlation between the distributions of parent and offspring fitness. In light of this, we will consider the  performance of $R_B(n)$ in a "worst case scenario." Let us assume that $w(B_{ij})$ is drawn from $f_c(S_{ij},w)$ independently of $w(P_j)$. This implies that *$w(B_{ij})$ is uncorrelated with $w(P_j)$*, which according to Price means that the selection of subtree crossover points, the transmission function, is resulting in *random search*. In this case the probability that $w(B_{ij}) > w(P_j)$ is just $1- F_c(S_{ij},w)$: qualitatively, this is related to how close $w(P_j)$ is to the "upper tail" of distribution $f_c(S_{ij},w)$. The probability that at least one offspring has $w(B_{ij}) > w(P_j)$ is then just one minus the probability that no offspring has $w(B_{ij}) > w(P_j)$. Under the simplifying assumption that the distributions $f_c(S_{ij},w)$ are independent for each subexpression $S_{ij}$ then the chances of  this occurring are:

6.
$$p\{\ [\mathbf{max}_{i=1,n}(w(B_{ij}))\ ]\ >\ w(P_j)\ \} = 1.0\ -\ \prod_{i=1}^{n} F_c(S_{ij},w(P_j))$$

Since $0.0 \le F_c(S_{ij},w(P_j)) \le 1.0$, the chance of producing a fitter offspring sharing a common subexpression $S_{ij}$ increases exponentially with brood size n. In practice, distributions of  parent and offspring fitness are certainly correlated: this quantity can be measured, but the mitigating effects vary on a per-problem basis. Likewise not all distributions $f_c(S_{ij},w)$ will be independent. These restrictions may be sidestepped by considering the search properties of $R_B(n)$ decoupled from selection, as described in the following section.

Although this figure 2 is just a sketch drawn for hypothetical distributions, it is possible to construct such diagrams using real data. Schemes for extracting all unique subexpressions from populations, along with their statistics, are described in detail in (Tackett 1994). While use of such methods to construct diagrams after Figure 2 holds potential interest for theoretical investigations, it is limited in practicality by the fact that the canonical fitness diagram requires enumeration of all programs of size less than k, which is a number of expressions exponential in k.

## 3. Search Properties of Greedy Recombination

Search is a primary tool in the field of Artificial Intelligence, and there exists a great body of related theory. Understanding genetic programming as a search on the space of computer programs provides insights into the properties of operators, particularly in this case the properties of $R_B(n)$. The classical model of AI search involves the traversal of a state-space tree (Korf 1987). Initially, the system is in a "start state" which corresponds to the root of the tree ("level 0"). Successor states are generated by applying some *operator* to the previous state, and they are represented as children of the previous state in the search tree. The process of generating the children of a parent state is called *expansion*. Thus operators are applied to level 0 to produce the states of level 1, the states of level 1 produce those of level 2, and so on.

The quality of a state in the search may be estimated by a function which can be applied to any arbitrary state: this function is referred to as an *heuristic*. Heuristic search typically chooses successor states in order to attempt to drive the heuristic toward some desired maximal or minimal value. By this definition, the fitness measure used in genetic programming is an heuristic, and the difference between the fitness value of a program and some "ideal" fitness value may be viewed as distance from a goal. Many variations of heuristic search, most notably the A* method, are concerned with preserving the path of states from the initial state to the goal. Conversely, genetic programming is only concerned with achieving a goal state, namely some program which produces a satisfactory fitness value.

Rather than searching the state space tree in some predetermined order, heuristic search proceeds in an order that is determined by the value of the heuristic function. A primary distinction between methods may be made by the amount of memory that they keep about the states that have already been visited. Hill-climbing is a memoryless method which embodies the graph search version of the *greedy algorithm* (Hu 1982). The successors of the current state are generated and evaluated according to the heuristic. If the successor state having the best heuristic value (closest to the goal) is better than the current state, that successor state is chosen to become the new current state, and the process is reapplied. Otherwise, the process terminates. Thus the name hill climbing, since the algorithm converges to the top of the nearest hill in the fitness landscape (that is, in the case of maximization: if performing minimization the algorithm seeks the bottom of the closest valley). There is no guarantee that this local extremum is the global extremum, and hill climbing may terminate without achieving a satisfactory value of the heuristic function. An alternative method is to store all states which have been heuristically evaluated but not expanded in a priority queue. These states are ordered in the queue according to their heuristic value, with the best being first, and the resulting algorithm is called "best-first" search (BFS). Best-first search always removes the state at the head of the priority queue for expansion, and so the next state searched is not necessarily a child of the current state (Figure 3). When the situation of finding an heuristic "dead end" occurs the search can back up to some previously unexpanded state even though that state may be less optimal than parents or ancestors of the terminated branch.

Although best-first search is guaranteed to find a globally optimal value of the heuristic function, the size of the priority queue can grow exponentially with the depth of search performed.  A compromise to this situation is "beam search" (Lowerre and Reddy 1980).  Beam search is very much like best-first search with the exception that the priority queue (memory) is set at some size limit, typically fixed (Rosenbloom 1987).  Thus there is a limit to which states the search can be backed up to.  The resulting tradeoff is that it is possible for states uniquely leading to the optimal state to be eliminated.  The imposition of limits which are high enough not to impede search is entirely problem dependent.

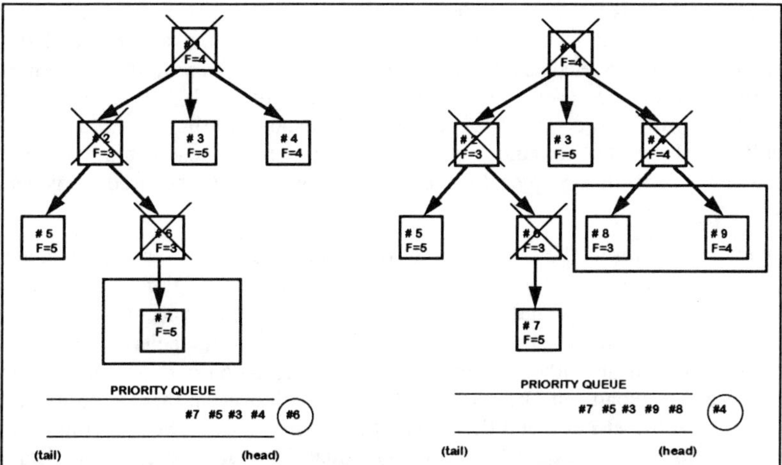

Figure 3: Beam search and best first search proceed by inserting states into a priority queue according to their heuristic worth, always choosing the state at the head of the queue as the next to be explored.  This example shows two successive stages of such a search, with lower heuristic value being more desirable.  On the left side of the diagram, state 6 is expanded to produce its single successor, state 7, which has a poor heuristic evaluation and is so placed at the end of the queue.  The next state to be explored is state 4, which has two successors, states 8 and 9, which are placed at the head of the queue due to favorable heuristic worth.  The only difference between Best First Search (BFS) and Beam Search is that BFS has an infinite queue size, or memory, in which to store unexpanded states while Beam Search has finite memory (after Rosenbloom 1987).

## 3.1. Genetic Programming as State Space Tree Search

Genetic programming may be posed as a variant upon state space search in which the nodes of the search tree are expressions.  What sets apart genetic programming and other GAs from many mainstream approaches to search is the joining of a strongly stochastic selection of successors with a multi-parent successor generator.  Initially, the population of N expressions are N randomly generated states.  A state is visited by being created and evaluated, as an expression, for fitness (Figure 4a). The selection operator (Figure 4b) works together with operators such as recombination, cloning, and mutation to create successors of expressions (Figure 4c).  Successors are created in batches of N new states, called a generation, with these new states replacing the N states of the previous generation. Among the set of N new states may be some arbitrary number of states also contained in the previous generation. The number of states which are different between the previous generation and the new generation is called the generation gap (De Jong 1993), which can range in number from 1 to N.

### 3.1.1. Selection and Stochastic Priority

The population of N expressions is analogous to a beam search priority queue with limited size N, ordered by fitness (Figure 4a). States are selected for partial expansion based upon order in the queue. The analogy is imperfect in the sense that the head is not necessarily chosen to have successors generated, but it is more likely to have successors than any other element. The selection process can be modeled as a transformation which maps *rank* in the original population into frequency of occurrence (FoO) in an *interim queue* (Figure 4b). In general, selection is performed N times with replacement to generate the N members of the interim queue, which is a fictitious entity used here for accounting purposes. The interim queue contain states for which successors will be generated, tagged by the operators which will be used to generate those successors.

The interim queue transforms the distribution of the population queue. States which are near the head of the population queue are represented (in probability) with a high frequency of occurrence in the interim queue, while those near the tail of the population queue occur with low probability (Figure 4b, 4c). The quantitative measure of the degree to which the behavior of genetic search mimics Beam Search (or any other method) lies in the correlation between the distributions of individuals chosen for expansion. In other words, how much overlap there is between the group of successors created by selection and the group of successors created by applying an equivalent number of iterations of node expansion under an actual (non-stochastic) Beam Search. Such measures are similar in quality to the culling function quality measure $\mathbf{Q}(F_B)$ described in Section 5.

### 3.1.2. Recombination as Search

Recombination is a binary operator which generates a successor for each of two open states by swapping subexpressions between (copies of) them. Considering a state as a "solution" to a heuristic problem, this operation can be viewed as combining partial solutions from states previously arrived at by search. In this respect it is probably the primary unique aspect of genetic methods which sets them apart from other varieties of heuristic search. We consider recombination in the context of search.

In the classical formulation of binary-string GA, the number of recombination sites is equal to the number of bits in the binary string representing the individual. This point is the same for both parents which participate in a given recombination, and so sets a limit on the number of possible unique successors of a mating pair. By contrast, in genetic programming the number of possible successors is the product of the number of alleles (function and terminal nodes) in each parent expression. We adopt the convention that one successor is generated for each parent, with parent and successor differing by the subexpression which was exchanged. It is easy to compute an upper bound $s_i$ on the number of possible successors for a specific node $i$ which can be derived in a given generation:

7.
$$s_i = SIZE_i \sum_{j=1}^{N} SIZE_j$$

Where $SIZE_i$ is the count of function and terminal tokens contained in expression $i$. Thus the number of successors of $i$ is the product of the size of expression $i$, the population size N, and the average size of expressions in the population. This is due to the fact that an expression contains $SIZE_i$ points into which a subexpression may be inserted from another expression, and likewise each of the N expressions $j$ in the population contains $SIZE_j$ subexpressions which may be donated to the insertion site of member $i$ in order to form a new offspring. Similarly, an upper bound on the total number of possible successors which can be generated for the entire population is given by:

8.
$$s = \sum_{i=1}^{N} s_i$$

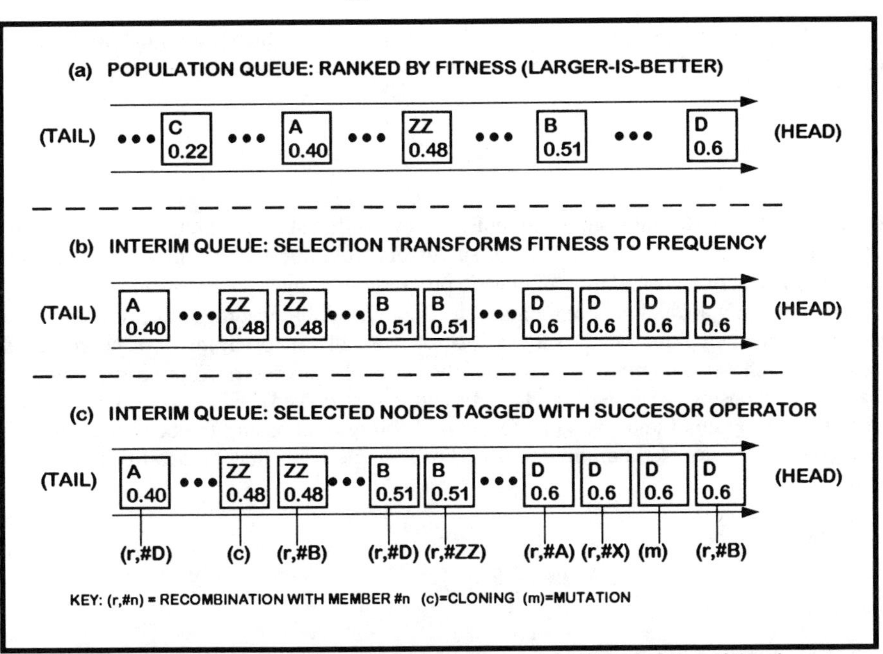


Figure 4: Genetic "beam search" on the space of programs: (a) The population of N nodes are ranked by fitness to form a "stochastic queue" in which members near the head are more likely to have successors generated. (b) Selection forms an interim queue of N nodes, drawn with replacement from the N members of the population queue. Those near the head of the population queue are drawn multiple times, on average, while those near the tail are not likely to be drawn. (c) Nodes selected into the interim queue are shown tagged with the operators which will be used to generate their successors. The recombination operator "r" is unique with respect to AI search in that it is a binary operator which combines parts of existing solutions.

Equation 8 shows that an upper bound on the number of successors which can be produced by recombination is the population size times the square of the average expression size. This upper bound, as well as that of Equation 7, are useful for analysis but are unachievable in practical systems. This is due to the fact that subexpressions consisting of a single terminal are guaranteed non-unique and comprise a significant fraction of subexpressions in the population. Furthermore, repeated selection over several generations guarantees that many other subexpressions occur multiple times according to Holland's schema theorem (Holland 1975; 1992). Regardless of these considerations, Equation 8 implies that even with many repeated subexpressions in the population, only a fraction of the possible successors of a single generation can possibly be visited by the population of the next generation. The purpose of $R_B(n)$ is to effectively sample a greater portion of this number of successors, with the intent of increasing exploratory power and improving algorithm performance. Other means of genetic search, most notably $(\mu,\lambda)$-Evolution Strategies (Bäck and Schwefel 1993) provide alternative approaches to oversampling of successors, but with a much different effect upon search ordering (Section 3.3.2).

## 3.2. Greedy vs. Random Recombination

$R_B(n)$ can be analyzed separately from the effects of selection. Once programs $i$ and $j$ have been selected from the population by arbitrary means, the number of possible successors of $i$ is given by:

9.
$$s_{ij} = SIZE_i \, SIZE_j$$

This is the same as the number of possible successors for state $j$ which can be generated by recombination, so that the total number of successors from one mating due to recombination is just $2s_{ij}$. In the classical formulation of genetic programming, one subexpression (crossover point) is chosen uniformly at random from among the $SIZE_i$ available in program $i$, and one is chosen randomly from among the $SIZE_j$ subexpressions available in program $j$. The result is that successors are chosen randomly from among the possible successors of programs $i$ and $j$. The probability of choosing the worst (i.e., least fit and lowest ranked) individual among the possible successors of programs $i$ and $j$ is equal to the probability of choosing the best individual among the possible successors of programs $i$ and $j$. For a single trial, that probability is given by the formula:

10.
$$p_{best} = p_{worst} = 1/2s_{ij}$$

Greedy recombination uses this same basic method to generate a randomly chosen subset of 2N possible successors from the total set of $2s_{ij}$ and discards all but the best two. This is virtually identical to tournament selection (Goldberg and Deb 1991) with tournament size 2N, with the exception that (a) two winners (not one) are selected, and (b) the selection takes place not from the population but from among $2s_{ij}$ potential successors. How does tournament selection improve the chances of finding fit recombinations? It is straightforward to compute the likelihood with which a tournament will draw the best, worst, or any intermediate individual in terms of its fitness ranking i (where 1 is the rank of the least fit individual and where $2s_{ij}$ is the rank of the most fit individual).  The probability distribution of this tournament selection is equivalent to making 2N rolls of an unbiased $2s_{ij}$ -sided die, and computing the chance that face i $\{1 \leq i \leq 2s_{ij}\}$ is the highest thrown.  This probability is just equal to the difference between the chance that no element with rank greater than i is generated in 2N trials and the chance that no element with rank greater than i-1 is generated in 2N trials.  Since these trials are independent, this can be exactly formulated as:

11.
$$p_i = (i / 2s_{ij})^{2N} - ((i - 1)/ 2s_{ij})^{2N}$$

Thus $R_B(n)$ imposes a power-law distribution on the choice of successors due to recombination rather than a uniform distribution.  Note that this result is quite similar in character to that presented in Equation 6, which was derived using a different approach and assumptions.  Also note that these formulae consider only the chance of drawing individual i as the highest ranked offspring, and do not consider for the 2nd highest ranked offspring, which also survives in the algorithm described here.

In (Tackett 1994) and (Tackett and Carmi 1994b) it was shown under a limited problem domain that using a reduced cost function set $F_B$ with $C_B << C_P$ (see Section 2.1) was effective in reducing CPU and memory resource use while improving the quality of solutions found.  A typical method of achieving this is to use a decimated set of training samples.  For example, in an induction problem with 200 training samples a subset of 30 or 40 samples might be used to evaluate the 2N members of the "brood," while a robot control algorithm might be tested in a very simplified environment relative to that used to evaluate fitness of a member of the population proper.  No quantitative theory is offered here concerning these properties under genetic programming, although the biological literature has developed sophisticated treatments in the context of living systems (Kozslowski and  Stearns 1989).  Quantitatively, the random recombination of portions of computer programs seems more likely than not to produce garbage code, and so even a crude filtering of potential successors may effectively cull entirely worthless individuals.  The principle of reduced-cost brood evaluation is applied in the experiments to be described here, and Section 5 discusses ways in which $F_B$ may be created adaptively and ways in which the quality of $F_B$ may be measured.

In summary, $R_B(n)$ substitutes a randomized version of greedy search for the otherwise random choice of insertion sites.  It does not affect the average branching factor due to recombination, nor does it affect the probability with which states will be selected to participate in recombination.  Once the two parent states are selected it does not affect the number of possible successors which can be generated from that pair through different choices of subexpression insertion and donation sites.  What it does affect is the probability with which those sites are chosen.  Therefore we may expect to see effects of $R_B(n)$ which are somewhat decoupled from methods of selection used.  Evidence of this is provided in Section 4.

### 3.3. Comparison of $R_B(n)$ to Other Methods

Having established greedy recombination in the context of genetic algorithms and AI search, it is worth briefly examining methods which use related principles. The idea of reduced evaluation $F_B$ for offspring is borrowed fairly directly from biology, however given the arguments of Section 3.2 it is possible to consider this principle as a form of *constraint satisfaction* (Waltz 1975). A second and equally important analogy can be drawn with Evolution Strategies, particularly the $(\mu,\lambda)$-ES method.

### 3.3.1. Constraint Satisfaction Methods

Constraint satisfaction is used in AI search in order to cut off branches of the search tree which involve a disallowed state. This is done by examining some relatively small subset of factors which are not allowed to exist in certain combinations. Only if this subset is legal --if the constraints are satisfied-- is it necessary to perform a more in-depth examination of a state in order to determine heuristic worth. The analogy to $R_B(n)$ is that if an individual performs very poorly on some fitness sample subset $F_B$, then it is likely that the same individual will have correspondingly poor performance on the general problem. This makes the basic assumption that there is strong correlation between fitness distribution induced by $F_B$ and that induced by the general population fitness evaluation function (Section 5).

### 3.3. 2. Differences Between $(\mu,\lambda)$-ES and $R_B(n)$

Evolution Strategies (ES) are a method for function optimization which were developed independently of the Genetic Algorithm, but share many common features which typically include population, selection, recombination, and mutation. One popular variety of this method is the $(\mu,\lambda)$-ES (Bäck and Schwefel 1993), in which recombination is used to produce a set of offspring of size $\lambda$ from a population of size $\mu$ where $1 < \mu < \lambda$. The best $\mu$ of these offspring are deterministically selected after all offspring have been generated. The algorithm for generating the new population can be stated as follows. Without loss of generality we assume that offspring are generated through 2-parent recombination:

**For i** = 1 to $\lambda/2$ do:

    **Select** 2 parents

    **Generate 2 offspring** through recombination

    **Evaluate fitness** of new offspring.

**EndFor i**. {There is now a set of offspring candidates of size $\lambda$}

**Cull** the $\mu$ fittest offspring from the global set of $\lambda$ new individuals.

By contrast, we can state $R_B(n)$ as follows. Without loss of generality we let brood size factor N (assumed to be an integer greater than 1) be equal to $\lambda/\mu$:

**For i** = 1 to $\mu/2$ do:

    **Select** 2 parents

> **For j** = 1 to $\lambda/\mu$ do:
>
>> **Generate 2 offspring** through recombination
>>
>> **Evaluate fitness** of new offspring.
>
> **EndFor j**. {There is now a set of offspring candidates of size $2\lambda/\mu$}
>
> **Cull** the 2 fittest offspring from the local set of $2\lambda/\mu$ new individuals.

**EndFor i**.

Under these conditions, both methods produce a population of $\mu$ new members from a population of $\mu$ old members, generating a total of $\lambda$ candidate offspring in the process. Examining the respective algorithms it is clear that although both select stochastically and cull deterministically, $R_B(n)$ does so on a local basis while $(\mu,\lambda)$-ES does so on a global basis. One direct implication of this is that while selection of a parent pair under $R_B(n)$ guarantees that offspring from that pairing will survive in the next generation, the same is not true of $(\mu,\lambda)$-ES. Effectively, under $(\mu,\lambda)$-ES some selected parents will have many offspring while other parents have none. This leads to speculation that $(\mu,\lambda)$-ES is a greedier technique than $R_B(n)$. Practical aspects of both methods confound some of these comparisons, such as the fact that selection is generally performed with a uniform random distribution in $(\mu,\lambda)$-ES while it is performed with a fitness proportionate or tournament method under $R_B(n)$. Likewise, $R_B(n)$ is specifically coupled to the recombination operator while $(\mu,\lambda)$-ES is applied across the board with all operators. Some of these considerations, such as the performance of $R_B(n)$ under uniform selection, will be addressed experimentally in the following sections, while others must be considered as areas for future investigation. Likewise, $R_B(n)$ may be of interest as an operator to practitioners of Evolution Strategies.

## 4. Experiments

### 4.1. Constructional Problems for Genetic Programming

Genetic programming has traditionally performed semantic evaluation of expressions in order to determine their fitness. Such problems do not lend themselves well to the study of how genetic programming may use building blocks, to paraphrase (Goldberg 1989), "[to] construct better and better [trees] from the best partial solutions of past samplings." The Boolean n-parity function (Koza 1992) is a scaleable difficult problem for which a solution *may* be recursively composed from partial solutions, but not *necessarily* so. Often, a problem sufficiently difficult to be interesting yields parsimonious yet "unexpected" solutions with no consistent set of intermediate building blocks: (Kinnear 1993) provides a good example of this. Other difficult problems such as the induction problem described in (Tackett 1994) may have no known solution whatsoever, and only comparative performance in relation to other methods may be measured. Finally, the difficulty which arises in a problem may not be structural: a subtle change in the atomic functions or terminals may yield easy solutions to a previously intractable problem (Reynolds 1994a; 1994b). In almost all cases, it is possible for genetic programming to construct programs with high fitness whose structure cannot be easily understood (Tackett 1994): in such instances it is hard to tell which subexpressions of a program actually contribute to fitness and which are "hitchhiking" (Forrest and Mitchell 1993). In the context of testing a new operator we wish to devise problems which minimize these sources of ambiguity.

Researchers in Genetic Algorithms have long turned to pattern-based problems in order to better understand the genetic search procedure: fitnesses may be assigned to particular bit patterns in order to create false peaks which render them *deceptive* (Goldberg 1989). Likewise, fitnesses may be assigned to building blocks in ascending order of complexity to yield a *Royal Road* problem that "should" be ideally solvable by a Genetic Algorithm (Forrest and Mitchell 1993). The genetic programming analogy we refer to generically as a *constructional problem,* defined by a set **T** of *target* expressions $T_m$ {m=1...M} to which are assigned fitness values $w_m$. In a constructional problem program P is searched for expression $T_m$, and assigned value $w_m$ when a match occurs. In the system implemented by the author a variety of wildcards are allowed, and the option exists to vary fitness value according to the number of times $T_m$ occurs within P. For the purpose of this discussion, however, a relatively minimal problem is implemented. A single set of patterns **T** is used, and the set of fitness values **w** is altered to produce variations upon a genetic programming analogy of the Royal Road problem.

Figure 5 depicts the pattern set both in expression and pictorial "tree" form. The goal is to construct an expression solely consisting of the pattern **(BAZ (BAR Z X) (FOO X Y))**. Any expression which matches this pattern exactly receives a fitness of 1.0 (out of a possible 1.0). Expressions which contain **(BAR Z X)** or **(FOO X Y)** (or both) are assigned a fitness of at least 0.125. Those which contain the more complex patterns **(BAZ $ANY (FOO X Y))** or **(BAZ (BAR Z X) $ANY)**, where the wildcard **$ANY** matches any subexpression, are assigned a fitness of at least 0.25. The two problems used here differ only in the fitness assigned when the expression **(BAZ (BAR Z X) (FOO X Y))** is matched to a proper subexpression of P. For the Royal Road a value of 0.5 is assigned, while for the deceptive problem a value of 0.125 is assigned. In the former case intermediate solutions are assigned fitness which increases monotonically, providing "stepping stones" to the solution. In the latter case there is a fitness "valley" between intermediate solutions and the final solution. For convenience we refer to the nonmonotonic case as a deceptive problem, although it is important to note that a truly deceptive problem requires rigorous definitions of the schema theorem and building block hypothesis applied to genetic programming, which do not currently exist. A more proper terminology might be a *"Royal Road with potholes"* as suggested by (Holland 1994).

In addition to the functions and terminals necessary to construct the fitness-producing target patterns, initial populations includes several "inert" functions: **NOP_1**, **NOP_2**, and **NOP_4**, have 1, 2, and 4 arguments respectively and do not match any pattern in **T** (except the sub-pattern **$ANY**). Numeric constants resulting from the pseudo-terminal RANFLOAT (Tackett 1994) comprise about 25% of the terminals of the initial population and they likewise do not match any target patterns.

### 4.2. Comparative Methods of Recombination and Selection

Three forms of selection are tested here, each alone and in conjunction with brood recombination for a total of six methods, or "breeding policies" (Tackett and Carmi 1994a). The three selection methods reflect differing degrees of greed, namely random selection (with no fitness bias at all),

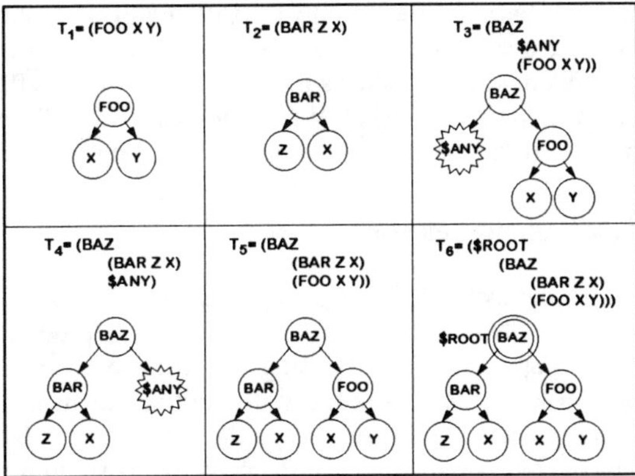



*Figure 5: Six patterns $T_i$ {i=1...6}. Each is matched against a program P sequentially, and if a match is made with some subexpression within P, then P is assigned fitness $w_i$. The pseudofunction $ROOT requires that its argument match the entire expression P. The wildcard $ANY matches any subexpression, including terminals. For the Royal Road the $w_i$ are {0.125, 0.125, 0.25, 0.25, 0.5, 1.0}. For the deceptive problem they are {0.125, 0.125, 0.25, 0.25, 0.125, 1.0}.*

tournament selection (a "standard" degree of bias towards choosing fitter individuals), and steady-state selection (strong fitness bias). For the three selection/recombination breeding policies that do not include $R_B(n)$ a population size of $N_1 = 500$ is used. Those which employ $R_B(n)$ use a population of size $N_2 = 250$ with n=5: each mating under $R_B(5)$ results in a total of ten offspring of which the best two "survive." The culling function $F_B$ consists of the patterns $\{T_1, T_2, T_3\}$ and their associated fitness values. The combination of population sizes and culling function $F_B$ are chosen a-priori based on experience using $R_B(n)$ on the donut problem, and inductive feature classification task described in (Tackett 1994, Tackett and Carmi 1994a). Brood-size factor n=5 is determined empirically so that runs with and without brood recombination run in approximately the same amount of CPU time. No attempt is made to optimize relative performance based on these parameters.

Selection and recombination are the only operators employed: mutation and other techniques are eschewed in order to reduce ambiguity of results. Those breeding policies which do not employ $R_B(n)$ instead apply crossover exactly as set forth in (Koza 1992) using the "crossover-at-any-point" method. Individuals in the initial population are limited to a depth of 4, and individuals resulting from crossover are limited to a depth of 6. When individuals are chosen via selection, 50% participate in recombination while the other 50% are cloned (generation gap = 50% of population size). The three selection methods are detailed below.

### 4.2.1. Random Selection

Random selection chooses parents according to a uniform random choice, and therefore is not driven by fitness. Individuals and the subexpressions which they comprise survive from generation to generation with distributions affected only by drift and by disruption/creation due to recombination. Under standard crossover there is no bias whatsoever to drive the population to greater fitness. Under $R_B(n)$ random selection allows the isolation of fitness effects due to greedy recombination. This latter method is somewhat similar to the $(\mu,\lambda)$-ES method, in which selection is random and only a global selection among an oversampling of offspring biases populations towards greater fitness.

### 4.2.2. Generational K-Tournament Selection

The tournament method is recognized as having improved properties relative to fitness-proportionate selection (Whitley 1989; Goldberg and Deb 1991). It proceeds by selecting K individuals at random from the population and choosing the fittest one. Individuals resulting from cloning and recombination are generated sequentially and stored in a list with no effect upon the population from which parents are drawn. When the list of new individuals is equal to the population size it replaces the old population. Tournament size is set to K=6; this value has been recommended as a good choice over a large range of conditions (Rice 1992), and corroborated by experiments documented in (Tackett 1994).

### 4.2.3. Steady-State K-Tournament Selection

Steady-State selection, is used here to represent greedy selection procedures. In genetic programming it has been used to advantage, for example, in (Kinnear 1993). Rather than creating a new population "batch" as described above, individuals are created and tested continuously. The key performance feature of this method arises from the fact that when new individuals are created they replace some existing member of the population: the "building blocks" comprising the replaced individual are lost in favor of those belonging to the offspring of some fitter (in probability) individuals. Performance depends critically on how individuals are selected for replacement (DeJong 1993). In particular, overly greedy replacement methods such as choosing the worst member of the population are typically detrimental to performance and should be avoided. The implementation performed here uses K-tournaments (K=6) to select "winners" for duplication and recombination, and to likewise select the "losers" which will be replaced.

### 4.3. Results for Constructional Problems

Each of the six breeding policies is run twenty times with the same set of twenty different random seeds. This results in the same twenty initial populations for all breeding policies with the exception that runs using $R_B(n)$ have half the initial population size of the non-$R_B(n)$ runs, and so are a proper subset. Each curve in the comparative performance plots shown here is a composite taken over the 20 runs.

### 4.3.1. Cumulative Probability of Success

This measure was described in (Koza 1992) and is used as a standard measure of relative difficulty for GP problems which possess an absolute criteria for "success," i.e. a known optimal fitness value. Cumulative probability of success (CPS) is defined for a given generation as the fraction of runs performed which found an individual with optimal fitness on or before that generation (in this case for example, CPS must increment in steps which are multiples of 0.05

since there are 20 runs). This measure integrates results both over time and across sample runs, so tending to reduce sample noise. For both problems, the CPS measure approaches asymptotic limits of success by the 24th generation. Due to convergence, it is unlikely that these curves would ever reach 100% cumulative probability of success even in a very large number of generations. For further details see (Koza 1992). CPS vs. Generation for each breeding policy against the Royal Road problem is shown in Figure 5, and CPS for the Deceptive Problem is shown in Figure 6. In all cases, $R_B(n)$ appears to speed convergence by a small amount, but for the case of the Royal Road all methods using non-random selection achieve roughly equal performance. The deceptive problem provides a different story: $R_B(n)$ with generational selection finds solutions more frequently than other methods.

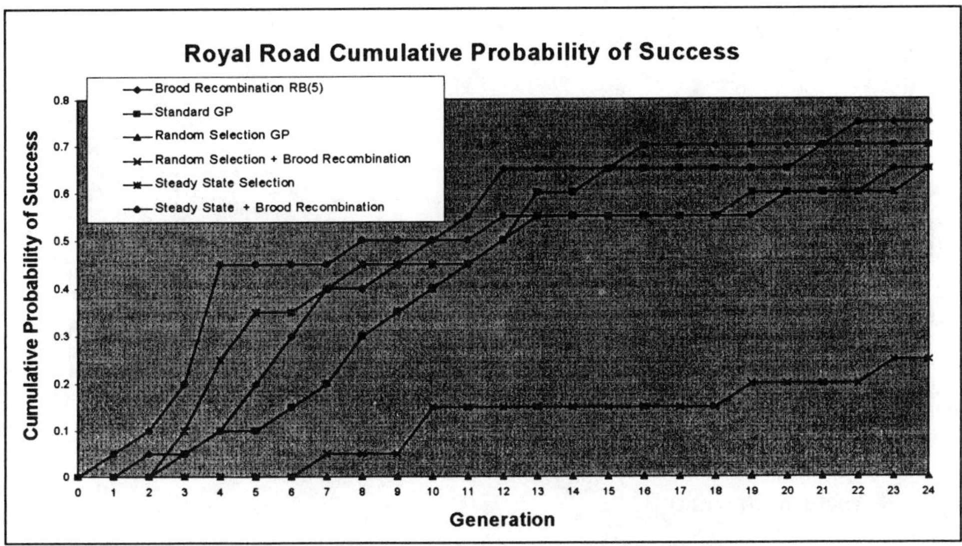


*Figure 5: Cumulative Probability of success for the Royal Road Problem.*

An interesting illustration of the exploratory power of $R_B(n)$ is provided by looking at the curves for CPS under random selection: whereas random selection by itself never finds a perfect solution, random selection under $R_B(n)$ does. As a matter of fact, in generation 24 of the Deceptive problem *it has the second-best performance!* Also note that the random-selection curves are the same for both problems: fitness values do not affect random selection, and $F_B$ is the same for both problems.

### 4.3.2. Standard Deviation of Population Fitness Distributions

According to Fisher's fundamental theory of natural selection (Fisher 1930; 1958) the ability of a population to increase in fitness is proportional to the variance in fitness of the population members. Standard deviation of population fitness, shown in Figures 7 and 8, is just the square root of variance and therefore similarly affects fitness. Figure 7 shows fitness standard deviation for the Royal Road problem. Standard deviation varies strongly with selection method, and $R_B(n)$ appears to have very little effect. Figure 8 shows population fitness standard deviation for the deceptive problem, which is again most strongly dependent upon method of selection. Note that the greatest fitness variation is always achieved using the tournament selection method.

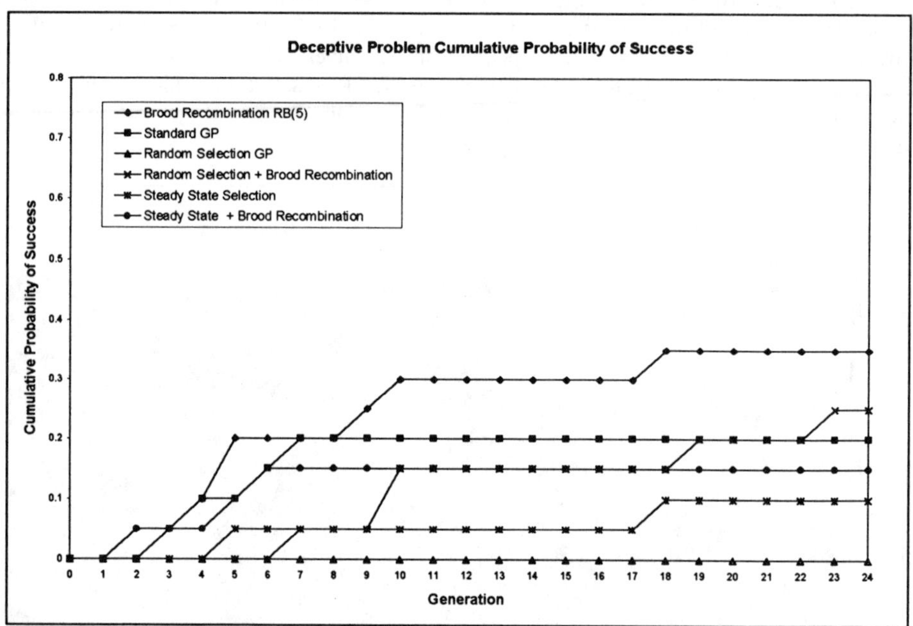


*Figure 6: Cumulative probability of success for Deceptive Problem.*

### 4.3.3. Structural Diversity

The final measurement made here is *structural diversity*. This describes the frequency with which new unique building blocks are formed as evolution proceeds. A list is made of all expressions and subexpressions occurring in the population based on an exhaustive search. The term "schemata" is used here to refer to expressions and subexpressions, duly noting that this is not a formal or binding definition. The list of schemata is maintained from generation to generation so that those schemata which are extinct (i.e., those which occur in the previous generation but not in the current generation) are removed from the list. A count is made of those schemata which are new to the list: they may be either entirely new or rediscovered after a previous extinction. Structural diversity is obtained by dividing the number of new schemata produced each generation by the population size. The result is the average number of new schemata per population member, which is an effective measure of the rate at which a particular breeding policy explores the space of program structures.

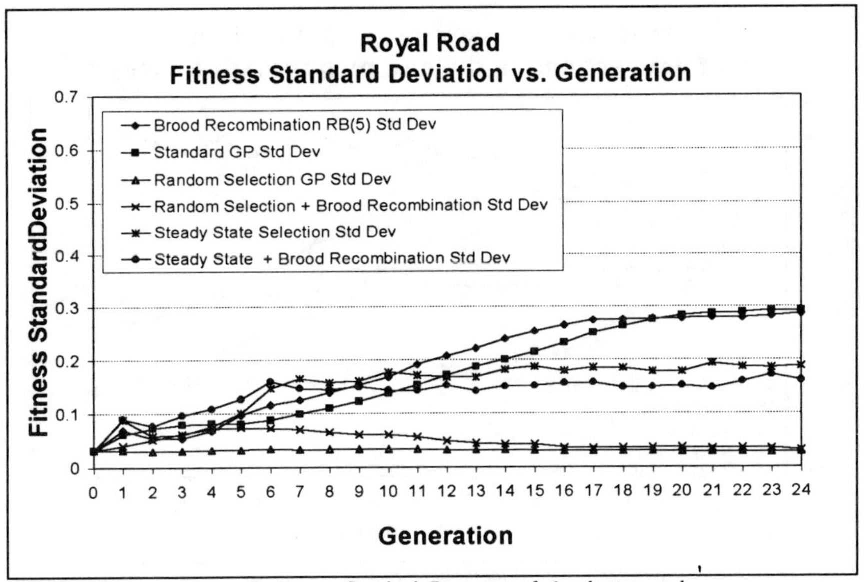


Figure 7: *Fitness Standard Deviation of 6 selection and recombination policies tested against the "Royal Road" problem.*

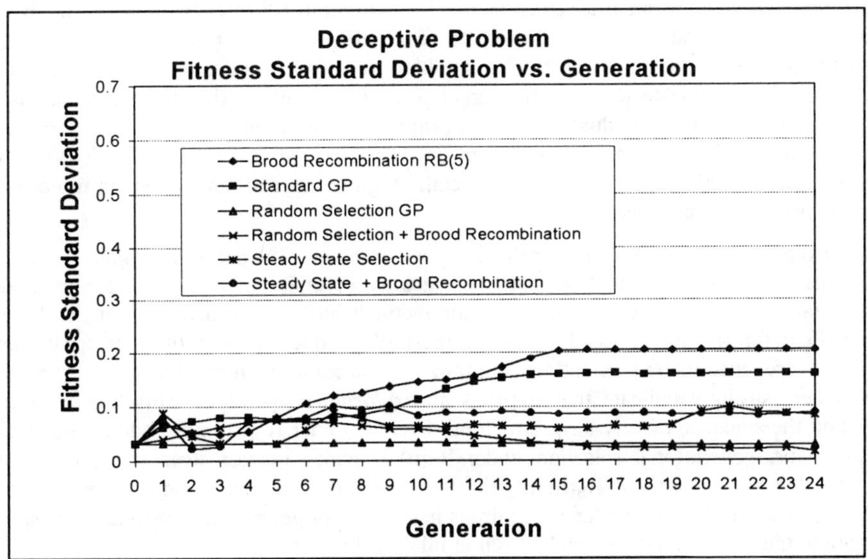


Figure 8: *Fitness Standard Deviation of 6 selection and recombination policies tested against the "Deceptive" problem.*

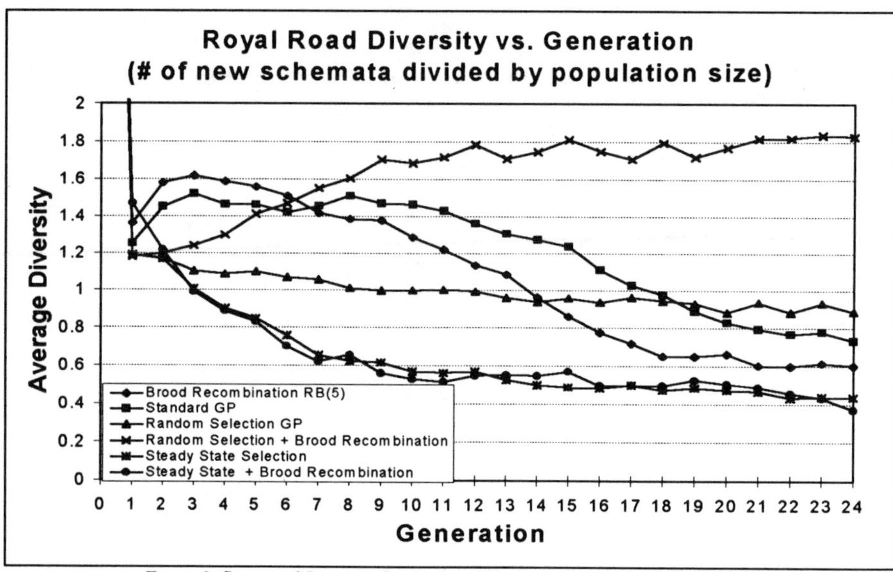



*Figure 9: Structural Diversity for the Royal Road problem.*

Figure 9 shows structural diversity for the Royal Road. Under random selection, $R_B(n)$ appears to produce new schemata at an increasing rate. Under random selection without $R_B(n)$ diversity slowly decays, presumably due to the effects of genetic drift. For other methods diversity continually decays with time as "perfect" individuals are formed and proliferate throughout the population. This is due to the fact that target pattern $T_6$ requires that no other schemata be present in the matching individual, and so its proliferation inhibits diversity. The intermediate targets $T_1$ through $T_5$ may appear within any greater structure and do not penalize structural diversity. Note that all methods have an artificially high number of new schemata in generation 0 since *all* are new at that time.

Figure 10 shows structural diversity for the deceptive problem. The curves are again the same for random selection. Generational selection has greater diversity than steady-state methods as might be expected, and all non-random selection methods have higher diversity for the deceptive problem than for the Royal Road. This is most likely due the fact that far fewer perfect individuals are encountered, therefore minimizing selection against diversity. The results obtained here strongly indicate that $R_B(n)$ is an *exploratory* operator. This may be initially inferred on the evidence of very large structural diversity under $R_B(n)$ and random selection. In both problems, generational selection under $R_B(n)$ provides greater structural diversity than generational selection without $R_B(n)$ for the first eight generations or so. After that point, however, structural diversity under $R_B(n)$ drops below that of generational selection, most likely due again to the fact that the "optimal" solution inhibits diversity.

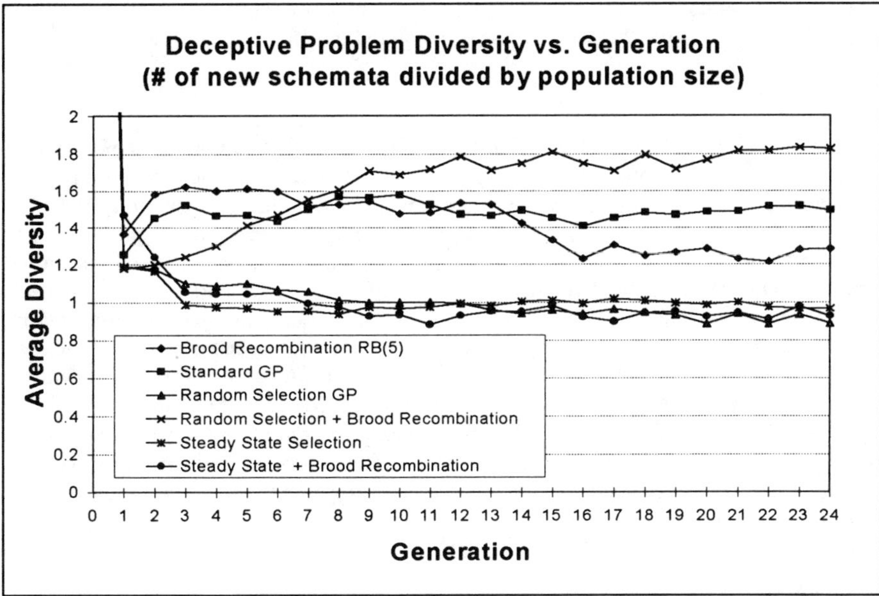


*Figure 10: Structural Diversity for the Deceptive Problem.*

## 4.4. Results Using Constructional Problems

Three measures were used in the constructional problems to measure algorithm performance. The problems themselves were differentiated through the alteration of a single parameter, changing a unimodal fitness landscape to a (quasi-) deceptive one with a fitness "valley." The first measure, cumulative probability of success (CPS), is essentially a measure of the likelihood with which the search procedure will produce a solution. The notable result is that while all methods did about equally well on the unimodal problem, when a degree of deception was introduced $R_B(n)$ became about 75% more likely to solve the problem. In both problems, the isolated effects of $R_B(n)$ in conjunction with random selection (i.e., no exponential allocation of trials to successful strategies) was able to find solutions, and in the case of the deceptive problem the random-selection $R_B(n)$ method outperformed some other breeding policies which employed selection.

The second measure, standard deviation, is proportional to fitness variance and therefore to the rate at which the population can be expected to evolve. The critical observation is that $R_B(n)$ does not appear to affect population variance, which is most strongly correlated to selection method. Finally, the measure of structural diversity indicates that $R_B(n)$ is beneficial to the production of new schemata, but at the same time illustrates a flaw in the formulation of the constructional problems used here, namely that an individual with perfect fitness has an exact form, and so is guaranteed under fitness-driven selection to inhibit diversity when found. Such problems may occasionally be encountered, particularly if size of expressions is incorporated as a fitness penalty, but this is not the general case encountered in genetic programming.

## 5. Discussion

Earlier work (Tackett 1994, Tackett and Carmi 1994b) provided encouraging demonstrations of greedy recombination on a type of problem typically encountered in genetic programming. These results indicated improvements in performance and a simultaneous reduction in CPU and memory costs as summarized in Figure 1. Here, a theoretical approach was taken in order to explain improvements in performance due to $R_B(n)$. A statistical analysis showed that improved performance could be expected, but this required simplifying assumptions due to interactions with the process of selection. In order to better understand $R_B(n)$ and genetic programming in general we then returned to first principles, posing these processes as beam search on the space of computer programs. This yielded an exact characterization of the expected improvement due to $R_B(n)$ when $F_B$ is the same as the population fitness function. Further analysis showed the relation of $R_B(n)$ to $(\mu,\lambda)$-ES methods. Finally, a demonstration of $R_B(n)$ was provided in the context of constructional problems, with fitness based upon syntax rather than semantics in order to show differential effects of operators with respect to changes in the fitness landscape. We now conclude with some observations concerning the methods used, their implications, and directions for future work.

### Genetic Programming as Heuristic Search

Search has provided a useful framework for analysis of $R_B(n)$. This is important due to the lack of a schema theorem and lack of a widely accepted formulation for building blocks in genetic programming. Search analysis allows the isolation of operators in order to consider their individual impact on overall performance. We suggest that the introduction of this methodology is important in its own right as a guide to the design of new operators and explanations of existing operators. As an example of this consider automatically defined functions (ADFs) in genetic programming (Koza 1994). In some problems, ability to find solutions can be greatly improved by using a genome which comprises a "main program" expression and one or more "sub-function" expressions, each of which may be called from multiple sites in the main. A program which makes M calls to a sub-function of size $SIZE_{SF}$, effectively contains $M \cdot SIZE_{SF}$ points (function and terminal nodes) which can vary in only $SIZE_{SF}$ degrees of freedom. This effectively projects the search space, which is exponentially vast in the size of expressions, to into one which is flatter by $(M-1) \cdot SIZE_{SF}$ dimensions. This theory explains results in (Kinnear 1994) wherein methods of sub-function generation that do not promote multiple calls do not show significant improvement in the generation of solutions.

The argument above illustrates just one example of how the search perspective may be applied in genetic programming. There are many others, ranging from population sizing and generation gaps to the creation of new successor operators beyond $R_B(n)$.

### Efficacy of Reduced-Cost Culling Function $F_B$

The results obtained here using constructional problems echo those of (Tackett 1994) in that reduced-cost fitness function $F_B$ is effective for achieving increased search performance at reduced computational cost. In the former case, $F_B$ was essentially chosen so as to be a subset of fitness cases which could not by themselves be used to arrive at the optimal solution. In the latter case $F_B$ was a fixed size subset of cases with an equal number chosen randomly from each class in an inductive classification problem. So then, how little investment of resources be can expended by $F_B$? Can $F_B$ be engineered or evolved to minimize the expense of the preselection process? An analytic theory of why reduced-cost $F_B$ is effective is not offered here. For most problems there are clearly useless or deceptive $F_B$ which can be constructed from some subset of the fitness cases. We can, however, formulate a direct measure of the effectiveness of $F_B$ and propose methods by which $F_B$ can be adaptively formulated.

The are many ways to formulate the quality of $F_B$, but most of them can be considered as some variation on the question: *how closely do the "surviving" brood members chosen by $F_B$ correlate with those which would be chosen by the full-fledged population fitness evaluation function $F_P$ ?* It is simple to quantify this measure by considering the choice of one offspring as the survivor $S_j$ from a brood of N offspring produced in brood recombination event $j$ $(1 \leq j \leq J)$. Let $Sj(F)$ be a function which returns a selected offspring from a brood of N as a function of the fitness evaluation criterion F. Consider then the vector **f** with J elements where:

12.
$$\mathbf{f}(j) = 0 \text{ iff } Sj(F_B) \neq Sj(F_P)$$

and

13.
$$\mathbf{f}(j) = 1 \text{ iff } Sj(F_B) = Sj(F_P)$$

Then the quality **Q** of $F_B$ is just the normalized degree to which the two criteria agree, which is the number of nonzero elements in **f**(j) divided by J, the length of the vector:

14.
$$\mathbf{Q}(F_B) = \frac{1}{J} \sum_{j=i}^{J} \mathbf{f}(j)$$

There are many possible variations on this theme, including sophisticated measures of fitness correlation and mutual information transmission between $F_B$ and $F_P$.

A major drawback to the methods outlined above is that they require the use of the full-fledged fitness measure in order to determine quality of $F_B$. This is good for providing an off-line assessment of $F_B$ but is at cross purposes to cost reduction of the on-line learning process. An alternative method for obtaining high-quality $F_B$ on-line employs a process of cooperative coevolution. Co-evolved training sets each include a "fitness tag" variable, which is initially zero. During a generation, each set is used to evaluate and select the offspring from some number of population members, which must be kept track of. After the new population has been evaluated, credit assignment is made to fitness tags of each training set based on relative fitness of the individuals which they chose. An alternative approach might be taken in which individuals of the $F_B$ population are single fitness cases instead of sets of fitness cases.

## Acknowledgments

Thanks to: Lee Altenberg for introducing me to the mathematics and biology of soft brood selection, to Jean-Luc Gaudiot for many discussions and readings of this manuscript, to Paul Rosenbloom for suggestions concerning the relation of genetic programming to search, and to Dave Andre and Scott Coon for providing a simplified formula for the probability distribution of $R_B(n)$.

## Bibliography


Altenberg, Lee (1993). Personal communication.

Altenberg, Lee (1994). "The Evolution of Evolvability in Genetic Programming." In Kinnear, K. E. (ed), *Advances in Genetic Programming*. Cambridge, MA: MIT Press.

Angeline, P. And Pollack, J. (1994) "Co-Evolving High-Level Representations." in Langton, C. (ed) *Artificial Life III, Santa Fe Institute Studies in the Sciences of Complexity, Proceedings Volume XVI*. Redwood City, CA: Addison Wesley.

Bäck, T., and Schwefel, H. (1993) An overview of evolutionary algorithms for parameter optimization. *Evolutionary Computation* v1n1, pp 1-24.

Darwin, Charles (1876) *The Effect of Cross and Self Fertilisation in the Vegetable Kingdom*. Murray, London, UK.

DeJong, Kenneth A. (1993) "Generation Gaps Revisited." in Whitley, L. D. (ed) (1993) *Foundations of Genetic Algorithms 2*. Morgan Kaufmann.

Fisher, R.A. (1930; 1958) *The Genetical Theory of Natural Selection,(2ed)*. Dover Press, New York.

Forrest, Stephanie, and Mitchell, Melanie (1993) "Relative Building-Block Fitness and the Building-Block Hypothesis" in Whitley, L. D. (ed) (1993) *Foundations of Genetic Algorithms 2*. Morgan Kaufmann.

Goldberg, David E. (1989)*Genetic Algorithms in Search, Optimization, and Machine Learning*. Reading MA: Addison Wesley.

Goldberg, D.E., and Deb, K. (1991) A comparative analysis of selection schemes used in genetic algorithms. In Rawlins, J.E. (ed) *Foundations of Genetic Algorithms*. Morgan Kaufmann.

Holland, John H. (1975; 1992) *Adaptation in Natural and Artificial Systems*. Cambridge, MA: MIT Press.

Holland, John H. (1994) Personal communication , Santa Fe Institute April 1994.

Hu, T.C. (1982) *Combinatorial Algorithms*. Menlo Park, CA: Addison-Wesley.

Kinnear, Kenneth E. (1993) "Evolving a Sort: Lessons in Genetic Programming." In *Proceedings of the 1993 International Conference on Neural Networks*. New York, NY: IEEE Press.

Kinnear, Kenneth E. (1994) "Alternatives in Automatically Defined Functions." In Kinnear, K. E. (ed), *Advances in Genetic Programming.* Cambridge, MA: MIT Press.

Korf, R.E. (1987). Search. In: Shapiro, S. (Ed.) *Encyclopedia of Artificial Intelligence, Vol. 2.* New York, NY: Wiley.

Koza, John R. (1992)*Genetic Programming.* Cambridge, MA: MIT Press.

Koza, John R. (1994)*Genetic Programming II: Automatic Discovery of Reusable Programs.* Cambridge, MA: MIT Press.

Kozlowski, J., and Stearns, S.C., 1989. "Hypothesis for the Production of Excess Zygotes: Models of Bet-Hedging and Selective Abortion." *Evolution.* 43(7):1369-1377.

Lowerre, B.T., and Reddy, R.D. (1980) The Harpy speech understanding system. In: Lea, W.A. (Ed.) *Trends in Speech Recognition.* Englewood Cliffs, NJ: Prentice-Hall.

Price, G.R. (1970) "Selection and Covariance.: Nature 227:520-521.

Reynolds, Craig W. (1994a) "Evolution of Obstacle Avoidance Behavior: Using Noise to Promote Robust Solutions." In *Advances in Genetic Programming.* Kinnear, K. E. (ed), Cambridge, MA: MIT Press.

Reynolds, Craig W. (1994b) "The Difficulty of Roving Eyes." *Proceedings of the First IEEE Conference on Evolutionary Computation, June 27-29, 1994.* IEEE Press.

Rice, James P. (1992) Personal communication, Palo Alto CA.

Rosenbloom, P. (1987). Best first search. In: Shapiro, S. (Ed.) *Encyclopedia of Artificial Intelligence, Vol. 2.* New York, NY: Wiley.

Stearns, Stephen C. (1987) "The Selection Arena Hypothesis." In Stearns, S.C. (ed), The Evolution of Sex and Its Consequences. Burkhauser, Basel, Switzerland.

Syswerda, G. (1989) "Uniform Crossover in Genetic Algorithms." In Schaffer, J. (ed) *Proceedings of the Third International Conference on Genetic Algorithms.* Morgan Kaufmann.

Tackett, Walter A. (1993) "Genetic programming for feature discovery and image discrimination. In Forrest, S. (ed) *Proceedings of the Fifth International Conference on Genetic Algorithms,* Urbana-Champaign IL. Morgan Kaufmann.

Tackett, Walter A. (1994) *Recombination, Selection, and the Genetic Construction of Computer Programs.* Ph.D. Dissertation. Available as: Technical Report CENG 94-13. Dept. of Electrical Engineering Systems, University of Southern California, April 1994.

Tackett, Walter A., and Carmi, A. (1994a) The donut problem: Scalability, generalization, and breeding policy in the genetic programming, Chapter 7 of: Kinnear, K. (ed) *Evolution of Genetic Programming.* MIT Press.

Tackett, Walter A. and Carmi, Aviram (1994b) "The Unique Implications of Brood Selection for Genetic Programming." *Proceedings of the First IEEE Conference on Evolutionary Computation, Orlando FL, June 27-29, 1994.* IEEE Press.

Waltz, D.L., "Understanding Line Drawings of Scenes with Shadows," in *The Psychology of Computer Vision*, P. Winston (Ed.), McGraw-Hill, New York 1975.

Whitley, D. (1989) "The GENITOR Algorithm and Selection Pressure: Why Rank-Based Allocation of Reproductive Trials is Best." In Schaffer, J. (ed) *Proceedings of the Third International Conference on Genetic Algorithms.* Morgan Kaufmann.

# Productive Recombination and Propagating and Preserving Schemata


**Larry J. Eshelman and J. David Schaffer**
Philips Laboratories
North American Philips Corporation
345 Scarborough Road
Briarcliff Manor, New York 10510


## Abstract


Stochastic sampling algorithms, the class to which genetic algorithms (GAs) belong, may be characterized by their sampling biases. A stronger bias will generally yield more efficient search, and thus better function optimization, but on a smaller class of problems than a weaker bias. We identify two biases for studying crossover operators—*recombinative bias* and *schema bias*—and demonstrate how they affect GA performance on specific problem classes. We show how a combination of high recombinative bias and low schema bias can combat premature convergence due to hitchhiking. However, high recombinative bias can be a liability for problems with competing conventions or traps. Competing conventions are a crossover-frustrating form of multimodality introduced by the representation. Traps lead to a phenomenon analogous to Gresham's Law in Economics where bad schemata drive out good schemata. We argue that it is susceptibility to this phenomenon that predicts whether a GA will be mislead and not the property of being fully deceptive. Finally, we present a method for automatically adapting the recombinative bias to the function being optimized.


## 1   INTRODUCTION

Only two search algorithms are bias free: random search and exhaustive enumeration. They work equally well, but equally inefficiently, on all problems. To improve efficiency of search one introduces some means of exploiting the information in previous samples to bias future samples. Such a practice will invariably divide the space of problems into two classes: those on which the bias is effective (or at least not ineffective), and those on which the bias will be deceived (the Achilles' heel of the bias).

What distinguishes genetic algorithms (GAs) from other types of evolutionary-based algorithms is the role played by recombination. Beginning with Holland's original work (Holland, 1975), recombination has been seen as the primary search operator and mutation has been relegated to a background operator needed to restore lost alleles. We believe that this stress on recombination is important, but that the traditional analysis of GA behavior, by focusing on schemata in a current population and their expected sampling in subsequent generations, tends to obscure rather than highlight the importance of recombination. Our first goal in this paper is to restore recombination to its proper place by focusing on what we call crossover's recombinative bias.

In the next section we identify two biases for studying crossover operators: recombinative bias and schema bias. In the third section we argue that a crossover operator with a strong recombinative bias and a weak schema bias will be better at combating spurious correlations. In the fourth section we identify two failure modes associated with strong recombinative bias. In the fifth section we present a mechanism for automatically selecting between two crossover operators with different recombinative biases.

## 2   PRODUCTIVE RECOMBINATION

The intuitive idea behind recombination is that by combining features (or building blocks) from two good parents crossover will often produce even better children. What we want a recombination operator to do is copy high valued building blocks from both parents, simultaneously instantiating them in the same child (Radcliffe, 1991). Characterizing these building blocks in terms of schemata makes this intuition more precise (Holland, 1975). In our opinion, however, the traditional analysis takes a wrong turn by giving undue emphasis to propagation—on how many schemata present in one parent are expected to survive recombination.

The reason for this emphasis is easy to understand. In the GA first analyzed by Holland, the parents are replaced by their offspring before the offspring are evaluated. Individuals 'live' for only a single reproductive cycle, or generation. Thus, good schemata can only be *preserved* if they are *propagated*. Thus, propagation and preservation must both be achieved simultaneously, usually by employing a crossover operator that is good at propagating schemata (i.e., is not very disruptive). As we have argued previously, however, such a GA is prone to a pernicious failure mode, premature convergence, by failing to disrupt spurious correlations (hitchhiking) (Schaffer et al, 1991).

The problem does not lie with recombination. The culprit is the revolutionary replacement strategy adopted by the 'traditional' GA. (Its basic policy toward parents is "Off with their heads!") The alternative is a conservative or elitist replacement strategy in which children replace the worst members of the parent population.[1] This replacement scheme guarantees

---

[1]It should be noted that this distinction is independent of whether one adopts an incremental or generational GA. Because the two best known incremental approaches, Syswerda's steady-state GA (Syswerda, 1991) and Whitley's GENITOR (Whitley, 1989), both use a conservative replacement strategy (offspring are added to the population one or two at a time, replacing the worst one or two members of the parent population), it is often assumed that such a replacement strategy goes hand-in-hand with an incremental GA. But an incremental GA need not adopt such a strategy: a parent (or two) could be replaced at random each cycle. On the other hand, a generational GA

the survival of all schemata in parents who are more fit than the new generation of offspring. By separating propagation from preservation, a conservative replacement strategy allows for a more vigorously disruptive form of crossover to be used with less worry about balancing exploration against exploitation. Instead the exploitiveness of the algorithm will adjust to the problem.

To understand why this is the case, first consider an algorithm where the only selection scheme is conservative replacement, applied without recombination or mutation (i.e., the offspring are identical to their parents). In such a case, the best individual will take over a population of size $M$ in log $M$ generations (Goldberg and Deb, 1991). However, when recombination is used, especially a vigorously disruptive from of recombination, the exploitiveness of the algorithm, defined in terms of the takeover rate, will vary depending upon the 'difficulty' of the problem. For problems where it is difficult to combine good schemata without disrupting them, very few offspring will be produced that are accepted into the parent population (i.e., that are better than the worst members of the parent population). Thus, the takeover rate will be quite low relative to the number of evaluations, and it will take a long time for the population to converge. On the other hand, if it is easy to find good combinations of schemata, many acceptable offspring will be produced, and the takeover rate will be high, and the algorithm will quickly converge to a good solution. In effect, the selection pressure of the algorithm will be self-adjusting, depending on the 'difficulty' of the problem. Of course, in so far as the difficulty of recombining schemata does not reflect the difficulty of the problem, such an algorithm can be mislead or stymied. (Later in this paper, we will discuss two classes of problems that have this property.)

With preservation of all the schemata in the surviving parents assured, we can now concentrate on the tradeoff between effective recombination and propagation. The nature of this tradeoff can be seen by examining the formula for the number of schemata ($N_s$) propagated via crossover, where $d$ is the Hamming distance between the parents, and $x$ is the number of differing bits inherited from the furthest parent:[2]

$$N_s = 2^x + 2^{(d-x)}$$

Note that the number of schemata guaranteed to be propagated is greatest when the operator does no recombining, i.e., when $x = 0$. On the other hand, the number of schemata guaranteed to be propagated is the lowest when $x = d/2$. A crossover operator that crosses over half the differing bits will be most likely to combine valuable schemata simply for the reason that the maximum number of schemata is combined from each parent, and assuming that we have no a priori reason for favoring some schemata over others. We shall refer to the expected proportion of the differing bits that a crossover operator copies to a child from its furthest parent (in terms of Hamming distance) as the measure of its *recombinative bias*.[3]

---

need not adopt a revolutionary replacement strategy. In the '$\mu+\lambda$' version of evolution strategy (Bäck et al, 1991) and Eshelman's CHC algorithm (Eshelman, 1991), a set of offspring are created and evaluated, replacing members of the parent population only if they are superior.

  [2]Note that $x \leq d/2$. Since we count only the $x$ bits that differ between the parents, the $N_s$ schemata we are examining do not include those schemata involving the loci where the parents agree. All crossover operators propagate those.

  [3]Recombinative bias equals $E(x/d)$. Recombinative bias is similar to what we called in an earlier paper distributive bias (Eshelman et al, 1989); however, we put more emphasis here on the expected amount of material that is exchanged, rather than its probability distribution. Also it should be noted that recombinative bias is not simply another name for disruption. It is true that one cannot

At one extreme is HUX, a variant of uniform crossover which swaps exactly half the differing bits. HUX has, by definition, a recombinative bias of 0.5, the greatest bias possible. This is because for HUX the expected (and, in the case of HUX, the actual) Hamming distance between a child and its furthest parent is half the Hamming distance between the two parents. The recombinative bias for regular uniform crossover's will vary, depending upon the rate at which the bits are swapped (Spears and De Jong, 1991). Two-point crossover (2X), on the other hand, has a recombinative bias of 0.25, assuming that it operates on the reduced surrogate, i.e., differing bits (Booker, 1987).[4] This is because the expected number bits that a child will inherit from its furthest parent will vary uniformly from 1 to $d/2$, and the mean of a uniform distribution is 0.5 of the range.

In order for a valuable schema to be recombined with schemata from another individual, it must be propagated. Likewise, in order for the performance of a valuable schema to be distinguished, it must be pried apart from other schemata.[5] Failure to pry apart the truly influential schemata from their hitchhiking neighbors results when a crossover operator privileges some schemata (e.g., those with short defining lengths) at the expense of others and can lead to premature convergence. We will call this privileging of certain schemata a recombination operator's *schema bias*. Schema bias is a generalization of positional bias (Eshelman et al, 1989). A recombination operator has no schema bias if all schemata of the same order are equally likely to be disrupted in a single mating of complementary strings. (Schema bias is closely related to what Radcliffe refers to as proper assortment (Radcliffe, 1991).)

One-point and two-point crossover have weak recombinative biases and strong schema biases. Uniform crossover (using a 0.5 probability of swapping bits) and HUX, on the other hand, have strong recombinative biases and weak schema biases. Hence, any empirical comparison of these operators will fail to discriminate between the contributions of these two biases. We designed shuffle crossover (SHX) to eliminate the schema bias of traditional segmented crossover (e.g., one or two-point crossover) while retaining the same recombinative bias (Eshelman et al, 1989). Shuffle crossover can be thought of as similar to traditional one-point crossover except that it randomly shuffles the bit positions of the two strings in tandem before crossing them over and then unshuffles the strings after the segments to the right of crossover point have been exchanged. Thus, crossover no longer has a single, consistent schema bias because the positions are randomly reassigned each time crossover is performed. Bits that are far apart are no more likely to be disrupted than bits that are close together. Alternatively, shuffle crossover can be thought of as similar to bitwise crossover operators such as HUX and uniform crossover except that the number of bits to be exchanged is first decided by choosing a random number $x$ (uniform distribution) between 1 and $d/2$ and then randomly picking (without replacement) $x$ loci for exchanging the bits. Thus, unlike uniform crossover, the number of differing bits exchanged varies uniformly from 1 to $d/2$ instead of being binomially distributed around $d/2$.

---

recombine schemata without disruption, but not all disruption is recombinative (e.g., the disruption produced by mutation).

[4] If the standard version of 2X is used, operating on the whole string instead of only the differing bits, then its recombinative bias will initially be 0.25, when operating on a random population, but will converge to zero as the population converges.

[5] Thierens and Goldberg (1993) refer to this as mixing.

# 3  SPURIOUS CORRELATIONS

We argued in the previous section that a strong recombinative bias coupled with a weak (or no) schema bias helps combat spurious correlations. Thus, one would expect that 2X would be the most subject to spurious correlations, HUX the least subject, and SHX in between. As a way of measuring the extent to which our three crossover operators are subject to spurious correlations, we tested all three algorithms on a 1000 bit Onemax problem (maximize the number of ones in the string).

Our basic test algorithm is CHC (Eshelman, 1991), using variant crossover operators (2X, UX, SHX). In our implementation of these three operators, each operates on the reduced surrogate, i.e., the differing bits, of the two parents. CHC uses a conservative replacement strategy as discussed earlier—the child population and the parent population are merged and the best $M$ (population size of 50 for all runs) individuals are chosen to make up the parent population for the next generation. Furthermore, this is the sole source of selection. In other words, when individuals are chosen for mating, there is no reproduction with emphasis—every member of the parent population is given an equal opportunity for mating regardless of fitness. However, if the two potential mates are too similar (defined in terms of their Hamming distance relative to a moving threshold), they are not allowed to mate—a form of incest prevention (Eshelman, et al 1991). Another feature of CHC is that it does not use mutation as a local operator, but relies solely upon recombination. Thus, there is no worry about mutation overwhelming the effects of the recombination operator. Instead, CHC uses restarts—i.e., the converged population is partially or fully randomized and seeded with one copy of the best individual found so far.[6]

For the Onemax problem, CHC's restart mechanism was disabled, eliminating CHC's only means of introducing new alleles. The runs were terminated when the population had converged (usually about 4500 trials). Table 1 summarizes the results averaged over 50 runs where the performance is the number of zeros in the string, and the goal is to minimize. (The last column shows the standard error of the mean.) Since the problem has no epistasis or local minima, differences in performance reflect premature loss of alleles whose values are '1'. As can be seen, 2X did the worst, with nearly a quarter of the 1000 bits zeros, whereas HUX did about four times as well, with SHX in between. The above results indicate that without mutation, 2X is more subject to spurious correlations (or hitchhiking) than either HUX or SHX.

More significantly, the results separate out two sources of spurious correlation. Unlike 2X, both HUX and SHX have no schema bias, so the difference in performance must be attributed to the fact that HUX exchanges more material, on average, than SHX—i.e., has a greater recombinative bias. On the other hand, the difference between SHX and 2X can only be attributed to the schema bias of 2X, since SHX was designed to have the same recombinative bias as 2X. Even though the Onemax problem is such that there is no schema

---

[6]One of the nice features of this combination of a conservative replacement strategy, incest prevention, and restarts is that a population size of 50 (parents), which was used in all experiments reported in this paper, works well for almost all problems, no matter what crossover operator is used. We believe that this is due, at least in part, to the algorithm's ability to self-adjust its selection pressure, discussed earlier. Thus, unlike a more traditional GA, a large population size is not needed to combat hitchhiking (Thierens and Goldberg, 1993). In a prior study we showed how incest prevention improved performance for both HUX and 2X (Eshelman and Schaffer, 1991). The only CHC parameter that is somewhat operator and problem sensitive is the restart rate.

Table 1: Onemax

| Best Performance | | |
|---|---|---|
|  | mean | sem |
| HUX | 68.5 | 1.8 |
| SHX | 127.8 | 2.4 |
| 2X | 237.2 | 2.1 |

Table 2: Performance Comparisons

| Mean number of trials to find optimum | | | | |
|---|---|---|---|---|
|  | 2X | SHX | HUX | sem | description |
| f1 | 1189 | 1254 | 1089 | 68 | parabola |
| f2 | 9681 | 6359 | 9065 | 964 | Rosenbrock's saddle |
| f3 | 1135 | 1349 | 1169 | 70 | stair steps |
| f4 | 4608 | 3966 | 1948 | 331 | quadratic with noise |
| f5 | 2207 | 1744 | 1396 | 117 | Shekel's foxholes |
| f6 | 15827 | 9704 | 6496 | 1231 | sine envelope sine wave |
| f7 | 10737 | 8051 | 3634 | 607 | stretched V sine wave |
| f8 | 15154 | 14315 | 7279 | 842 | FIR filter |
| Mean performance (minimizing) | | | | | |
| f9 | 452.6 | 451.1 | 427.1 | 4.1 | 30-city TSP, sort rep. |
| f10 | 3.55 | 2.04 | 1.60 | 0.52 | 64-node graph partition |

bias for 2X to exploit, 2X's schema bias is not neutral, but rather is a liability.

Of course, Onemax is a rather unchallenging problem, e.g., easy for bit-climbers (Davis, 1991). Most problems will be such that an operator's schema bias will have some relevance, although this does not mean that the schema bias will be such that it can be exploited by 2X—the correlated alleles may, in fact, be far apart rather than close. As a more representative test, we compared the three crossover operators, 2X, SHX and HUX, on a suite of test functions for which we have extensive data (Schaffer, et al 1989; Eshelman, 1991; Eshelman and Schaffer, 1991).[7]

Table 2 summarizes the results based on 50 runs of up to 50000 trials. For the first eight functions the average number of trials to find the global optimum are listed, or in the case of f4 to find a value prior to adding the noise that is within two standard deviations of the noise function. For functions nine and ten the average best scores are listed since the global optimum is frequently not found. The standard error of the mean listed is the largest among the three crossover operators. HUX stands out as the overall best performer and 2X as the loser. 2X wins only on f3 but is not significantly better than HUX. SHX does better than HUX only on f2, but does significantly better than 2X on six of the functions (f2, f4, f5, f6, f7, and f10) and significantly worse on two (f1, f3).

---

[7] For all subsequent experiments we used a divergence rate (i.e., restart mutation rate) of 35% for HUX and 2X and 50% for SHX. We tried other divergent rates for the operators, but these seemed to work best overall.

It is our hypothesis that it is HUX's stronger recombinative bias that explains its better performance. Evidence for this comes from the improvement ratios of the two algorithms. The improvement ratio is the number of offspring that are better than both parents divided by the number of offspring that are better than only one parent, calculated over the entire search.[8] One would expect a crossover operator that has a greater recombinative bias to have a higher improvement ratio than a weaker operator. After all, the whole point of recombination is that it will frequently combine the best features from both parents into a superior kid. On the other hand, an operator that has less recombinative bias, and thus is more prone to propagate schemata from one of the parents to the child, is more likely to produce children that are better than only one parent (by producing a child that shares a lot of material with the best parent, but has picked up a few bad alleles from the worst parent). HUX has a higher improvement ratio than 2X or SHX for each of the above functions.

## 4   RECOMBINATIVE BIAS'S FAILURE MODES

As we noted earlier, for any bias which makes search more efficient on some problems, other problems can be found for which it will be a source of failure. This phenomenon is fairly well understood in the case of schema bias. It is easy to create problems where the schema bias of 2X benefits search (e.g., problems consisting of a series of tightly coupled deceptive segments) and it is easy to make these problems difficult for 2X (by distributing the loci constituting these segments). Although it is always a good idea to try to exploit a representation's schema bias, it is our guess that such problems are mainly of theoretical interest. For large, complex, poorly understood search spaces, the kind of problem that GAs are supposedly most useful for as function optimizers, there will be little or no a priori knowledge about which bits interact, and so it will be highly unlikely that the problem can be represented in such a way that 2X's schema bias will be an asset. In the next two subsections we discuss two failure modes that operators with a strong recombinative bias are subject to: failure to propagate good schemata and failure to preserve good schemata.

### 4.1   FAILURE TO PROPAGATE

Once one adopts a conservative replacement strategy and, thus, separates propagation from preservation, it is harder than one might expect to produce examples where propagation is a problem. Consider, for example, a problem consisting of a set of needles-on-a-plateau segments. Provided the order of these segments is high enough, this would seem to be an obvious candidate to confound a crossover operator like HUX with its strong recombinative bias. To test this hypothesis we tried the three algorithms on a problem consisting of 20 10-bit segments, where each segment is worth one point if the loci are all ones and no points otherwise. As one might expect, 2X was able to exploit the schema bias of the problem and was the winner, finding on average 17.7 of the 20 needles over 50 runs (see Table 3). On the other hand, its performance plummeted when the 10 bit schemata where maximally distributed (2X-d). Contrary to the above hypothesis, however, HUX did significantly better (0.005 level) than SHX, finding 14.0 needles on average to SHX's 12.9. Thus HUX's stronger recombinative bias (and, therefore, higher rate of disruption) did not hurt its performance relative to SHX.

The fact that HUX has more trouble propagating good schemata is reflected in the accep-

---

[8]It should be stressed that this information is not used by the algorithm.

Table 3: 20 10-bit Needles-on-a-Plateau

| Num. of Opt. Segments Found | | |
|---|---|---|
| | mean | sem |
| HUX | 14.02 | 0.28 |
| SHX | 12.92 | 0.26 |
| 2X | 17.68 | 0.18 |
| 2X-d | 8.04 | 0.26 |

tance rates of the two algorithms—the percentage of offspring generated that are accepted into the parent population, calculated over the entire search. HUX's acceptance rate for this problem is 12% whereas SHX's is 15%. The difference in how the two operators work is also reflected in the improvement ratios of the two algorithms. HUX's improvement ratio is 0.60 whereas SHX's is 0.28. Thus, although HUX propagates fewer schemata that survive (i.e., are preserved), those that it does propagate tend to be better than those of SHX. Because crossover is used in conjunction with a conservative replacement strategy, it need not always propagate good schemata in any one generation in order for them to be preserved. The more disruptive operator lowers the acceptance rate, but this is more than compensated for by a higher portion of acceptances being offspring which have recombined good schemata from the two parents.

Of course schemata must eventually be propagated if search is to make any progress. It is easy to imagine a schema that is of such a high order and is not composed of any valuable lower order building blocks that it is nearly impossible for a recombination operator like HUX that swaps half the differing bits to propagate it. The trouble with this imagined monkeywrench in the gears of uniform crossover is that some account needs to be given to how this high order, brittle schema got into the population in the first place. Without such an account, one is, in effect, postulating a *miracle schema*.

We believe, however, that a credible account can be given of how valuable schemata might exist in the population which are nearly impossible for HUX to propagate, but that this happens only under special circumstances. A number of researchers have noted that crossover is not very effective for setting the weights on a neural network. The problem is one of multimodality introduced by the representation—what we call *competing conventions* (Schaffer et al, 1992). If there are only a few conventions, this will be no problem, since at least some members of the population will share the same convention and so when members sharing this convention mate they will have a good chance of producing improvements. But if there is such a vast number of incompatible conventions that it is highly unlikely that any members of the initial population will share (i.e., be close to) the same convention, and if the number of loci that determine which convention a particular individual is close to is high, then it may be very difficult for a GA using a conservative replacement strategy and a recombination operator with strong recombinative bias to make any progress.

To test to what extent competing conventions can frustrate our three crossover operators, we designed a problem that is trivial except for the competing conventions aspect: the goal is to find a set of $N$ parameter values that represent the integers from 0 to $N - 1$ in any order. Each individual is evaluated by sorting the parameters, labeling them from 0 to $N - 1$ (the targets), and calculating the variance from these target values (i.e., the sum of the squares of the differences). Since any order is as good as any other order, there will be $N!$ different ways of representing these integers. Not all these conventions will be that different, but there are so many of them that it is highly likely that the initial population will be distributed among conventions that will be incompatible and thus cause difficulties for a crossover operator with a strong recombinative bias. Our particular test problem consisted of 32 5-bit parameters. This is an easy problem that can be solved by a GA using mutation alone or by a bit-climber; yet, HUX was never able to solve the problem in 50000 trials, whereas both SHX and 2X found an optimum in an average of about 15000 trials. This confirms our hypothesis that a crossover with a strong recombinative bias will have more difficulties with problems whose representation contains many competing conventions.

We also tested our algorithms on a neural net weight setting problem. The problem is a 4-bit parity problem, and the neural net consists of 10 hidden layers with 10 units each. Each of the 1051 weights (including threshold weights) is represented by 6 bits, Gray coded, and scaled to range from -6.0 to +6.0. HUX could make little progress on this problem in 50000 trials, whereas 2X and SHX usually reached the halting criterion (less than one percent error on the worst training case) before 50000 trials. There was no significant difference in the performance of 2X and SHX. The reason that HUX did so poorly was that it hardly ever generated any new individuals who were accepted into the parent population. In 50000 trials HUX generated, on average, about 355 acceptable new individuals, and two thirds of these had been generated in the first 5000 trials. 2X and SHX, on the other hand, both generated nearly 8000 acceptable new individuals in 50000 trials. In brief, HUX had the same difficulties as for our simple competing conventions problem.

Finally, it should to be stressed that competing conventions cause difficulties for HUX only if the number of conventions is very high and are defined on schemata of sufficiently high order. For example, HUX has no difficulties on the simple competing conventions problem when $N$ is 8, doing as well as 2X or SHX.

## 4.2   FAILURE TO PRESERVE

Let us turn now to problems where preservation is the problem. A conservative replacement strategy separates preservation from propagation, but it does not necessarily guarantee that the good schemata, once represented in the parent population, will be preserved indefinitely. In particular, there are certain types of problems where something akin to Gresham's law holds for GAs: Bad schemata drive out good schemata.[9] These are 'trap' problems (Ackley, 1987) in which there are middle order building blocks that cannot be incrementally built from lower order building blocks, because the needed lower order building blocks have a lower value than their complements except when fully assembled. What counts as middle order will depend upon the population size—the order has to be low enough that there is a good chance that these schemata will be created randomly, either in the initial population or via recombination and mutation. This class of problems includes deceptive problems (Goldberg, 1987; Whitley, 1991) but also includes problems that are not fully deceptive, but still have this misleading element (Grefenstette, 1993). The difficulty of such problems will depend upon how much credit the (wrong) lower order building blocks receive relative to the (correct) middle order building blocks for which they are complements. As the total credit for these misleading lower order building blocks approaches that of the middle order

---

[9]Gresham's Law is an economic maxim that asserts that bad money drives out good money. It applies when there are legal tender laws that make it illegal to refuse the 'bad money' as payment.

Table 4: Trap

| Number of Optimum Segments Found | | | |
|---|---|---|---|
| 20 5-bit Traps | | 10 5-bit Decept. | |
| mean | sem | mean | sem |
| HUX | 19.34 | 0.10 | 1.88 | 0.09 |
| SHX | 18.80 | 0.13 | 6.44 | 0.17 |
| 2X | 19.94 | 0.03 | 9.76 | 0.07 |
| 2X-d | 12.84 | 0.20 | 4.10 | 0.11 |

building blocks the problem becomes increasingly difficult, and this difficulty is more serious for an algorithm using a crossover operator that has greater recombinative bias than one with less bias because such an algorithm will be more prone to climb the false peaks.

We initially tested our algorithms on a trap problem which consists of 20 5-bit segments. Each segment receives 5 points if it is all zeros; otherwise, it receives 0.5 points for each one. We were surprised that HUX did somewhat better than SHX as shown in Table 4. (Note 2X's better performance, when the deceptive bits are adjacent.) We also tested HUX and SHX on Liepins's and Vose's (Liepins and Vose, 1991) 10 segment, 5-bit deceptive problem and found that SHX did significantly better (cf. Table 4). (The performance values shown are the mean number of optimum segments found in 50000 trials over 50 runs.)

This is consistent with our hypothesis that SHX, because of its weaker recombinative bias, will do better than HUX on problems that consist of misleading segments. The question, then, is why did HUX do better than SHX on the trap problem? Does the problem have to be fully deceptive in order to have the predicted effect? To test this hypothesis we created a number of variants of the trap problem, that differ only in how much credit is given to the suboptimum segments relative to the optimum segments. In particular, the original trap problem gives a half point to each '1' in a five bit segment, and five points if the segment consists of all zeros (the optimum). Thus, the best suboptimum value is 50% of the optimum. The variants are in 5% increments. For example, in the first variant each one receives 0.55 points, for a suboptimum total of 2.75 which is 55% of the optimum (always 5). The following figure plots the results for HUX and SHX for the 10 variants. Although HUX does better than SHX when the suboptimum is 50% or 55% of the optimum, thereafter SHX does better. (All differences in performance are statistically significant, and are based on 50 runs of 50000 trials each.) Furthermore, although the problem becomes fully deceptive at the 62.5% point, SHX passes HUX before that point, so deception isn't the critical feature.

The clue to the puzzle as to why SHX does not consistently do better lies with the stairstep shape of the curves (especially visible for the HUX curve). It turns out that the 'flat' part of the steps are the regions where the number of additional ones (accumulated on segments that are suboptimal) required to compensate for the breaking up of a (different) segment that is optimal is the same. For example, in the original trap problem where each suboptimum bit receives 0.5 points, at least 5 additional bits are required to compensate for the loss of an optimum via recombination. This will be the case when an optimum segment in the parent is transformed to the highest valued suboptimum in the child (which is not very likely). If, instead, it is transformed into the worst value (only one '1'), then nine compensating 1's will need to be acquired on other suboptimum segments to compensate for this loss. It turns out that for the 55% version of the problem the same number of compensating bits are required (five to nine). On the other hand, the 85%, 90% and 95% versions of the problem require only one to five bits to compensate for the loss of an optimum segment. This accounts for the wide step at the bottom. The 60% version of the problem is the only one that is different from both of its neighbors, and so accounts for the steep drop in the curve at this point.

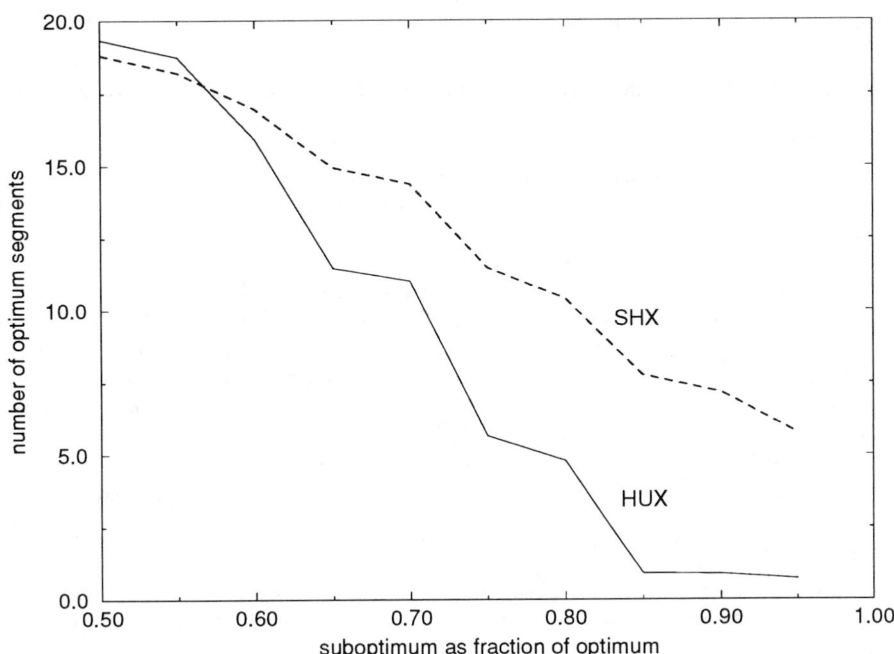



SHX's better performance on the harder versions of the problem (those where the suboptimum is a larger fraction of the optimum) is explained by its weaker recombinative bias. Because SHX tends to grab less material from the more distant parent, it is not so good at climbing the false peaks—i.e., it is less subject to Gresham's Law for GAs. Conversely, HUX's strong recombinative bias means that it is better at recombining the lower order (but misleading) building blocks into suboptimum segments—i.e., it is more subject to the crowding out of good schemata by bad schemata. (HUX's better performance on the Onemax problem supports this thesis.) Whenever HUX breaks up an optimum schema, it is more likely than SHX to recombine enough suboptimum bits (in other segments) to compensate for the loss. However, when the suboptimum is a low enough fraction of the optimum, the number of compensating bits is so high that not even HUX's strong recombinative power can pull in enough bits to compensate for the loss.

It might seem that an alternative explanation is that SHX is better at propagating the optimum schemata. This is true, but as we have argued above, high rates of propagation (and low schema disruption) is simply the other side of the weak recombinative bias coin. Furthermore, it should be stressed that propagation, per se, is not the main hurdle since each optimum schema is of the same order in all problems (five). For any pair of parents, HUX is just as likely to propagate an optimum segment to one of the offspring for the 90% version of the problem as it is for the 50% version. The problem lies with preservation. The middle order optimum segments are more likely to be crowded out by the lower order suboptimum segments (i.e., Gresham's Law for GAs) for the problems where the credit for suboptimum bits is a larger fraction of the optimum. By focusing on the crowding-out effect, rather than schema averages, we are able to explain why certain trap problems are easier for one operator than another.

## 5 SELF-ADJUSTING RECOMBINATION OPERATORS

Given that different recombination operators perform differently on different problems, it would be ideal if we could discover a mechanism that enables a GA to select the operators which work best—e.g., some technique that adapts the operator probabilities based on their observed performance during any run (Davis, 1989). We have experimented with a number of such schemes for choosing between HUX and SHX (as well as other operators), and have found that they are all subject to three difficulties. First, it is often difficult to find a reliable intra-run measure of an operator's performance. For instance, early in a run on a trap problem HUX will look better than SHX by most short run measures (e.g., the number of new best individuals found), even though SHX often is the better operator in the long run. Second, the dynamics of two operators operating on the same population is often quite different from that of either one alone. Again, on a trap problem, HUX, when used in conjunction with SHX, will often destroy the deceptive building blocks before SHX has a chance to exploit them. Finally, even when we can avoid the first two problems, the intra-run sample size may be so small, especially early on, that the statistics used for operator selection will be totally unreliable.

Although we have not found any *general* method for operator selection that overcomes these problems, we have found a simple method for choosing between HUX and SHX that works reasonably well. Recall that CHC uses restarts—when the population is (nearly) converged, the converged population is partially or fully randomized and seeded with one copy of the best individual found so far (the *elite* individual). During any convergence period between restarts (including the period leading up to the first restart), either HUX or SHX is used but not both. HUX is always used during the first two convergences. Subsequently, two rules are used for switching operators: (1) SHX is used for the next convergence (restarted with a 50% divergence rate), if during the prior convergence no individual is found that is as good as the elite individual. (2) HUX is used for the next convergence (restarted with a 35% divergence rate), if during the prior convergence, no individual is found that is better than the elite individual, but at least one individual is found that is as good as the elite individual (it may be identical). No change in the operator is made, if during the prior convergence, a new best individual is found (which will replace the old elite individual).

The rationale behind these rules is that since SHX is better at propagating schemata, it should be used if the algorithm is having trouble exploiting the elite individual (shown by the fact that it converged to individuals that are worse). On the other hand, since HUX is less prone to propagating schemata, it should be used if the algorithm is getting stuck in the same place (shown by the fact that it converged to individuals that have the same values as the elite individual). Since it has been our experience that HUX works better for most problems, it is used initially. How these rules address the first difficulty for an adaptive operator mechanism will be discussed below. Since HUX and SHX are never mixed during a convergence, the second difficulty is avoided. And since the decision as to which operator to use is based on the results of running the algorithm until the population converges, the third difficulty, if not avoided, is not quite so serious.

We found that the performance of CHC on most problems (e.g., f1-f10) is not significantly affected by this mechanism. This isn't too surprising since the condition that triggers SHX—converging to a worse individual—does not happen very often. But it does happen often enough in both deceptive and competing conventions problems, so that it improves performance. One would expect it to help on problems with competing conventions, since these are problems where propagation is a problem using HUX, including propagation of the elite individual. For both the simple competing conventions problem and the large neural net problem described in section 4.1, the HUX-SHX version of CHC performed significantly better than HUX alone but significantly worse than SHX alone, with performance values that fell about half way in between those of HUX and SHX alone. This reflected the fact that it did a lot of switching back and forth between HUX and SHX, making most of its gains when using SHX. We tried several variants of the switching mechanism which dampened this whipsaw effect. This helped somewhat on the competing convention problem, but lowered performance on problems where HUX is the best operator.

For deceptive problems, propagation per se is not a problem; however, propagation of the optimal segments contained in the elite individual becomes increasingly difficult as the other members in the population converge to the complements of these segments. For problems where this applies, one would expect the algorithm to often converge to individuals who don't contain all the optimal segments from the elite individual, and to sometimes be worse than this individual, triggering SHX for the next convergence. In fact, the HUX-SHX version of CHC performed significantly better on the Liepens's deceptive problem than HUX alone and significantly worse than SHX alone (finding 51% of the optimal segments versus 36% and 80% respectively). On the other hand, for the 50% version of the trap problem the performance of HUX-SHX is not significantly different from HUX alone, and significantly better than SHX alone.

## 6   CONCLUSION

It has been our experience that the most common failure mode for GAs is premature convergence, and that a crossover operator with a strong recombinative bias and low schema bias is an effective means of combating the spurious correlations that cause this problem (provided a conservative method of replacement is used). Nevertheless, there are problems where recombinative bias can be a liability and schema bias an asset. We have identified two types of problems where recombinative bias is a liability—problems with competing conventions and problems with traps. Both types of problems are problems where the difficulty of recombining schemata (into schemata that survive) does not reflect the difficulty of the problem. In competing conventions problems recombination is much more difficult than is warranted by the problem, whereas in trap problems recombination is much easier than warranted. The former type of problem is often easy to identify. Since the competing conventions are introduced by the representation, the researcher may have a good idea that there is a potential problem. Furthermore, if the GA is having difficulties in generating offspring that make it into the parent population, then competing conventions (or some other form of rampant multimodality) is a likely explanation. Trap problems are more difficult to detect, and the only suggestion we have is to always try a recombination operator with less recombinative bias (like 2X or SHX) on difficult problems. Alternatively, one can use a mechanism like the one suggested in the previous section to switch between operators based on the progress of the search, although no such mechanism is likely to be ideal. Finally, although it is always a good idea to try to exploit schema bias, this will often not be possible. In particular, it is our guess that problems where 2X's schema bias is an asset are mainly of theoretical interest. For real-world problems one is unlikely to have the kind a priori knowledge needed to represent the problem so that the interacting bits are close together. A better candidate for privileging certain schemata will be problems which are naturally represented as a set of continuous variables, and where a crossover operator that acts on real-valued representations can be used to exploit the gradualness of such variables (Eshelman and Schaffer, 1993).

## References


D. H. Ackley, *A Connectionist Machine for Genetic Hillclimbing*, Kluwer Academic Publishers, Boston, MA, 1987.

T. Bäck, F. Hoffmeister, and H. Schwefel, A Survey of Evolution Strategies, *Proceedings of the Fourth International Conference on Genetic Algorithms*, Morgan Kaufmann, San Mateo, CA, 1991, 2-9.

L. Booker, Improving Search in Genetic Algorithms, in *Genetic Algorithms and Simulated Annealing*, L. Davis (editor), Morgan Kaufmann, San Mateo, CA, 1987, 61-73.

L. Davis, Adapting Operator Probabilities in Genetic Algorithms, *Proceedings of the Third International Conference on Genetic Algorithms*, Morgan Kaufmann, San Mateo, CA, 1989, 61-69.

L. Davis, Bit-Climbing, Representational Bias, and Test Suite Design, *Proceedings of the Fourth International Conference on Genetic Algorithms*, Morgan Kaufmann, San Mateo, CA, 1991, 18-23.

L. J. Eshelman, R. A. Caruana and J. D. Schaffer, Biases in the Crossover Landscape, *Proceedings of the Third International Conference on Genetic Algorithms*, Morgan Kaufmann, San Mateo, CA, 1989, 10-19.

L. J. Eshelman, The CHC Adaptive Search Algorithm: How to Have Safe Search When Engaging in Nontraditional Genetic Recombination, in *Foundations of Genetic Algorithms*, G. J. E. Rawlins (editor), Morgan Kaufmann, San Mateo, CA, 1991, 265-283.

L. J. Eshelman and J. D. Schaffer, Preventing Premature Convergence in Genetic Algorithms by Preventing Incest, *Proceedings of the Fourth International Conference on Genetic Algorithms*, Morgan Kaufmann, San Mateo, CA, 1991, 115-122.

L. J. Eshelman and J. D. Schaffer, Real-Coded Genetic Algorithms and Interval Schemata, in *Foundations of Genetic Algorithms*, D. Whitley (editor), Morgan Kaufmann, San Mateo, CA, 1993, 187-202.

D. E. Goldberg, Simple Genetic Algorithms and the Minimal, Deceptive Problem, in *Genetic*

*Algorithms and Simulated Annealing*, L. Davis (editor), Morgan Kaufmann, San Mateo, CA, 1987, 74-88.

D. E. Goldberg and K. Deb, A Comparative Analysis of Selection Schemes Used in Genetic Algorithms, in *Foundations of Genetic Algorithms*, G. J. E. Rawlins (editor), Morgan Kaufmann, San Mateo, CA, 1991, 69-93.

J. J. Grefenstette, Deception Considered Harmful, in *Foundations of Genetic Algorithms*, D. Whitley (editor), Morgan Kaufmann, San Mateo, CA, 1993, 75-91.

J. H. Holland, *Adaptation in Natural and Artificial Systems*, University of Michigan Press, Ann Arbor, MI, 1975.

G. E. Liepins and M. D. Vose, Representational Issues in Genetic Optimization, *Journal of Experimental and Theoretical AI*, May 1991.

N. J. Radcliffe, Forma Analysis and Random Respectful Recombination, *Proceedings of the Fourth International Conference on Genetic Algorithms* Morgan Kaufmann, San Mateo, CA, 1991, 222-229.

J. D. Schaffer, R. A. Caruana, L. J. Eshelman and R. Das, A Study of Control Parameters Affecting Online Performance of Genetic Algorithms for Function Optimization, *Proceedings of the Third International Conference on Genetic Algorithms*, Morgan Kaufmann, San Mateo, CA, 1989, 51-60.

J. D. Schaffer, L. J. Eshelman and D. Offutt, Spurious Correlations and Premature Convergence in Genetic Algorithms, in *Foundations of Genetic Algorithms*, G. J. E. Rawlins (editor), Morgan Kaufmann, San Mateo, CA, 1991, 102-112.

J. D. Schaffer, D. Whitley and L. J. Eshelman, Combinations of Genetic Algorithms and Neural Networks: A Survey of the State of the Art, *COGANN-92 Combinations of Genetic Algorithms and Neural Networks*, D. Whitley and J. D. Schaffer (editors), IEEE Computer Society Press, Los Alamitos, CA, 1992, 1-37.

W. M. Spears and K. A. De Jong, An Analysis of Multi-point Crossover, in *Foundations of Genetic Algorithms*, G. J. E. Rawlins (editor), Morgan Kaufmann, San Mateo, CA, 1991, 301-315.

G. Syswerda, A Study of Reproduction in Generational and Steady State Genetic Algorithms, in *Foundations of Genetic Algorithms*, G. J. E. Rawlins (editor), Morgan Kaufmann, San Mateo, CA, 1991, 94-101.

D. Thierens and D. E. Goldberg, Mixing in Genetic Algorithms, *Proceedings of the Fifth International Conference on Genetic Algorithms*, Morgan Kaufmann, San Mateo, CA, 1993, 38-45.

D. Whitley, The GENITOR Algorithm and Selection Pressure: Why Rank-Based Allocation of Reproductive Trials is Best, *Proceedings of the Third International Conference on Genetic Algorithms*, Morgan Kaufmann, San Mateo, CA, 1989, 116-121,

D. Whitley, Fundamental Principles of Deception in Genetic Algorithms, in *Foundations of Genetic Algorithms*, G. J. E. Rawlins (editor), Morgan Kaufmann, San Mateo, CA, 1991, 221-241.

# The Role of Development in Genetic Algorithms

**William E. Hart**
Sandia National Laboratories - Department 01422
P.O. Box 5800 Mail Stop 1110
Albuquerque, NM 87185-1110
wehart@cs.sandia.gov

**Thomas E. Kammeyer**     **Richard K. Belew**
Computer Science and Engineering
University of California, San Diego
La Jolla, CA 92037-0114
{tkammeye,rik}@cs.ucsd.edu

## Abstract

The developmental mechanisms transforming genotypic to phenotypic forms are typically omitted in formulations of genetic algorithms (GAs) in which these two representational spaces are identical. We argue that a careful analysis of developmental mechanisms is useful when understanding the success of several standard GA techniques, and can clarify the relationships between more recently proposed enhancements. We provide a framework that distinguishes between two developmental mechanisms — learning and maturation — while also showing several common effects on GA search. This framework is used to analyze how maturation and local search can change the dynamics of the GA. We observe that in some contexts, maturation and local search can be incorporated into the fitness evaluation, but illustrate reasons for considering them seperately. Further, we identify contexts in which maturation and local search can be distinguished from the fitness evaluation.

## 1   Introduction

The genetic algorithm (GA) is often cast as a function optimizer, manipulating a population of solutions using recombination and mutation. This formulation omits mechanisms present in many genetic algorithms. Here we will be most concerned with the distinction between the space of *genotypes*, in which genetic operators apply, and the space of *phenotypes*, in which individuals' fitnesses are evaluated. *Development* is the process by which genotypes are transformed into phenotypes, where we intend this term to subsume two forms of within-lifetime individual change: maturation and learning. *Maturation* refers to the process by which a genotype is mapped into a phenotype, and *learning* refers to phenotypic plasticity remaining in the mature organism as evidenced by adaptive responses to the environment. "Development" is a useful, inclusive term exactly because these two forms of within-lifetime change are notoriously confounded in biological systems.

Maturation and learning have been used with GAs in several contexts. Learning has been studied under the guise of "hill climbing" [17, 18] and local search [8]. These authors use learning to refine solutions and speed up the GA. Gruau [4, 5] and Kitano [13] have used maturation in applications of GAs to neural networks. These authors used maturation to construct neural networks from a grammar representation. Similarly, Belew and Kammeyer [2] used maturation in an application of the GA to sorting networks.

In GAs, we have complete knowledge of all of the algorithm's mechanisms, and distinctions between "learning" and "maturation" may be considered matters of nomenclature. In this paper, we provide a framework in which learning and maturation have precisely defined roles. We argue that this framework captures an important class of GAs, and that it can be used to understand the relative success of some standard GA techniques (e.g., Gray coding).

We begin with the definitions for local search and maturation, and present a simple model of a GA using these mechanisms. Next we describe three examples that illustrate the variety of GAs that this model captures. The next two sections describe the relationships between local search and maturation, and between maturation and repair mechanisms. Finally, we illustrate several instances in which development affects the time complexity of the GA's search.

## 2   Definitions

We begin by providing definitions that provide a framework for our discussion of development. Let $\mathcal{G}$ be the space of genotypes and let $\mathcal{P}h$ be the space of phenotypes. $\mathcal{G}$ is the search space in which the GA's operators apply, while $\mathcal{P}h$ is the space in which the fitness of solutions can be evaluated. Let the function $f : \mathcal{P}h \rightarrow \mathbf{R}$ be the fitness function.

Genotypes are mapped to phenotypes via a maturation function, $\delta : \mathcal{G} \rightarrow \mathcal{P}h$. This is a restricted notion of maturation, as the phenotype is generated solely based on information that is available in the genotype. Thus the maturation process is not influenced by information derived from the rest of the population or from the fitness function. This simple model of maturation captures many aspects of maturation in current GA models. The inverse map $\delta^{-1} : \mathcal{P}h \rightarrow \mathcal{G}$ is also used in some GAs, but we do not require that $\delta^{-1}$ exist in general.

A local search algorithm iteratively improves its estimate of the optimum by searching for better points in some local neighborhood of the current solution. The neighborhood of a local search algorithm is the set of solutions that can be reached from the current solution in a single iteration. A local search algorithm employs information about the fitness landscape when performing a search. For example, the fitness values of individuals from previous iterations are typically used. For smooth, differentiable functions, sophisticated methods have been developed that use derivative information to guide the search (e.g., conjugate gradient [21]). Because information about the fitness function is employed, a local search algorithm can be modeled as a mapping $\lambda_f : \mathcal{P}h \rightarrow \mathcal{P}h$. If individual moves of the local search are defined using a local search operator $\mathcal{L}_f$, then

$$\lambda_f(ph) = \mathcal{L}_f^{(n)}(ph),$$

where the superscript $(n)$ indicates $n$-fold composition of the single-step function $\mathcal{L}_f$.

The use of fitness information differentiates local search from mutation, which depends only on information contained in the genotype. Mutation can be modeled as $\mathcal{M} : \mathcal{G} \rightarrow \mathcal{G}$. Because mutation does not use fitness information, it is forced to make a random selection among a set of possible genotypes. Further, the set of genotypes that can be generated by mutation is also invariant to the fitness information. While "mutation" is sometimes used to refer to any and all genotypic modifications, we reserve the term "mutation" for completely random, "blind" modifications.

We can imagine more general definitions of local search and mutation which use information about a GA's current or previous populations. For example, the definition of local search does not encompass the methods described in Hart [7] that use statistics from the population to selectively apply local search. Our notion of mutation does not include the dynamically adjusted mutation operator used in evolutionary strategies, in which the standard deviation is adapted using the frequency of previously successful mutations. Applying local search and mutation with additional information is certainly of interest, but the effect of this information is beyond the scope of the present discussion.[1] If we view $\lambda_f$ and $\mathcal{M}$ as stochastic functions, our definitions of learning and mutation *can* model local search and mutation operators that are applied with some fixed probability per individual.

Figure 1 illustrates the interactions between the various elements of the framework that we have described. This figure shows how mutation and local search take a genotype $g$ and generate new genotypes $g'$ and $g''$. The mutation operator simply generates another genotype; local search uses the maturation map to generate a phenotype, which is modified using fitness information. When local search is used, the initial genotype $g$ may or may not be modified. *Lamarckian local search* replaces $g$ with $\delta^{-1}(\lambda_f(\delta(g)))$. The name is an allusion to Jean Batiste de Lamarck's contention that (some) phenotypic characteristics acquired during a lifetime can become heritable traits. In our model, acquired characteristics correspond to phenotypic modifications due to the local search operator, and their heritability corresponds to the replacement of $g$ with $\delta^{-1}(\lambda_f(\delta(g)))$.

In the figure, a genotype $g$ is mapped to a phenotype $ph$ with a maturation function $\delta$. The fitness of $ph$ is measured with a fitness function $f$. The genotype $g'$ is generated by applying a mutation operator $M$ to $g$, after which the maturation function generates a phenotype whose fitness is evaluated. The genotype $g''$ is generated with a "Lamarckian" local search. After $g$ is mapped to $ph$, a local search operator is applied some number of times ($L$ abbreviates several iterations in the figure), and the resulting phenotype is mapped back to $g''$. Note that a non-Lamarckian local search omits the final step and does not create the genotype $g''$.

---

[1] Note that if the more general definition of mutation is restricted from accepting information about the current individual's fitness, as opposed to population statistics, then it is still possible to differentiate local search and mutation based on the kinds of information each uses.

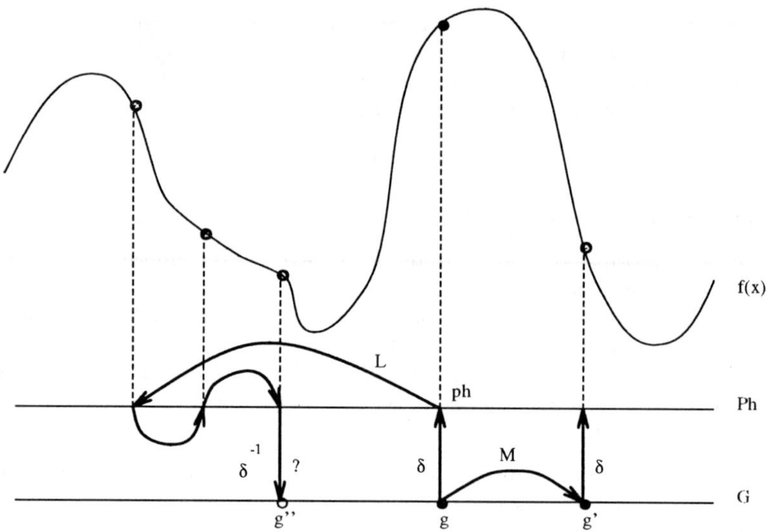



Figure 1: An illustration of the interactions among local search, maturation, and mutation.

There are a number of contexts in which $\delta^{-1}$ does not exist. For example, $\delta$ may be a many-to-one mapping, or $\delta$ may be stochastic. If $\delta^{-1}$ does not exist, then "exact" Lamarckian local search cannot be performed, though we could easily imagine using a stochastic choice or an arbitrary choice among possible inverses as a pseudo-inverse. *Non-Lamarckian* local search exploits information gained via phenotypic search without using it to directly modify the genome. In particular, non-Lamarckian local search is used to determine a fitness to be associated with $g$. Thus, non-Lamarckian local search is still useful in the absence of $\delta^{-1}$.

If $\delta^{-1}$ does not exist, it is sometimes possible to perform Lamarckian local search with approximations to $\delta^{-1}$ (e.g., see Hart [7, pages 105-110]). GAs using Lamarckian local search are typically more efficient than GAs using non-Lamarckian local search [3, 8, 11] when $\delta$ is invertible. Consequently, GAs using Lamarckian local search based on an approximation to $\delta^{-1}$ are of practical interest when computing $\delta^{-1}$ is impractical or impossible.

Figure 2 shows pseudo-code for a simple GA that uses maturation and local search.[2] Maturation and local search are applied in lines 13a-b. The GA presented in Figure 2 uses maturation and non-Lamarckian local search. We can describe GAs with different developmental mechanisms by modifying only these lines. For example, a GA using maturation and Lamarckian local search would replace lines 13a-b with

13a $\qquad ph_i = \lambda_f(\delta(\tilde{G}_t^i))$

---

[2] The code in Figure 2 implements a GA with a very simple model of the interaction between selection, mutation and crossover. For example, this GA replaces every member of the previous population, while many common GAs selectively replace a fraction of the individuals in the previous population. This simple GA is presented because these considerations do not affect the dynamics of maturation and local search.

```
1   For i from 1 to N {
2       G₀ⁱ = Random_Genome()
3       F₀ⁱ = f(δ(G₀ⁱ))
4       }
5   DO {
6          Gₜ = Select(Gₜ₋₁, Fₜ₋₁)
7          For i from 1 to N {
8             r1 = Rand(1,N)
9             r2 = Rand(1,N)
10            G̃ₜⁱ = M(X(Gₜʳ¹, Gₜʳ²))
11            }
12         For i from 1 to N {
13a           Gₜⁱ = G̃ₜⁱ
13b           Fₜⁱ = f(λ_f(δ(G̃ₜⁱ)))
14            }
15         }UNTIL Finished(Gₜ,Fₜ)
```

Figure 2: Pseudo-code for a simple GA using non-Lamarckian local search. $G_t^i$ is the $i$th member of the population at time $t$, and $F_t^i$ is the fitness of the $G_t^i$. Random_Genome() generates a genotype randomly. Select($G_{t-1}$, $F_{t-1}$) performs selection and returns a population of individuals selected from $G_{t-1}$. Rand(1,N) returns a uniformly distributed integer in $\{1,\ldots,N\}$. Finished($G_t$,$F_t$) performs a convergence check.

$$
\begin{aligned}
\text{13b} \quad & G_t^i = \delta^{-1}(ph_i) \\
\text{13c} \quad & F_t^i = f(ph_i)
\end{aligned}
$$

The temporary variable $ph_i$ is used to emphasize that although $\lambda_f$ and $\delta$ may be stochastic mappings, $G_t^i$ and $F_t^i$ are generated with the same phenotype.

## 3  Examples

We now describe three problems: a simple function optimization problem, a sorting network problem and a molecular conformation problem. These problems are used in subsequent sections to illustrate the relative roles of maturation and local search.

### 3.1  A Simple Example

Consider the function

$$f(x) = -1/(1 + x^2)$$

where $\mathcal{G} = \mathcal{P}h = [-10, 10]$. Let

$$\delta(x) = \operatorname{sgn}(x)\frac{x^2}{10},$$

be the maturation function. To perform local search, we use a simple gradient method that takes a step of $\eta$ times the gradient, where $\eta = 0.5$. For $f(x)$, each step of the local search performs the map

$$\mathcal{L}_f(x) = x - \eta f'(x) = x - \eta \frac{2x}{(1 + x^2)^2}.$$

We use 3 steps of local search, so $\lambda_f(x) = \mathcal{L}_f^{(3)}(x)$. This optimization problem is discussed further below.

### 3.2  Sorting Networks

Sorting networks are simple sorting programs. A sorting network operates on an array of integers, $A$, of length $N$, using only *compare-exchange* (CMPX) operations. $N$ is often called the *width* of the sorting network. Each CMPX specifies an operation on two locations in $A$. For $1 \leq i < j \leq N$, "CMPX $i$, $j$", more often denoted $[i : j]$, swaps the contents of $A[i]$ and $A[j]$ if $A[j] < A[i]$. Thus, executing the operation $[i : j]$ sorts the values at array locations $i$ and $j$, placing the smaller value in the array location with smaller index.

A *compare-exchange* network is a sequence of CMPX operations. A *sorting* network is a sequence of CMPX operations that are guaranteed to sort $A$'s contents regardless of their initial order. Formally, a sorting network is a CMPX network that operates on $A$ such that after executing the network's CMPXs, $A[i] < A[j]$ for $1 \leq i < j \leq N$. Sorting networks are often drawn as shown in Figure 3. The horizontal lines represent indices into $A$. The vertical lines represent CMPX operations by connecting the horizontal lines corresponding to their arguments. Thus $[1 : 2]$ is represented by a vertical line connecting the first two horizontal lines.

We *could* represent the sorting networks by enumerating their CMPXs. In this representation, each genome would be a series of integers and successive pairs of integers would be used to defined CMPX operations, with some care taken to insure that anomalous CMPX's were handled properly[3]. This representation, however, does not capture the *structure* of a network. For example, a sorting network can be built by building two networks of half as many inputs, renumbering their inputs so that one operates on $A[1], \ldots A[N/2 + 1]$ and the other on $A[N/2], \ldots A[N])$, and adding some CMPXs to the result.

Belew and Kammeyer[2] searched for small (width 8) sorting networks using a GA with a representation designed to allow the expression of such structural relationships. In their GA, each genome represents a nonterminal and a sequence of rewrite rules (i.e., grammar productions). Each rewrite rule specifies either how to build a small network or how to combine two networks into a wider one. Maturation, $\delta$, builds a CMPX network from a genotype by starting with the genotype's nonterminal and applying the first production on the genome which matches it. Any nonterminals in the result are expanded by applying the first rule which matches them. This process continues until some fixed derivation depth is reached or until no nonterminals remain.

In the genotypes each nonterminal, $N_S^W$, stands for an entire sorting network of width $2^W$. A wild-card symbol, \$, can replace $W$ or $S$ in the nonterminal on the left-hand side of a rewrite rule. Thus, $N_\$^\$$ matches any other nonterminal. The $S$ parameter has no predetermined semantics, and is provided so that two rules specifying the same value of $W$ in the nonterminal on their left-hand sides are distinguishable by something other than

---

[3] For example, we would have to deal with or eliminate operations like $[5 : 5]$ or $[7 : 2]$ or any operations $[i : j]$ with $i \geq j$, since such "backward" CMPX operations are not normally used in sorting networks.

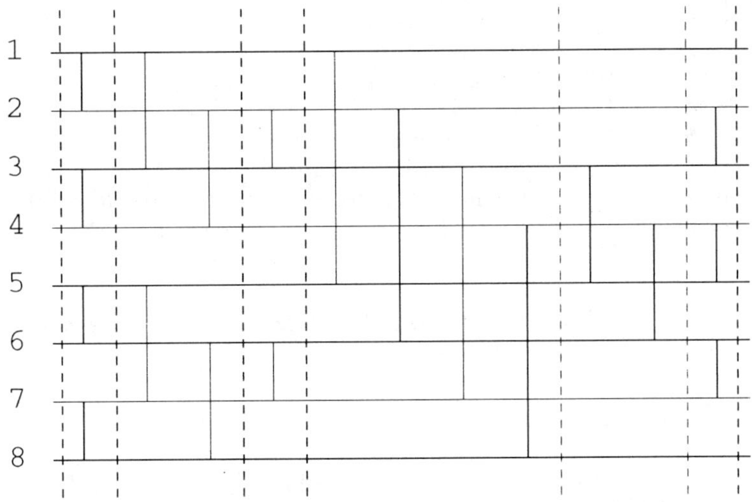

Figure 3: A pictorial representation of the sorting network: $[1:2][3:4][5:6][7:8]$ $[1:3][2:4][5:7][6:8]$ $[2:3][6:7]$ $[1:5][2:6][3:7][4:8]$ $[3:5][4:6]$ $[2:3][4:5][6:7]$ The dashed lines separate sets of CMPX operations which can be performed in parallel, since no two in any such set touch the same horizontal line. This network is a merge sort based on the well-known Batcher merge.

position on the genome. The grammars are restricted in two ways: there is a soft limit on the number of productions any one genotype can contain, and all of the productions were the result of filling in one of the eight "templates" shown in Figure 4.

Once $\delta$ is computed, the resulting network is tested to see whether it sorts all possible sequences of 0's and 1's with length equal to the network's width[4]. The percentage of such strings which the network can sort determines its fitness.

Although Belew and Kammeyer's GA performed no local search, it is possible to define a $\lambda_f$ on the space of CMPX networks. For example, local search could be performed modifying individual CMPXs in a phenotype. Such a search would probably be expensive, since the fitness evaluation is expensive, because the network must be tested on $2^{width}$ strings after each modification.

## 3.3   Molecular Conformation

A simple molecular conformation problem is taken from Judson [10]. Consider a molecule composed of a chain of 19 identical atoms which are connected by stiff springs. A simple

---

[4]A well-known principle, the "0-1 principle", assures us that the ability to sort all bit strings of length $N$ is sufficient for a CMPX-network to be able to sort all numeric sequences of length $N$. Knuth [14] contains an easily understood proof of this principle.

$$
\begin{aligned}
\text{Type 1:} &\quad N_S^W \rightarrow ([i_1 : j_1][i_2 : j_2], \ldots, [i_k : j_k]) \\
\text{Type 2:} &\quad N_S^W \rightarrow ((i_1, i_2, \ldots, i_k) + \text{offset}) \\
\text{Type 3:} &\quad N_S^W \rightarrow (\text{Repeat } N_{S'}^W \ R \text{ times}) \\
\text{Type 4a:} &\quad N_S^W \rightarrow (\text{Stack } N_{S'}^W \text{ and } N_{S''}^W \text{ before } N_{S'''}^W) \\
\text{Type 4b:} &\quad N_S^W \rightarrow (\text{Stack } N_{S'}^W \text{ and } N_{S''}^W \text{ after } N_{S'''}^W) \\
\text{Type 5:} &\quad N_S^W \rightarrow (\text{Concatenate } N_{S'}^W \text{ and } N_{S''}^W) \\
\text{Type 6:} &\quad N_S^W \rightarrow (\text{Interleave } N_{S'}^{W-1} \text{ and } N_{S''}^{W-1}) \\
\text{Type 7:} &\quad N_S^W \rightarrow (\text{Combine } N_{S'}^{W-1} \text{ and } N_{S''}^{W-1} \text{ using partition } P) \\
\text{Type 8:} &\quad N_S^W \rightarrow (\text{Combine two of } N_{S'}^{W-1} \text{ using partition } P)
\end{aligned}
$$

Figure 4: The templates for the eight rewrite rule types allowed in the genotypes of the GA used to search for sorting networks.

equation for the potential energy of this molecule is

$$
E = 100 \sum_{i=1}^{n-1} (r_{i,i+1} - 1)^2 + \sum_{i=1}^{18} \sum_{j=i}^{19} \left[ \left( \frac{1}{r_{ij}} \right)^{12} - 2 \left( \frac{1}{r_{ij}} \right)^6 \right],
$$

where $r_{ij}$ is the distance between the $i$th and $j$th atoms. The first term of $E$ accounts for the energy in the bonded interactions between atoms, and the second term accounts for the van der Walls forces in the non-bonded interactions. The distance terms in this energy function can be be parameterized in two ways: (1) using the coordinates of the atoms, and (2) using the bond angles and bond lengths. Figure 5 illustrates the relation of these parameters to the structure of a simple molecule. Analytic gradients can be calculated for either of these parametrizations, so gradient-based local search can be performed on either of these spaces. Consequently, either space can be used for the space of genotypes or phenotypes.

## 4   Fitness Transformations

The GA described in Figure 2 uses non-Lamarckian local search and maturation. In that GA, the effect of local search and maturation is limited to the computation of the fitness $F_t^i = f(\lambda_f(\delta(\tilde{G}_t^i)))$. Note that that GA is equivalent to a GA optimizing $h = f \circ \lambda_f \circ \delta$ for which the new phenotypic space $\mathcal{P}h'$ equals $\mathcal{G}$. Since these two GAs have the same genotypic space, local search and maturation do not modify the search performed by the GA. Instead, they transform the fitness landscape that the GA searches.

### 4.1   A Simple Example Revisited

To illustrate the fitness transformations performed by maturation and non-Lamarckian local search, we compared the performance of variants of a binary GA using the simple function defined in section 3.1. To do this, we take advantage of the observation that maturation and non-Lamarckian local search can be folded into the fitness evaluation. Because $\mathcal{G} = \mathcal{P}h$, in this example the *only* role of $\delta$ is to transform the fitness landscape.

Figure 6 graphs $f(x)$, $f(\delta(x))$, $f(\lambda_f(x))$ and $f(\lambda_f(\delta(x)))$. In this example, both maturation and local search broaden the shoulders of the minimum, and they widen the shoulders even

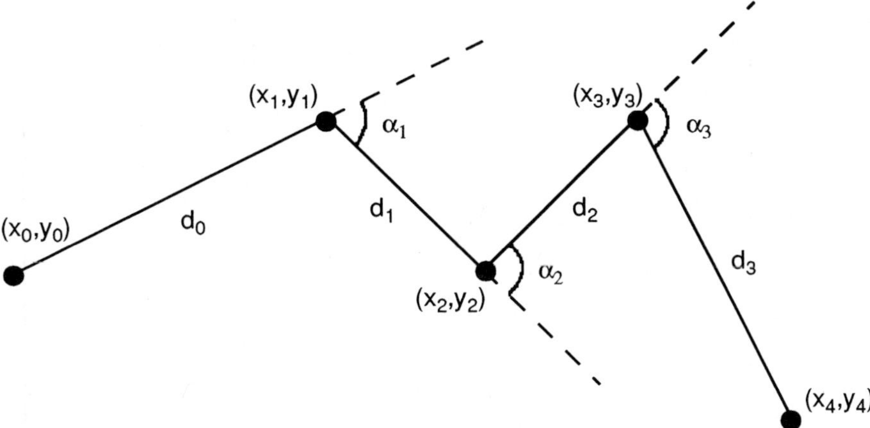


Figure 5: Illustration of a simple molecule showing the dimensions used to parametrize the potential energy.

more when combined. This should enable the GA to work with individuals whose fitness is clearly distinguishable, thereby increasing the convergence of the GA to the minimum.

To test this prediction, we applied a binary GA to these four functions. This experiment used $\mathcal{G} = \{0,1\}^{30}$ and $\mathcal{P}h = \mathbf{R}$. A small population of 10 was used to illustrate the effect. The average results of 10 runs are shown in Figure 7. As expected, the GAs converged to the minimum more quickly for the functions that incorporated the developmental transformations.[5]

Figure 6 also illustrates a hazard of these fitness transformations. While maturation and non-Lamarckian local search broaden the basin of attraction, they also flatten the bottom of the local minimum. The solutions at the bottom of the local minima are not identical, but they are so similar that the GA will have a hard time distinguishing between them. As a result, GAs using maturation and non-Lamarckian local search may have more difficulty refining their solutions near minima than the standard GA. The larger basin of attraction may, however, may make it easier for the GA to "track" a non-stationary fitness function. That is, if the minimum moves each generation, but only by small a amount, then the large basin of attraction for the minimum will tend to contain many of the same individuals from generation to generation. The broader basins of attraction resulting from the use of maturation and local search before and after a small perturbation of the minimum will tend to overlap more than the narrower basins of attraction for the raw fitness function, before and after the same movement, would overlap.

When optimizing a stationary function, it may be possible to avoid very flat minima by carefully selecting the maturation function. However, this problem is inherent for non-Lamarckian local search, since the "length" of the local search affects the fraction of a

---

[5] We realize that using the binary encoding in this experiment introduces complications due to the interpretation of the binary encoding, but we do not believe the binary interpretation affects our results in this case.

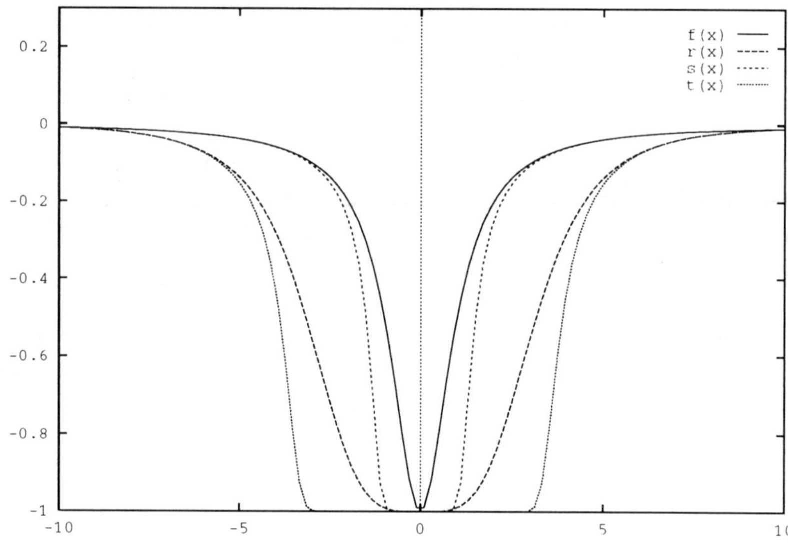

Figure 6: Transformation of the $f(x)$ fitness landscape, showing the function $f(x)$, along with $r(x) = f(\delta(x))$, $s(x) = f(\lambda(x))$, and $t(x) = f(\lambda(\delta(x)))$.

minimum that is flattened by the fitness transformation. For example, a local search algorithm is more likely to find a solution near a minimum when run for many iterations. Keesing and Stork [12] apply local search at several different lengths to alleviate this problem when using long searches.

## 4.2  Comparing Maturation and Local Search

Although maturation and non-Lamarckian local search perform a similar transformation of the fitness landscape in Figure 6, they offer distinctly different approaches to fitness transformation.

### 4.2.1  Non-Lamarckian local search

The fitness transformation shown in Figure 6 is characteristic of all transformations performed by non-Lamarckian local search. Non-Lamarckian local search transforms the fitness landscape by associating the fitness of a genotype with the fitness of the phenotype generated by a local search algorithm. This type of transformation tends to broaden the "shoulders" of the local minima [9, 6]. Hinton and Nowlan [9], Nolfi, Elman and Parisi [19], Keesing and Stork [12] have shown how this type of fitness transformation can improve the rate at which the GA generates good solutions.

Although non-Lamarckian local search really only offers one type of fitness transformation, there is a great deal of flexibility in the application of local search. In particular, there is

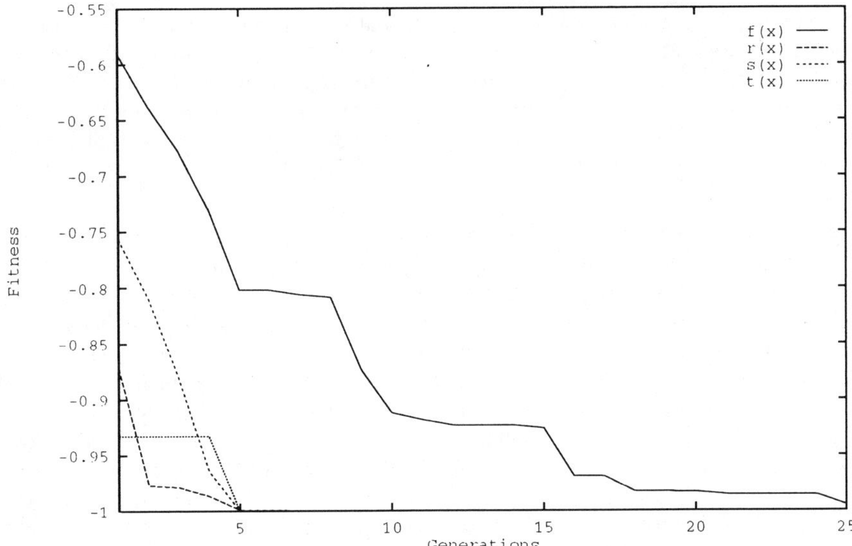

Figure 7: Transformation of the $f(x)$ fitness landscape, showing the performance of the binary GA on these functions, averaged over 10 runs. Comparison of these figures shows that the GAs optimizing functions with wider local minima converged more quickly.

often a trade-off between the information used to perform local search and the efficiency of the local search. Consequently, the quality of the fitness transformation can often be modified by changing the information available to the local search algorithm. (e.g. by incorporating the use of gradient information). One apparent drawback to the use of non-Lamarckian local search is that it is usually computationally expensive. The cost of the transformed fitness evaluation, $f(\lambda_f(x))$, may be substantially greater than the cost of the original fitness evaluation, $f(x)$. However, even given the cost of local search, GAs using non-Lamarckian local search *can* be more efficient than the GA alone [8].

### 4.2.2   Maturation

Maturation offers a variety of possible fitness transformations, since the maturation function can specify an arbitrary mapping between $\mathcal{G}$ and $\mathcal{P}h$. The following examples illustrate important types of maturation functions that we have identified.

Consider maturation functions that are bijections from $\mathcal{G}$ to $\mathcal{P}h$. These maturation functions can differ in the distribution of the phenotypes generated by the maturation function, as well as the association the genotypes to phenotypes. For example, the results for $f(x)$ and $f(\delta(x))$ shown in Figure 7 are a comparison of a GA using $\delta$ with a GA using a identity maturation function, $\bar{\delta}$. The difference between $\delta$ and $\bar{\delta}$ is that $\delta$ biases the distribution of phenotypes towards phenotypes near zero.

Application of binary GAs to functions defined on $\mathbf{R}^n$ show how maturation can affect the association of genotypes to phenotypes. The Binary GA's that interpret genotypes as Gray-coded integers typically perform a more efficient search than binary GAs that interpret genotypes as binary-coded integers. The maturation functions used by these GAs are both bijections using the same $\mathcal{G}$ and $\mathcal{P}h$ spaces. The different interpretations of the genotype affect the way that the maturation functions associate genotypes with phenotypes, thereby affecting the relative fitness of individuals in the search space. In this example, the fitness landscape generated by maturation using Gray-coded genotypes is often easier for the GA to search.

When symmetries exist in the search space, a surjective maturation function can be used to focus the search on a subset of the search space that does not contain symmetries by selecting $\delta$ so that $\delta(\mathcal{G}) \subset \mathcal{P}h$. Similarly, a surjective maturation function can also be used to focus the GA's search on a region where the best local minima (and global optima) are located. For example, Belew, Schraudolph and McInerney [3] argue that the best initial weights to perform local search for neural networks have a small absolute magnitude. With this in mind, they use a maturation function that maps a weight's binary genetic representation into a real-valued parameter in $[-0.5, 0.5]$, which is a surjective mapping because a neural network's weights may assume any real value. This maturational transformation focuses the GAs search on phenotypes with small weights. Belew et al. [3] observe that GAs which use this maturational transformation with local search find better solutions than GAs which use a uniform maturational transformation.

Similarly, a surjective maturation function can be used to bias the coverage of local minima in the search space. If the approximate locations of the local minima are available, this can be used to create a genotypic space that allows the GA to search with points that are closer to the bottoms of the local minima. This type of maturation function is interesting because it can affect the utility of local search operators. In particular, local search may not be cost effective if the maturation function maps genotypes very close to local minima.

This point is illustrated with an experiment using the molecular conformation problem. One common method of reducing the search of molecular conformations is to fix the bond lengths at an estimate of their optimal values. For example, in the molecular conformation problem described in Section 3.3, the molecules with a bond-length of one are close to local minima of the potential energy function. This suggests the use of a genotypic space containing bond angles, with a maturation function that defines the bond lengths to be one. Further, it suggests that local search may not be as important when using this genotypic space since the solutions are already close to the nearby minima.

We measured the utility of non-Lamarckian local search for this problem by varying the frequency of local search [7, 8]. The experiment compared GAs using the following two genotypic spaces: (a) the bond angles and bond lengths and (b) the bond angles. The space of atom coordinates was the phenotypic space for both GAs. A GA with floating point representation was used to search these genotypic spaces [7]. Local search was performed in the coordinate space, using the method of Solis-Wets [17, 22]. The performance of the GAs was measured as the best solution found after 150,000 function evaluations. Results were averaged over 20 trials. Table 1 shows the performance for the GAs using different genotypic spaces and different local search frequencies. As expected, the GAs using the bond angle genotypes performed better when local search was used infrequently, while the GAs using the bond angle and bond length genotypes performed better when local search

| Frequency | Angle/Bond Repn | Angle Repn |
|-----------|-----------------|------------|
| 1.0       | 0.119           | -3.373     |
| 0.25      | 3.473           | -6.472     |
| 0.0625    | 18.470          | -9.450     |

Table 1: Conformation experiments using a GA and varying local search frequency.

was used frequently.

## 5  Repair and Maturation

Given spaces $\mathcal{G}$ and $\mathcal{P}h$, it may be difficult to construct a reasonable maturation function such that $\delta(\mathcal{G}) \subseteq \mathcal{P}h$. However, it is usually possible to construct a function $\tilde{\delta}$ such that $\tilde{\delta}(\mathcal{G}) \supset \mathcal{P}h$. Given $\tilde{\delta}$, solutions mapped into $\delta(\mathcal{G}) - \mathcal{P}h$ need to be mapped back into $\mathcal{P}h$ for their fitness to be evaluated. This mapping has been called *repair* by a number of authors [16, 20].

For example, consider constrained optimization problems. In general, a constrained optimization problem solves for $x^*$ such that

$$f(x^*) = \min_{x \in D} f(x) \quad \text{subject to}$$
$$c_i(x) \geq 0 \quad i = 1, \ldots, m$$
$$g_j(x) = 0 \quad j = 1, \ldots, n,$$

where $c_i : D \to \mathbf{R}$ and $g_j : D \to \mathbf{R}$. Let $\mathcal{D} = \{x \mid c_i(x) \geq 0\} \bigcap \{x \mid g_j(x) = 0\}$. Solutions in $\mathcal{D}$ are known as *feasible* solutions, and solutions in $D - \mathcal{D}$ are *infeasible* solutions. Manela, Thornhill and Campbell [15] describe a GA that performs constrained optimization using a representational mapping (decoder) that maps from $\mathcal{G}$ to $\mathcal{D}$. Michalewicz and Janikow [16] observe that this type of GA can use a representational map that generates some infeasible solutions, which are mapped to feasible solutions by a repair mechanism. Since the representation map may generate infeasible solutions, it is equivalent to the $\tilde{\delta}$ function described above.

Taken together, $\tilde{\delta}$ and repair implement a mapping from $\mathcal{G}$ to $\mathcal{P}h$ that can be interpreted as maturation. However, it is important to consider whether $\tilde{\delta}$ and repair represent distinct steps of development. For example, in place of maturation and local search, we may have maturation, repair and local search, where maturation is modeled by $\tilde{\delta}$.

In fact, we believe that repair is not a distinct step of development, but is simply one aspect of maturation. In the context of constrained optimization, repair can be modeled as a function from $\tilde{\delta}(\mathcal{G})$ to $\mathcal{P}h$. In other contexts, repair may have other forms. For example, we could perform an initial "repair" which maps genotypes that would generate infeasible solutions to genotypes that generate feasible solutions. Also, repair may interact strongly with maturation. Consider the maturation function used to generate sorting networks from the grammar representation described in Section 3.2. The maturation function may generate infeasible phenotypes due to time constraints on the maturation process or because information in the genotype is incompatible with some fact about the network being built. A common problem of the latter type is the occurrence of backwards CMPXs. These are CMPXs $[i : j]$ for which $i \geq j$. These can be repaired by simply swapping the indices in the illegal CMPX. Because the maturation function for sorting networks is an iterative process, repair can be performed at intermediate steps of the maturation process, thereby allowing maturation to continue *after* repair has been performed.

## 6   Time Complexity Issues

Section 4 illustrated the different roles that local search and maturation play in the transformation of the fitness landscape. We observed that GAs using non-Lamarckian local search and maturation are equivalent to GAs optimizing $h = f \circ \lambda_f \circ \delta$. This formulation does not capture the possible time complexity advantages of GAs that use these developmental mechanisms. In this section, we describe two examples of how maturation can be used with GAs to improve their time complexity.

**Phenotypic Reuse**   In many applications of GAs, the fitness evaluation involves a number of independent tests of an individual's phenotype. An example of this type of fitness is the error criteria used in neural network problems. For a given network, the error criterion is calculated by summing the network's error on a set of independent trials.

When maturation is used with such fitness functions, the maturation function can be distinguished from the fitness evaluation for time-complexity reasons. The maturation function can be used to "decode" the genotype once, after which the fitness is iteratively evaluated on the phenotype. The maturation function used for neural networks in Gruau [4, 5] can be distinguished from the fitness evaluation on this basis. Similarly, sorting networks are evaluated with such a decomposable fitness function, since a sorting network's fitness is defined by its performance on several input sequences.

When the fitness evaluation is stochastic, maturation can be used to generate a phenotype that is evaluated several times. This increases the time complexity of each fitness evaluation, but makes the fitness evaluation more precise. Thus there is a trade-off between the accuracy of fitness evaluations and their costs. The more accurate fitness evaluations may, however, allow the GA to converge in fewer generations than would be possible with less accurate fitness evaluations.

**Local Search Complexity**   The conformation problem described in Section 3.3 is an interesting case where maturation can be used to reduce the time-complexity of the local search method. Recall that the potential energy can be parameterized using either atom coordinates or bond angles and bond lengths. Thus, there is more than one possible phenotypic space in which the potential energy can be evaluated. The gradient calculation using bond angles and bond lengths is more expensive than the gradient calculation using atom coordinates. The gradient can be directly calculated from the atom coordinates in $O(n^2)$ time steps. To calculate the gradient from bond angles and bond lengths, the bond angles and bond lengths are first mapped into atom coordinates, from which the gradient is calculated. With this additional step, the gradient calculation requires $O(n^3)$ time steps!

In preliminary experiments, GAs using the space of bond angles and bond lengths for $\mathcal{G}$ and $\mathcal{P}h$ had better performance. When solving this problem with GAs that used gradient-based local search, it is most efficient to use maturation to let $\mathcal{G}$ be the space of bond angles and bond lengths and let $\mathcal{P}h$ be the space of atom coordinates.

## 7    Evolutionary Bias

Maturation can also be used to allow a GA to search a genotypic space $\mathcal{G}'$ that is more easily searched than the phenotypic space. For example, Gruau [5] solves a neural network problem by searching for the network architecture and network weights simultaneously. The fitness evaluation is a function of the network, so $\mathcal{P}h$ is the space of network architectures with weights. Gruau [4] compares the performance of GAs in which $\mathcal{G}$ is a grammar with GAs in which $\mathcal{G} = \mathcal{P}h$. Gruau found that GAs that use the grammar-based genotypic space have better performance. The two GAs share the same phenotypic space, so differences between them depend on the dynamics of the GA on the different genotypic spaces.

Similarly, suppose we have a problem with a natural notion of complexity, and we are using the GA to solve incrementally more complex instances of our problem. Maturation can allow the GA to solve a problem instance by searching a space in which solutions to "complex" problem instances are related to the solutions to "simple" problem instances. *Evolutionary bias* refers to an influence on the solutions a genetic algorithm finds to complex instances of a problem based on the solutions it find to simpler instances of the same problem. The general idea is that solutions to simpler instances of a problem will bias the search for solutions to complex problem instances.

More concretely, imagine that a GA is being used to search a set $S$ and that $S = \bigcup S_i$ for $i \geq 1$, such that $S_i \subseteq S_j$ whenever $i \leq j$. In this case, we say that $S$ is *graded* by $i$. In many cases, $i$ will correspond to the size of a problem instance, such as the number of cities in an instance of the travelling salesman problem, or the number of literals per clause in a conjunctive normal form logic formula as in satisfiability for k-CNF, or the number of clauses in such a formula as in k-clause-CNF. In general, the problem instances in $S_{i+1} - S_i$ are "harder" or "bigger" than those in $S_i$.

A graded search space, $S$, is not sufficient for evolutionary bias to effect a GA's search. It must also be true that searching for a solution to a problem instance of "size" or "complexity" $i$ is somehow similar to searching for a solution to a problem instance of size $i + 1$. That is, the "fitness landscape" must display some self-similarity at different scales. Maturation can lead to such self-similarites in the fitness measure by allowing specification of the way in which elements of $S_i$ can be used or combined to arrive at elements of $S_{i+1} - S_i$. Two examples will help to illustrate this point.

Belew [1] noted an evolutionary bias in his work on evolving polynomials. In this work, the GA is used to search for polynomials to fit a chaotic time series. The search space is thus that of polynomials. Belew's representation used a set of rules that governed the growth of a "polynomial network" which computed a polynomial. The structure of these rules made searching for fine-grained solutions (polynomials that provided a very tight fit to the time series) a similar process to that of searching for coarse-grained solutions once a set of coarse-grained solutions was known. Belew's search space is, in the above terminology, graded according to degree of polynomial.

Consider the sorting network problem of Section 3.2. The search space, $S$, is the set all of CMPX networks. We can consider $S$ to be graded by the number of inputs to a network. The rewrite rules used to generate CMPX networks have the property that large networks are built from smaller ones, so searching for large networks is similar to searching for smaller networks once those smaller networks are known. Thus, once sorting networks of width $N$

have been found, the search for sorting networks of width $2N$ proceeds similarly. In this case, maturation provides a means of problem decomposition which leads to an evolutionary bias.

In order to determine whether evolutionary bias can improve search efficiency, we conducted the following experiment. We ran a GA 10 times using the grammar representation of Section 3.2 to evolve width four sorting networks. The final populations from these ten simulations were used as the initial populations, or "seed populations" for simulations which searched for width eight sorting networks. We then compared the number of generations needed to find a solution in the 10 seeded runs with the number of generations needed to find a solution in 10 runs which searched for width 8 sorters using random inital populations. Using a Wilcoxon rank-sum test we compared the number of generations for which the seeded and unseeded runs ran before either reaching a set limit or finding a sorting network. The two-tailed test was significant for $\alpha = 0.1$. When the number of generations required to generate each seed population was added to the number of generations for which the corresponding seeded run executed, the seeded and unseeded width eight runs were no longer significantly different. Thus, we have evidence that given the seed populations, the time (in generations) to find a solution was shorter for the seeded than for the unseeded runs, but the *total* number of generations needed to find a solution was not different for the seeded and unseeded variants.

## 8    Conclusions

This discussion has provided a framework in which maturation and learning have well-defined roles. We have also given examples in which it is useful to analyze the effect of maturation and learning. In each of our examples, an analysis of these developmental mechanisms provided useful insights into the behavior of the GA. Developmental fitness transformations explain differences in performance among alternative methods of decoding the genotype, and can be used to incorporate domain-specific information into the genetic search. Maturation offers computational advantages when performing phenotypic reuse, and can improve the search dynamics of GA's which use local search. Maturation functions offer a solution to constrained search problems, and can be used to introduce evolutionary bias into the GA's search.

Our framework for developmental mechanisms makes a clear distinction between maturation and local search. Specifically, it requires that maturation be a function of only the genotype. While this definition of maturation has clarified the discussion in this paper, it precludes other methods of maturation which may be interesting. For example, it precludes maturation methods for which fitness information can be used to evaluate the phenotypic representation even when the phenotype is incomplete. Gruau and Whitley [6] describe a similar developmental method which interleaves maturation steps with learning steps.

While we have illustrated the utility of developmental mechanisms, we have only described some of the computational costs which must be considered when using them. In specific applications, it is important to consider the cost of developmental methods, since it is possible for development to introduce a computational cost which outweighs the improvements in the GA's search. For example, Hinton and Nowlan [9], Nolfi, Elman and Parisi [19], Keesing and Stork [12] describe how using non-Lamarckian local search with GA's improves the rate at which good solutions are generated. However, the computational cost in these analyses is based on the number of generations of the GA, which ignores the costs introduced by the local search.

Above, we discussed a way in which GA's with a maturational component can implement "evolutionary bias" — a bias in the search for solutions to an problem instance based on already-found solutions to smaller instances. This is not the only way in which maturation could introduce bias into the GA. For example, if a given genome can be matured into many phenotypes, then our choice of phenotype represents a bias in the algorithm. This sort of bias comes into play above in our discussion of transformations of the fitness landscape, where we discussed biasing the GA by using maturation to map the $\mathcal{G}$ into some specific subset $\mathcal{P}h$.

# References


[1] R. K. Belew. Interposing an ontogenic model between Genetic Algorithms and Neural Networks. In J. Cowan, editor, *Advances in Neural Information Processing (NIPS5)*, San Mateo, CA, 1993. Morgan Kaufmann.

[2] Richard K. Belew and Thomas E. Kammeyer. Evolving aesthetic sorting networks using developmental grammars. In *Proceedings of the Fifth International Conference on Genetic Algorithms*. Morgan Kaufmann Publishers, Inc., 1993.

[3] Richard K. Belew, John McInerney, and Nicol N. Schraudolph. Evolving networks: Using the genetic algorithm with connectionist learning. In Chris G. Langton, Charles Taylor, J. Doyne Farmer, and Steen Rasmussen, editors, *Proceedings of the Second Conference on Artificial Life*, pages 511–548. Addison-Wesley, 1991.

[4] Frederic Gruau. Genetic synthesis of boolean neural networks with a cell rewriting developmental process. In *Intl Workshop on Combinations of Genetic Algorithms and Neural Networks*, pages 55–74, 1992.

[5] Frederic Gruau. Genetic synthesis of modular neural networks. In Stephanie Forrest, editor, *Proceedings of the 5th Intl. Conference on Genetic Algorithms*, pages 318–325, 1993.

[6] Frederic Gruau and Darrell Whitley. Adding learning to to the cellular development of neural networks: Evolution and the Baldwin effect. *Evolutionary Computation*, 3(1):213–233, 1993.

[7] William E. Hart. *Adaptive Global Optimization with Local Search*. PhD thesis, University of California, San Diego, May 1994.

[8] William E. Hart and Richard K. Belew. Optimization with genetic algorithm hybrids that use local search. In *Plastic Individuals in Evolving Populations*, 1994. (to appear).

[9] Geoffrey E. Hinton and Steven J. Nowlan. How learning can guide evolution. *Complex Systems*, 1:495–502, 1987.

[10] Richard S. Judson. Teaching polymers to fold. *J. Phys. Chem.*, 96:10102–10104, 1992.

[11] R.S. Judson, M.E. Colvin, J.C. Meza, A. Huffer, and D. Gutierrez. Do intelligent configuration search techniques outperform random search for large molecules? *International Journal of Quantum Chemistry*, pages 277–290, 1992.

[12] Ron Keesing and David G. Stork. Evolution and learning in neural networks: The number and distribution of learning trials affect the rate of evolution. In Richard P.

Lippmann, John E. Moody, and David S. Touretzky, editors, *NIPS 3*, pages 804–810. Morgan Kaufmann, 1991.

[13] H. Kitano. Designing neural networks using genetic algorithms with graph generation systems. *Complex Systems*, 4:461–476, 1990.

[14] D. E. Knuth. *The art of computer programming*, volume III. Addison-Wesley, Reading, MA, 1973.

[15] Mauro Manela, Nina Thornhill, and J.A. Campbell. Fitting spline functions to noisy data using a genetic algorithm. In Stephanie Forrest, editor, *Proceedings of the 5th Intl. Conference on Genetic Algorithms*, pages 549–553, 1993.

[16] Zbigniew Michalewicz and Cezary Z. Janikow. Handling constraints in genetic algorithms. In Richard K. Belew and Lashon B. Booker, editors, *Proceedings of the 4th Intl. Conference on Genetic Algorithms*, pages 151–157, 1991.

[17] H. Mühlenbein, M. Schomisch, and J. Born. The parallel genetic algorithm as function optimizer. In Richard K. Belew and Lashon B. Booker, editors, *Proceedings of the Fourth Intl. Conf. on Genetic Algorithms*, pages 271–278. Morgan-Kaufmann, 1991.

[18] Heinz Mühlenbein. Evolution in time and space - the parallel genetic algorithm. In Gregory J.E. Rawlins, editor, *Foundations of Genetic Algorithms*, pages 316–337. Morgan-Kauffmann, 1991.

[19] Stefano Nolfi, Jeffrey L. Elman, and Domenico Parisi. Learning and evolution in neural networks. Technical Report CRL 9019, Center for Research in Language, University of California, San Diego, July 1990.

[20] David Orvosh and Lawrence Davis. Shall we repair? genetic algorithms, combinatorial optimization, and feasibility constraints. In Stephanie Forrest, editor, *Proceedings of the 5th Intl. Conference on Genetic Algorithms*, page 650, 1993.

[21] William H. Press, Brian P. Flannery, Saul A. Teukolsky, and William T. Vetterling. *Numerical Recipies in C - The Art of Scientific Computing*. Cambridge University Press, 1990.

[22] F.J. Solis and R.J-B. Wets. Minimization by random search techniques. *Mathematical Operations Research*, 6:19–30, 1981.

# Author Index

# Key Word Index